Commentary on CONSUMER BEHAVIOUR

S.A. CHUNAWALLA

B.Com., (Hons.), D.Pharma, MBA (Marketing)
Communication Consultant,
Benzer, Borivali (W), Mumbai - 400 103.
E-mail: chunawalla@yahoo.com

THIRD REVISED EDITION : 2012

Himalaya Publishing House

• MUMBAI • NEW DELHI • NAGPUR • BENGALURU • HYDERABAD • CHENNAI • PUNE • LUCKNOW
• AHMEDABAD • ERNAKULAM • BHUBANESWAR • INDORE • KOLKATA • GUWAHATI

Millennium Edition	:	**2000**
Reprint	:	**2001**
Second Revised Edition	:	**2005**
Reprint	:	**2007**
Reprint	:	**2009**
Third Revised Edition	:	**2012**

Published by : Mrs. Meena Pandey for **Himalaya Publishing House Pvt. Ltd.**, "Ramdoot", Dr. Bhalerao Marg, Girgaon, **Mumbai - 400 004.**
Phone: 022-23860170/23863863, Fax: 022-23877178
E-mail: himpub@vsnl.com; Website: www.himpub.com

Branch Offices :

New Delhi : "Pooja Apartments", 4-B, Murari Lal Street, Ansari Road, Darya Ganj, New Delhi - 110 002. Phone: 011-23270392, 23278631; Fax: 011-23256286

Nagpur : Kundanlal Chandak Industrial Estate, Ghat Road, Nagpur - 440 018. Phone: 0712-2738731, 3296733; Telefax: 0712-2721215

Bengaluru : No. 16/1 (Old 12/1), 1st Floor, Next to Hotel Highlands, Madhava Nagar, Race Course Road, Bengaluru - 560 001. Phone: 080-32919385; Telefax: 080-22286611

Hyderabad : No. 3-4-184, Lingampally, Besides Raghavendra Swamy Matham, Kachiguda, Hyderabad - 500 027. Phone: 040-27560041, 27550139; Mobile: 09390905282

Chennai : No. 8/2, Modley 2nd Street, Ground Floor, T. Nagar, Chennai - 600 017. Phone: 044-28144004/28144005; Mobile: 09345345051

Pune : First Floor, "Laksha" Apartment, No. 527, Mehunpura, Shaniwarpeth (Near Prabhat Theatre), Pune - 411 030. Phone: 020-24496323/24496333; Mobile: 09370579333

Lucknow : Jai Baba Bhavan, Church Road, Near Manas Complex and Dr. Awasthi Clinic, Aliganj, Lucknow - 226 024 (U.P.). Phone: 0522-2339329, 4068914; Mobile: 09307501550

Ahmedabad : 114, "SHAIL", 1st Floor, Opp. Madhu Sudan House, C.G. Road, Navrang Pura, Ahmedabad - 380 009. Phone: 079-26560126; Mobile: 09377088847

Ernakulam : 39/104 A, Lakshmi Apartment, Karikkamuri Cross Rd., Ernakulam, Cochin - 622011, Kerala. Phone: 0484-2378012, 2378016; Mobile: 09344199799

Bhubaneswar : 5 Station Square, Bhubaneswar - 751 001 (Odisha). Phone: 0674-2532129, Mobile: 09861046007

Indore : Kesardeep Avenue Extension, 73, Narayan Bagh, Flat No. 302, IIIrd Floor, Near Humpty Dumpty School, Indore - 452 007 (M.P.). Mobile: 09301386468

Kolkata : 108/4, Beliaghata Main Road, Near ID Hospital, Opp. SBI Bank, Kolkata - 700 010, Phone: 033-32449649, Mobile: 09910440956

Guwahati : House No. 15, Behind Pragjyotish College, Near Sharma Printing Press, P.O. Bharalumukh, Guwahati - 781009, (Assam). Mobile: 09883055590, 09883055536

DTP by : HPH, Editorial Office, Bhandup (Shilpa S)

Printed at : Geetanjali Press Pvt. Ltd., Nagpur. On behalf of HPH.

PREFACE TO THE THIRD REVISED EDITION

Mostly in an organization, hard skills are valued more e.g. engineering skills, financial expertise, quantitative techniques etc. Soft skills like communication skills, human relations, and psychological basis, of human-consumer behaviour are considered passé. Of late, there is a paradigm shift in this thinking. Post-Hawthorne experiments, the significance of the human factor emerged as never before. In marketing too, apart from the glamourous topics of product-brand management and advertising, the top management understood the consumer behaviour. In fact, it facilitates organizational and marketing planning including advertising and product planning.

As new research concepts in this area were developed, it was felt that there is a need to revise the complete text. In this revised enriched form, the book will serve the needs of the students better.

— AUTHOR

CONTENTS

DETAILED CONTENTS

1

NATURE AND SCOPE OF CONSUMER BEHAVIOUR

Consumer behaviour obviously refers to the behaviour of consumers in deciding to buy or not to buy or use or not to use or dispose of or not to dispose of the products which satisfy their needs. Consumer behaviour also refers to the use of scarce resources like time, money, and effort on consumption items.

The term consumer is constantly evolving. There is a thin boundary line gap between a 'customer' and 'consumer'. A consumer, on some occasions, becomes a customer, and sometimes a customer plays the role of a consumer. A text book definition of a customer is = a person + the act of purchasing goods and services. A consumer is a person in the act of self-consumption. Marketers continue to treat the consumers as 'dolls' whom they can dress up in various brands. This doll is our person who purchases goods and services. Consumer is the person buying.

Consumer behaviour tries to answer the following questions:

- *What* products and services consumer buy?
- *What makes* them buy them?
- *When* are these bought?
- *From where?*
- What is the *frequency* of buying? *How often* are they *used?*

Let us take an ordinary example of deciding to buy a soap. We have a large choice of soaps (Janta soaps, premium soaps, special antiseptic soaps, transparent soaps, sandalwood soaps and so on). There are a number of brands available (Lux International, Lux, Lifebuoy, Hamam, Rexona, Pears, Mysore Sandal, Dettol, Savlon, Niko, Palmolive, Dove, Cinthol and so on). What prompts us to buy a particular soap? Because it is a complexion soap or deo soap, or moisturizing soap? From where do we buy it? From the neighbourhood grocery soap or a general store. We can buy it from a chemist shop or a departmental store like Akbarallys. How often do we buy soap? Once a week or twice a week. How often do we use it? Once a day or more than once a day? All these are dimensions of consumer behaviour.

Just consider another product, say a consumer durable like a photocopier. Who are the customers for photocopying machines? What do they look for in a photocopying machine? What types of documents are photocopied? What for are they photocopied? What incentive do they need to replace their old photocopying machine?

We will have to undertake what is known as consumer research to find the answers to the above questions. These answers will provide insight to the manufacturers in the design and development and further improvement of their product. It also enables them to design their promotional strategies.

Consumer research is not restricted to just buying decisions. After the purchase is made, what wind of experience do we have with the product? If it is a mobike, does it run without any problem? Is it fuel efficient? Does it have a good pick up? Does it deliver those values that it promised? Either we are satisfied, Post-purchase dissatisfaction has implications for the marketers.

What do the consumers do after using a product? Are they interested in throwing it off or in lending it to someone? They may gift it to somebody. They may sell it off. They may store it. They may rent it off. There are several possibilities. Replacement market is a very potential market. What the consumers do with a product is an indicator of the chances of the product being replaced. Replacements frequency or repeat buys are to be matched to production plans.

Consumers themselves are individuals who buy products for their own use or household use or as gifts. But there is one more type of consumers — *organisational consumers* which are business, government and instruments of government, and institutions who buy products to run their organisations. This book treats the behaviour of individuals consumers and omits organisational buying behaviour.

A purchaser or buyer is not necessarily a user e.g. stationery is bought by parents for their children. Sometimes a product bought may be used jointly. It is also to be noted that the decisions to buy may be influenced by a number of persons. A marketer has to direct his promotional efforts either to the buyer or the user or the influencers. Some think that the best audience is that of buyers, while some others think that it is that of the users. It is possible to play safer by directing the promotion to both the buyers and users. Medicines are promoted through the doctors, who take the product selection decision, but are neither buyers or users.

Importance of Consumer Behaviour

This subject is useful to the marketers, consumers and students of human behaviour. We as consumers gain valuable insights in our consumption-related behaviour. It makes us wiser consumers. Marketers benefit by understanding how consumers take consumption decisions which enable them to formulate suitable marketing strategies. They can anticipate the reactions of the consumers to various cues, both informational and organisational. It is likely to give them a competitive advantage.

As students of consumer behaviour, we learn the logic behind consumption-related decisions and motivations which propel them to take certain decisions. It becomes a fascinating subject, drawing from various disciplines like psychology sociology, social psychology, anthropology and economics. To begin with a consumer was conceived as an 'economic man' taking rational decisions. Later theories brought an end to this 'economic man'.

Initially, marketers thought that if they are able to predict consumer behaviour, they will be able to influence it. This is a *positivist* approach to consumer behaviour. Consumer behaviour was thus considered just applied marketing management. However drawing from diverse disciplines, consumer behaviour developed into an inter-disciplinary subject. It become a subject of study going beyond narrow marketing and managerial perspective. There is focus on simply *understanding* all nuances of consumer behaviour, and this approach is called *interpretivism* Experience plays a great role while buying and each such experience is affected by a host of factors. Therefore, interpretivism is also called *experientialism*. Both these approaches are complementary to each other. As students of management, we definitely are interested in this book in the positivist approach. But at the same time, enough care is taken to understand the consumption related decisions. This integration contributes to enrich our study of consumer behaviour, and formulation of better marketing strategies.

The area of consumer behaviour is related to the marketing concept which evolved in the late 50s. We have travelled from production-orientation (efficient economical production) to product orientation (best products) to sales orientation (focus on sales) to marketing orientation. Marketing orientation simply means producing those products which the consumers need and want. General Electric adopted this approach in mid-50's. It came to be known as the marketing concept which emphasises the needs and wants of the target markets, and delivery of products to satisfy these better than the competition. This concept spread widely, and so also the study of consumer behaviour. In order to produce want satisfying products it is necessary to assess those needs and wants. Marketing research was therefore, necessary. Consumers were then recognised to be extremely complex individuals with a variety of needs and wants. Each consumer segment had unique needs. Thus it was felt that in-depth study of consumers and their behaviour will be necessary to design suitable products and marketing them. Marketing concept is the fountain head of consumer behaviour studies, undertaken for formulation of the marketing strategies.

Consumer research has also two approaches, a more objective positivist approach which seeks causes of behaviour or a qualitative interpretivitst approach based on small samples.

Ethical Considerations

Consumer behaviour though quite a useful subject is open to criticism since it exposes the vulnerabilities of the consumers which could be exploited by the marketers. It thus imparts an unfair advantage to the marketers. The overall marketing ethics is now a matter of concern considering the marketing practices followed by reputed marketers with respect to products, prices, promotion and design with just one aim in mind — profit maximisation. Though what is ethical is debatable, ethics can be based on cost-benefit analysis, justifying those products which bring about 'the greatest goods of greatest number' though some segments can be adversely affected. Here the moral worth is checked against consequences. It is called *teleology*. It encompasses a kind of utilitarian approach in itself. On the other hand, *denotology* is concerned with out overall intentions. Greater emphasis is placed on non-economic values. Out actions equally apply to us. We do not do unto others what we do not like others to do unto us.

Ethics get ingrained early in life. If we as individuals have respect for values, the same will be carried to an organisation. Ethics is not to be practised only by the marketers. Consumers must also behave ethically. It is strongly advocated that business schools should include a paper on business ethics in their curricula. Consumer movement also makes it compulsory for business to be socially responsible. Corporate philosophy also determines the ethical behaviour of the employees of an organisation.

Societal Marketing Concept

Marketing has now acquired an added dimension — social responsibility. Marketing executives are expected to act in a socially responsible manner. They have to trade off between the consumer wants and interest and the long-term social welfare. External pressures of diverse nature influence the marketing programme of a firm. Marketing has to show concern for natural resources, shortages, deleterious effects of certain products, non-biodegradable materials, pollution, environment etc. Marketing has to offer a better quality of life — rather than a mere standard of living.

Growth of Consumer Behaviour

Consumer behaviour is a multi-disciplinary field which draws its concepts from several fields of study. It is useful to the marketing organisations, consumer groups and governmental authorities. It is an applied field since the concepts of behavioural science disciplines are applied to the understanding of human behaviour as far as consumption is concerned. By its very nature, it increases appreciative content of marketing, and leads to more effective and consumer-oriented marketing programmes. Consumer behaviour is interwoven with the emergence of the marketing discipline and has extended the motivation research of 1950s. By 60's consumer behaviour acquired a formidable body of knowledge. The following table summarises the growth of consumer behaviour as a subject of study.

CONSUMER BEHAVIOUR: GROWTH IN 1900's

Researcher	*Year*	*Contribution*
Katz and Lazarsfeld at Columbia University	1955	Information dissemination and interpersonal infleuence
Katona and his colleagues at University of Michigan	1960	Expectations and attitudes
Bauer at Harvard	1960	Communication and consumer response under conditions of uncertainty. Perceived risk.
Kuehen Howard	1962 1963	Learning theory
Evans Kassarjan	1959 1965	Personality and social character
Engel Kassarjan and Cohen	1963 1965	Cognitive dissonance
Cox	1967	Perceived risk
Steffler Green	1968 1969	Perception preference mapping
Levy	1959	Symbolic interactionasim

Day	1969	Attitude
Bourne Stafford	1957 1966	Reference groups
King Zaltman	1963 1965	Interpersonal communication and diffusion
Levy	1966	Social class
Wells	1966	Life style
Bauer Sturdivant	1965 1969	Sub-cultures
Kuehen Frank	1962	Model of consumer behaviour (limited aspects)
Niccosia	1966	Comprehensive consumer behaviour model
Howard and Sheth	1969	Comprehensive consumer behaviour model
David Laibson	1994	Will power and money. Explained overspending and undersaving. Behavioural economist.
Sendhil Mullainathan	1997	Integrated behavioural economics into mainstream theory.

Models which are integrative is a significant development to resolve contemporary problems of consumer research. As there is no single unified theory of consumer behaviour, several theories function for a single model. These models draw upon many theoretical areas such as social class, attitudes and perception. As many concepts of consumer behaviour are contributed by diverse disciplines, sometimes the research findings lack consistency and are disjointed, attracting the label of too academic for the entire subject. Consumer research should be related to the problems that are relevant for the managers and the findings must be communicated adequately.

Business executives should also learn to value the research findings, and use them in their decision making process. Researchers should not lose sight of the marketing realities while undertaking their research. We can think of having some trained individuals as links between the marketing practitioners and research workers. These individuals can be called 'social science technicians' or 'social engineers'.

Consumer Scene in India

India is a country of great diversity. India is unique because there is unity in her diversity. Indian consumers of 60's and 70's had seen the Independence struggle from close quarters. Some of them must have been 'mid-night children'. There was a streak of idealism running through them. They were inspired by a galaxy of freedom fighters. Nehru was influenced greatly by the Soviet experiment of socialism and wanted India to adopt a planned economy where public and private sector would co-exist. But the commanding heights were occupied by the public sector. India talked of social equality, and slogans like *Garibi Hatao* were popular. India wanted to be self-sufficient and Gandhi's Swadeshi had led to protective policies towards Indian industry. The emphasis was on core sector where government companies had a dominant role.

The teeming millions found that Indian's 6 lac and odd villages had little to offer by way of opportunities. It led to migration towards town and cities. People felt secure only when they got government jobs such as that of LIC, public sector undertakings and administrative services. It is out this sense of security that a huge savings rate was observed. People put a restraint on their acquisitive habits, and restricted their purchases to some white family goods. Cars, TV and fridge which are so common today were considered luxury goods, and were meant as status symbols only. The bread-earners were traditionally the males in the family, and women played the role of a home maker.

We now shift to the period of 70's and early 80's. Indira Gandhi declared the Emergency during this period. India was given a 20-point economic programme. In 1982, Asian Games were held in Delhi, and colour TV entered Indian market. Rajiv was sworn in as PM after Mrs. Gandhi's cruel assassination in 1984. India got a multi-party system. Haves and have-nots learned to co-exist. Equality was thought to be a utopian concept. India started slowly opening up of the economy. It wanted to be open to new technologies like computers. India wanted to catch up with the rest of the world, having realised that she has already lagged behind many other nations. India was a nation in a hurry.

The previous generation had worked hard and had provided a launching pad to the new consumer. He was already a secure person. He confidently invested in capital markets, housing and banking. He expected fair returns. Though the consumer was willing to take risks, he wanted immediate rewards and gratification. Private sector emerged as a strong but still an opportunistic, force. Consumers wanted indulgence, and had acquisitive tendencies.

In the late 80's, and 90's the consumer was exposed to a far more liberal economy. Eating out became a common thing. White goods are purchased to improve quality of life, and are no longer status symbols. Many of the luxuries of yester years have become necessities today. Consumers were no longer interested only in functional aspects of the products. They also wanted aesthetics. There are many double income households.

Man-woman roles now overlap. Foreign things are no longer a craze. In British India, the UK was the bench mark. Reference has now shifted to the US. Even South Asian giants like Japan are looked up to, though they have lost some of their sheen due to Asian currency crisis and stock market crash recently.

Indian consumer shows the following core values.

- family orientation
- value-seeking
- progress-orientation
- class-consciousness

Madhukar Sabanvis of O & M compares and contrasts the two generations of consumers in India.

Previous Generation	*Today's Generation*
Security	Confidence
Idealism	Practicality
Risk avoidance	Risk taking
Saving-oriented	Investment-oriented
Job security	Job satisfaction
Postponement of gratification	Instant gratification
White goods as stamps symbols	White goods for life-style
Considered decisions	Impulsive
Habitual	Experimentative
Gender roles defined	Gender roles overlap
Icons god-like	Icons are human
Filial betterment	Improvement of previous generations.

The consumer is more demanding today. He is experimentative; and is open to new products and ideas. For him, value is not just price, but price-quality combination. He is ready to fight against all odds. In promotion, there is emphasis on both rational and emotional appeals. We see an Ariel women tackling her MIL.

What Forces Drive the Change in Consumer Behaviour?

In this first decade of the new millennium, we can identify the four forces which drive the change in consumer behaviour. First of all, environmental changes such as *rising personal disposable income*, *facilities to finance* purchases easily and *rising rural wealth* have boosted demand. Social and cultural factors affect consumer behaviour. Kearney identifies four subfactors here – *globalisation*, *nuclear families*, *urbanisation* and *dual-income households*. Corporate organisations offer a greater and better *variety of products* which they *promote* in diverse media. *Media options* have increased, and media software has made media more consumer-oriented. The following diagram illustrates these four factors.

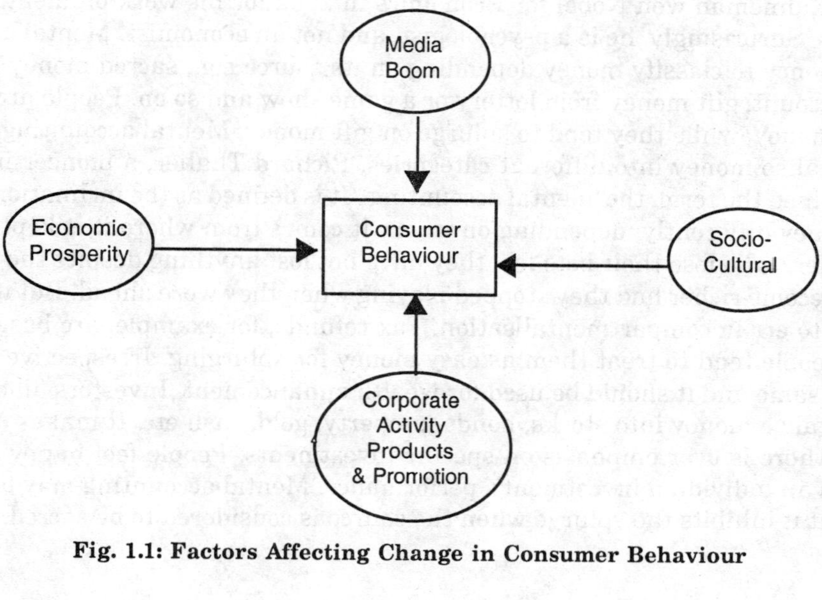

Fig. 1.1: Factors Affecting Change in Consumer Behaviour

Values Driving the Consumer Preferences

In pre-80's, consumer were just price-conscious. In mid-80's, they tried to trade off between price and quality. By the 90's, price-quality equation was supplemented by the enjoyment and time potential of the products. In the first decade of this new millennium, we combine quality with enjoyment or entertainment values and also at the same time put price, time, energy and stress as additional considerations in the value chain.

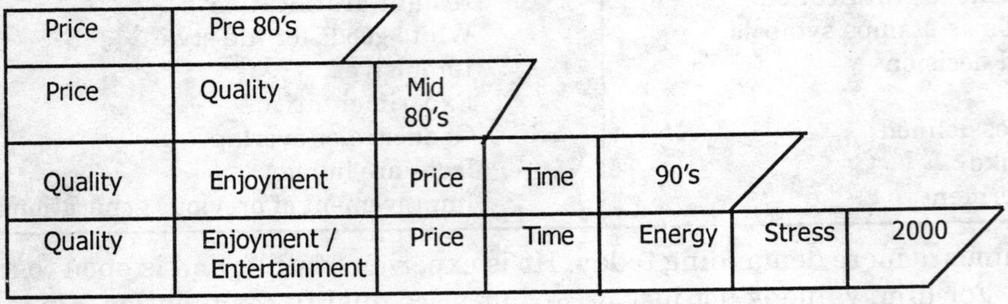

Fig. 1.2: Evolving Consumer Preference
Adapted after KSA Technopak

HYBRID CONSUMER

We come across a consumer who does not hesitate even slightly while buying a pair of sports shoes for Rs. 5000. But the same consumer haggles with the shop-keeper to reduce the price of socks costing Rs. 25. In other words, the consumer maps the value he gets from the products he is buying. In the process, he commoditises some brands or some categories. This trend in consumer behaviour challenges the retail practices and structures. Retailers have to learn how to provide more and better value.

Mental Accounting

Daniel Kahneman won Nobel for Economics in 2002 for his work on mental accounting, among others. Surprisingly, he is a psychologist, and not an economist. Mental accounting is a common tendency to classify money depending on its source e.g., sacred money received from VRS or PF account, gift money from lottery or a game show and so on. People are conservative with sacred money, while they tend to splurge on gift money. Mental accounting makes one to compartmentalise money into different categories. Richard Thaller, a pioneer in behavioural economics, coined the term, the 'mental accounting'. It is defined as the inclination to categorise and treat money differently, depending on where it comes from where it is kept and how it is spent. Gamblers who lose their bets feel they have not lost anything despite the fact that they would have become richer had they stopped playing when they were ahead. But while doing so, it is possible to err in compartmentalisation. Tax refunds, for example, are basically deferred salary, but people tend to treat them as easy money for splurging. Irrespective of the source, money is the same and it should be used for wealth enhancement. Investors all over the world compartmentalize money into stocks, bonds, property, gold, cash etc. It makes us blind to the big picture. There is over emphasis on specific investments. People feel happy or devastated depending on an individual investment's performance. Mental accounting may be beneficial in the sense that it inhibits the splurge when the source is considered to be sacred. A compulsive spender or non-saver may benefit by labelling some money as sacred. A missing ticket to see a movie may be considered a loss, and though another ticket is available, a person finds difficult to see a movie by buying it, because he will have to pay a price of two tickets to do so. A cash loss is however considered differently. Though it may be equal to the price of the ticket, a person is likely to buy a ticket because a cash loss is unconnected to the ticket. We do not know how Daniel Kahneman dealt with his Noble price money.

Paco Underhill

His book *Why We Buy* is an international best seller. He is a leading expert and pioneer on consumer behaviour. He is the founder and CEO of Envirosell Inc, a global research and consultancy firm. He is N.Y. based, though he spends a third of his time on the road.

Behavioural Economics

Traditional economic theory which deals with what people should do, assumes that people are rational. Behavioural economics examines what people actually do and discovers the depth and breadth of human irrationality.

Ariely has written a book *Predictably Irrational* where he dwells upon his experience as a burn patient whose dressings were hastily removed by the nurses thus subjecting him to a lot of physical pain. He felt that slow tearing off of the bandages would have caused less pain. He later proved this by research. People do unreasonable things. Ariely quotes several examples. Diners are influenced by the orders of co-diners. Some of them tend to be conformists, whereas some show deviant behaviour. They are less satisfied with their meals as a result. He believes contrary to the conventional wisdom that there is no free lunch, free lunches can exist when benefits of an action far outweigh its costs Suggestions do affect us strongly. People feel repelled by vinegar in a drink if so suggested. However, in the absence of such a suggestion, they may consider the flavour novel. Coke's taste has been registered in the brain, and thus Coke's mention anticipates great taste. Placebos with no therapeutic effect do work.

Stock Market Losses

A person multiplying his savings of Re. 1 lac by several lacs in the stock market only incur losses equal to one lac only due to mental accounting. It is the tendency to value some rupees less than the other. Money is fungible, that is the notion that one rupee is capable of being used in place of another rupee. Mental accounting is the tendency to give different values to the same amount of money depending upon how it is acquired when it is acquired and the amount of effort required to acquire it.

Tailor your Marketing Programme for the Customers

Harvard Professor Ranjay Gulati quotes a case of Best Buy, consumer electronics retailer, in his recent book *Re-organise for Resilience*. Best Buy faced stiff competition from Wal-Mart who became a No.2 in consumer electronics market by its aggressive low-cost model. Best Buy had to think smart to survive, and they exactly did so. They tried to figure our who their customers really are. They identified five groups — tech fanatics, home theatre connoisseurs, family men, busy moms and small business customer. A deeper research brought out the fact that women purchased 55 per cent of all consumer electronics and also influenced approximately 75 per cent of all such purchases. Yet, the retail marketing was geared up to suit male customers. It was due to male dominated decision making managers. Busy moms did not like loud music. They were put off by sharply contrasting colours. They did not like complex layouts. Best Buy designed stores with softer colours and made layouts more open. Women buy electronics in clusters. Women are not gadget freaks. Best buy, therefore, hired generalists as shopping assistants, instead of specialists devoted to specific departments. Consultants counselled busy moms one-on-one and served them individually Best Buy thus, countered Wal-Mart's threat. In other words, it tailored its marketing programme keeping their customers in mind. This is what marketing is.

❑ ❑ ❑

2

CONSUMER RESEARCH

Marketing research is a useful tool to find solutions to any problem of marketing. As crisp R.D. puts it, "Marketing Research (MR) is the systematic, objective and exhaustive *search for* and *study of the facts* relevant to any *problem* in the field of marketing." Surely, marketing research involves, as luck Wales and Taylor put, "the *application of scientific method* to the solution of marketing problems." Scientific method is primarily borrowed form the natural sciences, and consists of experiments, survey techniques and observation. The findings are generalized to larger populations. Mostly it is quantitative data. Marketing research later took in its stride qualitative research using projective techniques and depth interviews.

Marketing research has many branches such as advertising research, product research, sales research including distribution research, corporate research and consumer research. Thus consumer research is an extension of the field of marketing research with an emphasis only on consumer behaviour.

Just as marketing research is a tool that aids managerial decision making, the findings of consumer research too serve the same purpose. It enables managers to *understand* the buying decision making and consumption. It also enables them to *predict* how consumer would react to promotional messages. In a nut-shell, consumer (behaviour) research facilitates the formation of marketing strategies including promotional strategies.

Consumer Research Process

Consumer research has two dimensions — quantitative and qualitative. First *research objectives* are defined. If *secondary data collected* by other agencies relevant to these objectives is available, it is collected and analysed. If sufficient information is available as secondary data, there is no need to go in for primary data. *Primary data is collected* by observation, experimentation or survey if the secondary data is not sufficient. The data collected is *analysed and interpreted. A report is prepared* on the findings.

The following diagram illustrates the consumer research process:

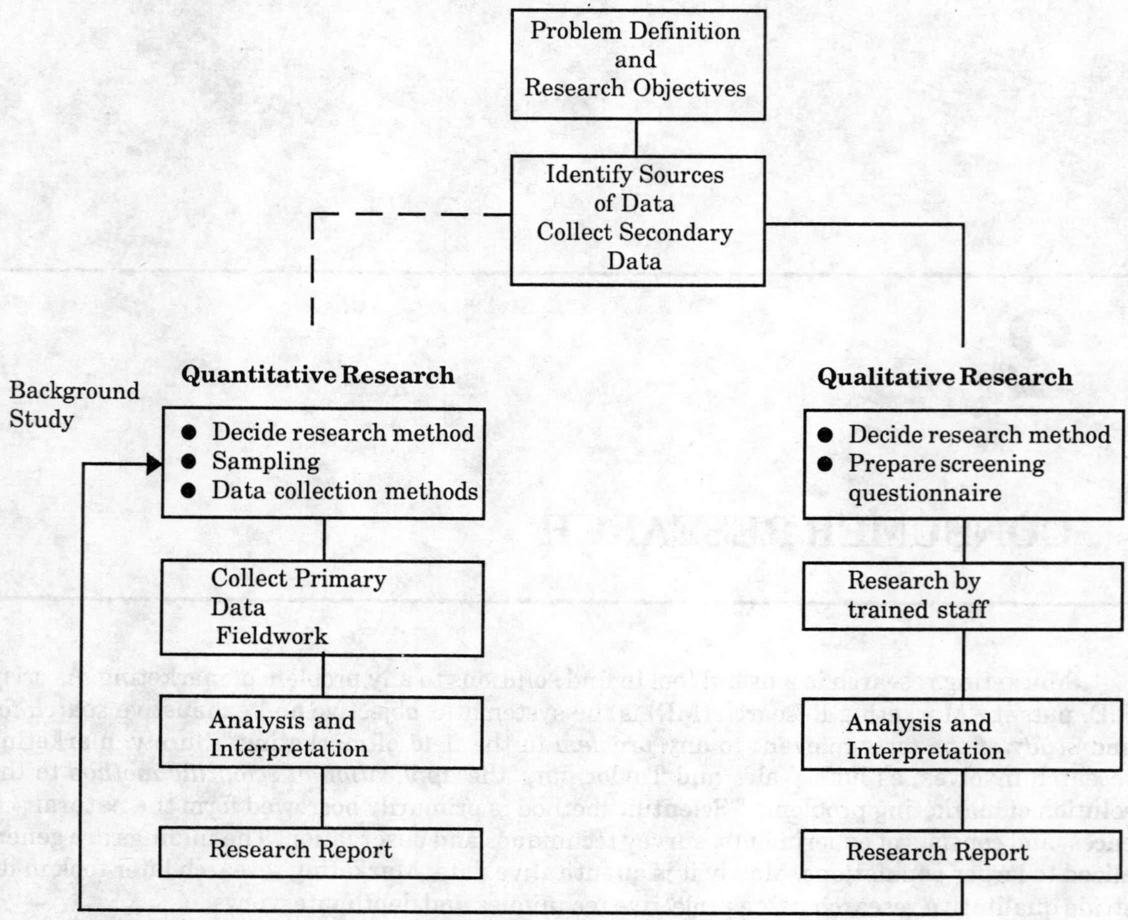

Fig. 2.1: Consumer Research Process

Research Objectives

There are many consumer behaviour problems in practice which are sharply defined. To illustrate, what percentage of men use deo sprays or what attitudes consumers have towards pre-paid mobile telephony. Sometimes, the problem is hidden and must be ferreted out. Students bunk college classes, but register overwhelming presence in the coaching class. Is it due to poor teaching in colleges and good teaching at coaching classes? Is it a problem of motivation? Why do students perceive coaching classes as better institutions? Has price something to do with it? Just because they pay through their nose for a coaching class enrolment they feel a compulsive urge to attend it? We have to identify the problem correctly so that we can frame appropriate research objectives.

Some typical research goals are:

(*i*) to segment the market of cellphone users

(*ii*) to identify the personality profile of different brands of cellphones

(*iii*) to understand the motivation of cellphone users.

If research goals are correctly set, it becomes easier to choose a research design. Thus if we want to know how a breakfast cereal is to be positioned a qualitative study could be undertaken in which the respondent is face-to-face with a highly trained professional interviewer. The sample is either a focus group or a panel. If the research objective is to find out how many people prefer changeable covers for their cell phones, we can undertake a quantitative study.

Collecting Secondary Data

We can collect our data from our internal records, library, directories, literature etc. The list of getting such secondary data is long. Secondary research sometimes eliminates the need for primary research. When our research project needs more data we will have to collect primary data. Primary data can be collected by our own research department or by an outside research agency.

Primary Research

Primary research can be quantitative or qualitative. First we shall acquaint ourselves with the quantitative research.

Quantitative Data Collection

There are basically three alternatives in collecting primary data — Observation method, Experimental method and Survey method.

(a) Observation Method

Observation is the process of recognising and recording the behaviour of people, objects, and events rather than asking for information. For example, instead of asking consumers what brands they buy or what television programmes they view, the researcher arranges to observe what products are bought and what programmes are watched.

Observational techniques can be classified in five ways as follows:

(1) *Natural Vs. Contrived:* Natural observation involves observing behaviour as it takes place normally in the environment, *e.g.,* shopping in a grocery shop. Contrived observation involves creating an artificial environment and observing the behaviour patterns exhibited by persons put in this environment, *e.g.,* having people shop in a simulated grocery store.

(2) *Disguised Vs. Undisguised:* "Disguise" refers to whether or not the respondents are aware they are being observed. The role of the observer should be disguised where people would behave differently if they knew they were being observed. Various approaches such as two-way mirrors, hidden cameras, and observers dressed as sales clerks can be used to disguise the observations.

(3) *Structured Vs. Unstructured:* Structured observation is appropriate when the decision problem has been clearly defined and the specification of information needs, permits a clear identification of the behaviour patterns to be observed and measured. Unstructured observation is appropriate in situations where the decision problem has yet to be formulated and a great deal of flexibility is needed. Structured observation is more appropriate for conclusive research studies. Unstructured observation is preferred for exploratory studies.

(4) *Direct Vs. Indirect:* "Direct observation" refers to observing as it actually occurs. Indirect observation refers to observing some record of past behaviour. Here, the effects, of behaviour

are observed rather than the behaviour itself. This involves the examination of physical traces, a process which includes such things as counting the number of empty liquor containers in trash cans to estimate liquor consumption of houses.

(5) Human Vs. Mechanical: In some situations it is appropriate to supplement or replace the human observer with some form of mechanical observer. The reason could be increased accuracy, lower costs, or special measurement requirements. The major mechanical devices used in observation include the (1) Motion picture camera; (2) Audiometer; (3) Psycho-galvanometer; (4) Eye-camera; and (5) Pupilometer. The *motion picture camera* can be used to record shopping behaviour in supermarkets, drug stores, and the like. The audiometer is a device to record when radio and television sets are turned on and the stations to which they are tuned. The psycho-galvanometer measures changes in perspiration rate from which inferences are drawn regarding a person's emotional reaction to stimuli present at the time of measurement. The stimuli presented might include brand names, copy slogans, etc. It is assumed, the stronger the reaction, the more favourable the person's attitude. The *eye-camera* measures the movement of the eye. It is used to determine how a person reads a magazine, advertisement, package and the like. The *pupilometer* measures changes in the diameter of the pupils of the eyes. An increase in pupil diameter is assumed to reflect on a person's favourable reaction to the stimuli being observed.

The observation method has several advantages. First, it does not rely on the respondent's willingness to provide the desired data. Second, the potential bias caused by interviewing methods is reduced or eliminated. Third, certain types of data can be collected only by observation.

The observation method has two major *limitations.* First, the inability to observe such things as awareness, beliefs, feelings, and preferences. It is difficult to observe a host of personal and intimate activities such as family games with children and late evening TV watching. Second, the observed behaviour patterns must be of a short duration, occur frequently, or be reasonably predictable if the data collection costs and time requirements are to be competitive with other data collection techniques. This requirement limits the observation method to a unique set of circumstances.

(b) Experimental Method

The second and least-used method of collecting primary data is that of controlled experiments. To date, the most common use of this method by marketers has been int test marketing.

Experimental method allows a maximum degree of control in comparison with other methods of collecting primary data. The method is also ranked as relatively high with respect to data accuracy since the ability to control the variables of interest tends to produce relatively error-free data. However, experimentation is limited to the collection of primary data on current behaviour and is, therefore, most restricted to primary data collection method in terms of flexibility and applicability. Besides, experimental method is usually costly and complex.

(c) Survey Techniques

Questionnaire or Survey Method: The survey technique is intended to secure one or more items of information from a sample of respondents or informants who are representatives of a larger group. The information is recorded on a form known as a questionnaire or a schedule or a blank form of inquiry. As data are gathered by asking questions from persons who are believed to have the desired information, the method is also known as the *questionnaire technique.*

The survey method is the most widely used technique in marketing research. It may be used at any one or more of the levels in the marketing process — at the consumer level, at retail, wholesale or manufacture level.

Reasons for Wide Use of Survey: There are a number of reasons for the very wide use of the survey techniques.

(*i*) It can secure both quantitative and qualitative information directly from the respondents, individuals or business consumers;

(*ii*) It is the only method of directly measuring attitudes and motivations;

(*iii*) It is quite flexible in terms of the types of data to be assembled, the method of collection or the timing of research.

It is presumed that respondents know the answers to the questions; have the authority to answer these questions; and are willing to co-operate in answering these questions in the best manner.

The versatility of the survey method, its speed, its relatively lower cost are its selling points when it is compared with the observation method.

Surveys are an effective way of gathering information (not already available) for the following marketing problems:

(*a*) Planning product features;

(*b*) Advertising copy;

(*c*) Media of advertisement;

(*d*) Sales promotion;

(*e*) Channel choice;

(*f*) Consumer research;

(*g*) Dealer research.

Use of Survey Method: There are three main uses of the survey or questionnaire method:

(*i*) We can have a factual survey together with facts; *e.g.*, "What brand of tea or soap do you use?"

(*ii*) We can have an opinion survey to secure personal opinions or thinking on a particular matter; *e.g.,* "Which design of the ornaments do you think is the most beautiful?"

(*iii*) Interpretative survey can be conducted to probe into the personal feelings, motives, attitudes, etc., of the respondent, who is not only a reporter but also an interpreter; *e.g.,* "Why do you use Brand X detergent?"

Types of Survey: In the questionnaire or survey method, we can have communication with the respondents to gather information in three alternative ways:

(1) Through the mail or post office;

(2) On the telephone; and

(3) At a personal interview.

(1) *The Mail Survey by Questionnaire:* This is a very effective and cheap method of conducting surveys. The contact is made by mail. An up-to-date mailing list is prepared. A printed copy of the questionnaire, with a covering letter and a stamped reply paid envelope, is mailed to the respondent on the mailing list. The covering letter, as a silent salesman, should create interest, convince and motivate or induce the informant to send prompt and accurate replies.

A gift incentive is provided to enlist co-operation and get a quick return of the duly completed questionnaire. A follow-up by a sweet reminder is necessary to secure the maximum response within a reasonable period.

The mail survey has no geographical limitation. It can reach even hard-to-reach respondents. It has, however, a few drawbacks. The response may be high as well as low. The questionnaire may not be carefully and completely answered. A higher rate of refusal and a lower degree of accuracy are the other important weaknesses of the mail survey.

(2) *Telephone Survey:* In big urban areas, we can interview the respondent on the telephone. It is an ideal method of communication when you need information on current activities; *e.g.*, on radio listening or TV viewing, while these activities are actually being carried on. If you need factual answers to a few questions, this method is very suitable. We can also have a large number of interviews in a short period. The telephone survey is quick and costs very little. The data collected are usually accurate. If respondents are concentrated in a city and are available on the phone, and if you require simple information, the telephone survey is the ideal choice. Of course, on the phone, people give non-committal answers, and they are unwilling to give personal information. Nor is a detailed investigation possible on the telephone. In India, this method has a limited scope, except in very big cities.

(3) *Personal Interview or Field Survey:* It is a direct form of investigation, involving face-to-face communication with a free feedback of information. It offers a sense of participation to the respondent. It is a more flexible form of data collection. The use of unstructured, open-end questions is possible. The rate of refusal is low. Depth interviews are possible. Complex questions can be asked. The interviewer may ask additional questions to secure more information. The observation approach may be combined to verify age, income, status, standard of living, etc. We can get accurate information. Visual aids in the form of pictures, advertisements, exhibits, etc., can be used to get views and opinions, and determine attitudes of the respondents. Literacy is not essential.

	Advantages	***Disadvantages***
(a) Personal interview	● Most reliable of the survey methods because of face-to-face contact.	● Most costly method.
	● Questions can be longer and more complex than with other methods.	● Some respondents such as high level business executives may be difficult to contact.
	● With skilled observation and probing, respondent can be encouraged to answer questions fully.	● Personal bias of individual interviewers can affect results.
	● Representatives of sample can be well-controlled.	● Reliability of face-to-face interviewing depends on integrity and skill of interviewers, which in some cases may be lacking.

Contd...

	Advantages	***Distadvantages***
(b) Telephone interview	● Fast, convenient method of obtaining even large number of responses in short time. ● Relatively low cost per interview. ● Sometimes good for reaching important people who are inaccessible. ● Respondents can be contacted at specific times of the day.	● Poor for obtaining large amount of information or for asking difficult questions. ● Securing co-operation not always possible. ● Obtaining a random sample may be difficult. ● Respondents cannot be observed while giving answers.
(c) Mail interview	● Interviewer bias is eliminated since no interviewer is present. ● Questionnaire may be answered more accurately since respondents can fill out forms at their leisure. ● Good for reaching people who are sometimes inaccessible. ● Comparatively low cost for reaching small and widely scattered groups.	● Extensive or complex questionnaire usually yield poor results. ● Respondent's interest in the subject under investigation has a direct effect on returns. ● Good possibility of biased or non-representative return. ● Respondents may be unable or unwilling to give answers without probing or stimulation from the interviewer.

However, we need trained, experienced and competent interviewers. This method, moreover, is a costly and time-consuming method of data collection. Special supervision is needed. The interviewer must be honest and loyal. It is possible that the data collected in an interview may be vitiated by the interviewer's bias.

Market Survey Techniques: Advantages and Disadvantages of Personal, Telephone, and Mail interview.

Qualitative Research Design

In qualitative research, the data can be collected by depth interviews, focus groups and projective techniques. The questionnaire consists of open-ended free-response questions of a probing nature to encourage the respondents to reveal their innermost thinking and beliefs.

Depth interviews are non-structured conversations of the respondent and a highly trained interviewer. Respondents are given the freedom to articulate freely about their activities, interest and opinions. They can reveal what they feel — their attitudes. The conversation is not restricted thus to the brand or product category under research. It takes some training to interpret the data so collected. Marketers gather valuable data which can guide them in product decisions.

Depth Interview and Focused Interview

Motivational Research Techniques: The motivational research techniques can be broadly classified as depth interviews and projective techniques. These techniques are designed to uncover information that direct questioning and observation methods cannot bring out. Their focus is on the reasons why individuals buy or use various products and what the act of buying, owning, or using the product, means to them.

In the discussion that follows, these two techniques are described briefly.

Depth Interview: Depth interviews are designed to uncover basic predispositions — unconscious feelings, needs, conflicts and the like. They achieve this result by creating a completely permissive atmosphere, in which the subject is free to express himself without fear of disapproval, admonition, or dispute and without advice from the interviewer. Depth interviews can involve one respondent and one interviewer or they may involve a small group of respondents, and a single interviewer. The latter type is called focus group interview and the former category is termed individual depth interview or just depth interview.

(1) *Individual Depth Interview:* Such interviews may be described as less-structured and more intensive than a standardised questionnaire-administered interview. There are three broad types of individual depth interviews:

(*a*) *True Depth or Clinical Interview* that corresponds to the psycho-therapeutic interview and requires far longer than a single session and is, strictly speaking, outside the scope of conventional marketing research.

(*b*) *Non-directive Interview* where, although the interviewer retains the initiative during the course of the interview, the respondent is given maximum freedom to respond in the manner he wishes, within reasonable bounds of relevance.

(*c*) *Semi-structured or Focused Interview* where the interviewer is required to cover a specific list of points and, although the respondent is allowed to respond freely, a much tighter control is exercised by the interviewer in order to maximise the collection of relevant data. Specific areas may be focused upon.

Individual depth interviews require great skill and considerable time. There are difficulties not only in establishing the right degree of confidence and eliciting answers but in interpreting the qualitative information provided. Analysis and interpretation are highly subjective. The technique is obviously expensive and in practice, group rather than individual interviews are more common place.

(2) *Focus Group Interview:* A variation of the depth interview is the focus group interview. A number of individuals (usually 8 to 12) are brought together rather than being interviewed one at a time as in the individual depth interview. Each group is designed to reflect the characteristics of a particular market segment of interest. The interaction among the group members is only loosely directed by the group interviewer, called the moderator. The moderator attempts to develop three clear stages in the group interview: (*i*) Establishing rapport with the group, structuring the rules of group interaction, and setting objectives; (*ii*) Provoking intense discussion in the relevant areas: and (*iii*) Summarising the groups' responses to determine the extent

of agreement. The moderator requires to perform the difficult task of guiding the discussion into the relevant areas while exerting minimum influence on the content of the discussion.

Focus group interviews are currently one of the most frequently used techniques in marketing research. They have been applied to: (*i*) Generate idea of new products; (*ii*) Explore consumer reaction to new product concepts; (*iii*) Explore consumer response to both advertising concepts and finished advertisements; (*iv*) Explore consumer response to package design and labellings; (*v*) Develop consumer vocabulary as a preliminary step in structuring questionnaires, and so on.

The Carnation Company (USA) provides an interesting example of the type of information focus group interviews can provide. Past research had revealed that many people did not drink powdered milk because of a perceived taste deficiency when compared with fluid milk. Carnation decided to reposition the brand to make it more appealing. First, Carnation conducted focus group interviews separately with users and non-users. Discussion with non-users confirmed that taste was a major barrier to use. Sessions with users revealed that a large percentage of them solved the 'taste problem' by mixing powdered milk half and half with fluid whole milk,

A GOOD FOCUS GROUP

QR uses 'focus groups' consisting of respondents whose quality does matter. A focus group should not include 'professional' respondents, or respondents belonging to the industry being researched. A focus group should have the right number, and last minute inclusions should not be used just to make up this number.

A focus group should be seated comfortably at a right venue with an opportunity for the moderator to maintain an eye contact. Videography facilities should be properly set up. A moderator should strike empathetic bonds. He should be sensitive to the body language and group dynamics. He should be able to make everyone talk naturally, without undue interruptions. In a good group, respondents talk more than the moderator. A moderator should avoid distracting behaviour, say spinning a pendant in hand.

The group discussion should be properly structured. Justice should be done to everything included in the study, e.g., attitude exploration, purchase processes, brand positioning, feedback to ads and products.

The participation should include all respondents. A dominant member should not overshadow an average respondent.

A group must provide good consumer insights. That is the very purpose of QR.

thus, producing a cheaper, better-tasting low-fat milk. Carnation hypothesised that non-users would be more likely to be converted if the company respositioned its product as milk extender. Quantitative research confirmed this hypothesis, and Carnation executed the strategy with an advertising and promotion campaign that told the milk extender story.

There are a number of *advantages* of focus group interviews over individual depth interviews. Each respondent is able to expand and refine his or her opinion in the interactions with the other members. Thus, the interaction process provides more detailed and accurate information than could be derived from individual depth interview. Snow-balling occurs when a comment, perhaps random, by one member triggers an idea or similar feelings in others. A group interview situation is generally more exciting and offers more stimulation to the participants than individual depth interviews. The heightened interest and excitement make more meaningful comments likely. In addition, the security of being in a crowd encourages some members to speak out when they otherwise would not. Because any question raised by the moderator is to the group as a whole rather than to individuals, the answers contain a degree of spontaneity not produced by other techniques. Furthermore, individuals are not under any pressure to 'make up' answers to questions.

However, there are a number of *disadvantages.* Both non-participation and non-response can be serious sources of error. Focus groups are expensive on a per-respondent basis. Without a sensitive and effective moderator, self-appointed participant will dominate the discussion. Participants may react negatively toward the dominant member and this may have a 'halo' effect on attitudes toward the concept or topic of discussion.

Projective Techniques

These techniques help to reveal the underlying motives of an individual despite his attempt to rationalize them unconsciously or conceal them consciously. They may consist of sentence completion tests, word-association tests, inkblot tests, picture tests. In Thematic Apperception Test (TAT) a picture is shown and the thoughts projected are likely to reveal the underlying needs, wants, fears, motives and aspirations. They expose their feelings without being aware of them.

Analysis

In quantitative research, the data is tabulated and analysed, either manually or with the help of a computer. In qualitative research, the responses are analysed by the test administrator.

Report Preparation

Each report summarises the findings as *executive summary.* The main body of the report consists of background study, research problem, research objectives, research design used, and findings. The data in the form of tables and graphics is appended to the research report. The questionnaire administered is also appended to the report.

Consumer Research Methods

The following diagram lists the method used for different aspects of consumer behaviour.

CONSUMER BEHAVIOUR VARIABLE

Motivation	Personality	Perception	Attitudes	Social Class	Culture	Opinion Leadership	Communications
• OB • S • PT • FG/DI	• S • PT	• S • PT • FG/DJ	• OB • S • PT • FG/DI	• S • FG/DI	• OB • SB • FG/DI •S	• E • OB • S • PT	• E • S • PT • FG/DI

Where OB = Observation, S = Surveys, PT = Projective Tests, FG/DI = Focus Group and Depth Interview and E = Experimentation.

Consumer Research Tools

The following diagram illustrates the various tools under the different research methods followed.

Experimentation
- Split Tests
- Copy Pre-testing
- Tachistoscopes

Observation
- Cameras
- Meters
- Content Analysis

Surveys
- Questionnaires
- Attitude Scales
- Value Instruments
- Inventories

Projective Tests
Sentence Completion
Word Association
Picture Sorting
Ink Blots
TAT
Other Person Characterisation

Focus Group/Depth Interviews
Screener Questionnaires
Discussion Guides

Mapping the Unknown

In this age of Internet, credit cards and mobile phones, we leave footprints all over the place, and the marketers follow these. Restaurants, air-lines and other consumer durables and non-durables companies track their customers after mapping their business needs. The data is captured after investing in technology. The database is utilised by the marketing people. It is a powerful medium to inform consumers of new products and services, cross-selling, targeted offers on the basis of clustering, and one-to-one offers. Most of these offers are made off-line, while the Net is also a powerful one-to-one marketing medium. The footprints also enable marketers to design relationship and loyalty marketing programmes, do telemarketing and personalize the offers. It is, however, difficult to map the complete life of an individual. Mapping also may cause a backlash from the consumers who would like to guard their privacy. They get irritated with unsolicited letters, phone-calls and mail. Indians are by and large tolerant, and a backlash is possible only when someone is obviously intrusive. Companies should not force the customer to answer questions they do not want to. Self-regulation is necessary, or else legislation will take over. Consumers should not share beyond basic demographic data. Indian consumers are also apprehensive that the data may reach the tax authorities.

Methods in Psychology

I. Statistical Method	Correlation
II. Descriptive Method	Interview, Introspection
III. Experimental Method	Clinical case study, Observation, Survey, Developmental.

I. Statistical Method

Correlation: A method is a procedure of studying human behaviour. The aim is to understand human beings but the approach is different.

Correlation is a method that requires a knowledge of the relationship between two or more psychological variables.

A variable is anything that can be measured and that can change. For example, intelligence is a variable as it can be measured and individuals differ in their levels of intelligence.

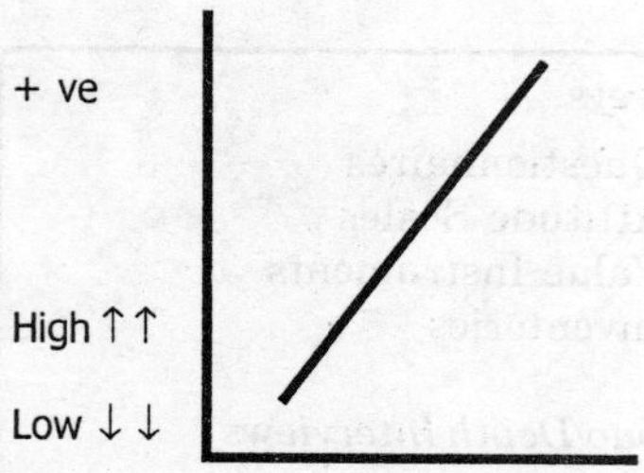

Fig. 2.2: Positive Correlation

Correlation coefficient expresses the direction and degree of such a relationship. It is symbolished by 'γ'. Correlation could be positive or negative. This indicates the direction. Positive correlation can be graphically illustrated as follows:

It means that high values of one variable go with high values of the other variable and low values of one variable go with low values of the other variable.

For example, high price goes with high quality and low IQ goes with low performance.

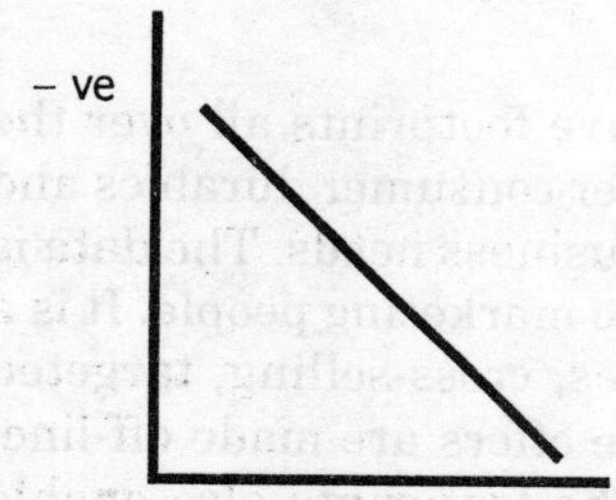

Fig. 2.3: Negative Correlation

Negative correlation can be graphically illustrated as:

It means that high values of one variable go with low values of the other variable.

For example, the more open or parking space in a city, the lower will be the accident rate.

The GOAL of correlation is to predict behaviour and understand mental processes. However, it does not mean causation, it does not reveal the direction of causality. A third factor could be responsible in influencing the result. In conclusion, it is a method of summarizing the relationship between two sets of statistical data.

II. Descriptive

(1) Introspection: It is self-observation focussing attention on one's thoughts, feelings, motives and reporting these to the researcher.

It is of two types:

(a) Casual: not used in research. The person just happens to notice how he is feeling. There is no deliberate attempt to focus on himself. Daydreaming, having fantasies are examples. Then we begin to remember the details of the daydream.

(b) Experimental: Observers are trained to attend to their own reactions, feelings, motives, etc. and describe them. It is a method of psychology.

(c) Titchener: perfected this method, when a subject is undergoing an experience (in a lab), he would ask him to introspect and report what he has been experiencing. For example, look at bulb for ½ min and then a white wall. He sees its image on the wall. This is what he reports when he introspects.

Disadvantages of Introspection

(1) The person may make judgements.

(2) No way of checking it is true or false because it is subjective.

(3) May differ from person to person.

(4) May give contradictory results.

(5) Emotions may cloud your introspection. "may come in the way of being scientific and objective."

(6) May be limited in scope because they can't be used with children or animals.

Advantages

(1) Can lead to further research

(2) Only source of knowledge of sensations, feelings and motives and so, can be used where scientific method is not possible.

(3) When there is a general agreement on the reports, we may rely on its results.

III. Experimental

(1) Case History: The method studies the behaviour of one person at a time. It is widely used by clinical psychologists (also by counselling and personality psychologists)

Steps involved are:

(i) Case history: Find out about their background, childhood, school performance, also through interviews with other People.

(ii) Administering psychological test: Of intelligence personality and Aptitude

(iii) Diagnosis: With both and DSM (Diagnostic & Statistical Manual)

(iv) Therapy or Treatment: Treated by psychotherapy, psycho-analysis.

(v) Evaluation.

Advantages

(i) Help overcome childhood problems.

(ii) Help treat illnesses of the client.

(iii) Get in-depth information about the client.

(iv) It suggests ideas of study by other methods.

Disadvantages

(i) While getting information for case history, interviewing others may get you faulty information, their loss of memory.

(ii) Is subjective, not scientific.

(iii) Depends on client's willingness to talk, dishonesty.

The data corrected may throw light on general problems of psychology. Freud's treatment of his patients led to a general theory of psychology "Dreams express unfulfilled wishes."

(2) Survey Method: Survey research studies the population by selecting small samples from it. A population is made up of all the persons, objects, events, etc. to be studied. Survey is used in social and community psychology. It is used to discover the relative incidence, distribution and inter-relation of variables. The study of public opinion, effect of advertising on purchases and the factors involved in success in work are some of its uses. Terman used this for determining the causes of happy marriage. His investigation of 792 couples showed that happy marriages depend upon how well-matched the couples are in their sex-drive.

The sample should be large enough and it should be representative i.e., it should contain the same proportion of different types of people that the population contains.

Example: With regards to a survey in FYJC Arts, there must be representatives from the Maths, History and Political Science, Hindi and French subjects. More girls than guys, etc. To find out Indians' attitudes to 'love marriages' the sample must consists of 75% villagers and 25% city dwellers as these are the relative proportions of population in rural and urban areas.

Surveys are of Different Types

(1) Personal interviews
(2) Panel interviews
(3) Mail questionnaires
(4) Telephone interviews

It is important in a survey for the questions to be properly framed, in the language of the respondent, generally avoid too awkward or personal questions.

Types of Questions

(1) Poll type (Yes/No) for quantitative analysis
(2) Open-ended (where the person has to write) for qualitative analysis.

Advantages of Survey Method

(1) It has wide scope and can gather a lot of information from large groups.
(2) It is economical compared to other methods.

Disadvantages

(1) It gives superficial information.
(2) Social desirability.

(3) Developmental Method: In this method, behaviour is observed at different stages in the process of growth. The observer needs to be trained and impartial. The value of this method depends on these Examples: Parent's observations of the development. of behaviour in their children are often unreliable as (1) parents are not trained observers and (2) they are likely to notice favourable points and ignore unfavourable ones.

Different Kinds of Studies

(a) Cross-sectional method: Here people of different ages are assessed on one occasion. It tells us about the differences in development among different age groups.

(b) Longitudinal studies: Researchers measure the same people more than once to see changes in development over time.

(c) Sequential studies: Here, people in a cross sectional sample are tested more than once. It is a combination of (a) and (b).

Disadvantages

(1) For studies done on one person, it is not possible to generalise.

(2) It usually takes a long time and is laborious.

(3) To study same groups for 5-10 years is difficult.

(4) Information obtained could be misleading and inaccurate.

Advantages

(1) Gives useful information about development and growth.

(4) Method of Systematic Observation (FIELD Study Method): It consists of the systematic observation of naturally occurring behaviours. Here, the researcher neither manipulates a variable nor does he control all relevant variables. There is no cause-effect link.

It is different from causal observation. It is planned. The observer is trained and knows what to look for and he has to ensure that his opinions do not affect his observations.

Time sampling is taking samples of the number of expressions of behaviour in the form of acts that occur in a given time period. Research can use video-cameras, one-way mirrors, so people can be observed without their knowledge. If people know they are being studied, they will behave so as to be in a favourable light. Example: to study mentally ill people, to study influence of heredity/environment on behaviour.

This method is especially useful because we can't manipulate all variables and because there may be ethical reasons against doing so For example, we can't deliberately place an infant in an orphanage to find out how his behaviour is affected by the environment in an orphanage.

Advantages

(1) It is realistic as it studies naturally occurring behaviours in natural settings.

(2) It can give insight into areas that can later be experimentally studied.

(3) Important variables that cannot be studied in the laboratory can be studied with this method.

(4) It can be used to study children and animals.

Disadvantages

(1) It does not give us information about cause and effect and can't test hypotheses.

(2) There is less control and less precision (accuracy).

(5) Interview Method: Interview is the oldest method of psychology. It is used for selecting persons for a given occupation or finding suitability for a certain course. It is also used by clinical and counselling psychologists and consumer and industrial psychologists. Interviewer notes what he hears and observes the subjects behaviour. He forms his judgement on the basis of his observations and replies to questions. Interview can be structured or unstructured and Panel or Personal. It can be casual or formal. The case may differ according to circumstances. The purpose is to collect data about the individual.

Structured: Set of some questions to lot of individuals; to recruit people to specific posts; specific format of interview

Unstructured: find out further qualifications. Modification may be made from individual to individual; finding out of details

Panel: to cross examine and recruit on unanimous decision.

Personal: by single individual of higher authority.

Advantages

(1) Allows correct selection of personnel.

(2) Comparisons are possible and so, there is a choice of choosing the best.

(3) Provides enough scope to observe verbal and non-verbal communication.

(4) Gives an immediate feedback.

(5) Gives you enough of time for clarification.

(6) Helps to observe candidates communication skills, inter-personals skills.

(7) Sometimes, it is possible to assess knowledge of the task.

Disadvantages

(1) It is not possible to assess knowledge of the task always. For example, a teacher's ability for class-control can't be assessed at an interview.

(2) Interviewer's bias i.e., attitudes, prejudice, likes and dislikes may work negatively against the individual.

(3) It is time-consuming.

(4) It is a disadvantaged situation because the individual is at the receiving end.

(5) It is highly subjective.

(6) It is too short a time to assess ability.

(7) Individuals may forget, fake, misinterpret or exaggerate details.

(8) When rating scales are used, this method suffers from defect.

(6) Experimental Method: It is observation which takes place under conditions controlled by the experimenter/investigator/researcher.

The subject is a person or animal on whom the experiment is done.

The experimenter is the person who conducts the experiment.

Variable is any factor that varies or changes qualitatively or quantitatively.

Three Types of Variables: Ideally, a variable is something which can be quantified and measured but in most cases it may be merely the presence or absence of the condition i.e., only two levels e.g., effect of alcohol on handwriting.

Independent Variable (IV): It is a condition created or selected by the experimenter. The investigator manipulates this variable to study its effect on another variable.

Dependent Variable (DV): It is the measure of the behaviour of the subject which occurs due to the independent variable. It is called dependent because its value changes or depends on the value or changes of the IV. Usually the hypothesis is formulated about the effect of one variable (IV) on another variable (DV).

Confounding/Relevant/Extraneous/Intervening Variable: These are other factors which are likely to affect the dependent variable. For example, age, gender, IQ. These variables must be controlled or kept constant.

Example: Effect of Alcohol (IV) on Speech (DV). ***Hypothesis*** more alcohol worsens speech. First group is given IV and other isn't. 1st group has more of 20 yr. olds and second has 50 yr. olds. The 1st group may be affected more but that could be because of age. Gender also may be a confounding variable, e.g., woman's reaction to distress may be emotional but man's practical.

Need for Control in an Experiment: There are two techniques to control confounding variables:

(1) Use of a control group: It is reference group i.e., a group whose behaviour is observed under normal conditions. The IV is presented to the experimental group but not to the control group.

The experimental group is a group whose behaviour is observed under experimental conditions. Ideally, the control group should consist of subjects who are matched with the subjects in the experimental group in every relevant way except one i.e., the IV. Only then, can we be sure that the differences in the DV are due to the IV and not due to other confounding variables. If factors other than the IV vary along different levels of the IV, the experiment is said to be confounded. The relevant variables which must be equated across groups include firstly (1) subject variables e.g., age, gender, IQ, etc. Secondly (2) environmental variables e.g. the room of testing, light, temperature, etc.

Steps in this Method

(a) Equate the two groups: the assumption of initial equality is important because the belief is that the groups initially are the same but will be different after special treatment of one of them (the experimental group).

(b) Experimental treatment: The IV is introduced in the experimental group and all other conditions are controlled.

(c) Evaluation of the outcome: the effect of the IV on the DV is measured. The two groups are compared.

Example: Studying effect of anxiety on memory test. Anxiety – → IV and performance of test → DV. CG is not made anxious but the EG is made. So, the EG may fare more poorly than the CG.

(1) ABAB Design/Before-After Method/Within Subjects Design

Here, there are no separate groups i.e., EG and CG. There is only one group.

Steps:

(a) *Observe baseline activity:* Before introducing the IV, the subject is observed and the measure of the DV is obtained.

(b) *Introduce IV:* The IV is introduced and the change in the DV is noted.

(c) *Return to baseline:* In order to check whether the change in the DV is due to the IV, the IV is withdrawn and any change in the DV is noted.

(d) *Reintroduce IV:* The special treatment is again given and the change in the DV is noted.

Example: Hypothesis = Ignoring tantrums help decrease them, IV = ignorance, DV = tantrums

Steps:

(1) Baseline Activity → Observing behaviour before IV is introduced.

(2) Introduce IV → Ignoring the tantrums on the next day.

(3) Observe the change if any → On 1st day, tantrums may be about 10 and on the 2nd day 5.

(4) Return to baseline → Withdraw the IV. Measure the number of tantrums again. There might be 8/9 tantrums.

(5) Re-introduce IV → to verify the hypothesis, count number of tantrums which may have reduced to 4 or 5. This helps to know if hypothesis is proved.

How to Establish Control in an Experiment?

There are several measures of control:

(1) Use of ABAB Design.

(2) Use of Matched Groups Design.

(3) Use of Placebo Design.

It is introducing an independent variable. Sometimes, it could mean introducing similar conditions to the control group. This helps to determine that the changes are a result of a particular independent variable only.

For example, if we believe drug *x* improves memory, drug *x* would be introduced to the experimental group and the control group would be given a sugar-coated pill which would resemble drug *x* in many ways.

Another example, effect of caffeine on sleep. Here, the placebo is decaf.

(4) Single Blind Technique: It is a condition where subjects are unaware whether they belong to an experimental or control group in an experiment. This reduces their ability to influence the results of an experiment. For example, the experimenter told the students to pick a card which instructed to pick a 2nd card. The 2nd card told them to calculate huge figures and then tear the card. The students diligently did this one by one. When asked why, they said they thought he was checking patience and so wanted to help him. In reality, he was checking frustration.

(5) Double-Blind Technique: In this, both the experimenter and the subjects are unaware which of the subjects belong to the experimental or control group. This is to prevent experimenter's bias in influencing the results. An assistant who would be helping the experimenter in the experiment would be aware of the classification.

For example, the experiment wanted to check humour. While reading the joke to the experimental group, he was very funny but was serious with the control group. This affected the result.

Disadvantages of Experimental Method

(1) All relevant variables in an experimental can never be controlled. Thus, the experiment is always likely to be confounded.

(2) Since the experiment is conducted in a lab under controlled conditions, the environment is artificial, subjects know that they are being studied and observed.

*Example.: **Hawthorne Effect:*** In Hawthorne studies in an experimental setup, the effects of environmental settings (IV) on performance (DV) were studied. Their performance was studied under extreme cold, heat, light, crowds. It was found that inspite of adverse situations, there was a high performance. So, the subjects knew that they were being studied and so, performed to their maximum capacities. This eventually manipulates the result of the experiment.

(3) Demand Characteristics: The experimental situation may interfere with the results because of the subjects attitude or motivation. The subject does what he believes is expected of him. He formulates his own hypothesis and behaves accordingly. Therefore, the results may be distorted. This is called Demand Characteristics.

To control this, the Single Blind Technique is used. Example: In Hawthorne's experiment, he was studying frustration. The subjects believed that something is demanded of them and behaved in a manner trying to prove their own 'hypothesis' i.e., they thought he wanted to check their patience.

(4) Investigator's Expectation: may also affect the results. He may unconsciously question the subject in an expected manner. This distortion of experimental results by the investigator's tendency to see, wished for results, in the data is called EXPERIMENTAL BIAS.

To control this, Double Blind Technique is used. e.g.: In *Masling's Rorschach Ink Blot Test,* there were 2 groups of subjects who were given ambiguous pictures and they were to say what 1st came to their mind. When the experimenter told them that when administered, people would tend to human forms, the results were mostly faces of people and when told mostly animals, they gave animal responses. There was a difference in the results because among each group, subjects did see what their responsible experimenters believed through non-verbal questions, nods, smiles, subtle questions and they made the expected response.

(5) The experimental method has limitations as it can't be used in all situations.

Advantages:

(1) *Since extraneous variables* are controlled, there is greater confidence in the results and greater precision. This method is therefore EMPIRICAL and SCIENTIFIC.

(2) *Through this method,* hypotheses can be tested. A hypothesis is an assumption of the effect of the IV on the DV. Thus, cause effect relationships can be established.

(3) *Repeatability:* If all relevant conditions are controlled, the experiment can be replicated by other investigators to verify the results.

Jam Study: Sheena Iyengar

It is harder and harder for us to make a choice when the number of options are more. To make the choice easier, the number of options must be reduced. Sheena Iyengar, Columbia Business School, quotes 'Jam study' with Mark Lepper conducted at Draeger's grocery store in Menlo Park, California to determine whether the wider choice of options actually result in higher sales. They set up a tasting booth near the entrance of the store at which they put either 6 flavours of jam or 24. They looked at two things. First, when people were more likely to shop at the tasting booth, and when they were more attracted to jam. In fact, 60 percent of the shoppers walking by stopped when 24 Jams were displayed. When only 6 jams were displayed, only 40 percent stopped. The second thing they looked at was in which case people were more likely to buy a jar of jam. They observed the reverse. Of the people who stopped when there were 24 jams on display, only 3 per cent actually bought a jar of jam. In contrast, when there were 6 jars of jam on display, 30 percent of the people who stopped ended up buying a jar of jam. Simple arithmetic tells us that when there were 6 jams on display people were over six times more likely to buy a jar of jam than when there were 24 jams on display.

We have cognitive limitations. As such, making a choice becomes increasingly difficult as the options increase. We might to decide to skip the choice altogether. Large assortments have three negative effects — people are less committed to making a choice, they make more errors and are less consistent in their choices. Even when they make objectively good choices, they could be less satisfied with the choosing process or their outcomes.

❑❑❑

3

MARKET SEGMENTATION

Let us first understand the concept of a market. First of all, we must find out whether there is a need for the product. Secondly, we must know whether those who need a product are interested in buying or using the product. After this the next step is to find out whether the interested and needy consumers have the wherewithal to buy it. Perhaps, they have the money, but it is necessary to find out whether they are willing to buy the product. In short, a demand for a product that satisfies a need becomes effective when it is backed up by the purchasing power and the willingness to buy. A market is thus by definition comprises people or businesses with a potential interest, purchasing power and willingness to spend the money to buy a product or service that satisfies a need. The following diagram illustrates this concept:

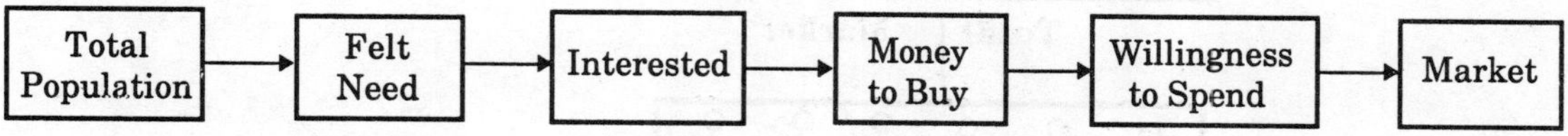

Fig. 3.1: What is a market?

Let us take an illustration. Tatas have started producing a Mercedes Benz car here in India. Many individuals have a need for a car but they may not need a luxury car like Mercedes. They are happy with Fiat or Ambassador or Maruti. Some might be interested in a luxury car, but may not be interested in Mercedes as it may attract the attention of tax authorities. They may prefer other luxury cars like DCM Daewoo, Ford Ikon, Opel Astra, Honda City and so on. Some may be interested in Mercedes but they are not able to afford a price of Rs. 32 lacs. Thus the market for Mercedes is a very small portion of luxury car markets which is a small portion of the total car markets.

Market Segmentation

At the beginning of the 21st century, we are in an era of micro-marketing which means knowing our customers well enough so as to give them products and services they need, and to direct promotional efforts to their needs and attitudes, and to build strong channel relationship.

Markets are today flooded with a wide variety of products, each for a specific need. Thus in soft drink market, we have two broad product classes — cola drinks and non-cola drinks. In both these classes, there are a number, flavours. Cola drinks which are sweet like Pepsi, and the real thing like Coke and want-my-thunder-type like Thums Up. In non-cola drinks, there are different flavours like orange, lime and kala-khatta. Soft-drinks are available from the fountain, off-the-rack returnable glass bottles, non-returnable PET bottles and aluminium cans. Sports Cola is for the cost-conscious, and Thums Up for young adventurous achievement-oriented customers. This is precisely what market segmentation is all about. It is a customer-driven focus.

Segmentation is the process of partitioning a large heterogeneous market into smaller groups of people or businesses which show similar needs and or characteristics thus resulting into a similar purchase behaviour.

There are two alternatives available to a marketer — treat the whole market as an entity or a collection of smaller sub-markets or segments with distinct characteristics. When the whole market is treated as one single entity, it is called *undifferentiated marketing strategy.* Such an approach is beneficial only to a few public utilities who operate as legal monopolies. Even these have to do some differentiation to meet competition from close substitutes. Thus couriers

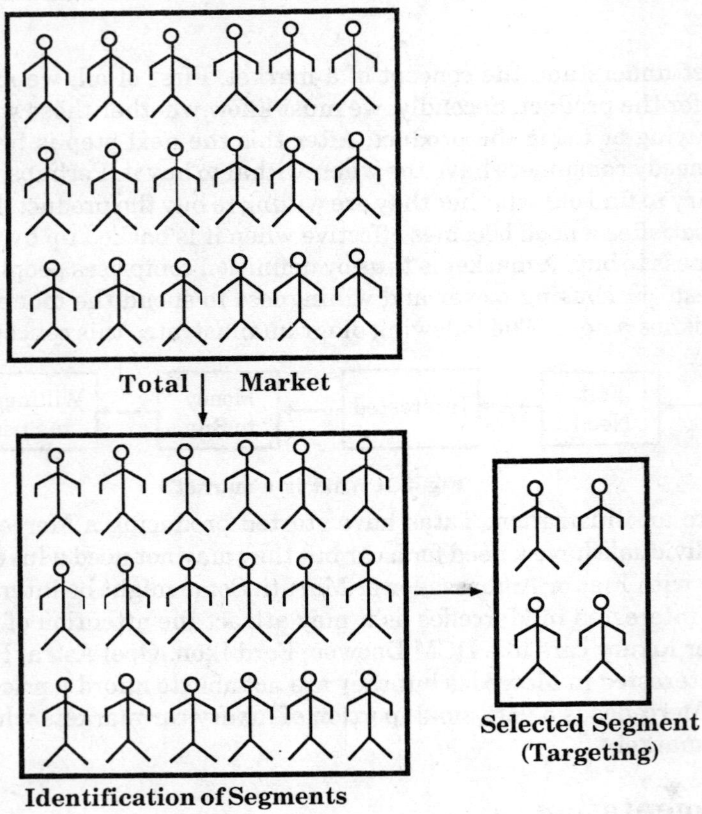

Fig. 3.2: Target Marketing

have influenced a monopoly like Posts & Telegraphs which now offers speed post service. In an undifferentiated marketing strategy, a single product is handled using a single marketing mix strategy directed towards all consumers in a market. It is also called total market approach. Here the organization depends upon mass production, mass distribution and mass promotion to reap the benefits of the economies of scale.

However, markets of today have a great amount of diversity. So the organisation uses market segmentation by identityfying two or more sub-markets based on their varying needs for targeting and concentration. Thus the target market is a group chosen out of the total market for whom a product is offered at a price that suits this group and to whom communication is directed and the product is made available to this chosen group through an appropriate channel. Thus targeting consists of addressing a specific group with a specific marketing programme. A target segment is that segment of the total market after which the advertiser decides to go. It is also called *target audience.*

Market differentiation is thus a segmentation strategy. It is practised in response to the nature of market demand. Product differention is not a segmentation strategy. It refers to creating different product versions on the basis of physical features of the product. It is suitable for commodities. Market differentation is broader. It is not restricted to product variants only. It goes beyond the product, and covers promotion, price and distribution aspects too. Thus in targeting, there is market differentiation and it is done on the strength of specific marketing programme, for the targeted group.

Out of the total segments of the market, if only one is chosen for targeting it is called *concentration strategy.* A publisher may decide to cater to taxation book segment of the total book market. Such a strategy is less expensive. If we carry out our segmentation exercise to its extreme, we finally reach the needs of an individual customer who may require a custom-made product, e.g., a super computer for a meteorological laboratory. Such a strategy is called an *atomization* strategy.

Benefits of Segmentation

Marketers indulge in segmentation exercise to exploit the diversity in the market. This way it serves its customers the best. It also defines the way it faces the competitors — its competitive positioning. Some benefits of segmentation are listed below.

(*i*) The market is defined on the basis of customer needs.

(*ii*) The products, promotion, price and place are all geared to changing consumer needs. It makes marketing responsive to the changing market.

(*iii*) The communication mix is specially prepared for a specific segment. The ad campaign thus becomes more effective. The media can be chosen to match the segment chosen. Personal selling is tuned to consumer needs. Marketing resources are better allocated.

(*iv*) In these days of globalization, organisation's face domestic and international competition. They have, therefore, to assess the strengths and weaknesses of competitors. A positioning stance of an organisation can decide its competition. We can design our competitive strategies better by choosing the segments and knowing the competition therein.

(*v*) Marketing objectives and strategies to exploit opportunities and ward off threats can be developed precisely. Marketing efforts are concentrated on a few segments rather than diluting them for the whole market. Performance can be evaluated against objectives set.

Two Approaches to Segmentation

There are two approaches to segmentation — divide the total market into homogenous sub-groups called segments. It is a breaking down of an entire market. Alternatively, the second segmentation approach starts with individual customers. Then the potential customers are identified with similar characteristics. When sufficient number of such customers are identified we have built up a segment. It should be appreciated that though segmentation divides the market in segments, it in reality is a consolidation process in which potential customers are put together on the basis of their common characteristics.

Limitations of Segmentation

Segmentation exercise suffers from several shortcomings. We should be aware that this mass marketing is less expensive than segmentation. While we segment, we have to devise a separate marketing programme, and we need additional resources to implement it. Segmentation is not a panacea for poor management skills and organizational defects. Segmentation requires a commitment of the organisation to implement research-based strategies. Segmentation profiles give an overall view of buyer's behaviour, but neglects individual differences. Two persons having the same income, age, education can show different buying behaviour depending on their psychological make-up. Psychographic analysis should supplement demographic analysis. An amazing diversity in consumer life-styles has made segmentation much more difficult. All customers may not fit in a slot created by market segment. Some of them are not slottable. These aberrations should give a group that is marginal and does not exceed 10 per cent of the total market. Any excess size of aberrant group calls for sub-segmentation.

Criteria for Effective Segmentation

A segment should satisfy three important criteria to be useful:

(*i*) it should be *substantial* in size and potential to justify the expenditure made on it.

(*ii*) it must be easily *accessible*, i.e., easy to reach.

(*iii*) it should show a distinct variation in responsiveness to marketing programmes in comparison with other segments.

Size

A segment ought to be of enough size so as to be viable. In some cases, even an individual customer is profitable especially when customized items like Rolls Royces and aeroplanes are sold. Generally, however, we have to decide whether there is such a number of customers which will justify its being treated as a target market. There can be a segment for cars designed specially for tall people or for that matter short people. But expenditures incurred in making and marketing cars for such segments when put against estimated sales will rule out such segmentation.

Accessibility

Sometimes there are enough numbers to make a segment but it is difficult to reach out to them either by promotion or distribution. Many products in India cannot be sold to rural consumers because of these very reasons.

Responsiveness to Marketing

All segments should not show the same response to a marketing programme. A segment has to differ from other segments in its response to justify its existence. If the same price concionsness is shown by all consumers, where is the necessity to offer premium and low-priced products? Segments are useful to marketers for selling only when they differ from other segments on marketing mix dimensions.

Segmentation Variables

There are several alternative methods of segmentation. The factors that describe and differentiate segments are called *segmentation variables.* In practice, all these parameters which enable to distinguish potential buyers and non-buyers can serve as segmentation variables. These variables have been distilled from consumer behaviour field. But consumer behaviour has both rational and emotional elements. The segmentation variables are thus a combination of these two—demographics, psychographics, motivational and need-based, perceptions, buyer habits and so on. Consider Air India who wants to attract non-flying passengers to its flights. First it will put its passengers into two segments — users and non-users. Here the segmentation variable used was *user-status.* Users are flying public and non-users are non-flying public. Non-flying public can be further segmented on the basis of their *attitudes* to flying — those who are scared to fly and those who are not. Some of them are indifferent to flying.

Only those who are not scared of flying and show a positive attitude towards it are chosen. Even here further segmentation is necessary. These who can afford to fly and those who cannot. The basis of segmentation is *income* here.

Let us see the target audience of Air India. It consists of those high-income group people who have positive feelings towards flying but have not so far flown. Here we have used three successive variables to identify our segment — *user-status, attitude and income.*

How to identify these variables which can be used in segmentation? A sample of consumers is interviewed and a hierarchy of variables is discovered. The consumers make use of these parameters while taking a purchase decision. The most common five segmentation variables are given below:

Geographic: An Oil Company can do a geographic analysis of its dealers.

Socio-economic: Credit card companies rate a customer on the basis of his income and social standing. A Gold Premium card of StanChart is offered to high income individuals employed in a responsible position or to self-employed professionals. An Executive card is offered to medium-income customers employed in junior cadre or small-time professionals. A classic card is offered to all those whose income is slightly above the taxable limit. It is no secret that a gold card customer differs from the classsic card customer.

Psychographic: Here the buyers are divided on the basis of their life-style and/or personality traits. People of the same demographic group are very much different in their psychographic profile. For example, the user of a lip-stick can be described as 'younger, better educated, working woman who is appearance-conscious and future-oriented.'

Product Usage: For beverages and liquors, buyers are classified into segments like heavy-users, medium-users and light-users. Heavy-users account for volumes. Many companies target their marketing effort to this segment. The heavy-users have their own demographic, psychoraphic and media-habit profile.

Benefits: Here the market is segmented on the basis of the benefits people seek from the product, e.g., lowest price, durability, use on special occasions. Benefit segmentation of toothpastes can be done on the basis of a flavour, price, product appearance, brightness of teeth, decay prevention. Forhans is for healthy gums, Colgate gives *Suraksha Chakra* and Close-up fresh breath. Naturally, Close-up is a craze with young people who like togetherness. A benefit to one customer, however, may be a drawback to another. If functions of a calculator are enhanced for one customer, the price increases, which the other customer resents as he may not have relevance for the additional functions. What is good for the goose may not so for the gander.

Segmenting Consumer Markets

Managers constantly strive to segment the market the best possible way. We shall now learn the alternative methods of segmentation available in consumer markets.

Geographic Segmentation

Most marketers consider geographic segmentation as the important basis of segmentation. It is a logical starting point, and is the simplest and less expensive. In this method, the total market is divided into different geographic areas like the sales districts, regions, zones, country, and the world. The division is based on our organisation's strength in coverage, marketing resources available, competition we are facing, competitor's strategies, corporate philosophy and capability to change the marketing mix variables to suit a geographic unit.

It goes without saying that our residence, place of work, and recreation do affect our buying behaviour. Geography decides the product consumption pattern. People in coastal areas of Konkan and Goa relish rice, a staple grain there and fish abundantly available from sea. Southerners are fond of coffee and north Indians like tea. People down south use body talc excessively, and apply it even on face, perhaps aspiring to look fairer like their counterparts in the north. When we market our products to international markets, we have to adapt the product to their needs. Rasna International gives an instant syrup when dissolved in a glass of water, and does not contain a lot of sugar. A complexion cream like Fair and Lovely sells only in India.

A multinational chooses several countries of the world as its market. While doing so, it caters to the international regions like the Gulf countries, the Warsaw countries, the Latin American countries, the European Economic Union, the South-East Asian countries and so on. The big organisation like Hindustan Lever decides to market products on all-India basis, but divides the market into north, south, west and east regions. Some smaller companies may choose a region or only some districts of a region to begin with and later on expand the market by adding other units. There are small-scale firms and retailers who operate in a local area which could be a city, a town or a village. Some companies operate in metropolitan areas only. There are very attractive emerging metros like Bangalore, Pune and Ahmedabad.

DEMOGRAPHIC SEGMENTATION

Segmenting a Market on Different Bases

Demographic Segmentation: Buyer groups differ in their requirements from the products and their marketing responses, e.g., low-income buyers prefer beedis for smoking, middle-income buyers smoke Wills Filter, and high-income buyers like 555 cigarettes. This is segmentation of the buyers on the basis of income. Such segmentation can be made on the basis of any relevant demographic variable, such as age, sex, life-cycle stage (single, married, married with children etc.), and occupation. Even education, race, religion and nationality can be the basis for demographic segmentation. Marketers generally do multi-variable demographic segmentation.

The following table illustrates the use of demographic variables.

TABLE 3.1

Variable	*Typical Break-up*
Age	Below 6 6 - 12 Teenage (13-19) 20 - 30 (Youngsters) 31 - 35 (Adults) 36 - 46 (Middle-aged) 47 - 60 60 plus (senior citizens) 70 plus (old)
Sex	Male, Female
Family Size	1 - 2 members 3 - 4 members 5 and above
Family Life Cycle (FLC)	Young, single Young, married, no children Young, married, children Young, married, older children Old couple Income - Below 5000 5000 - 10000 10000 - 15000 15000 - 20000 Above 20000
Occupation	Professional (MBA, CA, ICWA) Technical (B.E, B.Tech, B.Pharm) Government Servant Businessman Farmers Operatives Housewives Unemployed Retired/Pensioner
Education	SSC and less 12th/HSC Graduate Post-Graduate Doctoral and above
Religion	Hindu, Muslim, Parsi, Sikh, Christian, Buddhist, Neo-Buddhist
Nationality	Indian, Foreigner

FAMILY LIFE CYCLE

Concept of Family Life Cycle

People go through several phases in their lives. Family Life Cycle (FLC) refers to the series of life stages through which individuals proceed over a period of time.

In other words, FLC describes the process of family formation and dissolution.

To illustrate, a young man or a woman marry to form a family, in which children are born and live with the family till they grow up, and later move out. At last, the couple grows old and fends for itself. Each life cycle stage differs from previous stages in terms of (a) structure, (b) financial position, (c) consumption pattern, and (d) product need and preferences.

Traditional or Conventional FLC

The FLC is a progression of several stages.

(1) *Young and single bachelor stage:* The career has just started. However, in absence of burdens, they are free to spend as they wish. They tend to buy personal consumption items of food and clothing, are fun-loving and buy entertainment, have time to be on vacations and tours, move about on bikes, mobikes and other two wheelers, read novels and thrillers.

They buy some basic utensils and furniture.

(2) *Newly married couples* have household burdens and go through an expenditure phase in life. They generally buy consumer durables like furniture, wall paints, refrigerators, TVs etc.

(3) *Young married with child* directs their income to bringing up the child. They buy toys, medicines, tonics, baby foods, formula milk etc.

(4) *Older, married with children* are fairly stable income-wise. They like food products, music, educational services and a wide variety of other products.

(5) *Older married with dependent children* have high income, but do rational purchases. There is replacement buying.

(6) *Older, married with no children* become interested in self-education, saving schemes, hobbies, luxury appliances, magazines, health products.

(7) *Old, single, retired* people lead an economic life style. They are interested in health care and other services. They've budget constraints.

Revised FLC Concept for the New Millennium

Conventionally, family was considered a single unit throughout the life-time of an individual. However, this assumption is not true these days. There are families due to second marriages, with a legacy of children from previous marriages. There are deserted wives. There are divorcees. Several families are single parent family, where the parent could be either a father or a mother. Again, the ubiquitous working woman makes the traditional FLC model invalid.

Let us consider the following dimensions of Indian families in the new millennium.

Young, Married, with Child and Dual Income

Here both the husband and the wife work, and get two income cheques. The pace of the life is faster and there is less time for children and also for one another. The consumption pattern, therefore, shows preference for convenience goods like washing machines, grinder-mixers, rice cookers, grinding mill (gharghanti) etc. Women manage on two fronts — domestic chores and work. Husbands share the responsibilities of running the house to some extent. Instant foods, creches etc. appeal to such families. To compensate for the time babies miss with parents, there is a tendency to buy costly garments for kids, games for kids, prams etc.

Single Parent Families

The single parent family needs security and buys all the products that offer physical and psychological and financial securities — e.g., burglar alarms, teddy bears, insurance, saving certificates etc. When the child grows, he may be put in a boarding school/public school.

Divorced

They buy money saving products, lease or rental housing, child care, time saving appliances, instant foods. They are short of cash.

Older People, Married or Single

They are also cash poor, and health conscious. They need security. They also need recreation.

Middle-aged

They buy children's lessons (dance, music), dental care, furniture, autos, houses, dining out.

If there are no children, they are interested in luxuries, travels, gift products etc. Their cash position is good.

Segmentation Strategy on the basis of FLC

Product	*Segment*
(i) Cosmetics	Young single and young married women who are cash rich are a potential segment for beauty products like face creams, moisturizers, compacts, foundation make up etc. Middle-aged families need facials, sauna baths and such related products.
(ii) Vacations	Newly married couples are sold vacations at the time of marriage in the form of honeymoon packages. Middle-aged couples with no responsibility of children are the most attractive segment to sell vacations in the form of packaged tours. They are cash rich and free from encumbrances.
(iii) Housing	Young, married with children need starter housing. Middle-aged couples need housing — 2 bedroom flats etc. Bachelors need liberal and professional education. They are career minded. They can be sold courses like private secretary, computers etc.
(iv) Education	Middle-aged with children buy education for their children — home tuitions, coaching classes, public schools etc. They buy education for self also to improve their career — e.g., distance education programmes of IGNOU.

Psychographic Segmentation

The term was first coined by Emanuel Demby, a marketing researcher some 30 years ago. His definition of psychographics is: " the use of psychological, sociological and anthropological factors, self-concept and life-style to determine how the market is segmented by the propensity of groups within the market — and their reasons — to make particular decisions about a product, person, or ideology." Psychographic has come a long way since then.

Psychographic segmentation, either singly or in combination with demographic segmentation, is widely used these days, dividing the buyers on the basis of their social class, life-style and/or personality traits. The point to be appreciated is that people of the same demographic group are very much different in their psychographic profiles, e.g., young women show different psychographic characteristics.

Social class: In psychographic segmentation, buyers are divided on the basis of their social class, life-style and/or personality traits.

Many companies design their product offerings for different social classes, e.g., lower class, middle class or upper class. They build into their product those features that appeal to these social classes.

Life-style Segmentation

Life-style segmentation forms the basis of life-style advertising. Life-style is a mode of living, and helps us to understand those who are in the market in terms of their behaviour. The products which are often sold by this approach are cars, women's clothing, cigarettes, alcoholic beverages, cosmetics and furnitures. An automobile marketer can make a small-family car emphasizing safety, compactness, and economy and a car-freak for sportminded individuals who love manoeuvrability.

To use this segmentation, data are first collected for developing a profile of the consumer. One such approach is to make use of data concerned with three major characteristics — activities, interests and opinions (called AIO inventories). This is in addition to demographic characteristics.

Consider the following example:

Activities	*Interests*	*Opinions*	*Demographics*
Work Likings, hobbies Recreation Entertainment Shopping Geography	Job Home Food Media Community	Culture Social issues Politics Education	Age Education Income Occupation Family size Life Cycle

The researcher makes the consumer respond to a number of AIO statements, and then uses statistical techniques to group consumers into similar categories. The grouping facilitates marketer's job of composing relevant profiles of users / non-users.

For example, the user of a lipstick can be described as:

'Younger, better educated, working woman who is appearance-conscious, cosmopolitan and future-oriented.'

Thus the marketer gets valuable input for media selection and advertising content. In addition, we can identify likely uses of related products — the products which are consistent with this life-style.

Personality

Marketers have identified personality variables to segment the market. Motor-cycle buyers can be identified as 'independent, impulsive, macho, ready to change, confident people.' 'Charms cigarettes are smoked by young people who love the spirit of freedom.' Lipsticks are for 'young, out-going, beauty-conscious women.' Other products which cater to personality traits are liquor and insurance. The marketers try to adjust the brand's personality to the personality traits of buyers for whom it is meant. Consumers of different brands are subjected to personal preference tests to measure their different needs, and the differences in personality traits are recorded.

Personality characteristics, especially the self-image which ideally should correspond to the brand-image, are the basis of advertising appeals made to certain types of personality. Other personality characteristics used are changeability, adaptability, thriftiness, prestige consciousness, self-confidence, masculinity, conservativeness and sentimentalism.
Recently, consumer personalities have been put into five geometric shapes:

Shape	*Characteristics*	*Example*
Boxes	Neat, organised, highly structured	Accountants, Computer programmers
Triangles	Self-assured, respected, leaders	Politicians, entrepreneurs, executives
Rectangles	In a state of transition — they undergo life style changes. Hence, unpredictable	New employees, college graduates
Circles	Concerned about good interpersonal relationship, and peace	Secretaries, nurses
Squares	Creative, idea-oriented, eye for details	Scientists, artists

Adapted from *Market Segmentation,* Art Weinstein, Vision Books.

Since it is difficult to reach targets on the basis of traits like sociability, self-reliance or assertiveness, the classifications based on slots as given above become useful.

Behavioural Segmentation

In behavioural segmentation, buyers are divided into groups on the basis of benefits sought from the product, user-status, usage-rate, loyalty-status, attitude and readiness to use state.

Benefit Segmentation

Here the market is segmented on the basis of the benefits people seek from the product, e.g., lowest price, durability, use on special occasions. Benefit segmentation of toothpastes can be done on the basis of a flavour, price, product appearance, brightness of teeth and decay prevention. Forhans is thus for healthy gum, Colgate gives suraksha-chakra, and Close-up fresh breath. Naturally, Close-up is a craze with young people who like togetherness. In other words a benefit chosen is a pointer to their demographic characteristic. The benefit segmentation thus requires identification of major benefits which people look for, the kinds of people who look for such benefits and the major brands which offer such benefits. This approach is direct and customer-oriented.

The following table gives Benefit Segmentation of the Toothpaste Market:

TABLE 3.2

Benefit Sought	*Demographic Characteristic*	*Behavioural Characteristic*	*Psychographic Characteristic*	*Favoured Brand*
Low Price	Males	Heavy users	Price-conscious Independent	Babool
Decay Prevention	Big Families	Heavy users	Traditional Health-conscious	Pepsodent
Brightness of teeth	Teenagers Youngsters	Smokers	Outgoing Funloving	Colgate Promise
Good Flavour	Children	Mint lovers	Active Self-involvement	Colgate
Mouthwash	Youngsters Teenagers	Want intimacy and togetherness	Self-involvement	Close-up Gel
Gentler Toothpaste	Children between 2.5 to 7.5 years	Loves to taste	Fun Dependent on mother for good habits	Just for Kids

Adapted from Russel J. Haley, *Journal of Marketing*, July- '63.

Demographic variables correlate positively with purchase behaviour, e.g., income and luxury products. As the market matures, all brands are at the same level of performance and minor benefits distinguish them. Psychographic variables for consumer products offer more promise. The other two variables for segmentation are user rate (light drinker of beer, heavy drinker of coffee) and brand-loyalty.

Occasions

Buyers can be classified on the basis of the occasion on which they use the product, e.g., talcum powder is used after a bath, after a shave or before moving out for work. Thus a certain brand can be promoted as 'something that completes your bath.' Occasion segmentation can expand product usage. Formerly, thermos flask were used only to carry tea/coffee to in-patients of the hospitals. They are now promoted as picnic companions, office companions, lunch and dinner companions.

User Status

Every product is used by some, and not used by some others. The users and non-users are important for the company. Non-users can be the users of competitive products. There can be ex-users for a product. First-time users have just started using the product. Many in the target group are potential users. All management students who opt for optional Advertising paper are potential users of this textbook. Marketers are interested in converting non-users into users. Potential users and regular users require different marketing approaches.

Usage Rate

For beverages and liquors, buyers are classified into segments like heavy users, medium users and light users. Heavy users account for volumes. Many companies target their marketing effort at this segment. The heavy users have their own profile in terms of demographic, psychographic and media habits.

Loyalty Status

Brand loyalty status is also the basis for segmentation. Hard-core loyalty means constant brand loyalty over a period of time. Soft-core loyalty means loyalty divided over two or three brands. Brand-switchers change their loyalty often. They are non-loyal. Shifting-loyals shift from one brand to another, say from A to B.

In India, razor-blades market and toothpastes market, and to some extent toilet-soaps market is highly brand-loyal. It is difficult to gain market share for new companies. The entry in this market for new-comers is difficult.

A company can make an analysis of its brand-loyal customers to determine its target market. For instance, Colgate buyers are more middle-class, larger-families who are health-conscious. The study of soft-core loyalty gives an indication to nature of competition. Possibly, Colgate finds that Colgate buyers also use Promise. By making use of direct-comparison advertising, Colgate can improve its position. Brand shifters indicate our own marketing weaknesses. Non-loyals can be put on our brand by winning them.

Brand-loyal purchases may be due to other variables like price, habit, indifference or non-availability of other brands. It should, therefore, be carefully studied.

Buyer Readiness Stage

People at a given point of time are in different stages of readiness to buy a product. They are either totally unaware or aware. Some are informed and some interested. There are some who have a desire to buy or some who intend to buy. The quantum of these groups determine the marketing programme. To create an awareness of cancer is the first step in advertising before people can come forward for a check-up. Later, cancer check results are so dramatized that more people desire to have them. Infrastructure is created to handle the motivated individuals for check-ups. In other words, the marketing programme is tailored to the distribution pattern which changes depending upon the readiness of buyers.

Attitude

There are several attitude classes of buyers — enthusiastic, positive, neutral, negative and hostile. Vast reminders work for enthusiastic people. Positive attitudes are reinforced. Neutral people are carefully converted. Negatively inclined and hostile people are difficult to tackle. The attitudes are co-related with demographic descriptors.

Identifying the Target Audience or Groups

The identification of the target audience is the process of sub-dividing the market on the basis of geographic, demographic, socio-economic, psychographic bases and the market conditions. The most common descriptions of the target audience are in terms of geographic, demographic and socio-economic terms, e.g., our soap is meant for high-income bracket people in Western India or our talcum powder is for urban women of cosmopolitan outlook who are on the move. However, these days mere demographic description is considered poor predictor of buyer behaviour, though it is the most common method of identifying the target audience. Of late, psychographic base is used to describe the personality traits, life-style, self-image and other psychological variables of the target audience. In Mumbai, MRAS: Market Research Advisory Services conducted a study of life-styles of cigarette smokers in 1975, identifying distinct groups or clusters of customers. Wills Flakes Filter Kings and Four Square Kings are targeted at the same demographic audience. However, qualitative research of customers who were subjected to expressing reactions to 118 psychological statements showed a remarkable contrast between the overall personality of those who smoke Wills and those who smoke Four Square. The table gives illustration of how the Garden Saree buying women are psychologically different from Garden Vareli dress-material buying women. Consumer differences extend beyond demographics as the AIOs piece together the total market puzzle.

TABLE 3.3

COMPARISON OF GARDEN SAREE WOMAN AND GARDEN VARELI DRESS MATERIAL WOMAN

Garden Saree Woman	*Garden Vareli Dress Material Woman*
Older	Younger
Married	Universal, unpredictable
Softer, quieter, intensely feminine	Venturesome
Grace and dignity	Exotic
Dreamer	

Haley suggests a benefit-sought as a useful base for identifying a target audience. It cuts across all other bases. The example of toothpaste users illustrates this. Toothpaste market has four identifiable segments, e.g., one concerned particularly with tooth-decay prevention, one with brightness of teeth, one with flavour.

Targeting makes the marketing mix relevant; and effective. The product matches consumer profile. The promotional programmes remain in tune with consumer willingness to receive, assimilate and react positively to communication. It is a recognition of the fact that the market is not a single cohesive unit but it is seething, desperate, pulsating, antagonistic, infinitely varied sea of differing human beings — everyone of them as distinct from the other as fingerprints; everyone of them living in circumstances different in countless ways from those in which everyone of them is living.

In Search of an Ideal Audience

As opposed to mass marketing, we have to select specific target markets for practising a specific marketing programme in target marketing. Thus targeting decision is not just a choice of a segment or segments. It also has to design a suitable marketing mix of the product, price, promotion and distribution variables for the chosen segments. While selecting our target markets, we have to consider whether a segment is meaningful and attractive. Meaningful segments differ from other segments in the way they respond to a given promotional effort or the way this segment can be approached. If we want to sell music, we can identify age groups — old people, middle-aged and youngsters. Old people prefer old melodies and religious songs. Middle-aged people like songs that lift up their spirits, and make them cheerful like ghazals, quawalis, thumris and sugam sangeet and youngsters like pop-music, feet-tapping rhythm, electronic synthesizer tunes of Rehman, Daler Mehandi, Apache Indian and so on. These three groups respond to music advertising differently. We reach them through different media. It is, therefore, meaningful to treat them as three separate segments. Attractive segments are not only meaningful, but are consistent with advertiser's plans and resources. These segments must provide profitable opportunities and must have growth potential.

APPENDIX 1

POSSIBLE ADVERTISING ARCHETYPES BASED ON PSYCHOGRAPHIC PROFILE OF AMERICAN WOMAN BY KATHY ZIFF

- *The Sensuous Woman:* Eyes closed, luxuriating in unabashed self-abandon. Film model: Parveen Babi.
- *The Siren:* Sexy, provocative, using body language. Film model: Mandakini (Ram Teri Ganga Maili). Advertising model: Garden Vareli.
- *The 'Come Hither':* Shy and sexy. Film model: Sharmila Tagore.
- *The Exotic Art Object:* Personality subservient to mood. She serves as a decoration. Film model: Rekha (Umrao Jaan). Advertising model: Raymond's Suitings. Old Spice.
- *The Cheer Leaders:* Friendly, engaging, non-seductive. The girl next door. Film model: Jaya Bhaduri. Advertising model: Fair & Lovely.
- *The Serious Woman:* Key dimension: Attractive competence, real authority. Film model: Priya Tendulkar (Rajni). Advertising model: Lalitaji (Surf).
- *The Amazon:* Dominant by sexual allure. Film model: Zeenat Aman. Advertising model: Dimple Kapadia (Crowning Glory).
- *The Independent yet Vulnerable Woman:* A free spirit who invites protection. Film model: Kitu Gidwani (Air Hostess). Advertising model: Stay-Free.

APPENDIX 2

PSYCHOGRAPHICS OF INDIAN HOUSEWIVES

P : SNAP

Cluster	*P: SNAP I 1987 Proportion (%)*	*P: SNAP II 1993 Proportion (%)*
The Gregarious Hedonist	8.7	6.6
The Contemporary Housewife	19.2	22.1
The Affluent Sophisticate	7.3	9.1
The Tight-fisted Traditionalist	14.8	10.0
The Troubled Homebody	15.9	18.3
The Anxious Rebel	14.1	15.8
The Archetypal Provider	13.0	8.8
The Contented Conservative	7.0	9.3
Total	100.0	100.0

N.B.: Advertisers have tended to concentrate on the first and the third clusters. The relevance of ad message to other clusters was answered by one word — aspirational. Wrist-watch ads have concentrated on the top three clusters. Tight-fisted traditionalist and Archetypal Providers are heavy users of soft drinks, vanaspati, washing soap, cooking oil, detergents and talcum powder.

The survey is called the Nation's Attitude and Psychographics (P: SNAP). The first survey was released in 1987. The research has been conducted by Pathfinders, the marketing research wing of Lintas. The objective was to go beyond mere demographics, and to develop a data-base of life-styles and psychographic information for women. The survey defines the urban women according to their beliefs, attitudes and life-styles in addition to their demographic profiles. The second such study was conducted in 1993. The third study has been published in 1997. The definitions of the clusters are given below:

- The Gregarious Hedonist : More likely to be working. Liberal food habits, believes she's successful. Personal life is more important than the family. An extrovert who indulges herself and uses all personal products.

- The Contemporary Housewife : Well-educated, working and hence double-income. More active life-style. High level of investments. Servants used. Optimistic. Into all types of media.
- The Affluent Sophisticate : Most self-assured and confident of all clusters. Late marriage. Full-time work. Educational and investment levels are high. English media.
- The Tight-fisted Traditionalist : Above 40 years housewives in high proportion Low to middle-income monthly-household income. High family consciousness. Insular and introverted life-style. Focus on thrift and economy.
- The Troubled Homebody : Large family size. Young motherhood. High proportion of widows. Low monthly house-hold income. Low level of education. Low media penetration. High pessimism.
- The Anxious Rebel : Better educated. Desires to study further and work. However, a pessimist. Not satisfied with what she has. High penetration of home appliances, music systems.
- The Archetypal Provider : More gregarious and prone to outside influence. House-proud. Low servant usage. High level of affluence. Penetration of consumer durables.
- The Contented Conservative : Larger than average families with older children. Insular life-styles except in food habits Early marriage. Middle-income level.

APPENDIX 3

Life-style Marketing

Life-style analysis makes our understanding of demographic groups sharper. In India, the marketers these days are tapping 'the young and upwardly mobile' group that cuts across many barriers. Many advertisement appeals are meant for this group. The behavioural differences do not come alive in demographic descriptions, but do show themselves in life-style patterns. Life-style is a group phenomenon which pervades various aspects of life. It implies a central life interest such as family, leisure, religion, politics, sexual exploits etc. and this interest fashions our interaction with the environment. Variations in life-style are a result of social change. Working women and working couples do have very distinct life-styles.

In India, one of the agencies is trying to build a psychographic profile of Indian children. Pathfinders have identified 8 types of Indian housewives.

VALS System of Classification

Values and Life-style (VALS) classification was developed by Arnold Mitchell. The adults (18 plus) are classified into distinctive life-style groups. Each group has psychological needs (values) and behavioural response patterns (life-styles). Much of VALS is based on Maslow's Need Hierarchy. VALS blends together demographics, attitudes, activities, consumption patterns, brand preferences and media graphics.

Four Major Groups in VALS

(*a*) Need-driven poor and uneducated,

(*b*) Outer-directed upper and middle-class,

(*c*) Inner-directed due to inner motivations,

(*d*) Integrated — a combination of both outer — and inner-directed values.

The above model of Thomas puts these groups into nine specific VALS segments.

NEED-DRIVEN SUSTAINER SURVIVOR OUTER-DIRECTED BELONGER EMULATOR ACHIEVER I-AM-ME EXPERIENTIAL INNER-DIRECTED SOCIETALLY CONSCIOUS INTEGRATED

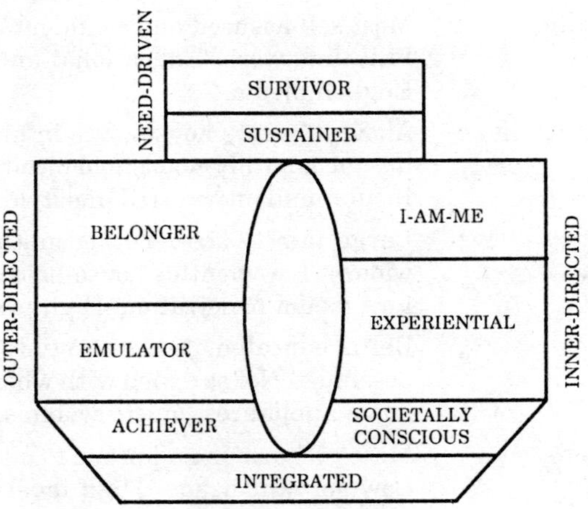

Fig. 3.3

Survivors are price-conscious, and not very knowledgeable shoppers. Sustainers are swayed by brands and guarantees and are impulse-buyers. Emulators buy to impress others, and to announce their status. Achievers buy high tech items and original top of the line products. Experiential buy for experimenting. Societally conscious want value for money.

Survivors are depressed; sustainers are strugglers. Belongers are conventional, emulators are status-conscious. Achievers are leaders and I-am-me are young, impulsive people. experientials pursue a rich inner life, and are interested in life's offerings. Societally conscious people are socially responsible and integrated mature psychologically. Thus an individual passes through several developmental stages. In India, we are now targeting selected life-style groups for a suitable niche for our product.

Applications of Life-style Marketing

It is useful for:

(*a*) positioning of new products
(*b*) re-positioning of old/existing products
(*c*) developing new product inputs
(*d*) creating promotional strategies

Life-style Advertising

A product which would add to the perception of one's life is a potential candidate for life-style advertising. Life-style advertising tend to be equal for different products and to break this parity requires time and effort of agencies. Genuine life-style advertising makes an aspect of a life-style intrinsic to the brand position and personality. In India, textile firms resort to life-style advertising that is not distinctive. Good life-style advertising should not become advertising for a good life. We should therefore focus on perceived product differentiation. Then only, life-style imagery works. In most cases, life-style advertising seems to be a safe, easy way out by creative people, without bothering to think of fresh ideas. Many have started using life-style advertising for me-too products. Sometimes life-style portrayed are absolutely unrelated to the target audience. They tend to become visual cliches.

❑ ❑ ❑

4

LEARNING TO CONSUME

It is very important for the marketers to know how cosumers learn about their role as consumers and about various produts. It pays them to know how cosumers learn about the product characteristics and benefits offered by the products. Consmers show a buying behaviour, and the fact that most of the behaviour is learned, teaches marketers and advertisers a lesson that consumers can be made to learn the desired behaviour, bringing into play a set of motives, stimuli, cues, responses and their re-inforcements. Consumers learn to buy, use and maintain their products. They learn to dispose of their products.

A baby sucking mummy's breast instinctive behaviour but a grown-up child's demand for a chocolate is learned behaviour. Much of the adult behaviour is learned. Though learning is an integral part of our life, there is no signle theory to explain it. We understand learning by examing two theories — behavioural and cognitive.

Behavioural theory tries to relate behaviour observed (responses) to our exposure to particular stimuli. In short it is called S-R theory or stimulus-repsonse theory. Cognitive theory treats learning as pure mental process.

It is difficult to define learning precisely. We quote three definitiions of learning.

Learning refers to a more or less permanent change in behaviour which occurs as a result of practice — G.A. Kimale (*Conditioning and Learning,* N.Y. Appleton — Century Crofts, 1961)

Consumer learning is the process by which individuals acquire the purchase and consumption knowledge and experience they apply to future related behaviour. - Schiffman and Kanuk (Consumer Behaviour, Prentice Hall, 1996)

Learning is the process by which an activity originates or is changed through reacting to an encountered situation. Hilgard and Bower (*Theories of Learning,* N.Y. Appleton - Century crofts, 1966)

Sucking in infants instinctive. While much of adult behaviour is acquired. The acquisition results from knowledge or experience. The source of our knowledge could be reading, thinking, listening or observation. Learning is a process of applying results of past experience to evaluate a new situation or modify future behaviour. It should also be noted that 'change in behaviour' extends to not just the behaviour that can be observed but the fundamental changes in attitudes, motives and even personality. Learning can be *intentional* or just *incidental.* Learning can be just simple and refletive or it can be highly complex problem solving.

LEARNING

What is learning?

It is a relatively permanent process or change in behaviour that occurs as a result of experience or practice. (Maximum work in the area of learning has been done by behavioural psychologists). Learning determines our nature and our behaviour.

The ***three elements*** involved in learning are:

(1) Change in behaviour
(2) It involves experience or practice
(3) It is a continuous process

The ***characteristics of learning*** are:

(1) It is a change in behaviour that is permanent:

The change may be in muscular movements, verbal behaviour, perceptual organization or thinking. That does not matter.
e.g. learning to drive a car, to play a flute or to knit involves muscular changes.
e.g. learning a language is a case of changes in verbal behaviour.
e.g. solving a maths problem involves change in thinking.
The change is permanent. You don't forget how to drive once you have learned to.

(2) The change occurs due to experience or practice:

This characteristic enables us to distinguish changes due to maturation from those due to learning.
At about the age of 4 months, a baby will babble; it does not matter how it is brought up.
This is due to maturation. However, development of language is a result of learning.
When a person says "Hello!" in response, or just nods his head to say "yes", he is giving a learned response. Experience has taught him to do so.
Practice makes learning more permanent. e.g. saying 'please, thank-you and sorry,' comes automatically as we have learnt to say it many times before.

(3) Learning is a continuous process:

— We continue learning various things throughout our life.

— We keep learning to do something, to adjust, etc.

(4) Maturation sets limits to learning:

It is said that we can learn more when we are younger till about 20 yrs. As we mature, we learn different things
As children, we learn to walk and talk.
Then as tenagers, we learn to make friends, to take part in competitions, to date, to follow rules at college.
As adults, we learn to do our job well to earn money.

(5) Learning can take place only if the individual has the capacity to learn:

Learning merely enables an organism to use its capacities. If it does not possess a capacity, it cannot learn to use it e.g., newborn baby does not have the capacity for learning language. Nor can we teach a cat or dog to talk.

Also, a mentally challenged child cannot cope with usual college studies.

Though there are differences in the view-points of learning theorists, they all agree that learning takes place in the presence certain elements like motives, cues, response and reinforcement.

Motivation

A housewife has the need to grind and blend so many things in the kitchen. When the need grows stronger, it becomes a *motive.* The motive is directed towards a stimulus object — a grinder mixer of say, Sumeet. This housewife will gather all information about the different grinder — mixers. Motive may be defined as an internal condition of the organism which initiates and sustains activity directed to a particular goal. Understanding motives is the primary task for marketers. They can teach the consumer how their product will fulfil her needs the best. Motivation makes a customer *involved* in the product.

Stimuli and Cues

A stimulus is defined as any physical event or condition that gives rise to the activity of a sense organ. It may be something external to the organism or internal. A response is the reaction of the organism to stimulus or stimuli. The stimuli are the various advertisements she reads sees and hears. Cues are minor stimuli determing her response in terms of time, place and method. Cues are the stimuli that give direction to her motives. Positive feedback about the mixie from her friend, watching it on display in a shop-window, a scheme reducing its price during festive season are the cues which influence her response to the motive of buying a mixie.

Arthur cites the example of wooing a girl. The boy can talk about his education, career to impress that he will do well in life. Or else he can take a rose, go on his knees to her and appeal to her emotions. Both are stimuli. One appeals to reason, and the other to emotions. Which works better? It depends on the target, the product category and several things. Arthur believes in the power of surprise. Stimuli should be imaginative which takes the customer to experience a certain level of emotion, a certain level of expectation and then to a different level of experience till the customer is compelled to say 'great!'.

Response

Response is our reaction to a cue. Though there are cues, they may not result in purchase. A favourable image of the product is conducive to its selection when the consumer is ready to buy. There are competing cues from the competitors. The response the consumer gives depends on previous learning. If she responds by buying a mixie and uses it satisfactorily, and she would continue to use if as often as possible. May be in future, she would buy another mixie or a better product like a food processor. Her response is thus, has been re-inforced.

Reinforcement

Reinforcement enhances the probability of a specific response in future as a result of particular cues or stimuli. Our housewife decides to buy Sumeet food processor. It is a result of her inference that a company making good mixers must be producing good food processors also. It is thus a generalisation of response.

A marketer can build up his brand by making the consumer learn that the brand is worth. He, therefore, associates his brand with strong motives and uses apt stimuli and cues and provides positive re-inforcements.

Behavioural Learning Theories

There are two types of learning theories as we have observed already — stimulus-response (SR) or behavioural learning theories. In SR theory, there is a link between responses and stimuli. Here our response to a particular stimuli indicates our learning. Thus what we learn are habits. In SR theory the process is not so important. The inputs and outputs are more important.

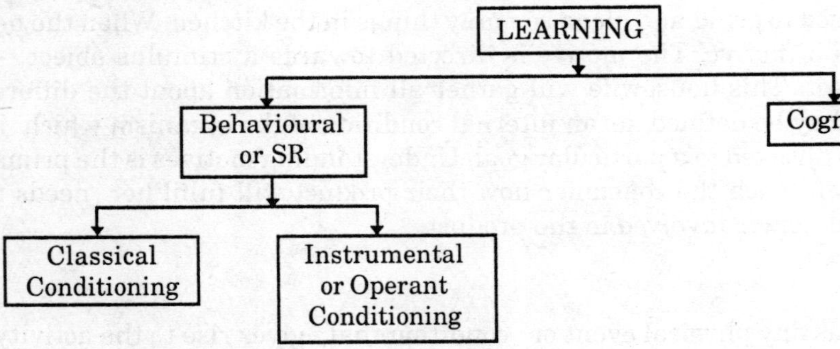

Classical Conditioning

Here the emphasis is on repetition or conditioning. The very thought of visiting a dentist insists fear in our heart. This apprehensive reaction is linked to our previous visits to dentists for tooth extraction and the pain we felt. Thus our reaction is conditioned. Through repetitive linkage of a response to a stimulus, the probability of the response being elicited increases. Thus if we keep on purchasing Aspro tablets each time there is a headache, we might buy Aspro next time there is a head-ache. In learning by classical conditioning, a response is associated with a neutral stimulus. A neutral stimulus is one which generally does not evoke a response. An individual thus will not respond to a neutral stimulus unless he has learned to do so e.g,bell and salivary response.

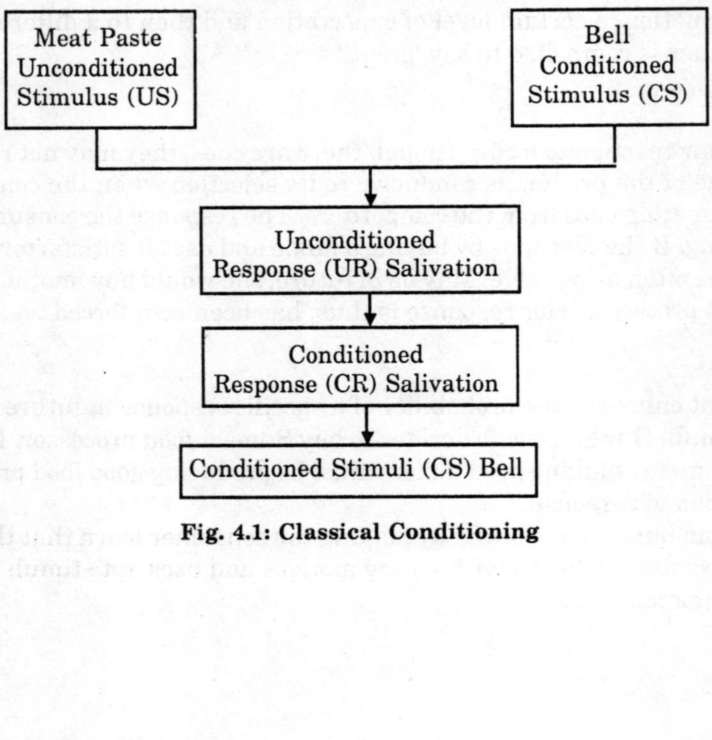

Fig. 4.1: Classical Conditioning

Pavolvian Theory

Pavolv, a Russian physiologist (1849 – 1936), explains how learning occurs. The kind of learning he examined is called classical conditioning or simply conditioning. Conditioned learning, according to him, occurs when two stimuli one unconditioned and one conditioned are paired so as to get a known response and the same response is produced when the conditioned stimulus is used alone. Consider two stimuli — one conditioned called CS and one unconditioned called US. When paired together they lead to a response that is unconditioned — UR. After repetitions, the CS will lead to the same response which is like UR but called CR. Pavolv used dogs in his experiment. He kept them hungry. He smeared meat paste on their tongues, causing them to salivate. Learning occured by conditioning. When the meat paste was smeared, a bell went off. After several repetitions, the bell alone could make dogs salivate. The dogs associated the bell to the meat paste and gave the same response to the bell alone which the were giving to meat paste. The above diagram 4.1 illustrates this theory.

A similar situation is that of Good Morning India programme on Star Plus TV channel in the morning at seven o'clock, which coincides with the preparation of breakfast in the kitchen. It makes our mouth water. After some time, even when no breakfast is being made good morning India causes our mouth to water.

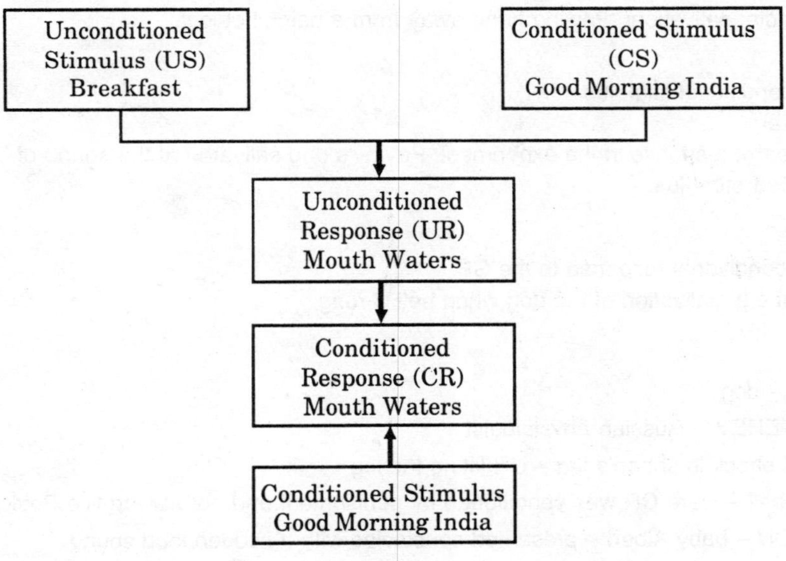

Fig. 4.2

It is now proposed that classical conditioning is a matter of associations between events. The association between stimulus and response occurs when the two occur together in time. In other words, they are contiguous to each other. The relationship or contiguity between CS and US influence dog's expectation, and thus lead a response — salivation.

Neo-Pavlovian theory considers consumer as one seeking information using logical and perceptual relationship amongst events as inputs. He merges his own pre-conception with these inputs and forms a representation of the world. Conditioning thus is learning as a result of exposure to relationship amongst events in the surroundings and this generates expectations about the structure of the surroundings.

We may now define classical conditioning as a process of forming an association between a conditioned stimulus and a response. The conditioned stimulus is repeatedly presented. Along with it the unconditioned (or natural) stimulus is presented.

TYPES OF LEARNING

(1) Classical Conditioning

It is given by a Russian physiologist – IVAN PAVLOV. He was not a psychologist.
It involves learning that takes place between a neutral stimulus and a response.
Some of the concepts that explain the experiment.

(i) US

It is the unconditional stimulus that is capable of eliciting a reflex-like response on its own, for e.g., - food. It evokes salivary response. Thus it is a normal or the natural stimulus. It is biologically certain to arouse a response.

(ii) UR

It is the unconditional response i.e. a response to the US, spontaneous and natural and unlearned. It is not a result of learning.

For example, salivation; drawing hand away from a painful object.

(iii) CS

It is the conditional stimulus.
It is neutral
It is the learnt response in the experiment. Pavlov's dog salivated at the sound of bell. The bell is a conditioned stimulus.

(iv) CR

This the conditional response to the CS.
It is learnt e.g. salivation of the dog when bell is rung.

Examples

(1) Pavlov – dog
(2) BEKHTEREV – Russian physiologist
— mild shock in sheep's leg – UR lifting the leg
— CS bell – Here CR was conditioned by punishment and not reward like Pavlov's.
(3) WATSON – baby Albert – presented spectacles with a sudden loud sound.

Implications of Classical Conditioning

(1) It paved the way for RESEARCH in the field of learning.
(2) Most of our responses are the result of CONDITIONING
(3) Certain PHOBIAS and milder forms of NEUROSIS are also the result of conditioning.
(4) Most of our likes and dislikes that relate to PEOPLE, PLACES, EVENTS or THINGS are the result of conditioning. For example, exam evokes fear and also of evaluation of exam – failure.

Feel hungry at 12.40 even on Sundays because of association with college break.

We come across in classical conditioning theory terms like repetition, generalization of stimulus and discrimination of stimulus. These concepts are examined below.

Repetition

We have to strengthen the association by repetition. Repetition also slows down the process of *forgetting*. Repetition has its own limitation. Though repetition and retention are related excess use of it leads to satiation and decline of retention. In the field of advertising, repetition is equated with frequency of the ad. The frequency depends on the nature of the media, *e.g.,* TV needs higher frequency of the ads than the press. If there are specialised market niches a brand is advertised on a programme that caters to this niche. A brand then needs higher frequency on this programme. Higher frequency leads to higher recall. Some theorists advocate just three exposures to an ad — one to create awareness, second to show the relevance of the product and third to act as reminder. More repetitions according to this theory, are advertisement wastage. However, other researchers advocate a higher frequency of say a dozen or so exposures just to ensure that the consumer will receive actually three exposures. When a new product or brand are launched we need higher frequency for complex products. When we advertise in a single medium, we opt for higher frequency. We can reduce the size of the ad, and increase its frequency. A dominant brand needs lesser frequency. If there is high usage in a purchase cycle, we need higher frequency.

In the final analysis, frequency is related to the creative involved. Each creative has its own *wear-out* or *irritational* level. Those creatives which use rational appeals have a low *irritational* level. *e.g.,* Lalitaji commercial for Surf. Emotional creatives have a higher irritational level, e.g. Hamara Bajaj commercial. Thus more exposures are needed before irritation sets in. However, such commercials are cloned and then consumers get quickly irritated. Entertainment ads have high irritational levels, but cloning lowers it.

Theme variation is a way out to avoid irritation and fatigue which are the two sides of the same coin. Sometimes the same theme is repeated but in a variety of formats. We can also use different advertising background or spokes persons.

Advertising attracts more new buyers rather than re-purchasers in the short-run. The higher the frequency of the ad, the higher the likelihood of attracting new buyers. The first ad's marginal value is the highest.

Generalization

Learning also depends on our ability to generalize i.e., the tendency to respond to a new situation the way we responded to similar past situations. In other words, the learned S-R link is extended to new stimulus situations. Pavlov noted that dogs not only respond to the sound of a bell, but to the sound of jangling keys — the response is salivation though to somewhat lesser degree. Much learning takes place on account of our ability to generalize. Consumers who receive satisfactory service in the electronics section of Akbarallys expect the same level of services in the appliances section. If we are satisfied with Cadbury chocolates, we also anticipate the satisfaction from Cadbury drinking chocolate. If we are not satisfied with a Bajaj toaster, we are likely to generalize this to Bajaj irons. Me-too products survive in the market because of generalization. Product line extensions are based on generalizations. The characteristics of parent brand rub off on the daughter brand. Family branding and franchising make use of generalization theory.

Discrimination

This is anti-thesis of generalization. When we generalize.we are responding to similarities. When we discriminate, we respond to differences. Here we select a specific stimulus from a set of similar stimuli. Positioning strategy is based on the consumer's ability to discriminate amongst the given stimuli. Those who make me-too products expect consumers to generalize, whereas market leaders expect them to discriminate. A brand leader discriminated on the basis of specific stimulus is difficult to dislodge. Perhaps, the leader being the pioneer got more time to teach the consumer a strong association between the brands and the product. Out of several brands available, a consumer selects a brand on the basis of stimulus discrimination.

Classical Conditioning Critical Evaluation

Though useful in advertising, brand management and marketing, it is not sufficient to explain the entire learning process. It assumes consumers as passive beings. Neo-Pavlovian model treats them as information seekers. Though ad frequency shapes part of our purchase behaviour, especially with respect to convenience goods, we have to still account for other purchase behaviour which evaluates different product alternatives. This evaluation of products is based on our rewards after using the product which means the theory of instrumental conditioning. Classical conditioning involves associative learning. Our response to people, places, situations and symbols (e.g. a flag) are a result of conditoning.

Instrumental Conditioning

As you will appreciate, classical conditioning was physiological in nature and dealt with the learning of reflex responses. In classical conditioning the organism is passive. Learning takes place just because a neutral stimulus happens to occur before a natural or unconditional stimulus. Most human learning is not of this type. Organisms are active. As against this, instrumental or operant conditioning deals with voluntary responses. It relies upon physiological as well as learned needs or motives. This theory was given shape by B.F. Skinner who contended that learning occurs in controlled environment which rewards the individual for apt behaviour. Learning is a trial and error process for consumers who opt for rewarding purchase behaviour rather than one that does not do so. A rewarding experience is *instrumental* in teaching the individual to repeat the same specific behaviour. Skinner had conducted his experiments like Pavlov on animals, like pigeons who were made to learn dancing and other things in the 'Skinner box'. Let us consider a college-going Mumbai girl selecting a western outfit for her. She tries several available brands and then selects one that suits her body contours (this is positive reinforcement). The brand of outfit that suits her structure is patronised. This is instrumental conditioning. This has been outlined in the following diagram.

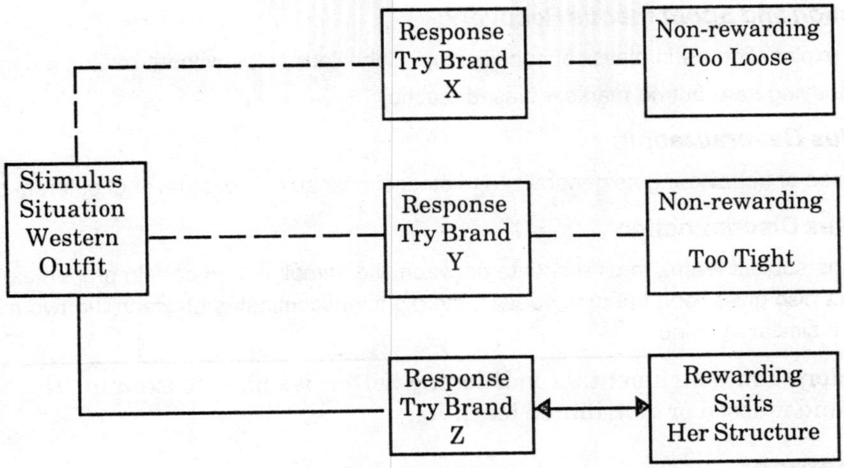

Fig. 4.3 : Model of Instrumental Conditioning

Thus to a conditioned stimulus (S) there is instrumental response (R) which receives reinforcement (Rn).

OPERANT LEARNING

It is given by B.F. Skinner (associated with behaviourism) It is also known as instrumental learning.

The experiment was conducted on a famous box known as the Skinner's box.

A pigeon, cat and a rat were used individually for the experiment.

Organisms are active and their behaviour is an attempt to introduce changes in their environment. The responses which are successful in doing so become fixed and thus learning takes place.

The response is instrumental in obtaining re-inforcement.

Experiment

(1) Hungry rat placed in Skinner's box (simple box with a lever at one end). After some time, it gets restless, moves about. When it happens to press the lever, a pellet of food is released. It doesn't notice this at first, continues to move, again. It notices and eats it. Later, it presses the lever rapidly and eats every pellet which is delivered. Now it has learned that by pressing the lever, it will get food.

(2) Rat gets a shock through the floor of the box. It presses the lever. Current is switched off – shock is avoided. Used for studying avoidance behaviour.

Associated Processes

(i) Shaping/Method of Successive Approximation:

It involves teaching a response through a series of steps that leads the learner to the final response.

Here, instead of waiting for a response to occur in its natural course, training can be given by rewarding the learning for any move in the right direction.

Gradually, the reward will be given for getting nearer and nearer to the desired response and finally, only when the learner gives the desired response.

For example, to train a rat to pull firmly on a string, the training will begin by reinforcing movements towards the string, next food is given only when the string is touched, then when the string is pulled and finally only a strong pull is rewarded.

For example, training a child to write the alphabet, training animals to do various tricks.

(ii) Extinction and Spontaneous Recovery:

Same explanation as in classical conditioning. Behaviour stops without reinforcement.

e.g.: studying hard but no marks – biased teacher

(iii) Stimulus Generalization:

Response or behaviour gets generalized to other similar stimuli. e.g., lever of different colour, length.

(iv) Stimulus Discrimination

Here, the subject learns to differentiate between two stimuli due to certain properties.
e.g., red disc gives food but pink doesn't; the pigion discriminates between the two even though they are similar in colour.

To understand instrumental conditioning better, we have to examine the concept of reinforcement, and massed or distributed learning.

Reinforcement

Skinner put re-inforcement or rewards which make us repeat our response in two categories. *Positive reinforcement* occurs when the individual experiences a reduction in the strength of a drive. Satisfaction of hunger or thirst is primary reinforcement. Approval by others is secondary reinforcement. A cap protects us from the sun. At the same time it makes us look fashionable. Thus it provides both the primary and secondary reinforcement. Positive reinforcement incline us towards a specific response. *Negative reinforcement* is associated with an unpleasant outcome thus leading us to a specific behaviour. An ad that shows a house on fire encourages us to buy a fire extinguisher. Negative reinforcement should not be equated with *punishment* which discourages behaviour.

Insurance policies, head-ache remedies, acidity tablets are sold by negative reinforcement. The advertiser advises us to ward off the unpleasant consequences by going in for the advertised product.

A learned response can be *un-learned* — this happens when it is no longer reinforced, and this leads to its extinction. A nail biting child may have some stress problem. His nails can be dipped into an inert but bitter-tasting liquid. This is primary negative reinforcer. Later, he was ridiculed in presence of other children. This was secondary negative reinforcer. Both led to extinction. It has been observed by researchers that extinction is not so easy to achieve. There are no studies as yet to know consumer behaviour of say brand choice with respect to extinction.

KEY CONCEPTS IN OPERANT LEARNING

(1) Reinforcement: The basic principle in operant conditioning is that if reinforcement is contingent (dependent) upon a certain response that response will be more likely to occur again.

(2) Reinforcement is any stimulus or situation that strengthens the response which precedes it.

(3) Primary reinforcement is unlearnt: For example, in animals, food is a primary reinforcer. To train a dog to jump over a stick, you give it a biscuit. A primary reinforcer is an unlearned reinforcer

(4) A secondary reinforcer is socially learnt: It differs from person to person. For some, it can be verbal praise. For others, money. Money is a secondary reinforcer as we have learnt the value of money. A secondary reinforcer is a learned reinforcer.

(5) In positive reinforcement, the presentation of a stimulus strengthens the response. Here, we reward the person to cause an increase in the occurance of his behaviour.

(6) In negative reinforcement, the removal of an unpleasant stimulus strengthens the response.

For example, animals are shocked in one area of the box and not in the other. So, animals move in the area where the negative stimulus (shock) has been removed.

"If you don't talk, I will not throw you out of class." By removing the negative stimulus, you increase the behaviour of keeping quiet.

(1) Punishment involves the presentation of an unpleasant stimulus to eliminate the response.

It is a kind of re-inforcement that is used to put an end to undesirable behaviour.

It is different from negative reinforcement.

(2) Contingent

The reinforcement is contingent upon (or depends on) the occurence of a certain response. (Persons behaviour is contingent on the stimulus)

(3) Operant

Operant means operating on the environment i.e., reacting to the environment.
It refers to the individual's behaviour.
It means operating on the environment through a system of reward and punishments and thereby influencing behaviour.

TYPES OF REINFORCEMENT

(1) Partial Reinforcement

This occurs when certain responses are reinforced.

The individual or the organism is not aware which response will be reinforced.

e.g. when you come to class always, but get attendance only sometimes.

Here the reward does not follow every correct response. Yet a person continues to give the cor rect responses.

(2) Continuous Reinforcement

Every response is reinforced.

e.g.: When you come everyday and get attendance everyday.

Partial reinforcement is more effective.

Because, in continuous, they know for sure that they will get attendance and so don't pay attention during class whereas in partial, you are not sure.
Gambling is a result of ***partial reinforcement***. There is a challenge, risk-taking.

SCHEDULE OF REINFORCEMENT

There are two major types of schedules.

(1) Based on Responses

These are also known as the ratio schedules.

These are of two types.

(A) Fixed Ratio Schedule: i.e., a fixed number of responses are reinforced. Every five times you answer a question, you get a sweet. This is fixed.

(B) Variable Ratio Schedule: where a variable number of responses are reinforced. Only sometimes you get the sweet.

(2) Based on Time

It is also known as the interval schedule.
It is of two types:

(A) Fixed Interval Schedule: Where after fixed amounts of time behaviour is reinforced. At end of one month, you get your salary. After studying 45 hrs., you watch T.V. You fix your schedule.

(B) Variable Interval Schedule: Where behaviour is reinforced after varying amounts of time.

Sometimes you have to work for 5 hrs, sometimes 3 hrs. This helps you because you continue working till you get paid.

Punishment

Definition

It involves presenting a negative stimulus that eliminates a response all together.

It has several negative consequences, it should be used with care.

It is necessary to exercise sensitivity while punishing others.

Factors Making Punishment Effective are:

(1) It is necessary to be consistent at all times. A child robbing Rs. 100 as well as Re. 1 should be punished.

(2) It should be immediate i.e., followed immediately after some wrong has been done.

(3) The degree and severity of punishment should not increase over time.

(4) There are gender differences, that need to be kept in mind while administering punishment.

(5) It should be focussed to the act itself.

There is no need to continue or re-inforce the memory of a punishment.

Shaping

It involves teaching a response through a series of steps that leads the learner to the final response.

This is also known as method of *Successive Approximation* e.g.: when a child learns to write the alphabet, when animal trainers train animals to do various tricks.

Application of Operant Learning

(1) Socially desirable behaviour is learnt through operant learning.

(2) The concept of reward and punishment was given by Skinner.

(3) Programmed learning that is used in computer is based on shaping.

(4) It can be used to train animals and birds.

A technique known as 'Token Economy' that has been used widely by mental health professionals in mental asylums where they try to change maladaptive behaviours and learn appropriate behaviour used in industry – mental asylum – stubborn, unwilling – not normal difficult – out of touch with reality – develop – if brush teeth, comb hair- given token – certain no. of tokens earn a phone call or desirable reward – very effective, cigarettes, relatives. Even cold drinks – caps – sp. no – even a music system, other prize – changes behaviour not comb hair, brush teeth, breakfast not grooming oneself – not adapting to surroundings by attending to their personal hygiene. (as an example) – industry – commercial sense.

Token Economy also effective for psychiatric parents and children.

Extinction: As in classical conditioning, if a response is not reinforced it become weaker and weaker till it drops out. This is called extinction.

DIFFERENCES BETWEEN CLASSICAL AND OPERANT

Classical	*Operant Conditioning*
1. In classical conditioning the response is involuntary	1. In operant conditioning, the response is voluntary.
2. Here, the reinforcement is the CS, US pairing which is presented regardless of the subject response.	2. Reinforcement depends on the subjects' response.
3. Here, the emphasis is on the stimulus which elicits the conditioned response.	3. The response is made or emitted by the subject.
4. Here, the organism is passive. For example, response on touching a hot plate (involuntary)	4. Here, the organism is active.

Trial and Error

(1) The concept of operant conditioning originated from the trial and error method of learning.

(2) When an organism is faced with a problem situation, it tries out many responses most of which are wrong responses.

(3) Accidentally, it hits upon the right response which helps it to reach the goal.

(4) After some trials, the correct response is learnt and the wrong responses drop out.

(5) Thorndike (1874 – 1949) the first experiments on trial and error responses. The apparatus used in these experiments was a maze.

- Cat hungry in a puzzle box (cage) – fish outside- press the lever and door opens.
- In the first trial, she has to learn after many trials and errors. In the second trial, the cat makes lesser number of unnecessary movements. In further trials, the useless movements are gradually eliminated.
- Rats – electric shock from floor
- Maze – series of alleys leading to goal/dead ends – choose from 2 alternatives – also paper and pencil maze is used to conduct experiments on human learning

(6) Involves the following stages:

(i) The organism is motivated.

(ii) The situation is blind to the organism. There is no easy solution to reach the goal.

(iii) The organism is free to move about and tries out many responses.

(iv) The right solution occurs by chance and the organism reaches the goal.

(7) Law of Effect"

"Law of Intensity"

"Law of frequency"

Insight Learning

Many human learning situations do not involve the specific manipulation of reinforcement. People may learn something simply by being exposed to it.

This is called cognitive learning.

Examples of cognitive learning are imitation, modelling and insight learning.

According to the principles of conditioning, the learner is passive.

Learning is a mechanical process which occurs automatically when reinforcement is associated with the response.

The Gestalt psychologists argue that the learner plays an active role in the learning process.

He must understand or correctly perceive the problem before he can solve it.

Further, once the solution is found, it is repeated without any trial and error.

So, learning is a sudden process which follows the insight or the "a-ha experience." e.g.: math sums where you learn the rules, steps, how to solve it – cognitive learning.

We are not mechanistic, machine-like creatures. Insight learning involves cognitive learning where we use reasoning. The individual suddenly 'sees' the solution. The moment this happens insight is said to have occurred. Before insight occurs, the individual's behaviour is similar to that in trial and error learning. He tries different ways, but fails, then suddenly a solution comes.

In insight learning, the learner plays an active role.

Here, once you have achieved a solution to the problem, you don't forget it.

It was Kohler who first suggested that learning takes place by insight.

Experiment by KOHLER – a Gestalt Psychologist

He used a chimpanzee 'Sultan' kept inside a cage outside which there were bananas.

There were also two rods in the cage.

The chimpanzee puts out his hand with one stick, tried, but failed.

Suddenly, he stopped, joined the sticks and brought the bananas inside.

Once he did this, he never forgot about it.

If the problem is beyond the individual's capacity, insight learning is not possible.

eg.: a cat can't do anything with sticks and so, will fail to use it.

Learning by insight generalizes widely to similar problems i.e., solution achieved through insight can be applied to similar problems. e.g.: chimpanzee has learnt to use a box to climb and reach a hanging banana – if not available, it will use a table, the experimenter's shoulders, etc.

Massed and Distributed Learning

How should we time our learning — is it to be widely spread over a longer period or is it to be compressed? If widely spread, it is called distributed learning. If compressed, it is massed. These considerations are important in media planning. A concentrated dose of advertising is necessary to educate the customer about a new product or to counter a competitor's onslaught. For established products expected to be bought repeatedly, we have distributed advertising. Sometimes a combination of concentration and distribution is used.

Evaluation of Instrumental Learning

Habits are formed as a consequence of repeated rewards for some specific response or behaviour. This model has extensive application. We learn about products, brands and shopping outlets through this type of learning. Critics point out, however, that learning occurs even when there is no reinforcement - either positive or negative. It is not necessary for a male gynaecologist to undergo labour pains to learn what the labour pains are at the time of delivery. He visualizes this vicariously. He has seen a number of women delivering babies. He learns by observation. Sometimes, we learn just for the sake of learning, and not with an expectation of rewards. Children are initiative, and do learn a number of things in this manner.

Instrumental learning is applicable to products which have no personal relevance. However, there are cases where it is applicable to products both having relevance and no relevance.

Cognitive Learning Theory

A great deal of learning occurs by our ability to solve problems and our ability to think with mental faculties. Some solutions flash before us in an instant whereas some problems need careful collection and evaluation of information to take decisions. Learning is thus a function of exerting the mind. This is called cognitive learning. A consumer as a buyer buys a brand, and learns by experience its performance. He next time buys the same brand if the performance is satisfactory rather than another brand which is stranger to him, and so riskier to buy.

Problem solving ability allows us some control over our environment.

DETERMINANTS OF LEARNING

Whether an individual learns something depends on three major determinants:

(1) Characteristics of the learning material.

(2) Method of learning.

(3) Characteristics of the learner.

They are explained in detail below:

(1) Characteristics of the Learning Material: (MIDPOF)

(i) Meaningfulness

The more meaningful the material is, the easier it is to learn it.

In experiments on different kinds of materials, it is found that nonsense syllables (e.g., bup, gup, foj) are the hardest to learn as they are absolutely meaningless.

Single words, being more meaningful than these, are not as hard.

But the learning of a prose passage, or a poem, is still easier as the material, as a whole, is meaningful.

(ii) Organisation

This might be present in the material itself or the learner may use some form of organisation that makes learning easier - e.g., In a book, the 1st few chapters are easier, related topics altogether etc.

(iii) Pronoucability

Words that are easily pronounced are learnt easily, Unlike for example: 'Pseudoher maphrodite.'

(iv) Frequency

Matter that is more frequently used or which becomes familiar over time is likely to be learnt easily - e.g., You remember the phone numbers of the friends you call frequently.

(v) Distinctiveness

Material that is distinctive in quality is learnt easily as it reduces confusion that is caused by similar material.

(vi) Imagery

Certain material lends itself to mental images more easily and this makes it easier to learn it.

Concepts that are abstract are more difficult to learn.

METHOD OF LEARNING (WDKRT)

Learning covers any change in behaviour due to experience or practice. However, the term is not always used in this wide sense.

When students talk of learning their lessons, or actor their roles, they are using this term in a more limited sense.

Their learning is done with the intention of recalling (or recognizing) the learned material.

The efficient methods for learning in this sense are:

Whole Vs Part Learning

- Whether it is better to learn a task as a whole or to break it into part depends on the complexity of the material and the learner.
- Part learning organises the material. It makes it easier to study as it is meaningful, structured and there is less matter. So, you have more concentration on it. If the different parts of a material are unconnected, the part method is better whereas if the different parts of a material have a natural connection, the "whole method" will be more efficient. But, poems need to be studied as a whole in order to retain the link between paras.

Distributed Vs. Massed Practice

Massed (or unspaced) practice involves learning continuously for a sustained period of time.

In distributed (or spaced) practice, learning is, spread out over several sessions.

Experimental evidence shows that this method is better for learning tasks. Total learning period of 120 mins, 1 group – without any break, 2nd 10 min periods, twice a day, 3rd – 20 min period once a day, 4th – 40 min periods on alternate days. The 2nd group gave best results.

However, what should be the length of a learning period, depends upon the nature of the material to be learned and the habits of the learner.

Knowledge of Results: (KOR)

Feedback regarding one's performance increases motivation and provides information about errors and so, it improves learning.

It tells us of what we have not learnt well so that we can relearn it and helps us to compare our performance to the ideal one. Experiment: chemistry class – group informed immediately about right and wrong answers — did better in next exams.

Reinforcement

If the activity involved in learning leads to the desired results, then learning is strengthened.

Success or failure also affects learning.

Reinforcement provides motivation to the learner.

Psychologists put it thus: Behaviour will persist if it has a satisfying effect. This effect may be either be satisfaction of a motive or escape from punishment.

Learning is more efficient in case of positive incentives (rewards) than in negative ones (punishments).

Transfer of Training: (TOT)

The effects of previous learning on new (or later) learning is called transfer of training.

Positive transfer is when the old learning facilitates the new one. Negative transfer is when old learning hinders the new one and zero transfer is when performance in the new learning situation is neither helped nor hindered by past learning.

Examples: Positive — drive one car, then another type, and learn Sanskrit, then Marathi.

Negative: drive a car (turn wheel to right moves in the right-hand direction, then boat (move the rudder to right, boat turns to left).

Negative: Learn to write Marathi (from left to right) and the Persian (from right to left).

Zero: Person learns Marathi, then to drive a car.

CHARACTERISTICS OF THE LEARNER

(1) Motivation

The motivation to learn should be INTRINSIC or EXTRINSIC

Intrinsic motivation leads to better learning and is not affected by any other factor like the need for success, money etc., done for the mere joy of learning.

Extrinsic motivation is affected by external factors.

(2) Age

Research shows that the ability to learn increases till about 20 yrs of age.

It stays constant between 20 and 50 yrs.

It then shows some decline.

(3) Gender

There are no general sex differences in learning ability but this factor interacts with the kind of material and leads to a difference. e.g.: girls are usually better in verbal abilities while boys are better at special and mechanical abilities.

(4) Intelligence

– It is positively correlated with learning.

– The greater the intelligence, the more efficient is the learning

Decision Process

The consumer as a first step recognises his unfulfilled need or want. It is called problem recognition. It actually leads to *information search* and *processing* of this information in the mind. The information search can be deliberate or prolonged or can happen without the consumer being aware of it. He can rely on past experience or can seek information from external environment e.g., friends, shopkeepers and advertisements. The consumer processes the information about the products on the basis attributes, brands, brand comparisons or any combination of these. The number of attributes and the availability of a number of brands contribute to the vigour of the processing. The more advanced the mental faculties of the consumer, the more rigorous his analysis and processing becomes. He uses his imagination his style and ability to fantasize while processing. The more knowledgeable and conversant with a product a consumer is, the more he appreciates the product information. Thus doctors appreciate the technical details of a remedy to be used in a disease. The consumer arrives at a purchase decision by evaluating the information. Having made a decision to buy, the consumer makes a choice regarding the outlet to buy from.

Storage, Retention and Retrieval of Information

Information processing has one key element — human *memory*. Memory has three components — sensory store where information is kept temporarily, a short term store where information is held for a brief period and a long-term store where information is held for a relatively longer period.

Sensory store accepts sensory inputs from the senses. Thus when we watch Madhuri Dixit on TV, our sensory store receives her image and even when she is no more on the screen, her after-image is retained. It is however, very short-lived.

We keep the informations in short-term store but for a brief period. Someone just tells us the telephone number. We keep on repeating it. However, at the time of dialling, we forget one or two digits. It is because the number is in our short-term store.

When we keep on repeating the number and dial it a number of times, it enters into our long-term store. This is because of our rehearsals. Later the same information is encoded e.g. a company is associated with a product — IBM and computers.

The following schematic diagram explains the components of human memory:

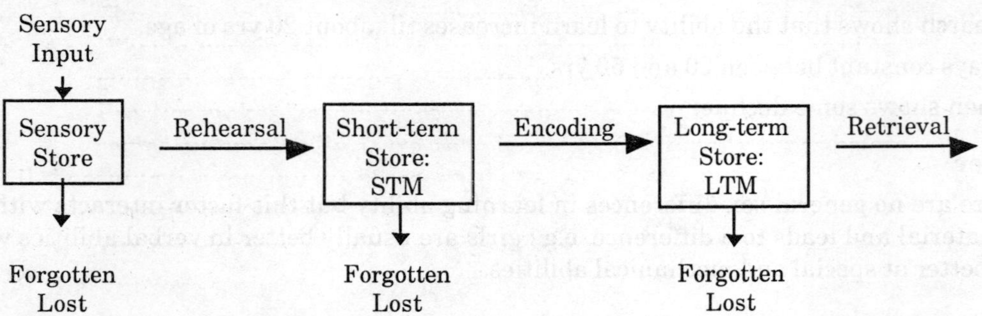

Fig. 4.4: Components of Human Memory

Encoding is the process of converting the information received from sensory input into some form or code which can be stored. Encoding is selective. Storage puts the encoded information into memory. Retrieval means the act of getting access to this stored information and bringing it up whenever needed. Distortion can affect all these three stages. The term rehearsal refers to the process by which items are kept at the centre of attention by repeating them either loudly or silently. The more the rehearsal, the more are the chances of the information getting into long-term memory. Mere repetion may not be sufficient to transfer the information to long-term memory. It is called *maintenance rehearsal.* But when material to be remembered is organised to make it meaningful and then repeated, it is called elaborative rehearsal.

Levels of Processing

Information is processed at the following three levels:

First Level	:	Superficial processing. Only awareness of the environment is created. This is called perception.
Second Level	:	Structural features of the input are analyzed. e.g., what it looks like or sounds like.
Third Level	:	Deeper analysis, meaning and associations of input are studied. Best Memory.

The Top-of-The-Tongue Phenomenon

TOT is an apt example of importance of organisation of information in long-term memory. Imagine we are asked to remember a brand of a cold cream but we cannot. It seems that it is just on the verge of being recalled. It is called TOT. The brand name is stored in memory but is not accessible.

Semantic and Episodic Memory

Memories of personal experiences is called *episodic* memory. It is the memory of events of our own life. Semantic Memory is the knowledge about the world around us. It also includes the knowledge of words and their meanings and relationship amongst them.

Implications of Cognitive Learning Theory

A picture is understood better than words. However, their combination contributes more to the mental image. A copy that has both visual elements and words has higher chance of being encoded and stored. Just a picture without any copy is less effective. Between pictures and copy, the pictures affect the consumer inferences more. A copy that uses imagery is more effective. When imagery is low, pictures take an upper hand. The software on TV itself needs processing of varying intensity. Dramatic situations require higher exercise of mental faculties. Therefore a commercial aired at such time is subject to lesser encoding and storage. Social situations contribute to a higher recall amongst women than in men. Tangible attributes can be processed in greater numbers than the intangible ones. Learning about a brand's attribute irrespective of their being positive or negative, affect our choice of brands.

When too much information is given to consumers in limited time, it is called an *Information overload* resulting in confusion. However, consumers have a high capacity to process additional information. It is difficult to decide the line of demarcation between adequacy of information and its overload. Can we rember 3 or 7 or 15 brands? More alternative choices given could be confusing. Overload is a Creative concept.

Retention

Information in long-term memory is always being organised and reorganised. When chunks of information are linked anew, we link additional information on a given issue, and create further linkages in the information stored. This is called *activation*. It consists of relating new data to the existing data. Many ads give us new information.

Retrieval

It is the process by which we recover information from long -term storage. Sometimes, we tend to forget certain familiar things, which can be considered as a lapse of the retrieval system. We tend to remember the benefits of the products rather than its attributes. We can recall different attributes under different conditions. Ad copies which blend the benefits and attributes together are more effective. Relevant information is more likely to be retrieved. Negative information is avoided in the retrieval process. Ad clutter contributes to difficulty in retrieving. Sometimes ads stimulate retrieval of competitive brands. New learning interferes with the recall of previously learned material. Old learning similarly affects the recall of newly learned material.

Limited and Extensive Information Processing

In buying, a consumer passes through several stages — awareness, preference, purchase and adoption or rejection. We have dealt with this topic again as the consumer adoption process (See Chapter 15) The sequential processing was thus assumed for all purchases. However, it was realised later that all purchases do not follow the same sequence.

Some products say salt or vegetables are purchased as and when the need is felt, without any extensive search and processing of information. These products do not have high personal relevance, and hence are treated as *low-involvement* purchases. However, while buying an automobile or TV, we do extensive search and these products are thus considered *high-involvement* products.

Involvement Theory: It is proposed that human brain has two hemispheres — the left and the right and each has a unique information processing capability. This is called *hemispheral laterlization* or *split brain theory*. The following diagram illustrates the specialisations of the two hemispheres.

This theory is extended to media, consumer's involvement with products and purchases. Visual images are analyzed by the right brain, without active involvement. TV therefore, is a right brain activity. Learning takes place because of repetition of a TV commercial by classical conditioning. Verbal information is processed by the left-side of the brain. Thus print media like press and magazines are high-involvement media. Print advertising is processed in sequential stages of information processing. Highly visual ads, packaging and store displays make us familiar with the brands and lead to purchasing. Visuals generate recall and verbal cues generate evaluation process.

It should be noted that such splitting may not always occur. Both the parts of the brain may process information simultaneously — *integrated processing*. Print ads are recalled better by such integrated process by individuals for both the visual and non-visual components. It is also proposed that both sides may have high and low involvement. High cognitive involvement engages left brain modestly and right brain intensely. Low involvement means either low cognitive or low-affective behaviour characterised by marginal involvement of the left and right parts of the brain.

Left Brain	*Right Brain*
(i) Cognitive activities. e.g. reading, speaking, information processing of attributes.	(i) Non-verbal visual information is processed. Holistic information is processed.
(ii) Verbal information is analzed by the left brain.	(ii) Emotional, intuitive, impulsive, metaphoric.
(iii) Rational, active, realistic	

Consumer Relevance: There are high and low involvement consumers and purchases. Consumer's involvement depends upon personal relevance of a product to him. High involvement products have high personal relevance and lead to extensive problem solving. Low involvement purchases are not so relevant and there is little perceived risk. Thus there is limited information processing. This is presented diagramatically below.

Automobile —High Involvement→ Extensive Problem Solving

Salt —Low Involvement→ Limited Information Processing

High involvement products adopt central route to persuasion which provokes considered thought about the product. Low involvement products adopt peripheral route to persuasion with little or no cognitive effort. Such products are sold on the basis of processing of visual cues. Holistic perception and learning occurs on the basis of repetition. High involvement products need quality arguments. Consumers buying high involvement products consider variety of attributes.

Social Judgement Theory: Our information processing is in line with our thinking on a social issue. Our high involvement with an issue and our positive opinion lead us to rejection of alternative propositions. Highly involved individuals treat an opinion that is compatible with their stand as more positive than it really is and one that is not compatible as more negative than it really is. Uninvolved persons are, however, open to arguments both for and against, sometimes they do not take any stand at all. We can extend this theory to marketing. Highly involved individuals have a very narrow set of brands for choice, as they find only a few brands acceptable. The brand messages are interpreted in keeping with their previously held opinions and experience. The uninvolved individual however is open to a variety of messages, and has a wider set of brands to choose from. He may switch his brand loyalty.

Evaluation of Involvement Theory: It is difficult to define involvement and more difficult to measure it. Involvement has the components of person, product and situation. There can be ego-involvement. Commitment also shows involvement. The more the search for information, the higher the involvement. The lower the search for information, the lower the involvement. There is a distinction, according to some, between product involvement and brand involvement. All said and done, it is an important construct of consumer behaviour. The degree of involvement is indicated by the decision time taken, and by the importance given to the product. Involvement is not a dichotomous construct, say high and low involvement. It is a continuum. Though there are semantic problems, involvement theory goes a long way in formulating our communication strategy.

Thorndike's Law of Effect: As we have learnt that learning occurs in presence of reinforcement. Reinforcement could be positive, say a reward or negative, say a punishment. This proposition is based on *Thondike's Law of Effect:*

(*i*) Other things remaining equal, of several responses made to the same situation those which are accompanied by *satisfaction* to the animal will be more firmly connected with the situation, so that when it recurs, they will be morely like to occun.

(*ii*) Those which are accompanied or closely followed by discomfort to the animal will have their connections with that situation weakened so that when it recurs, they will be less likely to occur.

(*iii*) The greater the satisfaction or discomfort, the greater the strengthening or weakening of the bond.

— **Edward L. Thorndike,** *Animal Intelligence* (N.Y. Macmillan, 1911)

In marketing parlance, we can say a satisfied consumer is likely to repeat the purchase of the same brand and vice versa.

Contributions

Buyer behaviour was first examined crudely by John A. Howard in his book *Marketing Management: Analysis and Planning* (Richard D. Irwin) in 1963. Later, Howard and Sheth jointly came-out with a model of buyer behaviour explained elsewhere in this book, and published as *The Theory of Buyer Behaviour* (John Wiley) in 1969. Howard Sheth model is basically a learning model which has drawn from the classical theory of Spence, Hull and Skinner. In Howard Sheth model, we come across the word *satisfaction* which is interpreted in terms of Thorndike's Law of Effect. Thus:

Outcomes of the Buying = Desired Outcome ⟶ Satisfaction

Outcome of Buying > Desired Outcome ⟶ Satisfaction

Outcome of Buying < Expected Outcome ⟶ Dissatisfaction

If a brand satisfies beyond our expectation, the consumer is inclined to increase its attractiveness. If a brand does not measure upto our expectations, the consumer is inclined to reduce its attractiveness.

Howard Sheth model has one contention. The level of satisfaction influences attitudes and choice criteria of the consumer. This can be traced to cognitive learning theory. Thus

Level of satisfaction = amount of reinforcement (intensity of motives)

We come across three stages of purchasing behaviours on the learning curves.

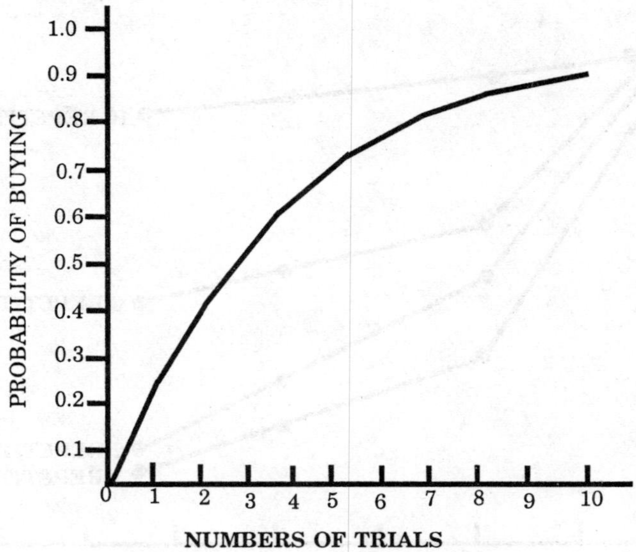

Fig. 4.5

We consider various brands on the basis of our experience. Our set of brands is wide. Our previous experience is generalized. We seek extensive information to solve our problem (EPS). Once we start using the brands, we gather more experience and then seek less information. This is called *limited problem solving.* (LPS) behaviour. We discriminate amongst brands and our brand choice is restricted. The probability of choosing each brand, therefore, increases. The last stage is that of routinized purchase behaviour (RRB). Only one brand here is chosen as a matter of habit. The probability, therefore, touches one. There is hardly any information search. Thus consumer learns to choose brands through repetitive purchasing and as he keeps on learning, he seeks less and less information.

Advertising Effect

In India we spend close to Rs. 5000 crores on advertising per annum. Still, business gropes in the dark about the effect of advertising on sales. It is believed that there is positive correlation between the two. In learning theory, we consider ad as a stimulus and the ability to recall it is its effect. The following graph shows how the frequency of ad messages affect the recall.

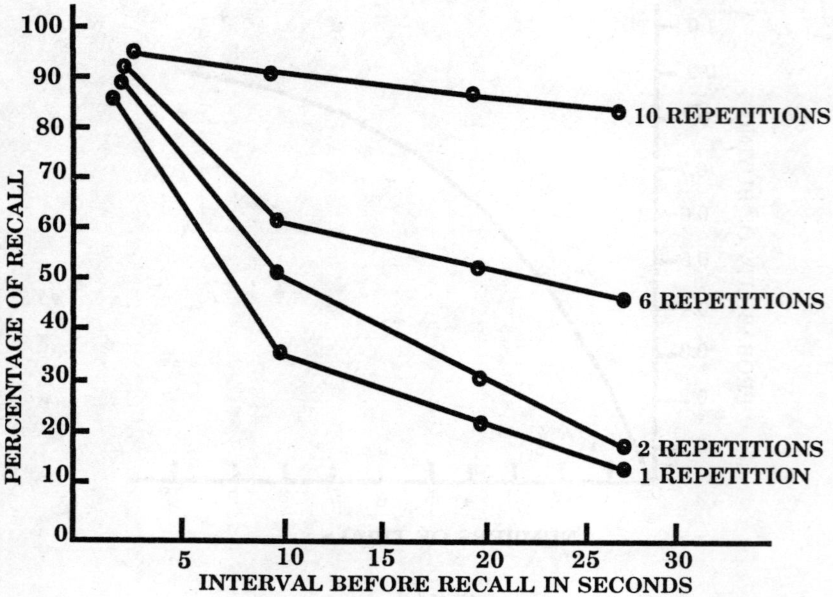

Fig. 4.6

Here we have considered four different frequencies. There are one, two, six and ten repetitions of an ad copy. In all four conditions, there is a decline in recall or forgetting. However the higher the frequency, the higher the recall because of increased reinforcements. There are studies the effect of repeated mailings of mail order companies on recall. The recall rate is higher when the mailings are repeated. We learn a useful moral from this that advertising should be undertaken on a continuous basis lest it slips out of memory.

❑ ❑ ❑

5

CONSUMER PERCEPTION

Perception can be understood as 'the way we look at' the objects, individuals, events and the world in general. Our sense organs keep on receiving messages such as sights, smells, sounds, tastes and sensations. All these are *stimuli*. We recognise these stimuli, select them and organise them. These are ultimately interpreted in our own way depending on our expectations, needs and values. This process is known as perception.

Perception can therefore, be defined as the *process of selection, organisation and interpretation of stimuli* into a *meaningful and coherent picture of the world.*

Since each individual is unique in his needs, expectations and motivations, each person's perception is also unique. Though subject to the same stimuli under the same conditions, two individuals can perceive things in their own individual way. Thus the response of two individuals to the same set of stimuli may be different because their perception may be different.

A *stimulus* is a unit of input to any of our five senses. As a sensory input, stimuli could be products, brand names, advertisements including commercials. Each product is a bundle of stimuli of shape, size, colour, fragrance, feel and taste. The promotion of the product — its packaging and advertising — is like providing stimulus to the consumer. If we understand the different perceptions with the above stimuli, we can emphasise those stimuli which provoke the most favourable response in most people. In respect of cosmetics, quality is perceived in terms of company image, good packaging and price. The study of perception is to a large extent the study of what we subconsciously either add to or subtract from the raw sensory inputs to produce our individualised picture of the world.

Sensation

Our response to stimuli which is immediate and direct is called *sensation*. We, thus, respond to stimuli like ads, packages and a brand name. Sensation is related to the quality of working of our sense organs. It is also related to the strength of the stimuli. Sensitivity of a blind person in terms of hearing is greater as he lacks the sensation of sight.

Sensation is related to the energy change it causes. It also depends upon how we distinguish the inputs. If the environment remains unchanged, it provides little or no sensation, whatever may be the strength of the input. We get used to the hustle and bustle of Navratri in Mumbai and thus do not respond to minor noises arising from vehicular traffic.

With decrease in sensory input, the ability to distinguish the changes increases. We, thus, respond most to the least stimulation. This reminds us how the Rolls Royce copy of Ogilvy talked of the highest noise which was the tick of the clock inside the car.

Sensation goes hand in hand with perception. Just sound notes are not what we hear. We hear Alisha Chenoy's 'Made in India' or Amartya Sen's advice on social inputs or the crying of a hungry baby. We cannot perceive random sensations. Our perception is an organised and meaningful pattern. A car driving down the road does not mean an engine fitted on tyres with a window pane in front. We perceive a driver, and his status. It is a 'Government of India' pilot car used by a VIP. We, however, may perceive a chauffeur if the driver is shabbily dressed. We thus are not overwhelmed by random sensations, but our cognitive structure allows a meaniful interpretation.

Threshold

Threshold indicates a level. The lowest of experiencing a sensation is called the *absolute threshold.* It denotes a point at which something is distinguished from nothing. We can see a hoarding on a highway from a particular distance. It is our absolute threshold. Individuals differ in their absolute threshold. It means two persons will be able to see the hoarding at different times; and at different distances. When there is constant stimulation, the absolute threshold rises up, indicating the numbness of the senses. If the avenue has a number of hoardings, we do not know whether any single hoarding will make an impact. It is, what is called 'get used to' feeling. Scavengers get used to the stink of the garbage. We get used to the odour in the fish market. This is called *adaptation.*

Sensory adaptation is a problem faced by makers of TV commercials. During the World Cup, many commercials compete with each other, and with the game of cricket itself. Adaptation has a lesson for advertisers. They should always create fresh campaigns, There should not be a getting-used-to-feeling for the commercials and print ad copies. In case there is, we no longer 'see' them. The sensory input is not sufficient to take notice of the ad.

To overcome the ad clutter, advertisers tend to increase the sensory input by buying larger space, by media innovations, by new media options, by in-movie placement etc. Fragrance samples can be put in the media, Ads print fragrance strips. Packages are made outstanding after determing the absolute threshold levels of the consumers. Crisp pages and currency notes makes us feel elated. Antiseptic smell of Lizol makes us feel clean and healthy. Detergent marketers can put 'scratch and sniff' stickers. Indian companies put their cosmetics with Filmfare and fashion magazines. Point-of-purchase devices can also be used to increase the sensory input.

Just Noticebable Difference (JND)

This concept is attributed to Weber, a 9th century German scientist. He put forward the concept of a differential threshold, which is the minimum difference noticed between two stimuli. This just noticeable difference is relative concept, depending on the intensity of the first stimulus. If the initial stimulus is intense, there is a greater need for higher intensity of the second stimulus. Then only we can perceive the difference. What amount of salt will make our potatochip packet saltier (JND) depends on the amount of salt used in the first place. Thus, marketers must make the additional stimulus equal to JND for people to perceive the difference. A slight increase in the price of a daily newspaper is immediately noticed. A slight increase, say of Rs. 1000 in the price of Maruti 800 is not noticed. Only when the car price goes up by several thousand rupees the difference will be noticed. Discount sales should consider JND, or else the discount will go unnoticed. Negative changes in products should be noticeable. The company knows how to make use of quantity reduction and price increase. Reduction in quantity should be below the JND. Formulation of coffee and chicory should be under the JND so that the consumers do not notice any difference in taste. Downsizing of a package without price increase actually amounts to an invisible price increase. It so happens that the consumers just do not notice the downsizing for which they are paying the same price. Package design is so changed that the differences are not noticeable. Changes are introduced in a phased manner, and the transition is not noticed, though the final package may be quite different from the original one. An abrupt change in packaging crossing the JND may make the consumer perceive a product which itself has undergone a drastic change. Improvements in products should not be above the JND, or else repeat purchases will be affected. Improvements should not be less than JND, or else they will go waste. JND enables us to determine the exact amount of improvements.

Weber has developed a mathematical formula valid for middle ranges of intensities of stimuli.

$$\frac{\Delta I}{I} = K$$

where

ΔI change in intensity sufficient to be noticed.

I original intensity

K constant that varies form one sense modality to another.

A difference below JND is called JNND, just not noticeable difference.

Sub-liminal Perception

We know people can be motivated below the level of their conscious awareness. In other words, people perceive stimuli without being aware of them consciously. Even weak and brief stimuli may be perceived by us. This is called sub-liminal perception. It is that perception where the stimulus is under the threshold or *limen* of awareness, but is certainly not under the absolute threshold of the receptors cells involved.

Consumer choices are influenced through sub-liminal messages. Wilson Bryan Key, an American communications professor, has done research on sub-liminal communications. In fact, according to him, sub-liminity is an inalienable attribute of all communication. Most junk food advertising utilises sub-liminal techniques. Life-style advertising of textiles is another instance. The cigarette advertising is associated with glamorous persons who smoke a particular brand. The sub-liminal message is that you can be like us if you smoke this brand. Sub-liminal messages play upon human fears, anxieties and desires.

However, it has not yet been proved conclusively that subliminity enhances sales. At the most, it breaks down the pre-conceived notions and melts the unreasonable aversion to the product. Prunes were endowed with all kinds of negative images in the US, but advertising was used to rid of that image by branding prunes as ones which bring colour to the blood and glow on the face. The visuals of desirable girls skating against cherry backgrounds enhanced this image. Thus interest in prunes was created. Sub-liminal messages might not be accepted. This is a risk that the advertiser takes. Sub-liminal messages are assaulted on moral grounds but human mind is influenced by subliminal content under varied situations, advertising or no advertising. For instance, a walk in the snow-clad Himalayas or deserts of Rajasthan pass on many sub-liminal messages to us. It is possible to ignore advertising, but not the chilly or hot weather. Subtle visuals, symbolic illusions (verbal, visual or phonetic) which can be interpreted at both the conscious and sub-conscious level, sensual images — all these are techniques of sub-liminal advertising. Sub-liminity is justified to differentiate products, to arrest attention and to gain visibility.

Half a century ago, James Vicary, a market researcher announced he had invented a way to make people buy things — whether they wanted them or not. It was called *sub-liminal advertising*

Sub-liminal advertising messages formally originated in 50s. In a New Jersy, New York theatre, 'Drink Coca Cola' or 'Eat Popcorn' was flashed for a short time which increased its sales. But this was not done using scientific method of using control groups. It is a moot point whether after perceiving below the level of conscious awareness, people are persuaded to act in response to such perception. Coke as a sub-liminal stimulus can arouse thirst but 'Drink Coke' cannot bring about a behavioural change. Marketers have used sub-liminal *embeds* which are nothing but disguised stimuli, not recognised by the readers in their ads. Liquor marketers use sexually suggestive symbols in the ice-cubes to increase sub-conscious appeal. This is an example of embedding. Individuals do differ in their to susceptibility sub-liminal stimuli. Audio sub-liminal messages played through cassettes are used by large retailers to discourage shop-lifting. They pass on messages like 'I am honest' or 'I will not steal'.

To improve the effect of sub-liminal messages, they are repeated so that they ultimately lead to a response. Sub-liminal communication can use sexual stimuli to arouse unconscious sexual motivations. How far these attempts are successful is a matter of further research.

Research is difficult as individuals vary in their susceptibility, and even the same individual shows a variation in his perception depending upon the time and mood. It is difficult to say what duration of time makes a weak stimulus. It is also true that embeds arouse the kind of images which one would like to see.

'Subliminal Message - Friends or Foes'? asked a newspaper headline in early 1959. People took sides. Some thought it is 'Merchandise hypnosis' or 'remote control of national thought'. Subliminal advertising can be used positively by flashing messages such as 'Drive Safely' or 'Join the Army'. In the late 1950s, brainwashing was a real fear. Messages can be used for indoctrination. Vance Packard's book the *Hidden Persuaders* (1957) warned people against mass psycho-analysis that was turning them into 'Pavlov's conditioned dog'. Vicary's experiment was repeated by Canadian Broadcasting Corporation which flashed the message 'Telephone now' 352 times on a 30-minute programme. It prompted 51% viewers to do something after watching the show. But that something related to eat or drink something. Only one felt like making a phone call. Later it was demonstrated that subliminal ads might move people to do something they like doing. They will never make a Democrat out of a Republican, or a Scotch drinker out of a teetotaler. In 1962, Vicary admitted in an interview that he had fabricated the results of the pop-corn test. Sub-liminal ads then were thrown into the trash bin. Vicary just succeeded in putting a new word into common usage.

Perceptual Selection

Countless stimuli bombard us daily. It is not possible to subject all of them to analysis. We have a screening system built into us that Selects and rejects stimuli called *perceptual selection.* The relevant stimuli are slected and recognised to the exclusion of all others. Selection of the stimuli depends upon the nature of the stimulus itself — previous experience of the consumer which affects expectations and motives at the time.

Contrast is considered valuable to get attention, and so it is made a part of the stimulus. Big ads, use of white space in ads, soundless commercial in the opening scene are all examples of the use of contrast to arrest attention.

Package design should be so distinguishable that it ensures rapid consumer perception.

Sometimes lack of contrast also leads to perception. An in-programme commercial is so broadcast that viewers do not feel that they are watching a commercial. *Infomercials* are long informative commercials like documentaries lasting for at least 30 minutes. Viewers get hooked to these. Similarly, in print media, advertorials resembling editorial matter serve the same purpose.

People see what they expect to see. The *expectation* is based on previous experience. A product is perceived according to our own expectations. Some products conform to our expectations. Some conflict with our expectations. They invite more attention. Topsy-turvy ads print half the ad upside down to attract reader's attention.

We develop a consciousness for the product which would satisfy our motives. A person who desires to have a car would be very much conscious of all the car ads. There is a heightened awareness of stimuli which are relevant to our needs and wants.

Advertisers like to have the stimuli provided by them to be recognised, interpreted and retained in memory. The following aspects of perception, therefore, need closer examination.

Selective Exposure: We tend to welcome those messages which we find palatable and avoid those which are either painful or threatening. Smokers avoid reports of nicotine being carcinogenic. They, on the other hand, like those reports which express doubts about such a declaration. We get selectively exposed to messages that assure us of our wisdom in purchasing a particular product.

Selective Attention: The consumer durables like colour TV, fridge or music system we might intend to purchase are widely advertised. The moment we decide to purchase any of these, we become conscious of the ads of these products, which till then we might have not noticed. This is called selective attention. We are more likely to notice simuli which relate to our immediate needs. The advertisers have, therefore, to tap the segment of customers correctly, since other segments are not likely to notice the stimuli. Once the customer segment is properly identified, the advertiser has to ensure that the stimuli are interesting enough to attract and hold attention.

People differ in terms of the kind of information they prefer. They also have varying preference for media. Some are more interested in appearance, some social prestige and some in price. Some prefer elaborate ads whereas some like simple messages. Consumers show wide variation in their selective attention to commercial stimuli.

Selective Distortion: Suppose a customer decides to buy brand A of a music system. Since now the decision has already been made, the customer seeks only that information which confirms the correctness of his decision to buy brand A.

On coming across some positive remarks regarding brand B, the customer tends to pick up some holes here and there to get a feeling that he is right in his selection of brand A. When in this fashion, we slot the information to our own ideas or meaning, selective distortion occurs. The advertiser might find his message is twisted in different ways by different customers.

Selective Retention: We tend to remember only the positive features of brand A confirming the correctness of our decision, and tend to forget the rest of the stimuli. The retained information confirms our values and decision.

Illustration of Cadbury: Change in Consumer Perception

Market stagnation was a major problem for Cadbury. In order to tackle this, it is attempting to change the consumer perception of chocolates. They wish to position chocolates as universal products any one can enjoy. Amul tried to reposition chocolates by promoting them as gifts to someone you love. The focus remains on gift, and does not cross across the age barrier. Cadbury is promoting chocolates by equating its consumption with natural spontaneous behaviour on the part of adults. The commercial lasting 60 seconds has the following clips:

(*i*) overweight mother in her 30s playing hopscotch with her daughter with gusto.

(*ii*) a middle-aged executive kicking out at a football on his way home from work.

(*iii*) an old grandfather blowing bubbles with his little grand children.

The Cadbury consumption clips are integrated:

(*i*) a man walking on a crowed pavement is about to cut a piece of chocolate when someone bumps against him, making him drop it. He picks it up, looks around if someone is watching him and pops it into his mouth.

(*ii*) pregnant wife pointing to chocolate bars and then to her belly.

(*iii*) sailor relishing a Cadbury bar while perched on his suitcase.

The message is "The real taste of life." Bring out the real self in you by natural spontaneous behaviour.

Perceptual Organisation

Stimuli are not treated as separate sensations, but are arranged in groups. They are treated as unified whole entities. This is the basic proposition of *Gestalt theory* Gestalt means form or configuration. Perceptual organisation consists of three elements — *figure and ground grouping* and *closure.*

We have to consider a figure against the background or ground. We preserve a figure since it is well-defined against the background. The ground is sub-ordinate to the figure. People organise their perceptions into a figure and ground relationship. Learning, however, decides what is perceived as figure and what as ground. Perceptual organisation also is influenced by our motives and expectations. Our communication should be planned that the stimulus stands out as figure. White background and silhouette figure ensures the clear perception of the figure. They should not be figure ground reversal. Consumers should not be confused about the figure and ground. Some ads carry a hidden figure. Music should not overwhelm a jingle. Background should not make the figure sub-ordinate.

A coffee ad can show a couple in a romantic mood near a hearth. Coffee thus gets associated with togetherness, warmth and romance. There is a tendency to perceive stimuli as groups which create an overall impression. We usually remember our cell phone numbers in two groups and our credit card numbers in four groups. We thus perceive chunks of information.

Fig. 5.1: Perception in Context
White considered figure. It's then vase. Black considered figure. It's then profile of two faces.

We tend to complete an incomplete picture by organisation of our perceptions. We tend to see a circle even if a part of it is left incomplete. We thus close it by our perception. An incomplete task causes tension and its completion results in satisfaction. There is a heightened memory for an incomplete task. A sound-track of a commercial can be put on radio. The consumers complete it by visualizing what they have seen in the commercial.

The principles of cognitive organisation state that perception is affected *stimulus* factors and *functional* factors. Stimulus factors are similarity, proximity, continuity and context. Similar things are perceived as belonging together, so also things near each other or proximate. Stimuli that form symmetrical or complete form are grouped together. Context or the setting also determines how things are perceived. A reversible figure given here shows a vase or goblet, if background is perceived as black And two black profiles, if background is perceived as white.

Perceptual Interpretation: Each individual interprets the stimuli in his own unique way depending upon his expectations based on previous experience and the motives and interests at the time of perception.

Mostly stimuli are vague or weak. Even strong stimuli show wide variations depending on placement, illumination and angle of viewing. Vague stimuli leads to a highly subjective interpretation as seen in projective tests. Our interpretations can be realistic or far from reality. It all depends upon what our expectations, interests and motives are.

Some distorting influences on perceptions are:

Stereotypes are formed by our impressions of the stimuli. We tend to generalize our perception according to these stereotypes.

Physical appearances: Models who are attractive are persuasive. Their very appearance pre-possess us. Stunning looks influences us. Good looking men are considered successful. All youth with long beards may be considered terrorists. The stimulus factor is similarity in physical appearance.

First impression is considered to be the best impression though we not know which stimuli are more important and relevant.

Irrelevant clues help us to take a complex decision e.g., buying a car on the basis of looks rather than engine performance.

Jumping to conclusions happens all the time. Copywriters, therefore, pack as much punch in their head-lines as possible.

Halo effect is judgement on the basis of one or few dimensions. Brands qualities are extended to extensions. It is also called *stimulus generation.* Franchises are also based on halo effect.

- **Movement:** Movement is easier to perceive than an object at rest. Neon signs which move at night, rotating outdoors and animated signs are used for this very purpose.

- **Optical Illusion:** Optical illusions or geometrical illusions also act as stimulus. Package shapes are so made that they give an impression of a large size.

- **Perceptual Defense:** Some words are taboo either socially or culturally. They are difficult to perceive. Words which are neutral or non-taboo are easily perceived. Socially valued words and concepts are more rapidly perceived than neutral words.

- **Perceptual Mapping:** In a perceptual map, we try to compare our products with other competitive products on the basis of one or more relevant characteristics. Let us take the market of washing machines. Different brands will be compared against the characteristics of *price* and *automation.* It results in the following perceptual map.

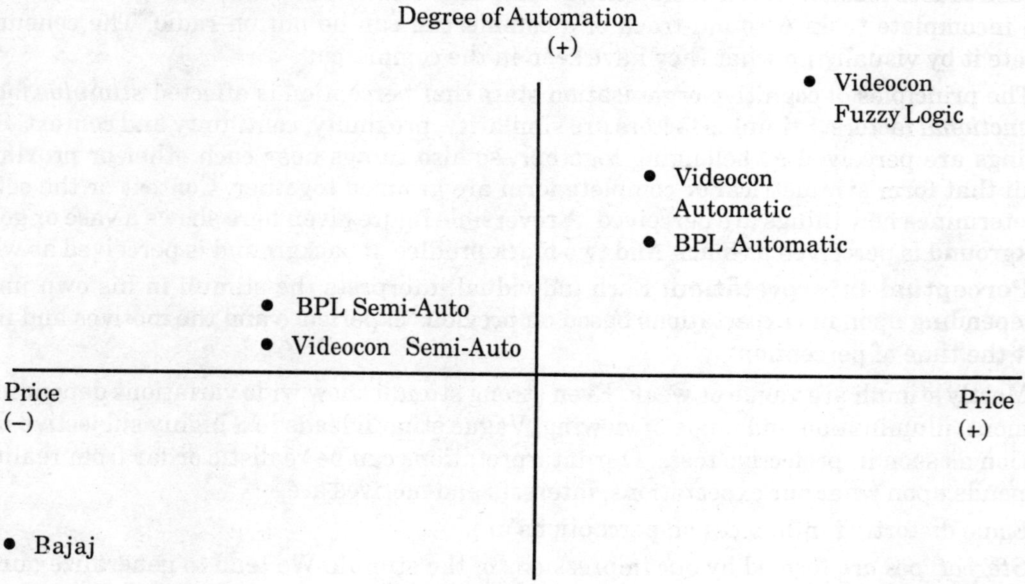

Fig. 5.2: Perceptual Map of Washing Machines

It is seen from the above perceptual map that Videocon semi-Automatic is a moderately priced washing machine and competes with a similar BPL semi-automatic model. Videocon Automatic is high on automation but moderately priced. Here also it faces competition with BPL automatic machine. Fuzzy logic models are highly expensive complex machines Bajaj and many unorganised sector machines are low on price and automation. Videocon has now identified a *gap* in the above map. It can introduce a low-priced model (below Rs. 3000) and low-automation model.

The economy and medium segments of the car market are shown on two characteristics of *fun-to-drive* and *safety* in the following perceptual map.

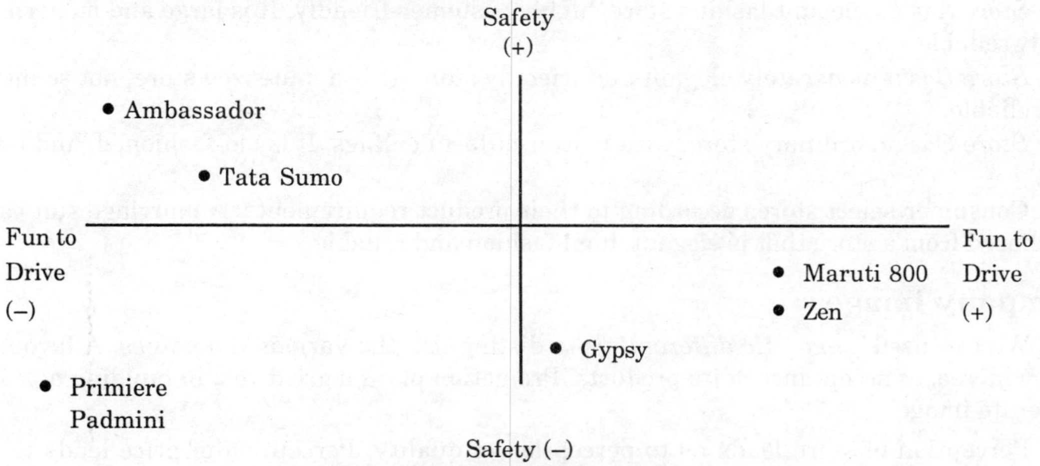

Fig. 5.3: Perceptual Map of Cars

Though Ambassadors and Sumos are safe, they are not fun to drive. Maruti 800 and Zen are moderately safe. We love to drive them too. Gypsy is very unsafe, but people enjoy to drive it to some extent. Primiere Padmini is low in safety, as well as low on fun to drive.

Perceptual maps indicate which products are similar and which dissimilar. We may collect information — from the consumers as *preference* data or *similarities* data. The question for preference data is — which of these pairs do you prefer? And for similarities data — if we take three brands at a time, which two are most similar and which two are least similar? Computer software is used to place the data in several dimensional spaces.

Volney introduced this technique to marketing.

It is used to assess the positioning of a new product. It assesses new product opportunities. It is useful in product and promotion strategies.

Store Image

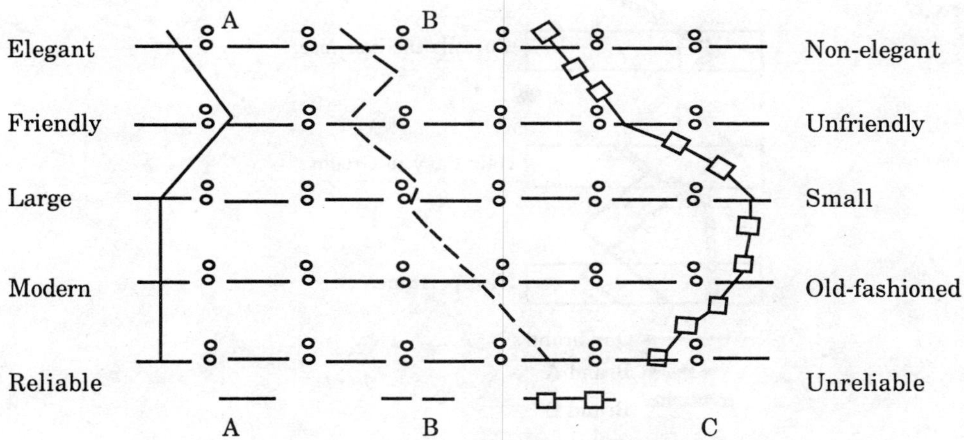

Fig. 5.4: Store Image

Retail stores project an image which influences the perceived quality of products they carry and the patronage of the customers. We can use *semantic differential* to obtain an image of a store.

Store A is an elegant fashion store, highly customer-friendly. It is large and modern. It is highly reliable.

Store B is a moderately elegant and friendly store. It is a mid-sized store, not so modern and reliable.

Store C is an ordinary store, with matter-of-fact dealings. It is old-fashioned, and unreliable.

Consumer select stores according to their product requirements. A marriage suit can be purchased from a store that is elegant, high fashion and reliable.

Company Image

We can used *semantic differentials* to distinguish the various companies. A favourable image increases acceptance of its products. Promotion plays a great role in building a positive corporate image.

Perception of store leads us to perception of quality. Perception of price leads to both perception of quality and perception of sacrifice needed to get this quality. The relationship between perceived quality and perceived sacrifice determines the perceived value, which if positive leads us to willingness to buy a product.

Snake Charts

Market research on consumer perceptions has become very important for brand image. How our brand compares with the other brands? To answer this question brand tracking exer-

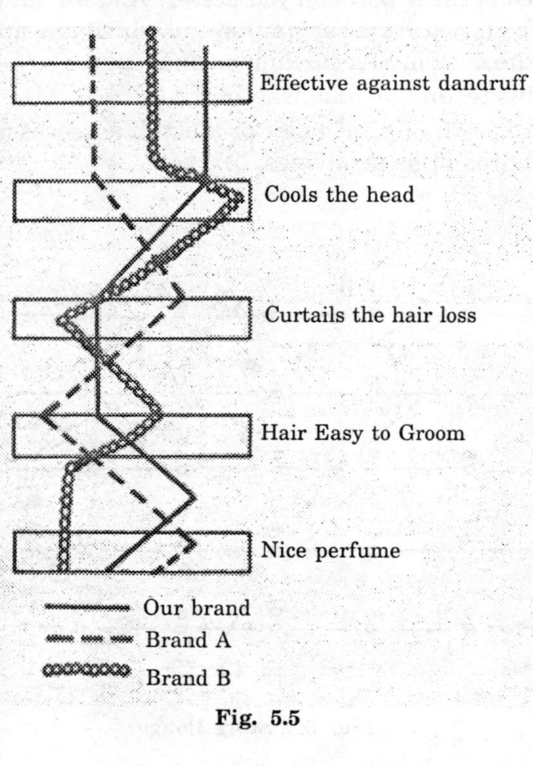

Fig. 5.5

cise is undertaken. Snake-charts provide useful information. Consider several attributes of the shampoo brand which have been compared with other two brands.

Snake-charts are however, difficult to read and provide no sharp insight.

> **BPCL'S CAMPAIGN**
>
> Bharat Petroleum Corporation Limited ran a campaign 'pure for sure' for six months to differentiate their gas stations and to redress the consumer grievance of not getting clean fuel. The perception about the gas station was very negative. This was to be changed. The consumer must be convinced. Once this is done, the value-added services like ATMs, laundry, food and convenience stores will pick up. The transit of fuel was, most vulnerable point for adulterations. Tamper-proof locking solved this problems. Underground pumps were sealed. Loose sales were stopped. Frequent lab testing was done. 'Pure and sure' certification was a stringent process. The audit and certification were entrusted to a third party. Modern looking gas stations gave a feeling to the consumers that they will not be cheated on quantity and quality.

Jack Trout on Perception

According to Jack Trout, marketing is a battle of perceptions. Marketing people are research-obsessed, and are secure in the belief that truth is on their side. They mistakenly believe that best product will win. It is an illusion. There is no objective reality here. There are no best products. All that exists in the world of marketing are perceptions in the mind of the customer or prospects. The perception is the reality. Everything else is an illusion.

APPENDIX 1

Perception

Definition Perception is the experience of objects and events based on the information provided by the senses. It is the meaningful interpretation of information received by these senses.

Stimuli → Sensory organs → interpretation → brain → age, experience, memory → individual differences.

It is very rare that two people share same opinions. Relationships suffer due to this
For example, two people of different ages will like different songs.

It is difficult for old people to change their perception.

Characteristics

(1) It is an internal process as it involves the sensory organs.
(2) It is active as it requires effort.
(3) It is relatively constant [esp. old people have rigid views].
(4) It is partly innate and partly acquired.
(5) It can be subjective (from experience) and objective (when information is read from sense organs).
(6) It is selective
(7) It involves organisation
(8) It has an affective (emotional) component. e.g., when you like/dislike something, it involves emotions.
(9) It involves past experiences and memories.
(10) It influences our behaviour e. g: when the teacher arrives, all students sit up straight.
(11) Change is the basis for perception. On a normal day, we are unaware of warmth or coolness. But with change in temperature, we perceive it as warm or cool.
(12) There are individual differences in perception.

Perceptual Organization

The natural organizing tendencies in our perception are termed as *principles of perceptual organization.*

Figure-Ground Relation

(1) It is similar to focus-margin concept of attention.
(2) We see objects as standing out from the background.
(3) The figure which stands out has some shape and object quality.
(4) The ground or the rest of the stimulus pattern is formless.
(5) The figure appears closer than the ground which extends beyond continuously.
(6) In some ambiguous stimulus patterns, we cannot be sure which part is the figure and which part is the ground.
(7) This indicates that the same stimulus input can be organized in different ways depending on the context to generate different experiences.
(8) Figure and ground can be reversible, e. g.: in the case of faces and vase.
(9) Camouflage

It is the blending of figure and ground, e. g.: Chameleon

Contour

We are able to separate objects from the ground only because we can perceive contour. A contour is a line of demarcation perceived by the observer whenever there is a marked difference in the brightness or colour of the background in one part of the visual field as compared to the other.

Contours give shape to the objects in our visual world because they mark off an object but they themselves are not shapes. e.g. in a song, the instrumental part is in the background while the singing is in the foreground.

Laws of Perceptual Grouping

They were proposed by the Gestalt school.

(1) Law of Proximity/Nearness

- Items that are close together in space or time are organized together.

  e.g. People perceive these as three pairs of dots and not 6 dots.

(2) Law of Similarity

- Similar items are organized together.

  e.g.

  × × 0
  × × 0
  × × 0
  × × 0

(3) Law of Symmetry (or good figure)

- It is the tendency to organize things, to make a balanced figure that includes all the parts.
- This law is more important than the law of similarity.

e.g:

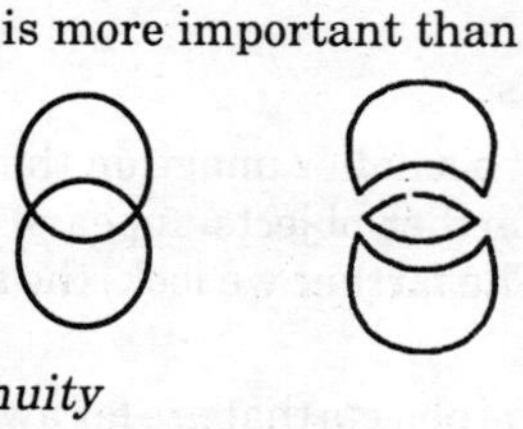

This is seen in terms of two circles and not three separate parts though they are similar because two circles are balanced and symmetrical.

(4) Law of Continuity

- Parts that are continuous with one another are perceived as together.
- We tend to see a line which starts in one way as continuous in the same way.

This is seen as a straight line and a wave and not as 5 lines and 5 arcs together. They are also seen as continuous.

(5) Law of Closure

- It is the tendency to perceive objects as wholes rather than separate parts.
- When a stimulus is incomplete, we fill in the gaps perceptually so that we see a meaningful whole.

eg.:

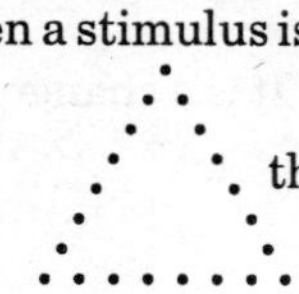

this is perceived as a whole triangle.

(6) Law of Common Fate

- Elements perceived as moving together form a single group.
- This applies to moving objects.

e.g.

We don't see them as 8 birds but as 1 group of birds.

Depth Perception

- It was of interest, to both scientists and philosophers, for several years.
- The ability to perceive depth is a major perceptual accomplishment.
- It depends on cues which are of two kinds
  (1) monocular cues
  (2) binocular cues

Bioncular Cues

Binocular cues come from the fact that two eyes receive a slightly different view of the world. It is of two types:

(1) Retinal Disparity: i.e., our eyes receive different images but these are united into a single perception and hence we do not see parts of an image.

(2) Convergence: i.e., our eyes converge towards each other to focus on objects that are nearer. This allows us to estimate the distance.

Monocular Cues

These can operate even when one eye is looking at objects.

(1) Linear Perspective: Objects that are far away project a smaller image on the retina than objects that are nearer. Also distance between images of farther objects appears to be smaller. This allows us to perceive distance e. g.: railway tracks. The farther we look, the smaller seems to be the distance between the two rails of track.

(2) Aerial Perspective [or Clearness]: The retinal images of objects that are far away and at a distance appear less clear and less saturated in colour.

When the object is nearer, it is possible to perceive details. This explains why more accidents occur when the weather is not clear. The car ahead looks hazy and so is seen as being farther away.

(3) Interposition: Near objects block off a part of the image of those objects that are far away. When this happens, the second object is perceived to be at a greater distance.

(4) Shadows: Inference about depth from shadows is based on the assumption that light comes from above.

Darker areas are perceived as deeper as compared to brighter areas.

When a dark area is seen on top of an object, it suggests that it has been painted as a shadow. It can't occur on top as light falls from top to bottom.

(5) Gradient of Texture : Gradient is a continuous change of something. It is a change without sharp differences.

— As the distance increases the objects are perceived to be smooth, having less details while those that are nearer are perceived to be rough and have many details.

This continuous gradation of texture gives the eye and the brain information for the perception of depth.

(6) *Motion Parallax (or Relative Movement):* It is used when our head moves in relation to objects.

Objects that are nearer seem to move faster in the opposite direction while those that are farther move slower in the same direction.

We have observed this when we travel by train or bus.

(7) *Accommodation*: Our ability to adjust to the distance of objects is called accommodation.

Our lens changes shape to adjust to the distance of objects. The changes in the lens shape are produced by ciliary muscles. Kinesthetic receptors in the ciliary muscles detect muscle tension when the eye is focussed on near objects. There is no muscle tension for farther objects.

Errors in Perception

When our perceptions do not agree with the nature of objects or events, we term them as errors.

These can be classified as illusions and hallucinations.

INDIVIDUAL DIFFERENCES IN PERCEPTION

(1) Perceptual Learning

Due to past experience, one can learn to extract more information from the sensory data.

For example, in a forest, a botanist will perceive the different kind of plants, leaves, etc.

(2) Mental Set

This refers to the expectations of the individual.

For example, in a dark room, if someone expects to see a ghost, anything white will appear to be a ghost.

Illusions	*Hallucinations*
(1) Illusions are experienced by all normal individuals.	(1) Hallucinations are experienced by abnormal individuals. e.g. Schizophrenics.
(2) They are influenced by past experiences, set or expectations. For example, a thirsty desert traveller sees water when it is shining sand. In a common auditory illusion, the echo of a sound is heard as coming from the opposite direction.	(2) They are influenced by drugs e.g. Under the influence of drugs like opium a person feels he is floating in the air.
(3) They involve perceiving the stimulus incorrectly.	(3) They involve falsely perceiving things in the absence of a stimulus.
(4) They are mostly visual. A traveller in a moving train may see the other train as moving – illusion of motion.	(4) They are generally accompanied by auditory stimuli.
(5) For exmaple, perceiving a water-pipe as a snake.	(5) For example, seeing a dragon in a class-room.

(6) In the same situation we experience same illustration e.g.: stick-water-bent A person who has read a ghost story may see a piece of cloth as a ghost. When we are anxiously waiting for a friend a stranger may be mistaken for the friend.	(6) Different persons experience different hallucinations in same circumstances. e.g.: one drunkard – pink rats – green elephants. A mentally sick person may hear bees buzzing around him or taste poison in his food.

(3) Motive and Needs

In deserts, people see mirages not only because of refraction of light on sand in the heat, but also because of his need of hunger, thirst etc.

(4) Cognitive Style

— This refers to the way in which one thinks.

— Some people are optimistic and some are pessimistic.

— Some people have abstract thinking while some concrete.

— Some people are rational while some imaginative.

— Depending on this, their perceptions also change.

Note: If the stimulus is concrete, you perceive it through your sensory organs but if the stimulus is ambiguous and vague, you are likely to perceive it by perceptual learning, mental set, etc.

Rorschach Ink Blot Test

The person is given 10 cards which have ink blots and is asked to note down what he perceives in those cards. At such times, the person projects his own motives, needs, etc. while interpreting it. The psychologist can study his personality through this.

❑ ❑ ❑

6

CONSUMER MOTIVATION

Why do we spend on products and services the way we do? What prompts us to take a vacation to exotic far off islands? Why do we aspire to be clothed in Versace outfits, or for that matter Ritu Beri's autumn collections? In order to understand human behaviour, we have to understand its driving force — motivation. Motivation impels us to action.

We all have some unfulfilled needs, wants and desires. This creates tension. We tend to reduce this tension consciously or subconsciously by behaving in such a way that we achieve our goal or satisfy our needs. To illustrate, a simple physiological process like 'feeling hungry' incites us to eat to satisfy the hunger because of the tension created in the form of low level of blood sugar. The goals we choose, and the behaviour we show are the outcomes of our individual thinking and learning. The following diagram illustrates the process of motivation.

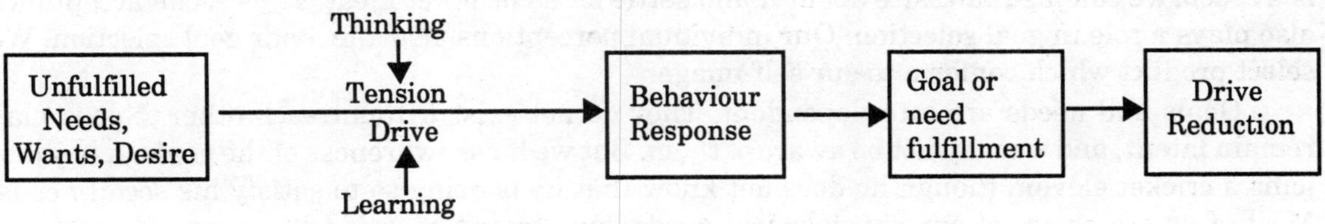

Fig. 6.1: Motivation Process

Motivation thus means all those drives induced by needs which incite an individual to action, and sustain the same till the goal is reached; or the tension is reduced. Motive may be defined as an internal condition of the organism which initiates and sustains activity directed to a particular goal. The ultimate satisfaction depends upon the course of action taken. One cannot become a heavy-weight boxing champion just by dressing like Mike Tyson but can certainly become one by taking rigorous training in boxing. The course of action taken and the goals chosen are in the context of our thinking process (cognition) and previous learning. It is thus simple to understand that we as marketers should influence the cognitive processes for the desired action.

Needs

We all have needs, some of which are innate and some acquired. We are born with *physiological needs* such as the need for food, water, air, clothing, shelter and sex. As these needs are necessary conditions for life to exist, they are called *primary needs.* As we grow, we acquire needs. A child needs protection and security. While growing up, it has to play with friends. It attends school and joins clubs. It dates the opposite sex, and finds a suitable partner to marry. Here, the social and psychological needs have arisen. They are called *secondary needs or motives.* They arise due to an individuals psychological make-up and his interactions with others. To illustrate, getting house to protect against elements is a primary need, but getting a bungalow enables him to throw parties, and fulfill his secondary social needs. Elite location provides a boost to his ego and fulfills his psychological need for prestige and recognition. Thus a place to live in not only satisfies the primary need of an individual, but also his secondary needs.

Goals

Motivated behaviour is goal-oriented. When a motive is aroused, it leads to such activity as will satisfy the motive. Goals can be *generic* like quenching the thirst in summer or can be *product-specific* like using Limca to quench the thirst. Marketers pay attention to both the types of goals. Eggs and milk consumption in general are being promoted. We may also come across promotion of a particular brand of milk like Amul.

Goal Selection

Each of the need directs an individual towards a goal. However, several goals can satisfy one need. Thus the need for status can direct an individual to acquire a car. Like Mercedes or a degree like MBA. Which goals do we select? It is a matter of our personal experience, physical capacity, the prevailing culture and values, and the accessibility of the goals themselves.

In order to satisfy our appetite, we may choose a vegetarian or non-vegetarian meal. It depends on what our attitudes are. We may find meat repulsive, and select a vegetarian meal. Sometimes, following a doctor's advice, we may choose a low-cal meal. While eating non-veg meal we may opt for red meat or white meat. Many Italian dishes are outside our realm of experience. We may, therefore, select Indian dishes. In a country like Saudi Arabia where pork is a taboo, we can just fantasize about it and settle for some other meat. Thus social acceptance also plays a role in goal selection. Our individual perceptions also affect our goal selection. We select product which conform to our self-image.

Goals and needs are interdependent. They do not exist without each other. Needs may remain latent, and we may not be aware of them. But we have awareness of the goals. A boy just joins a cricket eleven, though he does not know that he is doing so to satisfy his social needs. Most of us are aware of our physiological needs, but are not consciously aware of our higher social and psychological needs. Subconsciously, however, our behaviour leads us to satisfy these acquired needs.

Positive Motivation and Negative Motivation

Motivation operates in both the directions. Either we are impelled by the drives towards a goal or away from the goal. Thus we may avoid riding a motorbike to satisfy our safety need. Such negative drives are called fears or aversions. Though the sentiments and physical activity associated with positive and negative drives are different, essentially they initiate us into action and sustain the same. Both these drives or motives are, therefore, treated as needs, wants and desires.

Needs and Wants

Needs are mostly biogenic, but wants are product specific. Thus a beverage is used to satisfy our thirst which is a need, but Coke is wanted to satisfy it.

Positive and Negative Goals

Goals can be positive or negative. When behaviour is directed towards a particular goal it is called positive. We try to approach it. When behaviour is directed away from a goal, it is called negative. We try to avoid it. Whether approach objects or avoidance objects, goals are still goals. Fitness is a positive goal. Obesity is not liked by figure-conscious women, and is avoided, and so is a negative goal. We can join a gym to achieve fitness and a jogging club to avoid obesity. People also resent a threat to their 'freedom to choose' and react negatively to such threats. New Coke was resented by the consumers of the traditional drink.

Rational and Emotional Motives

Traditional economic theory considers a man to be rational in his economic choices — he is an economic man. His choice is based on objective criteria such as price, size, mileage or weight and such other factors. On the other hand, consumers can choose products according to subjective or personal criteria such as need for status, prestige, pride, individuality etc. These are called emotional motives.

Needs and Goals in a State of Flux

Is motivated behaviour due to properties in the immediate psychological field or to the influence of past experience? This involves the genetic and dynamic approaches. Lewin's concept of *Psychological Field* is useful in this connection. It consists of -

(*i*) the external physical environment
(*ii*) the internal physiological state
(*iii*) neural traces of past experiences.

Though man is the master of his own fate in one sense, the pressure of the ages is upon him in another sense.

Goals keep on changing, once the previous ones are attained. If the older goals are not achieved, some substitute goals may be developed. Need-directed human activity is a continuous process since —

(*i*) existing needs are never completely satisfied.
(*ii*) new needs and higher needs emerge when older needs are satisfied.
(*iii*) new goals and higher goals are set when older goals are achieved.

As we satisfy hunger once, we again become hungry after some time. Once our physiological needs are satisfied, we crave for security. Once these are satisfied, we tend to aspire to have recognition and prestige. Even though a Chief Executive Officer has the maximum power, he may like to become an owner with his own decision making power. Individuals continue striving to satisfy new and higher needs. A product has to satisfy the existing needs of the customers, and as customers show different needs, we have to reposition the product to keep it relevant. Today a car may be sold to satisfy prestige needs. Tomorrow, it may be repositioned to satisfy safety needs.

Achievement of goals changes our *level of aspiration* — we tend to set higher and new goals. It shows our added confidence to achieve higher things. Similarly, no achievement of goals lowers our level of aspiration. Success and failure thus affect our goal selection. Students who aspire to enter the medical profession may opt for paramedical courses, if they are not able to enrol themselves for the medical course. The chances of success decide our persistence. Past experience make us familiar with an activity, and we may have higher expectations of success. A successful amateur photographer may dare to buy a professional camera emboldened by his previous success. Marketers have several lessons here. They should frame realistic product promises and the product must live upto the expectations created. Unrealistic expectations are likely to cause dissatisfaction.

There are situations when it is not possible to attain a primary goal set. A person may aspire to have Mercedes, but may settle down for Ford Escort or Honda City thinking that these cars give the same status as that given by Mercedes. Thus a primary goals is replaced by some other goal, which is called subsidiary goal. This type of behaviour wards off frustration, and is essentially defensive in nature.

When we fail to achieve a goal, we are *frustrated.* The reasons for failure can be personal or environmental. Different individuals reflect differently to a frustrating experience. Some bypass it, or select a substitute goal. This is adaptation. Some experience stress and anxiety.

If we cannot cope with frustration, we may show aggression or rationalization — which are defence mechanisms. Frustrated consumers may show their aggression by writing complaint letters, to the newspapers. They may rationalize their behaviour by citing cogent reasons. An individual who cannot afford a snake-skin bag can proclaim that this product should not be favoured as it affects wild life and ecology. Other defence mechanisms are regression, withdrawal, projection, identification, autism and repression. *Atuism* is dreaming and fasntasizing. *Regression* shows childish immature behaviour. *Withdrawal* means a retreat from the frustrating situation. *Projecting* means extension of our own behaviour to others. *Identification* involves repressing a frustrating need. Such repressed needs can be *sublimated* in a socially acceptable way. Thus frustration can be dealt with in a variety of ways. It protects our self-worth from the anxieties resulting from the conscious awareness. Advertising appeals are chosen keeping in mind how frustration can be handled.

Multiplicity of Needs

Consumer behaviour is likely to satisfy a variety of needs. The very fact that some particular goals have been selected vouchsafes the presence of several needs. Clothes are worn to protect us and to reveal what we stand for. A dominant need initiates the behaviour. We get ourselves off alcohol to please our spouse primarily but also to avoid its adverse effects. But the first step in the direction of alcohol avoidance has been taken to satisfy the spouse — it is the pre-potent need.

Variation among Individuals Regarding Needs and Goals

People select one and the same goal, but their needs may be different. Similarly people may fulfil the same need by selecting different goals. Thus it is difficult to infer from behaviour the motives of people.

Arousal of Motives

Our specific needs remain latent for quite some time. They get aroused at a specific time by internal stimuli in the physiology of the person, or by emotional or cognitive processes or by outside stimuli.

Physiological arousal relate to a physiological condition and arousal of a need, say decline in blood sugar level and hunger. Mostly, these are involuntary. An ice-cream cone in a commercial may arouse us physiologically to desire the product.

Emotional arousal occurs because of dreaming, aspiring and fantasizing. A dream to be a business magnate may force one to join an MBA programme.

Cognitive arousal arousal occurs after cognitive awareness of the needs. Nostalgia about people back home results in the use of ISD.

Environmental arousal result from the specific causes in the environment. Smell of bakery products arouse the need for cakes and pastries. The very sight of a product may trigger off its need. A video of a birthday party captured on Handycam impels us to buy one. Exposure leads to a desire for many products. An environment that does not provide enough opportunities to see better and new products does not stimulate needs. TV viewing inspires audience to have a better life style, but also frustrate some, who do not have the means to sustain such a life style.

Behaviourist school considers arousal as a mechanical process of stimulus and response. *Cognitive* school considers behaviour to be goal-directed. There is reasoning, categorization, attitude formation and beliefs as predispositions to behaviour.

Human Needs or Motives

There are countless needs and motives, but all these fall into the basic categories of physiological, social and psychological needs or motives. Daniel Starch (1923) has prepared a list of advertising appeals for adults.

DANIEL STARCH'S ADVERTISING APPEALS

Taste	Ambition
Hunger	Respect for deity
Sex	Approval of others
Body comfort	Gregariousness
Physical activity	Efficiency
Curiosity	Teasing
Health	Possession
Personal appearance	Shyness
Rest and sleep	Co-operation
Home comfort	Respect for others
Play-sport	Domesticity
Love of offspring	Social distinction
Parental affection	Hospitality
Safety	Devotion to others
Economy	Warmth
Pleasure	Courtesy
Cleanliness	Imitation
Protection for others	Coolness
Managing others	Fear and caution
Construction	Manipulation
Style	Amusement
Humour	Competition

Murray (1938) has grouped 28 psychogenic needs into categories like needs for power; affection; asking and telling; ambition, prestige and achievement; acquisition.

Such lengthy lists are of little use to marketers. It is necessary to classify needs into distinct categories signifying generic needs which take care of the detailed human needs.

Hierarchy of Needs

Very seldom an attempt has been made to understand Maslow's theory of need hierarchy beyond a narrow perspective. It is important to look at it from a situational perspective and develop a frame of reference within which it would be possible to analyse specific situations. Maslow first presented his basic ideas on motivation in 1972 when he addressed a psychoanalytic society and stated that he wanted to "integrate into a single theoretical structure the partial truths I saw in Freud. Alder Jung, Levery, Fromm, Honey and Glostein." Maslow's thinking was also affected by the works of Murray, Gorden, Allport, Rogers and others.

Maslow's Need Hierarchy

Human motives can be put into five distinct catergories in the form of a pyramid as shown in Fig. 6.2. Perhaps, the five catergories over-simplify the human motives. This need hierarchy theory was the result of Abraham Maslow's work; and hence the name Maslow's Need Hierarchy. In fact, human behaviour is directed by several other needs and need combinations at a given point of time. It is however difficult to pinpoint them separately, and so a need hierarchy as shown in Fig. 6.2 simplifies the problem for our understanding.

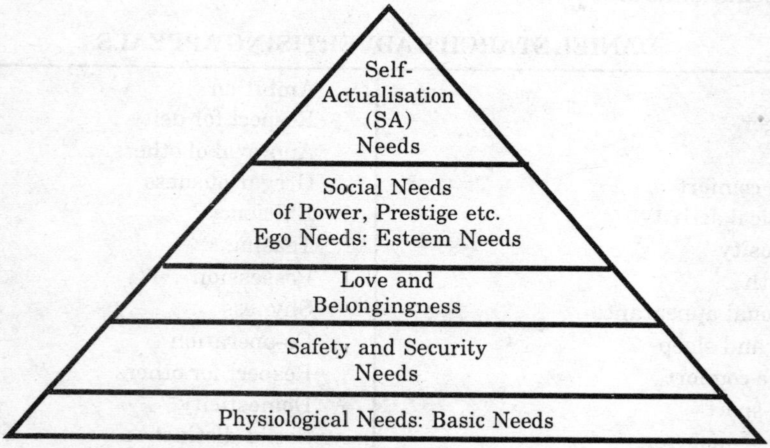

Fig. 6.2 : Maslow's Need Hierarchy.

Maslow advanced three important propositions about human behaviour:

(*a*) Men are wanting beings. Their needs are unlimited and as soon as one need is satisfied, another appears in its place, and this continues from birth to death.

(*b*) A satisfied need is not a motivator of behaviour; only the needs which are not satisfied are capable of motivating individuals.

(*c*) Needs of men develop in a sequential order and are arranged in a hierarchical order. Fig. 6.2 illustrates the concept.

Physiological Needs

At the lowest level of his need hierarchy are his physiological needs such as hunger, thirst, sex etc. These are called biogenic motives which arise due to some internal need or physiological condition withing the body. The main biogenic motives are temperature regulation, hunger, thirst, pain, sleep and sex. The body tends to maintain balance among its internal physiological states — it is called homeostasis. When the physiological needs are thwarted, they assume great importance. Consider a man who is very hungry. He may not like to think of status, or prestige but would like to find ways and means by which he can satiate his hunger. Maslow in fact referred to the potency of needs. Thus when physiological needs are potent, other needs like psychological are pushed into the background.

Further, it is important to undertand these sets of needs are independent of each other. For example, even while an individual is not thirsty, he needs food to satiate his hunger. These sets of needs are also repetitive in nature and re-emerge after a short time. To base motivation only on these lower sets of needs will have little meaning in a developed economy because of the fact that the satisfaction of such needs is guaranteed.

Security Needs

When the physiological needs are satisfied, the next level of needs emerge to motivate him. These are the security needs. An individual would like to work for the organisation to ensure continuity of employment. Security needs assume great significance in an organisation where the individual finds himself in a dependent relationship and where he fears arbitrary deprivation. Arbitrary action of management which shows favouritism and discrimination can be strong motivators of the security needs in the work-life relationships.

Security needs can be operative both at conscious and subconscious level. Too much emphasis on conscious needs can have a disciplinary effect rather than motivating the person. "Unconscious security needs on the other hand result from childhood experiences which depict life as either far too uncontrolable to make initiative worthwhile or far too benevolent to make initiative necessary."

Social Needs

When an individual's first two level needs, *i.e.,* physiological and safety, are relatively satisfied, then the social needs become an important motivator of his behaviour. He then seeks acceptance by the group and strives for affection and belongingness.

However, this need to belongingness may be stronger in one person than in another. Maslow distinguished the need for affiliation into two categories. In the less mature form, this need is manifested when one tries to relate or seek company with another in order to overcome loneliness or to kill boredom. Maslow called it as "D-love" or which is based on deficit need. In its mature form, which Maslow termed as "B-love," it is evident when a person wants to relate to another without any desire to use him any way and accepts the way he is.

According to Pathak, "When managers take a purely intellectual and economic view of people by ignoring their social needs, they develop a managerial style that is cold, elusive, and insensitive to non-economic concerns."

Quite often, managers perceive this only as a threat to the organisation. As a result, they try to exercise tight control. They constantly see that such informal groups do not emerge and actively try to break up existing groups. When the individuals find that their social needs and even the security needs are threatened, they may become resistant, antagonistic and unco-operative, thereby defeating the organisational objectives.

Esteem Needs

The next level of needs are perhaps of the greatest significance both to the organisation and the man himself. When the physiological, security and social needs are appreciably satisfied, the esteem needs emerge. These needs include those for distinction, achievement, status and independence.

Unlike the other lower needs, esteem needs are rarely satisfied. They are largely unsatiable. In a conventional type of management, managers give little attention to these aspects of human motivation which if properly utilised can yield high organisational performance. Some higher social needs and esteem needs are tabulated here for ready reference.

TABLE 6.1

HIGHER SOCIAL AND ESTEEM NEEDS

Motive	*Meaning*	*Behaviour Indicators*
Achievement	Desire to excel	Active, exert themselves, set high goals, accept challenges, derive pleasure from trials, strive for quality. They do self-evaluation. They imagine the accomplishments of tasks.
Power	Desire to influence others. Desire to exercise control on others.	Seek positions vested with power. Seek leadership opportunities. Always giving directions to others. Argumentative. Want to be the first.
Extension	Desire to be helpful to others. Desire to serve the orgsanisation, nation or any external agent.	Social workers. Enjoy helping others.
Aggression	Desire to dominate others. Desire to demonstrate strength, at times physically.	Argumentative. Loud-mouthed. Pick up quarrels. Want to be winners. Show strength.
Dependence	Need to consult others before deciding.	Seek directions from others. No independent decision. Need protection. No initiative.
Independence	Desire to do things autonomously.	Autonomous decisions. May consult others, but do not seek approval.
Status and Prestige	Desire to be respected in social set up.	Non-violative of social behaviour. Violates social behaviour only when it gives recognition. Selective interaction with others. Authoritarian tendencies. Run for offices.
Recognition	Need to be recognised for one's achievements.	Work hard. Motivation lost if no recognition. Visible. Attention-seeking.
Activity	Desire to be always doing something.	Active, hard worker. Opposite of passivity which is a need to relax.

Self-Actualisation Needs

On top of the individual's need hierarchy is the need for self-realisation. It is one of the needs discussed by Maslow about which little is known to the behavioural and social scientist. This is mainly because people try to satisfy these needs in many different ways. It is, therefore, extremely difficult if not impossible to pinpoint or identify the self-actualisation needs. Once the other lower level needs are completely or partly satisfied, the person tries to realise his own potential. Though the identification of these needs is not easy, there are at least two motives which seem to be related to it. They are acceptance and competence.

Self-Actualisation Concept Reviewed

Maslow borrowed the term 'Self-actualisation' from Kurt Goldstein and it refers to the desire for self-fulfilment, namely, one's tendency to become actualised in what one potentially is. 'A musician must make music, an artist must paint, a poet must write, if he is to be ultimately happy. What a man can be he must be.' This need we may call self-actualisation. At the end he shows how nebulous this need is: "Since in our society, basically satisfied people (*i.e.,* people who are satisfied in the physiological, safety, love and esteem needs) are the exception, we do not know much about self-actualisation, either experimentally or clinically. It remains a challenging problem for research."

Maslow has discovered the following six characteristics in self-actualised human beings : *(i)* They can accept the way things really are. *(ii)* They are not afraid to get close to others. *(iii)* They are efficient judges of situations. *(iv)* They are creative and appreciative. *(v)* They march to different drummer. *(vi)* They are willing to learn from anyone.

Rogers has suggested four personal characteristics in self-acutalised persons: *(i)* willingness to accept experience for what they are; *(ii)* trust and confidence in their own ability and judgement; *(iii)* greater reliance on self than on society or friends; *(iv)* willingness to continue to grow as persons. McGregor refers to self-actualisation as "the need for realising one's own potentialities." Rensis Likert calls it "the desire for growth and significant achievement in terms of one's own values and goals."

Keith Davis has used the synonym 'self-realisation' for this need and writes,"... which means to become all one is capable of becoming. This need is less apparent than others because many persons have not unleashed it.... If to the degree that the need can be unleashed, people will find their work a challenge and an inner satisfaction." Warren Bennis writes that "the concept of self-actualisation is, at best, an ill-defined concept..." (and that) self-actualised man seems to be more myth than reality.... Paul Hersey toes the line of other behaviourists and writes, "Of all the needs discussed by Maslow, the one that social and behavioural scientists know least about is self-actualisation. Perhaps, this is because people satisfy this need in different ways. Thus, self-actualisation is a difficult need to pin down and identify...little research has been done on the concept of self-actualisation...."

Robert M. Fulmer observes, "Only a few people ever achieve the true concept of self-actualisation." Atchison and Hill have also written about the self-actualisation needs. "Maslow believed that what a person can be, he or she must be. This means that people have a full range of potential (talents, knowledge, emotions, and so forth) that must find expression. When people begin to actualise their potential, they begin to preceive themselves, others, and the environment creatively, spontaneously and appreciatively." But, these observations are prefaced by the sentence, "the need for self-actualisation is somewhat more complex than the others."

Amongst the very recent observers (1979), Richard M. Hodgetts includes under it "Self-development, and creativity in the broadest sense of the word." But he admits, at the same time, that "of all five needs, the least is known about self-actulisation." As such, this need appears to have defied a correct analysis so far.

Comment

When the lower level of wants are adequately satisfied, the person moves to a higher level and the lower level of wants becomes less important in his total system of wants. Once the lower level of wants becomes less potent, the individual is free to realise his higher level of wants which increases in number and variety.

Maslow's need hierarchy model helps the marketers in developing suitable advertising appeals for their product. An appeal satisfies a particular need experienced by a substantial portion of the population. Need hierarchy also helps in product positioning.

Need hierarchy model is useful in segmentation. Soft drinks ads use social appeal, and are directed to fun-loving youngsters. Need hierarchy also helps positioning by taking advantage of the fact that a product has to satisfy an unfulfilled need. Luxury cars are meant for prestige and status. Mid-sized cars are meant for the whole family. Some cars are sold on safety. Maslow's model has versatility. A single product can be sold against various appeals.

Basic Trio

Psychologists have identified three basic needs in human beings — the need for power the need for affiliation and the need for achievement.

Power need makes an individual exert control over his environment consisting of persons and things. This corresponds to the ego need or need for self-esteem. Affiliation need has a desire for friendship acceptance and belonging. It shows dependence on others. This corresponds to the social needs of Maslow. Achievement need emphasises personal accomplishments. It corresponds to the ego and self-actualization needs. Persons with different need sets receive different kinds of products in keeping with their need pattern. Appeals work on individuals depending on their need requirement.

How Motives are Measured?

First, we have to identify the motives. Which are the motives at work when we behave the way we do? It is not something that can be seen with the naked eyes. Its a matter of observation and inference. Projective techniques can be employed, to know the presence of these motives and their strength. We have discussed these methods elsewhere in this book The whole process is not very precise. The criteria of *validity* and *reliability* are not met. Validity ensures that the test measures what it purports to measure. Reliability ensures consistency of results. Projective technique is subjective. It cannot be relied upon exclusively. There should be combination of observation, self-reports and projective tests. The research output is qualitative.

MOTIVATION RESEARCH

Motivation research techniques have become a standard part of most marketing researchers' repertoires. Broadly classified, there are two types of techniques: depth interviews and projective techniques. Depth interviews are unstructured, non-disguised and intensive methods to uncover basic predispositions, unconscious feelings, emotions and so forth. They can be either individual or group interviews.

Projective techniques are indirect (unstructured disguised) means of questioning respondents. The methods are based on the premise that an individual's description of real or imagined events required interpretation and this interpretation can only be based on the individual's own background, attitudes and values. Some common projective techniques are : word association, sentence completion, thematic-apperception test and third-person technique.

Motivation Research: Motivation explains why people behave as they do, but there is rarely a simple, single explanation for human behaviour. This is especially the case with the type of consumer behaviour studied by market researchers.

Since it is questionable whether people themselves can identify the whys and wherefores of their buying, it became evident to marketers that a technique was required that could discover and evaluate the drives which cause people to purchase particular products or specific brands. Motivation research has introduced such techniques.

Motivation research uses social science techniques to find and evaluate the forces which cause certain behaviour in the market place. *It involves penetrating analysis of the thinking and attitude of consumers to discover the subconcious reasons why consumers buy particular products and specific brands.* To illustrate, Hall-mark sold many cards having the image of a savaged bare tree. This tree was symbolic of the lonely person sending this card. Similarly, yellow colour only on the Surf package makes it too astringent. Blue only makes it less effective as a washing powder. Blue and yellow together pleases the consumers. Chrysler convertible cars suggested to the consumers a fantasy mistress and the Sedan a symbolic wife. They naturally settled down with it.

It is important to note at this stage that motivation research is not synonymous with qualitative research. Very often motives are sought and explored by qualitative techniques but these techniques are used for a wide range of purposes other than being concerned with motives.

Motivation research became popular among researchers in the 1950s. During that period, some of its supporters made such enthusiastic claims for the capabilities of the techniques that other researchers listed "over-expectations" as one of the major problems with motivation research. As a result of overenthusiastic claims and misuse of the techniques, the use of motivation research has declined considerably. However, motivation research techniques (namely, projective techniques and depth interviews) have become a standard part of most marketing researchers' repertoires. They have been successfully applied to problems such as product design, package design, advertising etc.

Motivation Research and Advertising: Human needs are the basis of advertising appeals. We can know about human needs (physiological, safety, love, esteem, and self-actualisation needs) through motivation research. We also would be able to concentrate on supply motives (hunger and thirst), avoidance motives (avoidance of negative consequences — illness, death etc.), species maintaining motive (reproduction, nutritive motives). We could also concentrate on acquired or learned motives, recognition and affiliation needs. We would know how the message would be developed, or rational basis of quality, price, durability, performance, convenience, resale value, operational economy etc. or an emotional appeal, either negative (fear) or positive (love, humour, pride, prestige, joy, exclusiveness). The motives used are desired to be different, desire to conform, desire to attract the opposite sex, and desire for prestige. We also are guided about the moral appeals we can use for social awareness advertising.

Mostly motivation research is qualitative research. Let us learn some salient features of Qualitative Research (QR).

Media research is no more a number game — words like psychographics and life-style segmentation have become acceptable and necessary too.

QR is an understanding of the perceptions, attitudes and pre-dispositions of a certain target segment towards a product, service, advertisement concept or a need area. The underlying assumption is that there is a common thread that unites every segment of the consuming public. QR tries to set the feel of this common thread. A small sample (say 4 groups of 8 respondents each) is enough to appreciate this common thread. QR selects a few focus groups — say of those who use conventional blades and those who use twin blades. We then study the motivation of these groups.

QR at its best is subjective. Rather than being a weakness, QRs subjectivity is its main strength. QR is interpretative in nature. The exploration of the unknown requires personal skills of the researcher. Subjectivity of the researcher should contribute to positive understanding of the problem.

Probe Qualitative Research is a division of IMRB. Quest is the qualitative research division of MARG.

Quantum is an Marketing research company run by women — Dr. Meena Kaushik, Srilekha Aggarwal and Meera Vasudevan (all ex- MARG). It was set up in Sept. 1990 with H.O. at Bangalore and branches at Mumbai, Madras and Delhi. This company also delves into consumer's psyche and tries to analyse the reasons and motives of brand preferences.

Qualitative Research

It is an exploration of the grey zones of human mind. It fills the gap between columns marked 'yes' and 'no' and 'don't know' in quantitative research. Qualitative research resorts to indirect interviewing. It traces the hidden motivators. The results of this research are not quantifiable, but the indicators it provides are startling. For products like cigarettes psychographic data, rather than mere demographic data, is invaluable. For cigarette marketing, attitudinal research is necessary. Another area for qualitative research is new products/concepts. Here the researcher himself knows very little about the product in question. Qualitative research is also helpful for a consumer's perception of a brand and imagery. For personal products like contraceptives, sanitary napkins, hair dyes which otherwise might cause embarrassment, Qualitative research gives more dependable results.

Qualitative research is considered a 'soft' science. Good analytical skills are required to make Qualitative research work. Qualitative research should complement other research data, and should not ignore the larger picture. Qualitative research should be substantiated later by quantitative research.

The choice of research group should be carefully done. It should be microcosm of the target market. The group may have a I-know-it-all person who is assertive and colours the view of other group members. It is, however, a microcosm of the market. The researcher's ability is tested here. He has to monitor the discussion without any obtrusion from one person. He has to trade-off between being provocative and totally unobtrusive. Mostly the approach is impromptu. There are chances that quantitative research and qualitative research findings are at variance. We have to examine the total research base then. In quantitative research, the research instrument like the questionnaire makes the critical difference. In qualitative research, it is the ability of the researcher to create a rapport and still keep a safe distance.

TECHNIQUE OF QUALITATIVE RESEARCH

1. Brand Maps.	Blank sheet of paper given to consumers. They are asked to map out brands of a particular product category. Certain brands form a cluster. Certain brands are distanced.	Brand perception of consumers. Competitive threats to researched brand.
2. Neuro Linguistic programming/unique trait sorting.	An exhaustive list of attributes associated with the product is prepared — sensory, emotional and physical qualities. Sorting game: which brand can make a claim to what extent on each of the listed attribute.	Larger share of unique attributes possessed by a brand makes it a strong brand or equity. Absence of unique trait indicates the contrary.
3. Brand personification.	Ask them to describe the brand. Ask them to talk to me brand.	*Perception.* Brand is projection — how far is it close to the desired positioning.
4. Chinese Portrait.	Supposing a brand is an animal or a flower, or a star or a deity, which one would it be?	*Perception.* Common perception (say strength or gentleness) indicates a fix on the brand image.
5. Bubble Drawing.	Cartoon-strip like characters are shown in conversation/action. Speech is omitted. Bubble is shown instead which the consumer has to fill up, imagining what the characters are saying. Characters may be brands in question or, people discussing a brand	Brand perception.
6. Bank Accounts.	Identify all values related to a brand. Ask consumers to invest, save or spend these value as they like. Values put in fixed deposit.	Precious values protect these.
	Values put in savings bank account.	Save them and consolidate them. They are not part of the core brand, though important.
	Values in current account.	Can be transacted with — changed, modified, reused. Peripheral values. Not critical to brand equity.
	Loose cash values.	Incidental to the brand. Not relevant for the brand/consumer.

APPENDIX 1

Emotion

Introduction

Emotions involve cognitive and psychological components deeper than feelings as emotions are a psychological and multi-dimensional expression. It has physiological and also subjective aspects.

Our brain consists of three separate brains — the original sensory brain, an emotional brain and a rational brain. First mover advantage goes to the cmotional brain. It sends 10 times the amount of data to the rational brain that it receives in return. Value is determined emotionally Brand attributes are merely assertions unless consumer's emotional brain finds them valid and worth embracing.

Definition

Emotion is a 'stirred up' state of the organism as a whole. (Person is in excited on aroused state – increased amount of energy. Under strong emotions, people feel more motivated/driven/pushed to do certain thing towards a goal. Experiment – depression due to decreased amount of energy.

Characteristics

(I) There is *an increase in the amount of excitation*. This is seen in various ways:

(i) *Electroencephalogram:* It measures the electrical activity of the brain which is measured in the form of brain waves. It records faster brain waves during emotions. (used in hospitals to measure increase in amounts of energy).

(ii) *Galvanic Skin Response (GSR):* It is the decrease in the resistance of the skin to the flow of mild electric current. In an emotional state, this is reduced i.e., skin passes electric current faster.

(iii) The pupils dilate (upto 10 times their normal size) i.e., they increase in size.

(iv) Heart rate increases and faster rate of breathing.

(v) Pulse becomes faster

(vi) Blood pressure increases

(vii) Stomach contracts and there is interference with digestion.

(viii) 'Pilomotor Response' – Goose pimples when there are strong emotions.

(ix) Increase in activity of adrenals.

(x) Increased muscular tension.

(II) *Emotion is Energising:* Due to the increased activity of the adrenals, there is greater supply of energy.

In an emergency situation, strong emotions can help us to use maximum strength for a short period or sustain activity over a longer period than ordinarily possible or to lessen sensitivity to pain.

e.g.: (1) When two persons are wrestling and one really wants to win, his strong emotions drive him to use maximum strength.

(2) When one is hanging from a cliff, one is so scared that one's strength is diluted.

(3) A courageous person can take on more pain – lesser sensitivity.

(III) Emotion can be considered as a response to external stimuli — a sudden loud noise, a physical injury, insult. However, emotion is the product of external stimuli interacting with subjective patterns.

There is no one-to-one correlation between emotion and stimuli because response may be different due to organism.

(IV) Emotions may be pleasant or unpleasant. The situation arousing the emotion may be favourable or harmful e.g., lottery – joy, snake – fear.

(V) Emotions motivate the individual. They give rise to activity towards a goal. The activity persists till the goal is reached. Fear motivates us to escape from feared object and avoid contact with it.

(VII) Emotion is a conscious experience. (as it is active and takes place with awareness of even subjective factors).

(VIII) Emotion is subjective in nature e. g., anxiety. There are individual differences in the nature of emotional response and the intensity of the response to the same situation. In a scary situation, soliders are not equally afraid. Some may remain outwardly calm and some shake with fear. The differences in emotional response are party due to cultural differences among people. The Japanese and Chinese are taught to control their emotions, while the Spanish and Italian to express them freely.

Emotional Development of Children

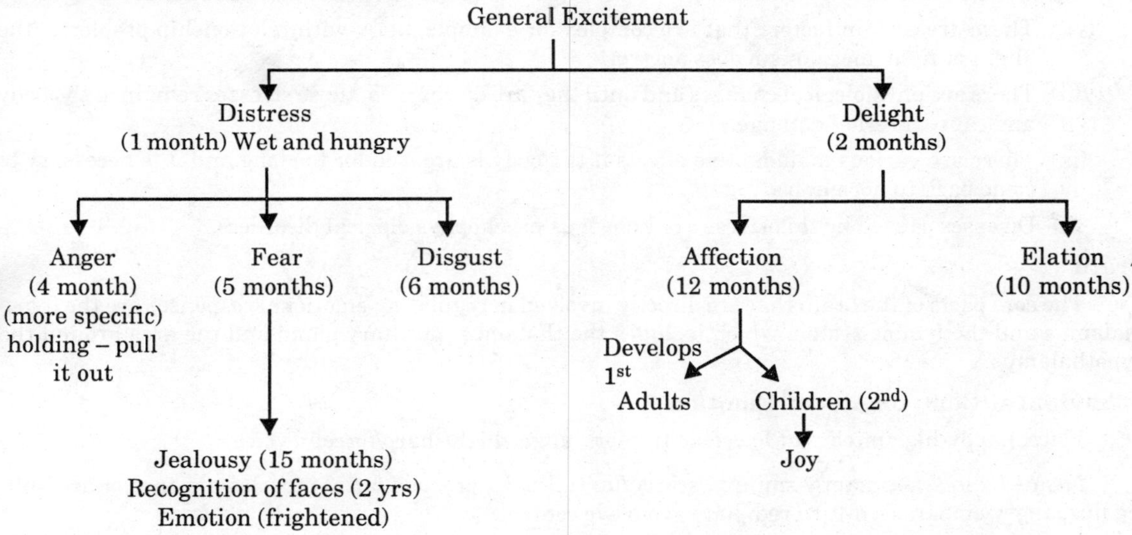

Some of the emotions are negative while others are positive. Disgust is not explained properly:

- The earliest emotion is distress which is seen when the child is wet or hungry.
- Anger is a more specific form of distress especially when you prevent a child from doing what it wishes.
- Fear of loud sounds is experienced.
- Jealously is seen when the child grows up in the environment and learns to recognize faces.
- A child develops affection for adults first as it is in their company more often.

Characteristics of a Child's Emotion

- Their emotions are brief.
- They are very intense.
- They are frequent.
- They are easily detectable as children do not control them.
- They change in strength.

Changes

(i) Physiological changes take place e.g. goose pimples, tears, high BP, dilation of pupils.

(ii) During a profound emotional experience, several physiological changes occur.

(iii) Most of these changes are produced by the ANS (Autonomic Nervous System) – breathing, etc.

Sympathetic and Parasympathetic Activity

(i) The Sympathetic nervous system is active during aroused states.

(ii) It releases hormones like adrenalin which provide more energy.

(iii) The parasympathetic system tends to be active when one is calm and relaxed.

(iv) It helps to build up and conserve body energy.

(v) The pattern of bodily activity characteristic of emotion is a blend of sympathetic and parasympathetic activity.

(vi) Pulse rate and heart rate changes are brought about by the ANS for an increase in energy.

(vii) There are certain factors that are complex for example, here, with relationship problems, the 'flight or fight' mechanism does not work.

(viii) There are physiological changes and until they are discharged, these stresses remain in the body and cause internal damage.

(ix) There are various maladaptive effects if the body is aroused for too long and it is necessary to come back to normal body state.

(x) Diseases caused by this stress are known as psychophysiological disorders.

Brain

The core parts of the brain that are directly involved in regulating emotional responses are the hypothalamus and the lymbic system which includes the thalamus, pituitary gland and the area around the hypothalamus.

Behavioural Components of Emotion

Voice: happy-high pitch, sad-low, fear-tremors, anger-high/sharp/forceful voice

Facial Expression: happy-smiling, scared/unwell-pale, anxious-facial muscles are taut, scared-biting lips, angry/embarassed-turn red, liars avoid eye contact.

Postures: Paying attention — sit up straight, nervous-keep shifting, excited-jumping, tired/unhappy – shoulders slouched.

Gestures: nervous-fidget with fingers, angry-clench fists, surprise lower mouth, sad/embarrassed – cover face, show appreciation-pat on the back.

These can be manipulated.

These are the factors by which expressions are manifested/expressed in our behaviour. e.g: anger, depression, elation, etc.

Cognitive Components of Emotion

These are how a person interprets or perceives a situation.

It is a conscious experience or perception of emotion.

Any individual is aware of the emotions that he experiences. He is also aware of the intensity of the emotional experience.

The situation in which the emotion occurs i.e., the context also gives us information for judging what emotion is experienced.

However, people often express several emotions at the same time and these blends of emotion are difficult to judge accurately.

The cognitive components bring out the awareness of the emotion e.g., when one feels a lump in his throat while crying, e.g.: when a person is about to give a speech, his hands may be cold, trembling, etc. He will interpret this according to the context and say it is anxiety or 'stage fright.'

However, the physiological changes in the body may be the same for two emotions e.g.: trembling – for fear and nervousness, tears – for sadness and happiness

The death of a terminally ill may cause sadness and relief. A friend's comments may cause anger and hurt.

Rational Emotive Therapy (RET)

- It was propounded by ALBERT ELLIS.
- The theory behind this is that the interaction between A and B leads to the emotion where

  A is the ANTECEDENT CONDITION,
  B is the BELIEF SYSTEM and
  C is the CONSEQUENT EMOTION.

'A' × 'B' → 'C' [+ 'D'] → 'E'

  Where E is the effect experienced and
  D is the dispute belief system.

- It is not just the situation which determines the emotion but also the belief system i.e., the person's perception and reasoning skills.

For example, a student fails in the examination.

Here, A → failure
& B → self talk (importance, crux of everything)

Positive (challenge) ↓ then C will work hard

Negative (self-piteous) ↓ C → depression, helplessness, disappointment.

'B' i.e., belief system is important because if the situation cannot be changed, the client's interpretation/perception can be changed (D).

THEORIES OF EMOTION

1. James Lange Theory

- It was proposed by William James (1884) and Carl Lange (1885).
- According to them, the consciousness of bodily disturbances constitutes the experience of emotion.
- An emotional event brings about physiological reactions of the body.
- These reactions send different impulses to the brain where they are interpreted in terms of emotional feeling.

Flaws

- Many physiological reactions are slow but we experience emotions immediately.
- Often the bodily changes are the same but the perceived emotions are different.

Example: When a person is crossing the road, a car comes speeding towards him. He remains stuck to the ground and starts trembling and physiological reactions takes place in the body. These send impulses to the brain where they are interpreted in terms of 'fear.'

2. Cannon-Bard Theory

- This was proposed by WALTER CANNON (1927) and PHILLOP BARD (1934).
- According to Cannon, the perception of an emotional situation triggers a nerve impulse in the thalamus.
- The impulse then splits with one signal travelling to the cerebral cortex which causes the conscious experience of emotion and the other signal travelling to the viscera bringing about the physiological changes.
- Thus, the subjective experience of emotion and the bodily changes occur simultaneously.

3. Schachter-Singer Theory

- This was put forward by SCHACHTER and SINGER (1962)
- It is called the cognitive theory.
- They proposed that given a state of physiological arousal for which the individual has no immediate explanation, he will label this state and describe his feelings in terms of the cognitions (context) available to him.
- Precisely, the same state of physiological arousal could be called joy, anger or any other emotion depending on the cognitive aspects of the situation.

SOME BASIC EMOTIONS

1. Anger

- It is most frequently expressed in childhood
- It is never without a reason.
- It is difficult to control.
- The longer we think about what makes us angry, we are likely to build up more anger.
- It is expressed differently by different groups of people e.g. children throw tantrums, males express anger physically and females verbally e.g., — using abusive language.
- *The two important aspects of anger are:*
  - — Frustration of motives.
  - — It is a response to injury or threat.
- The most universal trigger for anger is a sense of physical threat or threat to one's self-esteem.
- Hostility is a strong response to anger.
- Aggression is an expression of anger that has a high physiological and emotional component that is specific towards an individual or thing.
- Not expressing anger is bad for mental health. e.g. suicide
- Anger blocks out our sense of reasoning. [After coming tired, mom says that the room must be kept clean].

Timing to express anger. Appropriateness — explain with a sense of reasoning and not just shout. Suicide – angry with someone – unable to handle the hurt by others and so hurt themselves.

2. Fear

- It is a response to any stimulus that is harmful.
- It is a learnt response.
- The maximum fears an individual experiences are from ages 7 to 11: developmental psychologists
- Media plays an important role in influencing our fears.
- The reasons of what we are afraid of change with age. (e.g. – children are afraid of loud sounds, of getting lost, complaints from teachers or doing badly in class. Adolescents – being embarrassed, insulted, losing friends. Adults – losing a spouse/job, insecurity or if their children might let them down).
- Unlike anger, fears may not necessarily drive an individual to action.
- Infact irrational fears that interfere with normal functioning are known as 'phobias.' – psychological problem e.g., - fear of dogs, you freeze when you see one. Needs psychological treatment. Learning (through media, other's experiences) frightens us.
- Fear is used as a form of control. Once fear is tested and nothing happens, fear disappears.
- Fear for child of being in a new place may make child very sociable or an introvert

3. Love

- Affection is characterised by:

  Caring: active concern for the other, unconditional care.

  Attachment: a commitment that is life-long.

  Intimacy: physical contact that is influenced by cultural norms, learning and values that a person may have.
- It is positive emotion, socially desirable, highly motivating, indicates warmth or friendship. It is need of every individual.
- It is generally very spontaneous among children.
- It is directed today towards people, animals and things.
- Girls are found to be more expressive with love than males.
- Human beings are the only species that have the capacity to love associated with sex and can separate the two.
- Individuals who have been deprived of love are likely to be affected physically, emotionally, socially and intellectually.

Children without love are emotionally quiet, cold, unable to express love. If unable to establish relationship with another person, they will develop 'It' with things.

Love – is to care unconditionally.

Attachment – time spend, spend quality time to know each other, talk first about common interests – general stuff, later talk about yourself (e.g., they don't like children)

Trust – talking builds up trust. Teenagers need to learn. Jealousy used often. Can't two-time people.

Touch – governed by culture, marriage, sanctions sex, teenagers don't know and go directly to touch. Largest sensory organ — skin.

Drawing a line in a physical relationship is not possible. Brain/conscience governs our values. Only use each other.

Love must be a gift of yourself to another. Gift must not be used.

Sex doesn't mean commitment.
Every choice has consequences.

4. Guilt

- It is generally associated with shame as anger is with hurt.
- Experience, education and one's religious beliefs influence our feelings of guilt.
- It needs to be dealt with tact and responsibility.
- If it is not done, it can prove to be traumatic and create adjustment problems.

  Sometimes a clarification is required whether the individual is really responsible or he/she needs to experience guilt. I feel guilty about breaking the vase and putting the blame on my brother.
- If damage can be repaired, guilt is not as great.
- We feel guilty for what we are not responsible like a child whose mum dies with his birth.
  - At times, the child feels the parents have separated because of him.
  - Guilt is also caused if you are sexually abused. The victim is unable to fight the oppressor and freezes, becomes immobile. Therapeutic intervention is needed for these people.
  - Their interaction clarifies whether or not guilt is necessary.
- Emotional baggage – caused by guilt or anger. This will not allow you to progress. An understanding parent may help.
  - 'Forgetting about it' will not help.
  - One monk carried pretty girl to other side. – When other monk asked – the first one said 'Why are you still carrying her?'

5. Jealousy

- An individual experiences jealousy when he senses a threat especially loss of affection.
- It is commonly experienced by children.
- It is learnt emotion.
- Sometimes emotional factors are likely to support and provoke jealousy.
- Adults are likely to use this emotion to the best of their advantage. Many of the games that an adult plays arise out of jealousy.
- It is commonly associated with females. Possible that girls express their emotions more and that's why it is said they are more jealous.
- It is potentially a destructive emotion.

- First born child experiences jealousy at the birth of the second child. The first child is threatened. Parent's behaviour might add to this threat.
  - — Guys might flirt around so that their girlfriend might get jealous, angry.
  - — Jealousy is a very seductive emotion.
  - — It is not necessary to make people jealous for them to like you.

6. Sadness

- It is normal to experience this emotion on a temporary basis at some point in our life.
- It is generally associated with a loss of something.
- If the individual continues to experience this for long periods of their life, they need help. e.g. - loss of spouse, child.
- Grievance must be for a short period only.
- If this takes a physical and emotional toll on you, it is not good for health and you need help.

According to modern research in neurobiology it is confirmed that people are primarily, even overwhelmed, emotional decision makers. How real the benefits of the product feel to consumers is actually the key. Emotions are more significant than thought to successful marketing.

Daniel Goleman, an internationally known psychologist has put forward the concept of emotional Intelligence and has argued that non-cognitive skills matter as much as the IQ for success in the workplace.

❑ ❑ ❑

7

PERSONALITY AND CONSUMER BEHAVIOUR

It is difficult to arrive at a single definition of personality. Some relate personality to certain traits while others see it as a unified whole. Socialization plays a great role in personality development. Personality continues to develop over a period of time.

We can think of personality in terms of man's consistency in coping with his environment. Personality represents *inner psychological characteristics* which decide and reflect how an individual responds to the environment. The key word in this definition is *inner psychological characteristics*. Essentially, it means specific qualities, traits, attributes, facts, mannerisms which distinguish an individual.

Personality, as we have observed, indicates consistent pattern of responses to the world that affects an individual from both internal and external sources.

Characteristics of Personality

We consider three essential characteristics of personality.

1. Personality reflects individual differences: Each individual has a special set of inner characteristics, and is thus unique by himself. However, individuals may just have a dominant single personality characteristic, which make them similar. This single characteristic makes him react in a consistent or stable fashion in a variety of environmental situations. A methodical and careful person while doing studies remains methodical and careful while driving a vehicle. Some individuals are highly sociable, whereas others are low on sociability. We can thus slot individuals on the basis of a single trait or a combination of few traits. This is the foundation of segmentation, and of target marketing. It is interesting to note that inconsistency in response from an established pattern is quite striking. If a dog bites a man, it is no big deal. But if a man bites the dog, it certainly is great news. A tipsy professor starts lecturing. It is just expected of him. But it is unusually interesting to see him circulating amongst the fair sex.

2. Personality is consistent and enduring: There is a lesson here for the marketers. They should not expect the consumers to change their personalities to suit the product offering. They should try to understand which characteristics of the personality affect their response, and, make an appeal to these characteristics. Though an individual has enduring personality, his consumption behaviour shows variations on account of a variety of other factors like motivation, attitudes, pressure groups, and the new products. It should be remembered that personality is not the only factor which influences consumer behaviour.

When a mother remarks that my son is stubborn right from the birth, she is proclaiming the consistency and stability of the personality.

3. Personality can change: There are some circumstances which have the capacity to change even enduring personality. These may be a major event like the death of the beloved, the birth of a child, a significant progress in career or separation of husband and wife. There are changes in personality as a man matures slowly. We find many aggressive persons mellow down as they advance in years.

Personality Theories

There are three major personality theories viz. (1) Freudian theory, (2) Jungian theory and (3) Neo-Freudian theory. We have selected these three for discussion out of many other theories, as they pinpoint the relationship between personality and consumer behaviour.

1. Freudian Theory

Modern psychology has been greatly shaped by psycho-analytic theory of personality put forward by Sigmund Freud. Human motivation according to this theory, is largely a result of *unconscious needs and drives,* especially sexual and other biological drives. Human personality is also shaped by these drives. Freud used data of early childhood recollections, dream analysis and adjustment problems of his patients to construct this theory.

Freud suggested that human personality consists of three interacting systems — the *id,* the *super-ego* and the *ego.*

Id: This is the storehouse of primitive drives consisting of impulses. They relate to basic physiological needs of thirst, hunger and sex. The individual seeks immediate gratification of these needs. Id releases libidinal energies. The unrestrained pleasure seeking energies originate in the id. What is represented by id is animalistic. It is restrained by a second system called super-ego.

Ads of many personal products like perfumes use basic instincts to provide the 'iddy' punch.

Super-ego: It controls the id by channelizing the instincts into socially acceptable forms. It is an individual's expression of social and moral code of conduct. It has inhibitive influences on the impulses of the id. It is moral arm of personality. It represents the traditional values and ideals of society. Sexual satisfaction through marriage is socially acceptable, and is seen as super-ego over-riding the id.

Ego: It is the balancing form between the id and super-ego. It balances the impulsive behaviour represented by the id and socio-cultural constraints of the super-ego. In other words, it is a conscious control mechanism of an individual. It obeys the *reality principle.* It is the executive of personality. The following diagram illustrates the relationship between these three systems.

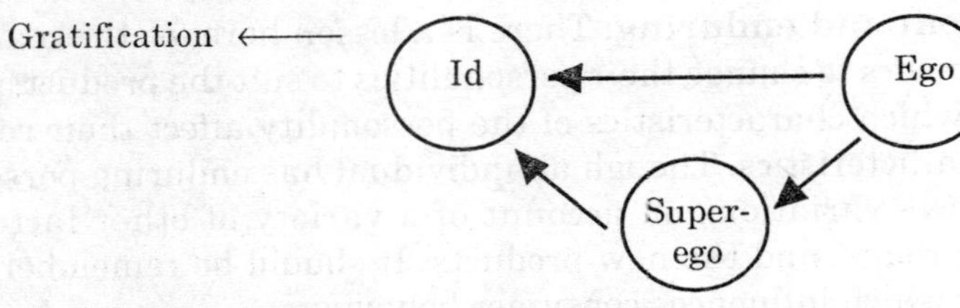

Fig. 7.1: Interactions between personality systems

Freud further suggested the stages of personality development. These stages are related to human anatomy where he believed a child's sexual instincts are concentrated.

Oral stage is the first stage of development represented by a suckling infant being breastfed. The outside contact is through the mouth. Even a bottlefed baby uses mouth as a contact point. The crisis occurs when the child is weaned away from this stage.

Anal stage provides child with pleasure when he defaecates. The crisis develops when the child is toilet-trained.

Phallic stage makes a child aware of his genitals. It is a pleasure by itself. The crisis occurs when it experiences a sexual desire for the parent of the opposite sex. The resolution of this crisis ultimately affects his gender relationships in future.

Latency stage speaks about the dormant sexual instincts from the age of five till adolescence. This stage does not display any important personality changes.

Genital stage On puberty, the child sexually desires members of the opposite sex. It goes beyond self-oriented love and affection for parents.

Freud believed that an adult's behaviour is largely affected by how he coped with crises during the above-mentioned stages especially the first three stages. Thus a person whose oral needs are not adequately satisfied becomes fixated at this stage and develops tobacco-chewing or smoking habits. An adult fixated at anal stage shows an excessive need for neatness.

Marketing Application of Personality Theory of Freud: As we know now, human drives are mostly unconscious. It means we do not know why we buy certain things. We can see purchases and consumption as extensions of personality. In other words, the way we look and conduct is a reflection of what we are. It shows our grooming. Matching of product and brand personalities and consumer's personality is considered later in this chapter. Freudian researchers use the techniques of projection and depth interviews. They render advice on packaging, colour, distribution and the need for the product. They also render advice on brand image. Nokia 5110 cell phone is designed like a model with a perfect 10 body. It has Freudian nuance.

2. Jungian Personality Theory

Freud and Carl Jung were contemporaries. His theory puts consumers into *personality types*. Myers-Briggs indicators make these types more relevant for marketers. Here pairing is done on the basis of Jung-inspired psychological dimensions. They are:

1. Sensing — intuiting
2. Thinking — feeling
3. Extroversion — introversion and
4. Judging — perceiving

	Thinking (T)	Feeling (F)
Sensing (S)	ST	SF
Intuiting (N)	NT	NF

The two different poles are distinct in each of these pairs. It shows consumer response to the world they live in. Permutations and combinations of these four types would make it cumbersome. If we take the first two pairs and cross tabulate four personality types, we get the following.

Let us summarise the characteristics of these four types.

ST are rational, logical, objective. They extensively search information. They consider economic criteria. They avoid risks. They identify with materialism. Time-frame is short in making decisions.

SF base decisions on experience and personal values. They are subjective. They are influenced by others. They are status conscious. Time-frame is short in making decisions.

NT have a broad view-point, and consider many options. They are imaginative as well as logical. They consider the options mentally. They are willing to take risk. Time-frame is long for making decisions.

NF have also a broader viewpoint. They also consider wide range of options. As they are highly people-oriented, they consider the views of others. They are subjective. They are least price sensitive. They are venturesome and seek innovations. Time frame is indefinite in making decisions.

The above gives an insight to the marketers as to how this affects the various stages of buying behaviour. It also enables marketers to understand how each type will choose the different products. It also enables communicators to address their message to a specific personality type.

3. Neo-Freudian Personality Theory

Freud was obsessed with the instinctive and sexual part of the personality. Neo-Freudians countered this, and said that *social relationship* contribute a great deal in personality development. Adler talks in terms of *style of life* to realise rational goals. He also emphasises how an individual tries to surmount a feeling of inferiority by striving to excel. Sulivan writes about an individual's attempt to forge social relationships with others. An individual also tries to reduce anxiety which causes tension. Horney, a lady researcher, puts individual into three personality groups:

Compliant individual has a desire to be loved, to be wanted and to be appreciated. He prefers brand names; and uses mouth washes and toilet soaps.

Aggressive individual has a desire to excel and compete with others. He tends to use, manual razor, more cologne and after-shave lotion. He likes Old Spice and Van Heusen shirts.

Detached individual is independent and self-sufficient. He is least aware of brands.

Horney's research was supplemented by Joel Cohen. Because of Cohen, we learn that Horney's Work has marketing application. Aggressive individuals tend to like products with masculine appeal. Detached individuals are non-conformists.

Eric Fromm studied loneliness in social context. Man tends to escape, and seek love. His book *Escape from Freedom* (1941) is published by Holt, Rinehart and Winston; New York.

Trait Theory

Both Freudian and Neo-Freudian theories are qualitative in nature. Trait theory by contrast, is quantitative. It measures personality characteristics or traits by empirical experimentation. Its theoretical base is that personality consists of a set of traits or factors. Some traits are common. Some are individualistic. These traits are measured against personality scales. Single-trait personality tests measure just one trait e.g. self confidence. These help us understand how the consumers make their choices, and how a product category is consumed or purchased. Personality of a washing machine user rather than personality of videocon machine user forms the basis of such studies.

Specific Personality Traits

We shall examine some specific personality traits.

Consumers can be innovators or non-innovators. *Consumer innovativeness* shows his willingness to innovate. His rigidity is shown by *dogmatism.* Dogmatism can be low, making a consumer open-minded or high, making him closed-minded. David Reisman has type consumers on the basis of *social character.* Social character here means 'ways of behaviour' or 'modes of conformity to the culture and society'. The three major types of social character are *tradition-directed* individuals who are slow to change, *inner-directed individuals* who rely on their own inner values to evaluate new products and *other directed* individuals who are guided by others and show social mobility. Inner-directed individuals prefer informative promotion, whereas other-directed individuals prefer social setting. Some are calm and some prefer excitement. The *optimum stimulation level* (OSL) indicates the desired life style. Those with high OSL have the readiness to take risks and try innovations. OSL and life-style can match, making a consumer satisfied. If OSL is greater and current life-style is under-stimulated, there could be boredom. If OSL is smaller, and current life-style is over-stimulated, there could be desire for rest and relaxation. Product choices and time-management are thus affected by OSL. *Variety novelty seeking* personality trait is also important.

Apart from innovativeness, another trait that is important is *consumer susceptibility* to inter-personal influence. A scale can be constructed to measure this susceptibility. It shows how social influence stimulates or depresses the acceptance of new products.

Cognitive personality factors like visualizer and verbalizers and need for cognition (NC) are useful in understanding some aspects of consumer behaviour. *Visualisers* prefer visual information and *verbalizers* prefer verbal or written information. *Need for cognition* (NC) measures a person's desire to enjoy *thinking. High NC* indicates the need for more information-packed promotion. *Low NC* indicates affinity for subsidiary aspects of promotion like the appealing model.

Consumer materialism indicates what value the consumers place on the products they possess. Some consider them to be essential for proving their self-worth and enrichment of life. Some think that products are secondary. Materialistic people have a luxurious conspicuous consumption life-style, and are selfish. Their possessions do not make them satisfied or happy. *Fixated consumers* like to show off their possessions. They search for their cherished possessions. They are passionate about these possessions. Generally, hobbyists and collectors show such behaviour. They love to hunt for their possessions. But all said and done, fixation is normal and socially acceptable behaviour. *Compulsive consumption* is, however, abnormal. They are addicts.

Consumer ethnocentrism is a scale developed to measure the receptivity of the consumers to indigenous and foreign products High ethnocentricity makes consumers averse to foreign products. Low ethnocentricity make them objective about foreign products.

Personality and Consumer Behaviour

Researchers distinguished users of Ford and Chevrolet on the basis of their personality traits. Ford users were macho, impulsive and confident. Cheverolet users were conservative, frugal and status-conscious. Evans (1959) refuted the distinction on the basis of personality traits. Westfall found differences between owners of convertible and compact, standard cars. Kamen could find no relationship between personality variables and toilettries and fashion goods. Koponen, however, could find significant differences between smokers and non-smokers. Bank depositor's study by Claycamp found no personality differences amongst savers. Dogmatism does affect our choice of new product (Jacoby). Personality scales enable us to have a comparative view of consumption pattern.

Self and Self Image

The inner core of a person is 'self'. Human personality, like an onion, has several layers. One by one, we can peel off the layers, and each layer reveals a certain aspect of self. Thus there are several selves in a personality. The concept of self-image is, defined as the perception of 'self' or how one sees himself. We tend to buy products or patronize retailers whose images correspond to our own self-image. Brands, products and distributors thus show a consistency or otherwise with our own self-image. This consistency is called congruence. Some products match our self-image and some remain alien to it. Congruence preserves our self-image or enhances it. Thus we prefer it. Non-congruence leads to avoidance of those products.

Let us consider the popular four kinds of self-image model.

How I see myself (Actual Self Image)	How I would like to see me (Ideal Self Image)
How others see me (Social Self Image)	How I would like others to see me (Ideal Social Self-image)

Fig. 7.2 : Self images

Thus actual self image indicates what the consumers are, and ideal self image what they would like to be. Social self image is the perception of others, and ideal social self-image is the desired perception by others. One more type is *expected self image* at a future date showing what consumers expect to see them as in future. This is somewhere between the actual and ideal self-images. It shows an opportunity to change the self. Thus in product design it is much more valuable.

Different product groups provoke different self images. We are guided for daily necessities by our actual self image, but for luxury products by social self image. We aspire to have products to satisfy our ideal self images or ideal social self images. Right now, we just fantasize about them.

Self image can be used strategically by the marketers. It gives good basis for segmentation. Marketers position their products to satisfy segments based on self-images.

Extended Self

There is a relationship between the self-images and our possessions. An exerciser like a Bullworker enhances the self-image of a person of athletic leanings. He is likely to feel fitter and confident. A gold bangle given to a daughter-in-law by the mother-in-law is a prized possession. Its loss may affect the psychological make up of the possessor. Perhaps, it is loss of protection too. Thus these possessions either *confirm* or *extend* our self-images. We establish an emotional attachment to these possessions. Such an extension can be symbolic making you feel better *e.g.*, an award or reward, problem solving *e.g.*, a computer, status giving *e.g.*, an object of art, magical *e.g.*, something inherited from ancestors. Products like watches can appeal to our extended self.

Self Alteration

We do love to change our 'self' for the better, say by using cosmetics, clothes and accessories. Thus some products help us to alter the self. A new self is created, while the existing one is maintained. Or else, the self is extended. Self-altering products can be used to take on the appearance of a particular type of person or to conform. Contact lenses, hair-style, cosmetic surgery, dying of hair, Ray Ban glasses make us an 'improved' person. Image consultants provide valuable inputs about such desirable improvements in self-image.

SELF-WORTH
Men and women these days want to look good, and smell good. It is an unarticulated sensual statement. They want to be desirable. It is derived from an increased awareness of one's self-worth. Diana Hayden while promoting L'oreal says, I love L' Oreal, because I am worth it. It shows how today's youth want to discover their inner worth. They are not just after external presentation. People tend to suffer from a lack of self-worth. Universally, today's youth are discovering self-worth.

Brand Personality

Just as we human beings have a personality showing a summation of characteristics, a brand also has a personality with a set of characteristics which are human in nature. These characteristics are demographic, *e.g.*, sex or gender, age, and socio-economic class. To illustrate Samsung and LG are considered new brands in consumer electronics in India, Weston is an old brand. Similarly, mopeds are feminine, whereas mobikes are masculine. Surf Excel is upper-class, whereas Nirma is a down-market product. Other classic personality traits are concern warmth and sentimentality. Garden is for the sophisticated modern women, whereas Poonam Saris are commonplace. American Express is a prestigeous card, whereas cards issued by nationalised banks are down-to-earth.

Brand personality lasts for years and is distinctive. Coke is the 'real thing' and Pepsi young in spirit. This distinction has remained unchanged for years.

It is observed that users and non-users have different perceptions about the personality of the brand. Users associate a brand with a strong personality, whereas non-users do not do so.

People often invest in brands human characteristics, and interact with them. Many people whisper a thing or two to their bike or car, and many have a lot to say to their garments. They may refer to their products as if they were human.

It takes image characteristics of a brand and renders them in human terms as seen by the consumer. Brand image is broader than brand personality because by the time we enter the personality realm, we are dealing with feelings and emotions that the consumer takes away from communications. A well-established brand has a clear brand personality. It may remain unstated. But it can play a strategic role in brand wars. Closely positioned brands may also acquire distinct personalities as a result of exposure to the product, packaging, service, word-of-mouth and advertising. Brand is thought as being friendly, boring, funny, rude, caring, stylish etc. Consumers need to think of brands in human terms. Memorability of a brand personality comes through consistency and other props.

Brand personality should not be confused with the description of target audience. The gap between these two is filled by aspirations that are sought to be addressed by the brand, e.g., the Dettol soap user is hygiene-conscious but the brand personality is that of a person who is fastidious, clean and sensible person.

In consumer eyes, Close-up is the attractive girl next-door, Colgate is the mother, whereas Cibaca Top is someone who lived on the 17th floor and about whom no one knew. Cibaca does have a personality problem.

Brands are much like people. They have certain physical characteristics (how they look and sound); certain skills and abilities (what they can do and how they perform), and certain associations and attitudes. Like an individual, a brand too is a blend of all these. The brand therefore, appeals to senses, to reason and to emotions. For the consumer to be at home with our brand, she must be comfortable with its personality. Brand personality must be consistent over a period of time.

Some common examples are the Liril girl under the waterfall, the muscle man for MRF tyres, *tandurasti ki raksha* for Lifebuoy, Charlie Chaplin for Cherry Blossom Polish and lightening flash with Rin. This is called brand property—the audio or visual tie that summarises the essence of brand personality.

BRAND PERSONALITIES

Just as the human personality is important, brand personality too is important for its success or failure. Brand personality may represent a brand's best shot at differentiation or connection with the consumers. It is a sum total of a look, an attitude, a pattern of behaviour and a style. Reinhard thinks that endowing a brand with a set of appealing and differentiating traits is the key to its success. The brand acquires then a personality which no competitor can copy. However, this personality takes off when all channels of communication right from personal selling, sales promotion, publicity, public relations, and advertising to the whole working of the organisation are steeped into brand culture. Advertising is one of the key elements in building a brand personality.

Measuring Brand Personality

A simple method to describe brand personality is to state it in terms of demographic characteristics life-style and personality traits. Researchers have identified five personality factors called the Big Five — sincerity excitement, competence, sophistication and ruggedness. Each factor can be extended by a set of traits.

Brand Personality Scale

Sincerity (Kodak)	Excitement (United Colours of Benetton)	Competence (Citi Card)	Sophistication (Revlon, Chambor)	Ruggedness (Ruf and Tuf)

The traits under sincerity could be honesty, wholesomeness, cheerfulness and down-to-earth quality. The traits under excitement could be imaginative, spirited, trendy and daring, contemporary and aggressive. The traits under competence could be reliability, intelligence and success. The sophisticated traits include up-scale and charming, sexy and feminine brands. Ruggedness denoted athletic, Western, macho, no-nonsense brands. Though brands can be put on this scale anywhere, they can have a complex personality that spread cuts across different factors. This scale is also used to measure attitudes towards a brand. Those who put sophistication trait on Lexus are likely to have a favourable attitude towards it. Some factors like sincerity generate positive attitudes. Some factors generate both positive and negative attribute, e.g., ruggedness is all good in a jeans trouser, but all wrong in food-products.

CELLULAR PHONE PERSONALITY

There was a small pilot study conducted on business executives to probe the brand personalities of the available hand-sets. The following personality profiles have been identified.

Nokia: The charming European. A widely-travelled global citizen, with a sense of humour. Practical technology. Likes to interact with people, and explore what they expect, and fulfill those expectations. Approachable, as he does not put on airs.

Motorola: The live-wire American executive. Powerful as well as resourceful. He believes in hard-sell. Command over technology. Respectable Reliable.

Ericsson: The aristocrat. Slim and elegant. He keeps his distance from the masses, Proud. Technology for him matters as far as it delivers. The electronics is for the engineers.

— Sengupta, McKinsey Adaptation

Brand Personality — How Created?

Various factors influence a human being's perceived personality, e.g., family, friends, neighbours, school, religious institutions, socialization in general. Similarly, various factors influence the formation of a brand personality — they are either product-related or non-product related factors.

Product class like a 'courtroom' creates a stereotype personality (serious, competent, honest). A denim trouser is rugged, daring and extrovert, as well as young and spirited. A package can affect a brand personality, e.g., Nirma's transparent polythene bag stapled at the top gave it a down-to-earth personality.

Product attributes affect the personality. To illustrate a drink with more fizz like Thums Up makes it *a drink* young and adventurous. Tanishque jewellery which is high-priced makes it stylish and rich; almost bordering on vanity.

User imagery, a non-product related characteristic, does influence brand personality. Users can be actual or ideal users shown endorsing the product. Beautiful film-stars using Lux makes Lux glamorous. User imagery has made Mercedes a sophisticated car. Another non-product related factor contributing to brand personality is sponsorship of the event. Femina magazine becomes young and intelligent by sponsoring Femina Miss India beauty pageant. Symbols like Maharaja for Air India, kangaroo for Patel Roadways, Amul girl for Amul contribute a great deal to their personality.

Advantages of Brand Personality

It is provides an added insight into the brand. By knowing what the people think about the brand, we can guess what their attitudes towards the brand are. Brand personality is either a part of core identity or extended identity. In both the cases, it is a basis to differentiate a brand. This is more so when brands have more or less the same attributes. Brand personality statement can be used in positioning strategy. Brand personality makes promotion easier.

Brands have expressional value for people. Brands they use show what type of people they are. A person buying low-priced brand is apparently close-fisted. Brands have a socio-cultural context. The context keeps on changing. People tend to use brands that fit their actual or ideal self. Brands are also aspirational, their use denoting what we would like to be, rather than what we are. The use of brands having distinct personality generate certain feeling and emotions to emerge. Brands are used to make personal statements. This is true in respect of clothes, cosmetics and car. A sports car user is making a statement that he is daring, and dashing and out to go. Sometimes, brands become an integral part of the self, e.g., a brand of a pen and a writer.

The research hypothesis which was tested was a person's self-image and the brand personality of brands bought would match each other. There is a relationship between the two, but it is not so strong. This is perhaps due to a number of self-images a person has — how he sees himself, how others see himself, how he would like others to see himself. Besides, a person plays several roles in different social situations. The dominant personality depends upon the role being played and the situation. Just like a person, a brand can assume different personalities in different settings.

Just as two persons can have relationship, a person can have a relationship with a brand as a person. The relationship with a sincere brand is that of respect. Exciting brands create a friendly relationship. Competent brands nurture a relationship based on expertise. Sophisticated brands foster a relationship like one with a rich relation. Rugged brands and an outdoor loving friend are on par. Brand relationship can be based even on the basis of functional benefits, which is purely a professional relationship. A brand can have friendship relationship, which any brand personality can offer.

Imagine if a brand talks to us. What statements would it make? A credit card in a restaurant may say, 'oh your taste is fantastic!' The card is so sophisticated. Perhaps it could say, 'what a spendthrift you are!' It is intimidatory. The first reaction was supportive and the second derisive. Though the product is the same, and users have the same socio-economic characteristics, they can have different kinds of relationship with the brand.

Thus up-scale brands can be snobbish, performance brands derisive power brands arrogant. Some brands suffer inferiority complex. We have to soften the brand imagery by suitable communication.

We can segment the customers an the basis of relationship. The segments could be those who like the brand, those who are neutral and those who dislike it.

A brand's behaviour shows its personality traits. A brand that is constantly on sales promotion becomes cheap in the eyes of the buyers. A brand associated with sponsoring good cultural programmes shows its cultural awareness. Extensive advertising makes a brand approachable.

Loyalty of highest order can be created in certain segments. In such a relationship a personal commitment to the brand is seen. Absence of a brand means missing out. A brand makes one nostalgic. A person becomes intimate with it.

The brand personality and product attributes should complement each other. A particular personality indicates certain benefits. Benefits can be copied and assaulted, easily, but it is difficult to do so with a personality.

Brand Personality and User Imagery

Human beings as users of various brands show certain characteristics which we call user imagery. A typical wearer of jeans today is a college-going, young student in his teens. As a product or brand, jeans are associated with cowboys and ruggedness. A marketer's job is to synchronize a brand's personality and user imagery.

Recap: A brand's personality is an important concept. Through it, a customer tends to express himself. It also becomes the basis for establishing a relationship with the brand. It also communicates product benefits. A brand personality has the potential of becoming product differentiation in the long term. A marketer has to try to enhance brand personality. It should become an important part of brand identity.

BRAND CHOICE AND PERSONALITY

Need	*Choices*
Core Need of Clothing	Jeans, shirts, dhotis, kilts
Two-legged garments	Trousers, Jeans
Denim-blue material, rugged cut, metal zippers and buttons, and a tough piece of clothing	Jeans
Product augmentation; fancy pockets, double stitching, wider range, designs.	FM Jeans

Brands make personality statements. FM Jeans declare your anti-traditional intentions, and find a cause in life. The onlooker may like your attitude and share it.

Multi-layered Personality

Indians have been exposed to a variety of influences, and thus their personality has become multi-layered. There are many Indians in each Indian. We have a layer of Americanised life-style and symbols. The British legacy leaves behind a layer where the Indian motifs are reinterpreted. There is a layer of post-colonial suspicions. The regional diversity gives its own layer. The social diversity leaves a layer of caste and class identity. The religious diversity also puts a layer of its own. Though advertising and marketing address to a horizontal layering of Indians by creating a universal concept and execution for all Indian audience, it has still to take notice of its vertical multi-layering.

We have in Mumbai a secular gentleman going to office in western outfit, reading Mills and Boons and Drucker, operating computers and fax machines, seeing English movies. The same gentleman in the privacy of his home offers *Puja,* puts a caste-mark on his fore-head, and reads the *Bhagwat Gita*. He returns home to be a part of either Maharastra, Kerala, Tamilnadu and Bengal.

A brand manager finds that his brand appeals to one layer of the psyche. He has to put it across the other layers. There are many inherent contradictions. The childhood values of 'avoid waste' are violated by a money-splurging consumerist attitude. The status symbols come in conflict with the ascetic values of self-denial. Coke assaults our culture and does not provide value for money. Such a plural psyche is difficult to address. Such a multi-layered society is more relationship driven.

APPENDIX

Socialization

Meaning

Socialization is the training of the younger generation to conform to society's norms.

→ Twins in Madhya pradesh that got kidnapped by a she-wolf had received culture shock when returning to civilization and died consequently. (Kamala & Amala).

Children that do not undergo the process of socialization are called 'feral cases.'

→ Case of Anna who was an illegitimate child — was thrown into attic with mother – found by neighbours 5 years later — could not talk — later on mother died – Anna was sent to school – adjusted with time.

Socialization is teaching the raw human organism to function like a social being. It is learning to adjust and communicate in society.

Teacher → Socializer and leaner → socialize. The term social refers to that inherent need that is there in every human being to interact with other people. However, this quality is not nurtured, equally among all people. When this quality is nurtured, the person becomes sociable. This quality of being social is nurtured through the process of socialization. Some people are more sociable than others.

Process of Socialization

Socialization as a process serves two major functions.

(1) Individual function.

(2) Societal function.

Individual Function

— helps individual to adjust to different situations by providing necessary norms and behaviour patterns.

— helps to develop personality.

— helps to develop survival techniques in society.

— prepares an individual for the various roles that he has to play and for the various statuses he will get.

Societal Function

- helps to transfer cultural heritage from generation to generation.
- gives individual an exposure to other cultures and thus brings various cultural groups in contact with each other.
- serves as an instrument of social control when various agencies like family, media, school take up this task for society.
- provides people in society with role-models for limitation.
- society channelizes the drives, instincts and urges of the members through the socialization process by providing norms and values for people to follow.

Both these functions take place through the process of INTERACTION. Interaction, therefore, becomes many-sided as people, groups are interacting. People have to perform several roles simultaneously and occupy various statuses. This shows that socialization is a complex and mutli-dimensional process. It also shows that people cannot function in isolation and must function in groups.

STAGES OF SOCIALIZATION

According to Sigmund Freud, there are two stages of socialization. They are:

(1) Pre-genital stage

(2) Genital stage

Pre-Genital

It has four substages. It lasts from birth to adolescence.

(1) Oral Stage: It is from birth to about 1½ years of age. There is tremendous oral dependency for the child. There is an extreme manipulation of the mouth. The child is too young to be involved with the whole family. He is only involved with that sub-system consisting of him and his other or surrogate mother. Many authors say that the child doesn't know it is apart from the mother and that it is a separate unit. This stage is termed as a stage of Primary Identification i.e., the child is able to identify his primary needs like hunger, thirst, kept clean and wants his needs to be fulfilled. If the child's need to manipulate the mouth is suppressed for a long period, it may experience oral fixation and may have a problem in later years.

(2) Anal Stage: (1 or 1½ to 3 years): At this stage, there is an 'anal' crisis. The focus here is on toilet training. There is an imposition of new demands. The child, now, begins to internalise his and his mother's roles. The child realizes he is a separate person and likes to use his name. The child needs a lot of care and the child reciprocates this a lat. The mother faces a traumatic phase here as she performs a dual role. She has to train the child gently as well as please the family and society. This dual role is given importance because the child is being trained to fit into society. The child has to function independently from the societal viewpoint and so it may be very painful.

(3) Phallic Stage (Oedipal) Stage: (4-5½ years): Here, the child becomes aware that it belongs to a particular sex. There is an 'oedipal' crisis. It has to follow a particular sex role. The child is a member of the family as a whole. He has to internalise roles of all family members and has to identify with his role which is ascribed to him. The child is now adjusting to its biological role. The son will imitate his father, girls imitate their mothers. It is important to note that the child of 4 or 5 has no appreciation of sexual functions but the child has a rivalry towards the parent of the same sex. The child imitates the parent to please the parent of the opposite sex to be accepted. There is a mutual attachment between the child and mother. There is Oedipus and Electra complex.

(4) Latent Stage: (6 years to Adolescence): It is so called because the child achieves an independence for himself, imbibed values, internalised roles and is a disciplined member of the family. The child has no attraction towards the opposite sex. Infact, they detest the opposite sex.

Genital Stage (Adolescence)

Starts roughly at puberty. Child is around 12-13, develops news ideas of his own, starts seeking independence from parental authority. The individual is neither a child nor an adult. It is a transition stage and so, is very crucial. The child has matured biologically and is starting to mature mentally. But, to the family, the individual is still a young child. This leads to conflicts, generation gap, strain in values, ideas as parental norms are obsolete to the child.

Development on 'Self'

— One of the most important concepts in socialization as it is connected with personality development.

- 'Self' may be defined as the ability to be conscious that one is an object distinct from other objects.
- It is the individuals awareness about his own personal and social identity.
- It is the individual's conscious experience of having a distinct personal identity that is separate from all other people and things.
- At birth, the human infant (almost till 6 months) has no sense of self, no awareness of a separate identity.

- Around the age of 2 yrs, children begin to use words like I, Me, My, Mine. The child now begins to realise that everyone has a distinct self, role, need, perspective and identity.

HOW DOES THE SELF EMERGE IN CHILDHOOD AND HOW IS IT CONTINUALLY MODIFIED THROUGHOUT THE LIFE CYCLE?

(1) Theory by C. H. Cooley (1864-1929) of 'looking-glass' self.

Cooley was an American economist turned social psychologist. He believed that self is a social product and it emerges in society largely through the process of interaction. According to him, a person interacts with his primary group and derives certain ideas from them about himself. These ideas get adapted into developing a self-image about oneself, one's character and one's personality. This self-image is the 'looking glass' self. He calls it this because the individual looks into society for an image of himself. So, society becomes the individuals' mirror for self-reflection. In the process of 'looking-glass' self, there are three steps: [According to Horton and Hunt].

1. An individual's imagination of how he appears to others.
2. An individual's imagination of other's judgement of him.
3. The Resultant feeling. By observing the responses of others, we imagine what their opinions would be of us and accordingly we are able to evaluate ourselves and our actions.

If the image/reflection we see in our imagination is favourable, then our self-image is enhanced. If not, then the self-concept is diminished and our actions are likely to change. According to Cooley, the concept of 'self' develops very gradually throughout one's life and it can develop only through interaction with people. Further, the young child is much more affected by the reactions of others than adults. Many research studies have shown that there is a definite difference between the Individual's Perception of How others view him and the Actual views that people really hold. He says that it is this perception that actually changes an individual's personality and not actual views of others.

(2) Theory of George Herbert Mead of Generalised Other (1863-1931)

He is one of the most prominent American social scientists. He never wrote a single book or article. His colleagues compiled his theories and put them down. He introduced for the first times in social sciences, the concept of Symbolic Interaction. This is interaction through gestures, facial expressions, sounds, all which lead to language which is important to man. Language is a form of expression that is socially learned. It is necessary for all forms of thought because you think in that language. In this sense, the MIND is a social product. Hence, the self is a product of society. He has defined 'self' as something that has a development, not initially there at birth but arises in the process of social experience and activity. Through the process of socialization, the individual looks at himself from the stand-point of the community to which he belongs.

In very early childhood, the individual learns to internalise the roles and expectations of SIGNIFICANT OTHERS (your primary group) and afterwards of the GENERALIZED OTHER. All this is achieved through the process of role-taking and role-playing.

The process of role-taking takes place in 3 stages:

(1) Preparatory Stage: (from 1-3 years): The child inculcates roles by imitating adults and their behaviour but without understanding it.

(2) Play Stage (from 3½ - 4½ years approx): The child has developed some understanding of adult behaviour but imitation of roles is erratic.

(3) Game Stage (from 4 years – adolescence): Here, role-play achieves a consistency and it becomes more purposeful. The individual now develops the ability to sense people's roles more clearly. According to Mead, here, the self begins to emerge. Mead divided the self into 2 dimensions – I and Me

I → The active part of the self i.e., the biological self, urges, drives, impulses.

ME → consists of societal values attitudes that the child develops over the years. It is developed through the significant and generalised others. It puts an individual on the prescriptive path of society. The ME is that part of the self which incorporates the requirements of the genralised other. ME is also called the *social conscience*. The ME tries to control the I but the I is never completely controlled by the ME.

3. Theory of Sigmund Freud Theory of Anti-Social Self (1856-1939)

He was one of the founders of modern psychology. Till today, he is one of the most original and profound thinkers of the past century. Several versions of his theories are still influential. Freud was one of the first to challenge the concept of 'Social-Self.'

He believed that self and society are opponents because society constantly pressurises and suppresses the self and the self is always trying to break free.

Freud's major insight into personality development was that the motives for human behaviour are largely unconscious.

According to him, human personality can be compared to an ice-berg. Just 1/10th of our personality can be observed by society and the rest is hidden in the unconscious not known to anyone and is motivated by unseen forces. He believed that very early childhood experiences are important in personality development. Though these experiences may be lost to memory in later years, their impact is still felt and is seen in the development of the personality. Society makes continuous demands on the individual channelising his drives and motivating socially accepted behaviour which leads to personality development. According to Freud, personality is developed largely in the unconscious. These may be divided into 3 interacting parts:

(1) The Id: It consists of the basic instincts and drives of man. This is the reservoir of urges which is present in the individual right from birth and continues throughout life. For example, hunger, thirst, sex, anger. They are unsocialized desires. A very young child's personality mainly consists of the Id.

(2) The Super-Ego:

— It consists of the person's social conscience.

— Consists of social values, attitudes, behaviour patterns, norms and other societal requirements.

— It refers to that Internal Vision of the moral authority of society.

(3) The Ego:

— It surfaces when the individual learns that the Id has to be suppressed. It is the conscious part (1/10th) of the self.

— It rationally attempts to mediate between the demands of the social environment (super-ego) and the deep unconscious urges (Id).

— The ego has two tasks to perform:

— To counter-balance the demands of the Id for socially acceptable behaviour coming from the Super-Ego.

— To mediate between the personality as a whole and society at large.

Society continually restricts the Id. However, sometimes the Id breaks open in definance of the Super-Ego and person commits crimes. It can also find expression in disguised forms – beating children, painting, crying loudly.

Agencies of Socialization

— Human personalities are shaped by socialization. Hence, it is a 100% never-ending process from birth to death.

— Training of the child and transmission of cultûre takes place through various agencies.

The five main agencies are:

(1) Family:

It is one of the first agencies that the individual comes in contact with. It is an agency of informal socialization. In the family, the child passes through various stages.

(1) Infancy Stage: The closest ties the child has with the family is here.

- The child is involved largely with the sub-system consisting of itself and the mother.
- The mother plays the role of the intermediary between the child and larger society.

Here, the child's personality consists mainly of the Id part of the self.

(2) Stage of Emergence of Self

- Approximately during 4-6 years of age.
- The child interacts with the entire family and has began to internalise roles but the focus is on interaction wherein the child realizes that he has to act all to societal expectations.

(3) Role Taking:

- Here the child learns that the roles performed by people in society are all different
- In the process of role play, the child develops role models. Initially the parents and then others.
- The child also learns roles by observing the authority structure in the family. The entire process of decision making (who makes what decisions) is observed by the child.
- The child identifies with his sex role very dearly and also internalizes the superiority and the inferiority of the sex role.
- The family experiences also carry special importance in shaping he childs personality.
- Agencies like crèches, schools, peer group, mass media are taking over the family's role in socialization.
- But, the family still remains as the primary agency of socialization and is still influential in shaping the child's personality.

(2) Peer Group: (Age-mates):

- Today, the peer group is an agency of informal socialization. The child in the peer group learns to function independently to acquire skills that will include him/her in the group. The child tests these skills and once these tests are passed, the child earns a status in the group do develop new outlooks and approaches and to share things. Due to all this, the peer group, in contrast with the family which is more authoritarian, is more egalitarian (permissive, more freedom).
- When the child becomes an adolescent, the peer group acquires more importance in the child's life because during this stage, parental norms tend to become obsolete and peer culture gains more importance.
- Why does peer culture become more important?

  Because the adolescent has participated in the making of rules. This group has a shorter life span as compared to the family. That's why their immediate pleasures of being with them become more important. Peer groups offer an alternative to adult authority and adult standards. The adolescent gets a different type of emotional support.

(3) School:

- Formal agency of socialization.
- Today, education is a basic necessity.
- As society gets modernized, the role of school as an agency of socialization becomes more and more important

The Role of School

- Helps to prepare individuals for adult life. Helps to prepare individuals for a vocation/career.
- It provides role-models.
- It helps to bring some kind of uniformity not only within education but also in the process of socialization.
- But school is not always successful in carrying out its tasks because
  - — Poorer children get poorer quality education and they find it difficult to live up to middle-class values and so gap between rich and poor widens.
  - — Children are more at home than at school and so, home values are stronger.
  - — Large numbers in schools leads to lack of co-ordination between teacher and students.
  - — Teachers may not be given their due importance and school may not be equipped.

(4) Mass Media:

- Formal and direct agency of socialization (direct because they have no intermediary to explain to them).
  - — Hence, the media is a very powerful agency.
- Also, because it can pass messages (-ve or + ve) in a capsule form to children and adults.
- In these messages, the essence of our culture is contained.

Role of media

- It makes all kinds of information available to the individual.
- It provides direct role-models for people to imitate.
- It offers a wide exposure to other cultures.
- It can re-inforce or strengthen values of society.
- It can weaken or dilute social values.

(5) Neighborhood

- Basically refers to the social environment of an individual. It could be of a upper class, middle class, village or slum environment.
- It provides an individual with the social atmosphere that he is living in For example, A person living in a slum environment is brought up in a culture of poverty.
- Neighbourhood can refer to physical and social environment.
- The type of people, their homes, the religion they practise, the education they get affects the child's life opportunities.
- The neighbourhood also affects one's attitude to public opinion. In village environment, public opinion and reputation are important.

ADULT SOCIALIZATION

Meaning

It refers to socialization of an individual who is already socialized. Child socialization refers to primary socialization whereas adult socialization refers to secondary socialization. This occurs when an individual enters any new group and is exposed to a new set of norms, ideals and cultural values.

Socializing the adult, however, is much easier than socializing the child because

(1) For the adult, large part of the socialization process has already been completed and the adult is already motivated to work towards his goal.

(2) The new role of the adult will have many similar traits like the previous roles which he has already played.

(3) The socializing agent i.e., the socializer can communicate much more easily with the socializee or learner.

However, adult socialization can also have its negative aspects. This is when there is a role conflict.

But, adult socialization is still much more purposeful and meaningful than child socialization because the adult already has the goal and he is working towards it.

There are several socialization agencies for socializing the adult. With respect to them, there is a meeting point. According to ALEX INKELES, this meeting point is none other than societal demands.

Adult socialization never terminates. It continues into old age and till death.

- old age is not defined very clearly in many societies.
- In some societies, it begins with retirement, in others much later.

The older members of society face difficulties with respect to the socialization process as there is always a feeling of being unwanted and lonely.

But, in modern society, older people are still very active.

❑ ❑ ❑

8

THE NATURE OF CONSUMER ATTITUDES

Most of us as consumers have attitudes towards products and services, organisations, promotions and issues. We say we like Pepsi or the services of Citibank. We express our approval for the way our our Jawans fought at Kargil. We love the slogan 'Yeh Dil Manage More.' In all these we are just expressing our *attitudes*.

Attitudes are the most basic constructs leading to behaviour. Attitude is an inner feeling which reflects how we are predisposed to some object. Our predisposition could be favourable or unfavourable. There are staunch vegetarians who are negatively predisposed to a meat diet. India loves cricket and cinema. It is positively predisposed to both these. Attitudes are, however, not directly observable. They are judged from what we express and do. Consumer research is necessary to infer a positive or negative predisposition towards objects.

Beliefs and opinions are held about objects on the basis of our *knowledge.* This knowledge is based on facts considered true from our own point of view and as perceived at a given point of time. Beliefs thus are emotionally neutral. Attitudes, on the other hand, are not neutral but dynamic. If we just treat a cup of tea as a product that exists to refresh us, we hold an opinion or belief. But our fondness for this cup whenever our spirits are down shows an attitude. It is, necessary to have a belief to hold an attitude. Attitudes do not exist in isolation. We can be pro and anti something, for and against something, positive and negative while expressing attitudes. Attitudes have this stirred-up characteristic.

Let us define attitudes. *An attitude is a learned predisposition to behave in a consistently favourable or unfavourable way towards a given object.*

Alternatively, attitude can be defined as "an enduring organisation of motivational, emotional, perceptual and cognitive processes with respect to some aspect of the individual's world". — Krech Crutchfield.

What is an Object?

Attitude objects are interpreted broadly. In marketing context, these could be both a product or product category. It would be a brand even. Promotions like advertising also form an object. Media and price could also be an object. Our object could also be a retailer. Attitude research is object-specific. When we want to assess the attitude of domestic passengers towards inflight services, our object is Air India, Indian Airlines, Jet Airways, Sahara Airways. While examining women's attitudes towards undergarments, our object is VIP and Loveable. We understand the attitudes of garment buyers by taking Shoppers Stop, Roop Milan, Kala Niketan and Sheetal as objects.

Learned Predisposition

We learn about a product by using it, or through media and advertising. This information develops our attitude which may either be favourable or unfavourable.

Consistency of Attitudes

Consumer behaviour is consistent with their attitude. This consistency is relative because attitudes may change. It means a favourable attitude towards breakfast cereals would make us buy Kellogs and a negative attitude towards artificial sweeteners would make us avoid soft drinks with such sweeteners. Thus if we are free to act as we desire, we tend to choose products which are consistent with our attitudes. But there are some constraints on this consistency, say our purchasing power is so poor that we cannot afford to use Kellogs daily. Situation plays a role in shaping our purchase behaviour. A brand may be purchased not because of a favourable attitude but because of the pressure of the situation which forces us to economise. We sometimes have to purchase 'out of reach' brands on health grounds.

Junk food becomes acceptable when we are out for a stroll on the sea beach. But can we accept it when a marriage ceremony is being celebrated? There is a time and place for everything. Our attitude towards junk food corresponds to a particular situation. We thus have to consider the situation in which the behaviour takes place to assess the attitudes correctly.

Salience

Attitudes do not hold the same relevance or *salience* for an individual under different conditions. Our negative attitude towards non-vegetarian food is not relevant while watching a Hollywood movie in which the characters relish meat dishes. Under these conditions, the negative attitude towards non-vegetarian food has a low degree of salience. Usually, attitudes towards products and brands are not salient to the average consumer. There are slight preferences for the brand. There may be or may not be some attitude. Even if there is some attitude, it is not relevant. Robertson considers attitude towards a product or brand as a result of a number of attitudes towards different attributes of the product such as price, safety, performance. All these have varying salience. Thus fragrance is highly salient for a perfume but not for a medicine. Price may be highly salient for food products but not for trivial items like salt. Styling is valued much for a car but not for a gharghanti (domestic flour mill).

Components of Attitudes

Some writers do not try to distinguish between attitudes and beliefs. They consider attitudes themselves consist of three components: a *cognitive* or belief component, an *affective* or feeling component and a *conative* or action-tendency component. (see Fig. 8.1)

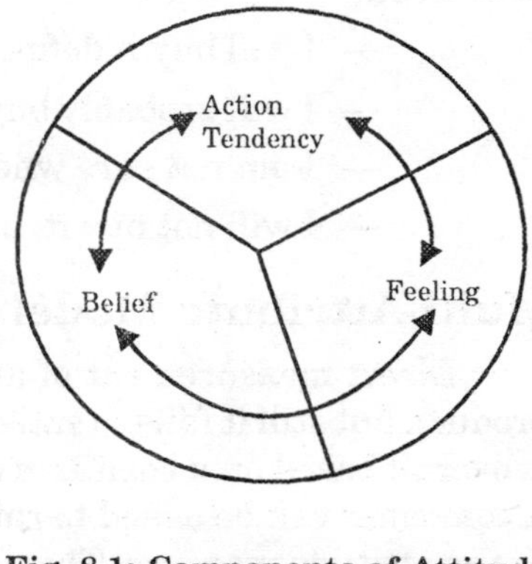

Fig. 8.1: Components of Attitude

Cognitive Component: The first component consists of a person's cognitions leading to a whole set of beliefs which he holds about the object. The beliefs are regarding the various attributes the attitude-object possesses. Attitudes about a perfume like *Fire and Ice* include beliefs about its lingering presence, unique smell, and use occasions.

A consumer may believe that she can wear this perfume for special occasions like marriage, has a fragrance that lasts long and is specially suited for fashionable women. These beliefs are *evaluative* in nature. They are either favourable or unfavourable, positive or negative, good or bad.

Affective Component: This is a feeling or emotional component of the attitude. These feelings are about the attitude object, say a product or a brand. The feeling are *evaluative* in nature, say love-hate, like-dislike, positive-negative or good-bad. The affective component leads to a stirred up physiology or an emotionally charged state like disgust, fondness, resentment, happiness, sadness, amazement. In a two-polar world of yesterday, much that went wrong elsewhere in the world was attributed to the Communists.

Emotionally charged state increase a positive or negative experience. When this is recalled later, the behaviour is affected. When the Taj Mahal is seen against the back-drop of a moonlit night, our viewing is enhanced by our mood at that time. Our joyous mood leads to a greater enjoyment of the Taj. Moonlight and the beauty of the Taj are pleasantly recalled later. We strongly recommend others not to miss the Taj on a moonlit night.

Conative Component: It represents the potential or readiness to respond. It shows the likelihood or tendency to behave or act in a particular way with regard to an attitude-object. A positive attitude is most likely to lead to recommendation or purchase. A negative attitude is likely to lead to attack, punishment or destruction of the object, or things associated with it. In marketing the buying-intention is considered to be a conative component.

Illustration

How likely are you to buy *Fire and Ice* perfume during the next week?

— Very likely

— Likely

— Unlikely

— Very unlikely

Which of the following statements best describes the chance that you will buy *Fire and Ice* next week?

— I will buy it definitely.

— I will probably buy it.

— I am not sure whether I will buy it.

— I will not buy it, definitely.

Multi-Attribute Model

Direct measurement of attitude is possible by asking liking or otherwise of a particular product, but still it fails to satisfy us completely as to why a brand is liked or disliked. The liking is overall based on a cognitive evaluation of the underlying attributes or benefits of the brand. A consumer can be asked to rate the brand on these attributes, and take the mean of the score as the attitude measure. This is called *multi-attribute evaluation of the brand.*

Fishbein's Model

Basically, this is a model developed by social psychologist Fishbein, and is called *attitude-toward-object* model. In this model attitude is considered in two components — *beliefs* about the attributes of the object and *evaluation* of these beliefs. If other conditions are present, a consumer moves towards the brand for which he has the most favourable attitude and moves away from the brand for which he has less favourable attitudes.

Mathematically, we use the following equation

$$A_o = \sum_{i=1}^{n} B_i \times a_i$$

where

A_o is the attitude toward some object

B_i is belief *i* about *o*. It means probability that the object *o* is related to some other object (the belief that the brand has some attribute e.g. Coke *refreshes* us)

a_i is the evaluation dimension of B_i, the evaluation of specific belief. The brand that possesses this attribute is good, e.g. how refreshing Coke is.

n the number of salient attributes or beliefs.

Theory-of-Reasoned-Action Model

It improves upon Fishbein's research. It is integrative since it takes the cognitive, affective and conative components in consideration.

Behaviour can be traced back to *intention to act* which itself results from *consumer's attitude towards the behaviour* and *subjective norm*. Diagramatically, it can be represented as follows:

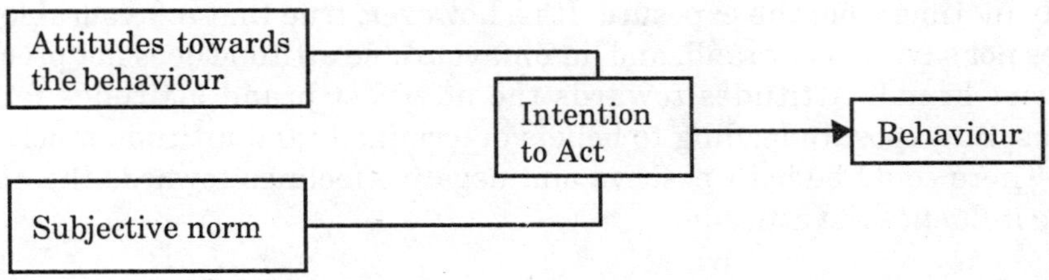

Fig. 8.2 : Reasoned-action Model

Attitude towards behaviour represents overall favourability towards the purchase. Subjective norm influences an individual's intention to act. Subjective norm has two components - *favourable or unfavourable thinking* of contemplated action by family, friends and colleagues and *motivation* to comply with their thinking. Thus while purchasing a moped like Scooty, we shall certainly consider what our parents think about it or whether our class-mates approve such a purchase.

We can see all these elements have inter-connection. Actual behaviour is preceded by intention which in its turn is preceded by attitudes and subjective norms. We also learn that an intention predicts behaviour better than attitude.

Attitude-Towards-the Ad Model

Advertising influences consumer attitudes towards brands and products. The following diagram outlines the attitude-toward-the-ad model.

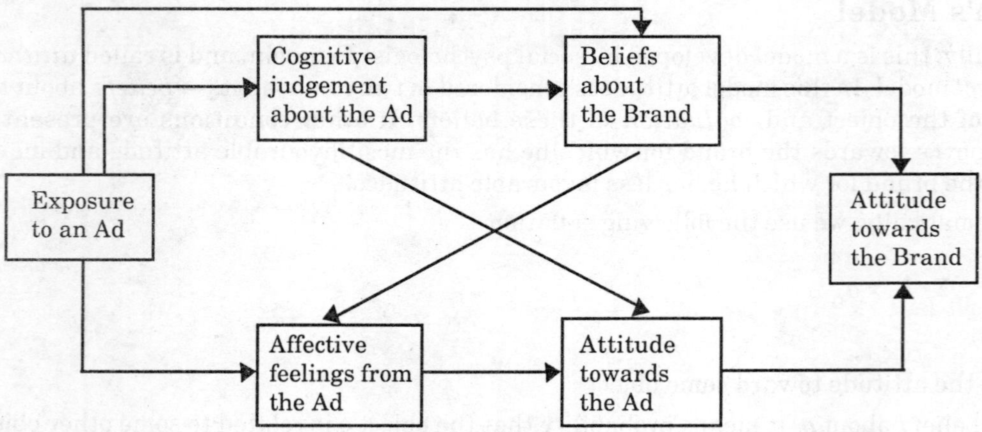

Fig. 8.3 : Attitude-Toward-the-Ad Model

Consumer comes to acquire various feelings and judgement about the ad after exposure. This influences the attitude to the ad and the beliefs about the brand. This consequently affects the attitude towards the brand.

Consumer attitudes towards the ad must be distinguished into cognitive and affective aspects.

Affective responses describe what we feel after seeing the ad *e.g.,* amused, sad, inspired, joyous etc. Cognitive evaluations describe our judgement regarding the ad e.g., humerous, interesting, believable, horrible etc. Both affective and cognitive responses can be measured on a five-point scale.

The favourable attitude shown towards a brand after exposure is likely to wear off as we move away in time from the exposure. It is, however, true that a favourable attitude towards the ad does not save a poor brand, and an unfavourable attitude does not preclude the selection of a superior brand. Attitudes towards the ad affect brand attitudes far more in case of innovations. Ad exposure leading to beliefs determine brand attitude much more for familiar products. There could be both positive and negative feelings towards the ad simultaneously. Both these influence the attitude.

Attitude Formation

We know by now that people hold attitudes towards objects. We have attitudes towards garments like jeans, soft drinks like Pepsi, and mineral water like Bisleri. What factors influence these attitudes? Are we influenced by celebrities endorsing certain products? What effect mass media like TV and newspapers have on attitudes? Do friends and family members affect us? Some attitudes last for a long time. Some keep on changing. Why so? Marketers must understand the formation of attitudes, so as to affect these in a desired manner.

Essentially, attitude formation is a *learning process.* Secondly, there are some *sources* of influence on attitude formation. Lastly, *personality* affects attitude formation. We shall cover these three aspects one by one.

Learning Process

There is a condition of *no attitude* towards an object in question from which we can shift to *some* attitude toward it. Learning causes this shift or attitude formation.

Cognitive learning theory is related attitude formation. A brand name that is favourably viewed is associated with an innovation. We tend to purchase it then. At the start, the attitude towards the brand is neutral. Once we start using it, it provides repeated satisfaction. It created a favourable attitude. This attitude influences our acceptance of the new product. In terms of learning theory, an *unconditioned stimulus* (brand name) leads to an *unconditioned response* (favourable attitude) by *repetition* and positive *reinforcement.* Celebrities bring about a positive association between them and the neutral new product. Celebrities enjoy goodwill and prestige (positive attitude). This is transferred to the product. The customer thus develops a positive attitude towards the product.

Instrumental conditioning is observed when the experience of using a product towards which we have no attitude leads to some attitude on getting satisfied.

Cognitive learning theory is seen in situations when a consumer forms attitudes while seeking information for problem-solving for need satisfaction. The attitudes formed may be positive or negative. The basis is information collected and our own cognition — knowledge and beliefs.

Sources of Influence

Attitude formation is highly influenced by family, peer and groups, personal experience, direct marketing and mass media.

Family Influence: By far, it is the most prominent influence. There is a direct correlation between the attitudes of the parents and children. Our political beliefs, social values, preferences for foods, social hygiene are all acquired through the family. Family gives us many basic values, and a whole variety of less central beliefs.

Peer and Group Influence: We interact without friends. We have respect for some individuals whom we admire. They influence us in attitude formation. Individual belongs to groups or aspire to belong to them. Group has its norms. We conform to these norms. Menzel and Katz studied prescription behaviour of doctors, and found that they were primarily influenced by their peers and opinion leaders and secondarily through journals and medical representatives.

Though peers and groups affect our attitudes, it is also true that we make friendship with those peers or join such a group which has a value system similar to our own. Larger groups like social classes, ethnic groups and entire cultures also influence our beliefs and altitudes. Wine as a product is acceptable to Catholics, whereas others may not readily accept it.

Experience: Direct experience regarding products through trial and repeat purchases affect our attitudes. Incentives are often given to try the products.

Direct Marketing: A specialised segment is targeted thereby increasing the chances of influencing the attitudes favourably.

Mass Media: There us proliferation of both print and electronic media. We are exposed to new ideas and product innovations. We come to know what others think. We come across a number of advertising messages. Mass media does have a profound effect on our attitudes.

Personality Influence: Human beings are not computers. Computers are programmed to act as per instructions. Human beings though influenced by others, have their own individual personality. Attitude formation has affected the personality. Open-minded individuals and closed-minded individuals differ in their overall attitudes. A closed-minded individual is dogmatic, not ready to listen to the viewpoint of others. Several personality traits like aggressiveness, conservatism, introversion and extroversion influence the attitudes of a person. A high need for cognition or information makes us appreciate information-packed ads. A low need for cognition makes us like ads using presentable models or renowned celebrities. Attitudes towards product innovation is also influenced by the personality of the individuals concerned.

Attitude Change

A change in attitude is also influenced, like attitude formation, by learning, sources of information and personality. In marketing, the leading brands wish to retain the positive attitudes of their consumers towards them; whereas the market followers and others want to change the attitude of the customers of the market leader. Several strategies are adopted to bring about a change in attitude. Ad agencies exist primarily for the purpose of attitude change. Consider several thousand crores of rupees being spent on advertising in India. Attitude change is thus an area of major concern.

Change in Basic Motivation

We can bring about a change in attitudes by making new needs more prominent. We can do so by initiating a change in basic motivation by what is known as a functional approach put forward by Daniel Katz.

Instrumental Function: Our attitudes are a result of our tendency to maximise the rewards and minimize the penalties. The brands which are instrumental in satisfying our needs make us hold positive attitudes towards them. What punishes us draws our negative attitudes. We do not like the brands which require frequent repairing and are of poor quality. If we can prove that the brand is in a position to satisfy the needs of the consumers or is utilitarian, the attitudes formed will be positive or the attitudes will change favourably.

Ego-Defensive Function: We tend to protect our self-image from anxieties or inner feelings of doubt. We express these feelings by choosing an object which becomes a convenient outlet. Ads for cosmetics and personal hygiene products bring about a favourable attitude change by bolstering the self-image of the consumer. These products give us desirability, confidence and safety from offending.

Value-Expressive Function: Each one of as has a personal value system, an individual life style, and an outlook. Attitudes give expression to these. A bibliophile loves books. He holds attitudes which support his love for books. He derives satisfaction by expressing these attitudes. Marketers should understand the attitudes of target segment to anticipate their life-style. They can make use of this in their ad messages.

Knowledge Function: The world around us pass on several stimuli, and is full of chaos. We make it meaningful by holding attitudes. Attitudes serve as standards or frame of reference to arrive at meanings. There is a need to know exactly for this purpose. Positioning products satisfy our need to know and enable us to choose among the competitive brands. Informative ads also satisfy our need to know. They improve our attitudes by doing so.

Consumer can display positive attitude towards products and brands, but the functional framework may be different for different consumers. Some may consider a brand instrumental, some others ego-defensive and still others value-expressive.

Change Agents

We belong or aspire to belong to groups, and thus change our attitudes as per the group norms. A child is aghast to see a drunkard father at home. But soon after he becomes a teen-ager, and finds his college-group enjoying booze parties his attitude towards alcohol changes. Similarly, we change our attitudes to clothing. Our conservatism gives way to liberal dress habits by conformity to group values. Most of the products we use today are used because they are also used by peers and the group to which we belong. Attitudes are shaped not only by the groups we belong to, but by the groups we want to belong to.

Communicator and the vehicle used for communication also act as change agents for our attitudes. We have to consider the style of the communicator, the diction used, his reputation and his professional standing. The media used and the method of presentation are also relevant for attitude change. Sometimes, a communicator is not able to have an impact on our susceptibility to persuasion. There are studies on the differences in influence of two types of sources — high credibility sources and low creditability sources. High credibility sources, to begin with, bring about a larger change of opinion than low credibility sources. As time elapses, however, we observe a *sleeper effect*, and notice a decrease in the amount of agreement of reliable source and increase in the amount of agreement with the non-reliable source. Over a period of time, the difference between two sources in their opinion change ability is not seen at all. Perhaps, the content of communication becomes more important than the source of communication. At times ads can be effective irrespective of the communicator.

Communication Content

There are techniques of content analysis and copy-testing. First we shall discuss one-sided vs. two-sided communication.

One-versus-two-sided Communication

This raises the question whether the advertiser should only praise the product or should also mention some of its shortcomings. The most common approach in sales and advertising is a one-sided approach. However, on deep analysis, it is found that one-sided messages tend to work best with the audiences which is initially favourably predisposed to the claims made in the ad message. Two-sided arguments go well when audiences have an unfavourable opinion about the communicator's position. Also, a two-sided message tends to be more effective with educated audiences capable of sound reasoning, particularly when they are exposed to counter propaganda. A two-sided communication produces the greatest attitude change when people are opposed to the point of view presented. Also, a two-sided communication is effective in maintaining the belief level against a counter-attack by competitors. However, it is the single-side communication which is commonly used, for it is difficult for the advertiser to refer to the product's shortcomings and still effectively persuade prospects to buy it.

Order of Presentation

What should be the order of our communication amidst a whole lot of competitive communication? There are several research studies on this subject. We tend to remember the last thing best. But we also tend to be most attentive when the first thing is told. However, irrespective of its location, it is the superior ad that wins the day. It goes without saying that when all ads are equally good in terms of quality, the results are equivocal. Further research is necessary to arrive at some conclusion.

Whether to put the strongest argument first or last in the advertiser's presentation is equaly important. Sometimes this is considered a part of copywriting strategy. In a one-sided argument, it is advisable to present the strongest point first, for it will result in better attention and interest. This is done with the objective of achieving the primary effect. However, when an audience necessarily requires a two-sided communication, it is better, at least initially, to start with the other side's argument and slowly disarm the audience which is opposed to the communicator's position, and then to conclude the message with the strongest argument.

The change that is produced depends on the change that is advocated. The greater the change advocated, the greater the change that is produced. It is not certain how far this is valid for the core attitudes. There may be an effect opposite to what is being advocated called *boomerang,* especially when the positions of the communicator and the recipient are markedly different.

Effects of Fear

The *fear appeal* is most important among emotional appeals, and also the most effective. It is said that the message's effectiveness increases with the level of fear it generates. The use of fear appeal in getting people to start doing things they should is very common. Many ad messages of toothpaste employ this appeal. They present the fear of tooth decay or unhealthy gums or bad breath, and then suggest the use of a specific brand of toothpaste to get rid of such fears. A recent ad of "Promise" shows a boy weeping because of severe toothache, and then suggests the use of "Promise" to avoid a recurrence of toothache.

A fear appeal of this kind is used in a wide variety of product categories. When products are designed to protect an individual from some loss of health (medical or life insurance), the fear appeal of the type illustrated above can be effectively employed. Then there are product designed to protect an individual from loss of property (automobile or home) which successfully employ fear appeals to induce a particular buying behaviour.

Fear appeals are at times used in ad messages in connection with getting people to stop doing the things they shouldn't do. The advertisements relating to prohibition, prevention of losses and conservation of energy fall in this category. The warning on the cigarette packet that smoking is injurious to health is a typical example, even though this is a statutory warning and advertisers themselves would not like to include it is the ad on their own.

Then there are many products which are, directly or indirectly, involved in the avoidance of a fearful situtation. Think of that popular advertisement of "FERODO," depicting that hundreds of road accidents are avoided because Ferodo brake liners have been fitted to the automobile. A large number of advertisements employ the fear appeal in their ad messages of products which relate to more subtle social and psychological motivations, such as loss of status, friendship, job, position, and so forth. Personal-care products (soaps, cosmetics, deodorants, shave lotions, mouthwash, etc.) fall in this category. Fear is the higher level of tension; but anxiety has been used to promote the sale of a large number of instant foods, other food products and home appliances. Think of ads wherein the housewife's anxieties are fully exploited to get the message across to the target audience.

The more carefully fear is built, the greater is the tension resulting in a greater drive from within to reduce the tension. Research studies have proved that extremely great fear appeals are less effective than moderate ones in motivating people to adopt the product and eliminate fear. However, very weak fear appeals are not effective in evoking the desired response. Therefore, a selection of the appropriate fear level is important; it should be strong enough to heighten the drive of the people to buy a paticular product. But if an excessively strong fear is pictured, it is possible that people would exhibit a defensive behaviour, and try to avoid the ad, and may not be prepared to accept the threat. They may even take the view that the solution recommended in the ad may be inadequate to deal with so great a fear. However, some researchers have found cases where strong fear appeals have worked beautifully. They feel that buyers have different tolerances for fear and that, therefore, different levels of the fear messages should be set for the various segments of the audience. However, the underlying concept that every message should promise to relieve, in a believable way, the fear it arouses should be the ultimate guide in the selection of the levels of fear appeals. A general principle of "not too much and not too little" is most relevant in the selection of appropriate fear appeals.

A methodical study in rural north India (mainly UP) was conducted by CARE (an American ad agency) to discover which of the two appeals — positive or negative—would work better in getting a nutritive food accepted. The positive appeal was love of children and the negative one was fear of the consequences of malnutrition. The "love" campaign featured a proud mother rearing her thriving child on the prescribed food. The "fear" approach created a frightening devil (*rakshas*), symbolizing the disease and misfortune arising from wrong food habits. These campaigns were run for a full year in two different areas. The evaluation of these campaigns clearly showed that the fear appeal created a great deal more awareness of the value of the nutritive food. The negative proposition aroused immediate reaction because of the fact that an unpleasant bang is more likely to make one sit up than the melodious strains of soothing music. Some authors and experts in the field of advertising, however, may disagree with this view. But fear appeals are seldom composed entirely of negatives. The warnings generally pave the way for positive advice and exhortation, and in this form the negative appeals appear to be just as effective on the average as positive appeals.

Take, for example, the recent advertisement of Khaitan Kitchen fans employing a negative appeal. The headline states: "Are you cooking or being cooked?" It goes on: "Every housewife knows how miserable she feels when she cooks. It makes her irritable and saps her energy . . Khaitan presents a simple, efficient and inexpensive answer. The Khaitan Fresh Air Fan. It drives out smoke, smells and heat, and brings in fresh air. Not only that; thanks to the continuous inflow of fresh air, the chances of dampness are eliminated. And this prevents cockroaches and other insects from breeding in your kitchen."

The headline and the initial part of the body of the copy effectively create fear; but the later part of the copy presents the solution and the positive appeal of the product. This is the most common form of the advertising message — first building up fear and then offering a solution with other positive appeals of the product advertised. On the level of fear, Aaker and Myer, in their book, *Advertising Management,* rightly state that fear or anxiety has two kinds of possible effects on message reception and yielding. As a *stimulus,* its effect tends to be negative; and as a *drive,* it tends to be positive. Furthermore, too little anxiety tends to provide an insufficient drive, and too much anxiety tends to make the stimulus aspect predominant. The net result of these two factors is to make the relationship between anxiety level and message effectiveness non-monotonic, with maximum effectiveness occurring at the intermediate levels of anxiety.

And, lastly, so far as appeals to fear are concerned, this approach is useful for products which are of little interest to consumers when rational appeals are employed. Even in cases where the product fulfils a generally recognised need, fear appeals are effective. Take the case of life insurance. Fear appeals are still required to sell policies. However, fear appeals fail in the case of the cancer hazard of cigarette smoking, which is often rejected by most smokers.

Fear Appeal and Market Segmentation: We have just now stated that, in some cases, big doses of fear are recommended, whereas, in others, the use of low levels of fear is the logical strategy. We have also given examples of an ad about dental health, where the degree of associated fear is high, and an ad about smoking and cancer, where the level of fear is low. Furthermore, apart from the differences in product categories, the age and personality differences in the target audience vary the effectiveness of each level of fear appeal. That is why it has been recommended that both the market segment and product category groupings should be taken into consideration before designing appropriate fear appeals.

Let us take an in-depth look at the use of fear appeals and their relationship with the market segment, for this will provide a valuable insight to advertisers. It is important to note that although people generally prefer positive arguments, a fear appeal can make an advertisement stand out from others. For individuals whose aroused fear or anxiety about the product is low, and those who would not normally search for information about the product, the fear appeal can be particularly effective if these individuals have been previously exposed to positive arguments.

It has been found that it is better to put fear first in the order of presentation, to threaten someone close to the prospect rather than the prospect himself. While advertising a helmet for scooter-riders, the fear of injury to the head is the most appealing to the wife and to someone close to the rider. The rider himself may not accept the idea promptly because of self-esteem and of ego-consciousness. The appeal of intense fear might be best for people who tend to be of low-anxiety and high self-esteem people, who exhibit a copying behaviour, and who find the product to be of low relevance. There are many who have a low vulnerability to fear and anxiety. For example, life insurance companies find that fear appeals work beautifully with those who feel that they do not need a coverage for their lives. Fear appeals are appropriate for breaking into new market segments. In fact, the susceptibility to fear appeals is one more approach to the market segmentation process. A careful analysis of those potential fear appeals, designed to arouse emotion in a group or audience, should be made a part of advertising strategy, wherein all ads addressed to this audience will incorporate such fear appeals. Thus, if appropriate fear appeals are defined, they become a useful tool in market segmentation.

Audience Characteristics

There is interaction between the message content and the audience for whom it is meant. We have already made references to these by discussing how fears appeals operate for helmet buyers showing different characteristics.

Attitude Change and Behaviour Change

We presume that there is a relationship between attitude change and behaviour change. So far experiments have proved that behaviour change often culminate in attitude change. But whether the anti-thesis of attitude change leading to behaviour change is valid or not has not been settled for certain. Ads may make consumers favourably disposed to the products, but it does not necessarily mean that they will buy these products. There are only indications to predisposition to purchase or what we call intention to purchase. Whether this results in actual purchase or not, we do not know for certain. Attitudes are clustered together, and they may lead to one behaviour. But specific attitudes could lead several behaviour patterns. This discussion, however, does not undermine the importance of the study of attitudes and attitude change for business and commerce.

More on Attitude Change

Marketers associate products with events or personalities to bring about a change in attitude. We can take advantage of conflicting attitudes to bring about a change in attitudes. Diet Pepsi is a good drink and is still not fattening. We structure the market into benefit segmentation, each having brands with different features and beliefs. Toothpaste market example quoted in segmentation chapter is a good example of this. This strategy in fact amounts to change the relative evaluation of conflicting product attributes. Marketers attempt cross-overs between these segments *e.g.,* a person taking non-colas can take either lime beverages or fruit beverages. We can also change attitudes by changing brand beliefs or perceptions of the brand itself. We can introduce a previously ignored attribute or add an attribute that makes the product technologically superior. Instead of concentrating on individual attributes, some companies try to change the overall brand rating. Instead of changing beliefs about our brands, we can change beliefs about competitive brands or their attributes.

Cognitive Dissonance

After a decision is taken, there can be discomfort or inconsistency called dissonance. Such a feeling is common when a consumer holds conflicting thoughts about either a belief or an attitude-object. It is observed that a parent who puts a child in a costly coaching class experiences cognitive dissonance when he thinks of other classes *not* selected, though they were reasonably good and economical. Dissonance after purchase is called *post purchase dissonance* which is quite a normal thing if it happens to be small. The feeling of discomfort is resolved by changing the attitudes to conform to their behaviour. This attitude change is a result of behaviour.

This theory has been first put forward by Festinger. When others admire our purchase, they infact are endorsing our purchase decision. This is reassurance to as about the sensibility of our purchase. According to Festinger the product that we do not purchase and their positive attributes are dissonant with our purchase and its negative aspects. Admiration of others reduce our cognitive dissonance.

Dissonance increases our receptivity to the ads inserted by the manufacturers. These bolster our decision. In a research study it was observed that car purchasers were more receptive to the ads of the car which they purchased, than those of the competing brand they did not purchase.

Dissonance can be reduced or consonance can be achieved, by:

1. eliminating or re-examing one of the cognitive elements or responsibility or control over the act or decision.
2. by denying or distorting or forgetting the information.
3. by minimizing the importance of an issue that led to dissonance.
4. by adding new cognitive elements to buttress the decision.

Marketers on their part can contribute to reduce dissonance by appropriate ad messages, by providing guarantees/warranties, by providing back up of technical literature and by increasing consumer services. Beyond the reduction of dissonance, marketers have started practising what is known as "relationship marketing."

❑❑❑

9

COMMUNICATION AND PERSUASION

The Communication Process

In marketing communication, there is a transmission of a message from a sender to the receiver. The end result of the communication process is the understanding of a message. The message is transmitted through media or certain channels. The response to the message is known by receiving the feedback from the recipient of the communication. The communication sometimes fails to accomplish its purpose — creation of an appropriate response or understanding when the message is distorted by 'noise' elements. The following diagram illustrates the communication process.

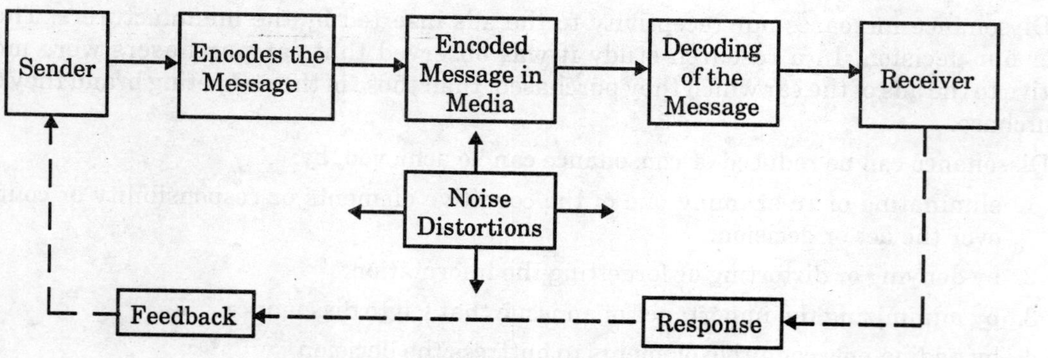

Fig. 9.1: Communication Process

The sender is the source of the message. It puts the message in symbolic form say a letter or advertising copy. It is called 'encoding.' The message is carried by the media, say the postal department or TV or newspapers. The message is received by the receiver who shows a particular response which is communicated back to the sender.

The message must accomplish three tasks in order to be effective:

(*a*) It must gain the attention of the receiver.

(*b*) It must be understood.

(*c*) It must stimulate the needs of the receiver and suggest appropriate method to satisfy these needs.

Senders must be aware of the receivers or audiences they want to reach and the responses they want. They must be skilful in encoding the message, taking into account how the receiver or the audience is going to decode the message. Since the sender wants the receiver to understand the message, the sender must know as much as possible about the receiver before the message is designed. The sender puts the message through efficient media that reach the audience. The response of the audience is known by developing the feedback channels. In this process, noise may distort the effectiveness of communication. Noise includes poor message planning, busy audience members or careless feedback of response.

Marketing Communication

Modern marketing is the management of the four 'P's — product, price, promotion and place or distribution channel. In a sense the entire marketing process has a large content of communication. For instance, the product communicates a distinctive image such as youthfulness, glamour or prestige. The brand name communicates physical and psychological attributes of the product, e.g., Dreamflower talc. The package communicates to the consumer what the manufacturer thinks of his convenience and sense of beauty. The price communicates the quality of the product. There are communications between buyers and sellers, i.e., the distribution channel. Thus each element of the marketing mix either helps or hinders communication and ultimately the sales effort. Marketing communication is thus a broader term than promotional strategy. However, the most important element of marketing communication is the planned promotional communication.

The marketing communication mix (also called promotion mix) consists of *four* major tools:

- *Advertising:* Any paid form of non-personal communication of ideas, products and services by an identified sponsor.
- *Sales Promotion:* Short-term direct inducements to encourage sales of products and services.
- *Publicity:* Non-personal stimulation of demand for a product/service or business organisation as a whole by putting commercially significant news in media to create a favourable image. It is not paid for by the sponsor.
- *Personal Selling:* For making sales, a salesman interacts orally with the buyer or buyers in the form of a sales presentation.
- *Public Relations:* Marketers engage in public relations to develop a favourable image of their organisations in the eyes of public — public at large, customers, suppliers, government, media, competitors, shareholders, employees and the society.

The Process of Marketing Communication

The following diagram (Fig. 9.2) illustrates the marketing communication process as applied to promotional strategy.

The marketing manager or the organisation is the sender of the message. The message is encoded as advertising copy, publicity material, sales promotional displays or sales presentation by sales people. The media for delivering the message may be the print media like press and magazines or the electronic media like TV, radio and films or a salesman who makes a presentation. The decoding step involves the consumer's interpretation of the message. This is often

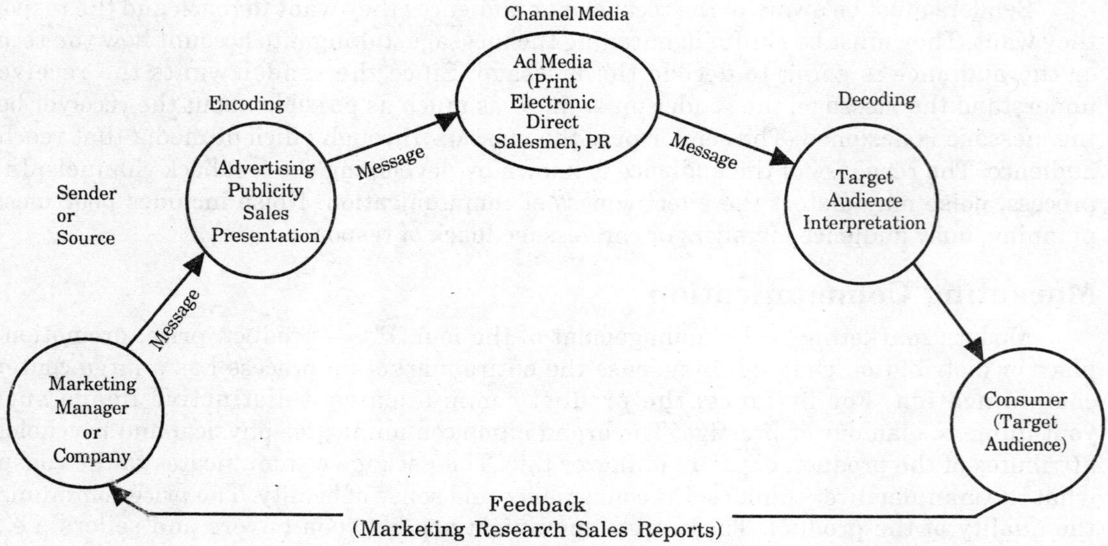

Fig. 9.2: The Marketing Communication Process

the most challenging aspect of marketing communication as consumers may not always interpret the message the way the sender wants them to interpret. As seen previously, the fundamental difficulty in communication process occurs during encoding and decoding. This may happen because the meanings attached to various words and symbols may differ, depending upon the frames of reference and the field of experience between the sender and the receiver.

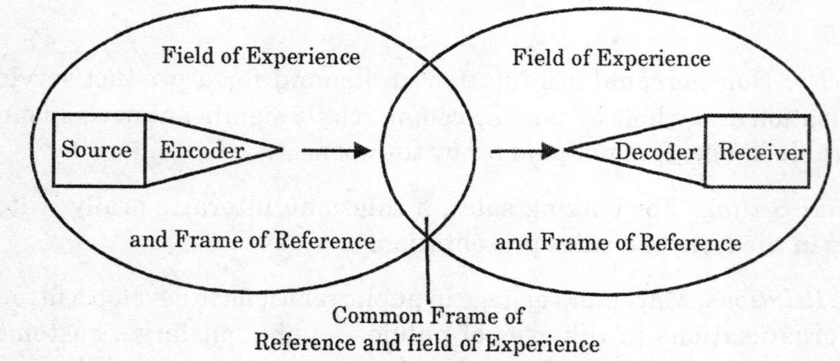

Fig. 9.3: Communication and Field of Experience

This is explained by the Fig. 9.3. The overlapping of field of experience and frame of reference makes the communication possible. If there is no overlap, communication may be bad or impossible. The consumer or audience response is known by undertaking a market research study or by analysing the sales reports. The noise element is in the form of competitive promotional messages. There may be random noise factors like people fast forwarding a video casette when advertisements are shown. Errors in communication may be minimized by knowing the relevant market dimensions, the needs and attitudes of potential buyers.

In total corporate communications, the marketing communications are the most important part. Advertising as we have seen is a part of marketing communication. Advertising as a tool of communication has certain important characteristics which distinguishes it from other tools of marketing communication like personal selling, sales promotion, publicity and public relations.

Advertising and Personal Selling

Advertising is communication with many consumers of products and services. To communicate with a large group, we put the advertising message through mass media like the press, magazines and TV. Advertising is thus one form of mass, communication. Advertising communication is non-personal. We communicate with the buyers through the media. There is no face-to-face conversation. Personal selling is personal communication where a salesman talks person to person with a prospect. Advertising aims at a group, i.e., mass while personal selling aims at individuals. Personal selling is not mass communication but individual communication. These days products are mass produced for mass consumption. It is not possible to contact each customer individually. Therefore, advertising a mass communication tool is a must for modern marketer. But industrial products and complex pieces of machineries can be sold better by personal selling where the salesman is in a position to explain the characteristics of the product to the buyer. Salespersons are in a position to tailor their messages according to unique characteristics of each prospect. In modern marketing, the marketing manager decides a judicious mix of advertising and personal selling. It is difficult to measure the effectiveness of advertising, however salespersons receive immediate feedback during their interacting and can see how their messages are getting across. They may, therefore, adjust the message or presentation quickly.

Personal selling is a very intense means of communication. People may skip an advertisement on TV but find it difficult to dismiss a salesperson. It is the most effective communication tool as it is inter-personal. But this is its major weakness as well as strength. It is terribly inefficient for mass market producers, where advertising a mass communication tool scores over it.

Advertising and Sales Promotion

Advertising predisposes a person favourably for a product/service/idea moving him towards its purchase. Sales Promotion takes over at this point. It makes the consumer take a favourable purchase decision by providing one or other kind of direct inducement, e.g., discount, price off, gift, coupon etc. Mostly advertising is indirectly concerned with sales. It either informs or persuades or reminds about a product or service. Most of the times, it is indirect in its approach and has a long-term perspective, e.g., building up a company image or brand image. Sales Promotion is a short-term approach, a direct approach and expects an immediate response in terms of sales. Sales promotion is an important adjunct to selling. Advertising is more frequent and repetitive than Sales Promotion. Sales Promotion are non-recurrent selling efforts. They supplement the advertising and personal selling. Displays are effective method of sales promotion. Contests are also another effective method of sales promotion.

Advertising and Publicity

Publicity is defined as non-personal stimulation of demand for a product/service/ business unit by *planting commercially significant news* about it in a published medium or obtaining *favourable presentation* of it on radio, TV or stage *that is not paid for* by the *sponsor.* Two significant distinctions emerge. Publicity is not openly paid for. Secondly, presentation is not programmed.

Marketers have less control over publicity than they have over advertising. Publicity is left to the discretion of the media in terms of whether to present it or not, contents of presentation and the format of presentation. Publicity may be negative as well as positive.

Advertising and Public Relations

The ultimate aim of Public Relations is to develop a favourable image in the eyes of the public. It refers to a company's communication and relationships with various sections of the public — customers, suppliers, shareholders, employees, governments, media, society at large. PR can be formal or informal. PR, unlike advertising, is personal.

Advertising is not the only form of persuasive communication. Very closely allied to advertising are sales promotion and public relations. In fact both are important parts of advertising, and are often 'managed' by the same people or agencies or departments. All three are vital to the 'marketing' of a product, service or idea.

While advertising is termed 'above the-line' communication, sales promotion may be termed 'below-the-line' communication. The ultimate goal of all three is to sell products, services, reputations, projects, programmes, people, politicians, beliefs, ideas — indeed everything and anything.

The institute of Public Relations, London, defines Public Relations as "the deliberate, planned and sustained effort to establish and maintain understanding between an organization and its public." Public Relations is low-cost compared to advertising, for the publicity obtained, say in the press, through public relations is not directly paid for. Indirectly, the expenses involve keeping in close touch with people in the media through press conferences, press visits and press releases. Besides, media persons have to be 'entertained,' and some of them expect 'gifts' from companies.

According to Edward L. Bernays, the 'father' of Public Relations, and the author of ' Engineering of Consent,' the phrase Public Relations means, "quite simply, the name of the engineering approach, i.e., action based on thorough knowledge of the situation and on the application of scientific principles and tried practices in the task of getting people to support ideas and programmes."

There are four elements to the mechanics of PR:

1. The message to be transmitted
2. An 'independent' third party endorser to transmit the message
3. A target-audience that it is hoped will be motivated to buy whatever is being sold, and
4. A medium through which the message is transmitted.

Advertising and PR are different from the point of view of their objectives. Advertising is an aid to selling and it improves the bottom line of business.

PR, which is the business of image management, cannot replace advertising. Of course, PR can in some way push up sales because it changes the way consumers perceive the company and hence the product. Advertising and PR are complementary in most cases but sometimes a dvertising is not necessary. PR can do the job. If a new manufacturing facility is started by a company, it cannot be advertised. A PR effort is more effective.

PR no doubt is valuable. Edit space is far more important than paid ad space. Of course, what has been achieved by PR must be adequately supported by the product and service. If PR is professionally handled, it can achieve benefits for an organisation at a fraction of a cost of advertising.

Advertising has a greater role when we are selling a tangible product. In a service industry, however, PR has a greater role, since the product is intangible.

Advertising and PR can't replace each other. By PR we create a good image. Advertising is necessary to take advantage of that good image for actual selling.

PR has higher degree of credibility since it is not paid for. Advertising, however, creates a brand personality. Only advertisement can add value to a product.

PR has now slowly evolved into an integrated approach called corporate communications.

Uncontrolled Communication

Out of the four major elements of promotion, personal selling advertising and sales promotion are within the control of a marketer who pays for all these. The only element that is outside his control is publicity which is not paid for directly by him. Media coverage may generate both positive and negative publicity. Aspirin received negative publicity for its side effects. It is sometimes out of control of the marketer.

Another communication that is beyond the control of a marketer is word-of-mouth communication. Here the consumers talk about their experiences with the products or services they have used to other consumers. Do we not tell our friends about the shopping malls we like, the movies that we dislike, and the CDs that we like to listen to? Sometimes there are rumours about the product and these must be fought actively by the company.

Corporate Communications

There are papers on corporate communications in American Universities and there are departments of corporate communications in different companies including our Hindustan Lever. In the 90s, business seeks to communicate positively in terms of clarity of identity to a wide range of people — financiers, those in autority, the general public, among others. Corporate communications is not limited to mere PR. It includes crisis communication, e.g., corporate identity programmes, re-imaging, media relations, corporate advertising, sponsorship for image building, and communicating during takeover. Corporate communications is not re-stricted to image management but considers corporate philanthropy, media dealing and crisis management.

Communication Model

Marketing communication, especially advertising is meant for a group of users of products called the target audience. After identifying the target audience, we must determine the response desired. The ultimate response desired is of course the buying of the product or service. We must know the decision-making process that leads the target audience from its present position to a higher state of readiness-to-buy.

The effectiveness of advertising depends upon to what extent the advertising message is received and accepted by the target audience. Research has identified that an advertisement to be effective has to (i) attract attention (ii) secure interest (iii) build desire for the product and finally (iv) obtain action. All advertisements obviously do not succeed on these counts. This is one solitary reason behind the great divergence between the number of people exposed to the advertisement and those who ultimately take the purchase decisions. At this stage, however, other elements of the marketing mix, especially distribution become crucial.

Advertisement communicates an idea, a message or a belief. An advertisement would be effective only if the media audience accepts that message and is motivated to take the required action. Several models have been developed which have specifically identified the sequence of events which must take place between receipt of the message and desired action.

AIDA Model: A somewhat simplified model based on the identical principle of sequential stages of consumer action is known as AIDA model. AIDA stands for:

A — attracting attention
I — rousing interest
D — building desire
A — obtaining action

Advertising as a communication medium can in most cases effectively perform the first three functions. In the case of direct-action advertising, it also must translate desire into action, unaided by any other promotional instruments. In the case of indirect-action advertising, however, the action can be aided at the time of purchase by two-way communication between the intending buyer and the sales staff.

Let us examine the attention, interest, desire and action components in more detail.

Attention: The layout is the most important factor that directs attention to an advertisement. Typography and colours used in the layout can rivet us. The size of the advertisement also compels us to get attracted to it. Contrast by white space is a good attention-getter. Movement is a vital element for getting attention. Movement can be physical or emotional. The position of the advertisement also adds to its attention value. Celebrities in the advertisement, dramatization, model selection, illustration all this contribute to attention. A detailed appendix on attention appears at the end of this chapter.

Interest: Ad seen does not mean *ad* read. Mostly people see the illustrations and do not read the copy. Here illustrations have to work hard. They should together with headlines must provoke further reading. The selection of the illustration and its integration to life are thus very important. Even copy format is important for interest creation. Some people get worked on by a scientific copy and some by a humorous copy. Here there is a dilemma for a copywriter. He has to satisfy maximum number of people so he has to search for a common denominator of interest.

Desire: The basic purpose of advertising is to create a desire for the product or service being advertised. It is function of appeals used for the motivation of people. Vivid description or copy always helps. Buying motives, physiological as well as psychological, make people purchase products. The copy of the advertisement must kindle these motives. There are certain barriers here — certain reservations in the mind of customers. We have to overcome them. We have to convince by giving evidence, testimonials, endorsements, facts and figures. On arousal, people become prone to buy the product.

Action: The logical end of the desire aroused is to buy the product.

1. Products are associated with the company.
2. The message is repeated.
3. Certain immediate action appeals are used.

The attention stage is the cognitive stage. In this stage, the target audience is exposed to the message, which when received by them causes a cognitive response awareness. The interest and desire stages are the affective stages which affect the attitudes and bring about an intention to buy. The final action stage is the behaviour stage. In practice all the ad copies do not lead the consumer through awareness to purchase. AIDA model suggests only the desirable qualities in an advertising copy as a communication tool.

Promotional Tools and Consumer Response

AIDA is an acronym given to the stages a consumer passes before he buys a product. The stages are:

1. *Attention*: to get the attention of the consumer or to create an awareness about the product.
2. *Interest*: to arouse interest in the product and hold it.
3. *Desire*: to create desire for the product.
4. *Action*: to motivate a consumer to buy the product.

This model is further elaborated to cover a number of more steps: awareness, knowledge, liking, preference, conviction and purchase. It is called *hierarchy of effects.* AIDA and hierarchy of effect models are inter-related as illustrated in the following diagram.

Stage	Response	
	AIDA	Hierarchy & Effects
Cognitive	Attention	Awareness
	↓	Knowledge
Affective	Interest	Liking
	↓ Desire	Preference
Behavioural	↓ Action	Conviction
	↓	Purchase
Outcome	Satisfaction Level	Satisfaction Level

Fig. 9.4: Relationship of Response Models

While relating them, we have put the stages into three broad psychological stages — cognitive, affective and behavioural. Cognitive refers to awareness and knowledge. It also refers to attention. Affective refers to liking and preference corresponding to interest and desire of AIDA model. Behavioural refers to conviction and purchase corresponding to action of the AIDA model.

The additional stage of outcome shows the response to the model. These models help us understand the tasks the promotion must perform.

We find the effects of different tools of promotion on hierarchy are different. The following diagram shows the effects of various promotional tools on the stages of AIDA model.

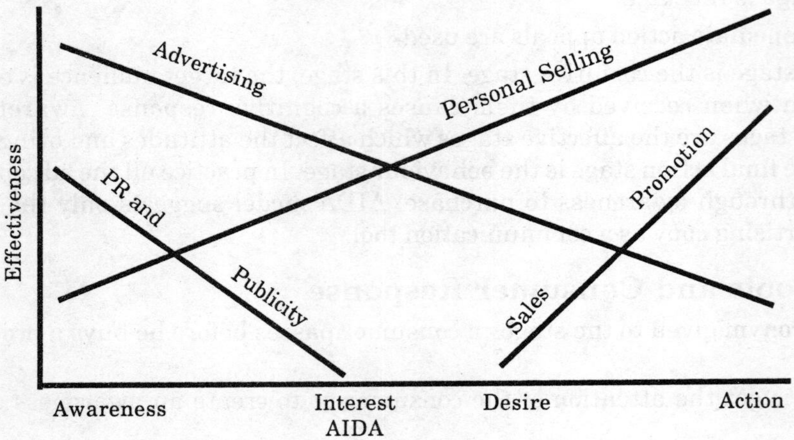

Fig. 9.5 : Effect of Promotional Tools on Consumer Response

Advertising has the capacity to generate highest awareness. It is also higher in arousing interest. However, it is not so effective in leading the consumer to action. Personal selling works exactly the opposite way. It is highest in making people buy and creating a desire for the product. It is, however, low in generating awareness. Sales promotion is highest in inducing action. Public relations and publicity are confined to creating awareness and a low level of interest.

Interpersonal vs. Mass Communication

Marketing deals with interpersonal and mass communication. Personal selling makes use of interpersonal communication whereas advertising, sales promotion and public relations are mass communication techniques. The following table summarizes the merits and demerits of both these modes.

TABLE 9.1: COMPARISON BETWEEN INTERPERSONAL AND MASS COMMUNICATION

Factor	*Interpersonal Communication*	*Mass Communication*
Speed with which a large audience is reached	Slow	Fast
Cost of reaching a large audience	High	Low
Attention-arresting capability	High	Low
Content Clarity	High	Moderate to low
Accuracy of Message	Low	High
Message flow traffic	Two-way	One-way
Feedback	High	Low

Adapted from *Promotional Strategy* by Engel, Warshaw and Kinnear (Irwin - 1987)

Mass communication, as the name itself indicates, takes the message to a large audience with a great speed. Advertising is mass communication. A sales presentation of a salesman is interpersonal communication. Each time a salesman can adapt the message to his prospective buyer. Mass communication is cost effective. However, it is a one-way communication. The feedback is not reliable many a time. Interpersonal communication provides immediate and accurate feedback. A buyer can ask questions and raise objections. He gets immediate response from the salesperson. It is much more effective than mass communication. But this communication is painfully slow when a large number of customers are to be contacted. It is very expensive.

Though mass communication has some demerits, it enables us to reach a large market economically. This leads us to a paradox that advertising is efficient promotion but inefficient communication.

The following table outlines the communication process for each component of promotional mix.

TABLE 9.2: COMMUNICATION PROCESS IN PROMOTION

Promotional Mix Element	*Source*	*Encoding*	*Media*	*Receiver*	*Decoding*	*Feedback*
Advertising	P & G ad for Ariel	Audio and Video in colour	TV Commercial	Housewives	Consumers learn about the product's stain removing capacity	Purchase of Ariel sales rise up
Personal Selling	Eros Pharmaceuticals anti-inflammatory Diclofenac	Words, body language, personal appearance	Personal visit	Doctors	Safe Anti-inflammatory properties of Diclofenac	Prescription flow
Sales Promotion	Shoppers stop	Discount offer at a sales festival	Local Newspapers, direct mailings	Women, Children, Men of middle and upper class	Consumers judge the benefits	Consumer avail of discount offer
Publicity	Interviews of the chairman of Hindustant Lever	Words gestures appearance	TV show	Viewer in India	Viewers unerstand how Lever brings useful products for the consumers	Viewers favourable image about Lever

Role of Marketing Communication

Marketing communication plays a multi-dimensional role. We can understand it better in terms of marketer-buyer communication, marketer-market communication and communication by non-profit and social organisations.

Marketer-Buyer Dyad

Marketing communication brings a marketer and a buyer close to each other. A marketer has certain goals to achieve. Similarly, the buyer has his own goals — keep himself well-informed about his choices, better consumption and a desire to have a better quality of life. The common thread between these two is the need satisfaction exercise through mutual efforts.

A product is the medium through which the duality of goals must be satisfied. A product is bought since it has need satisfying attributes. Products are offered, because the marketer has to achieve his own goals through them.

Marketing communication allows sharing of the organisation's product offering with the consumers so as to help them realise their own goals, while at the same time move the organisation closer to its own goals. The following diagram illustrates this.

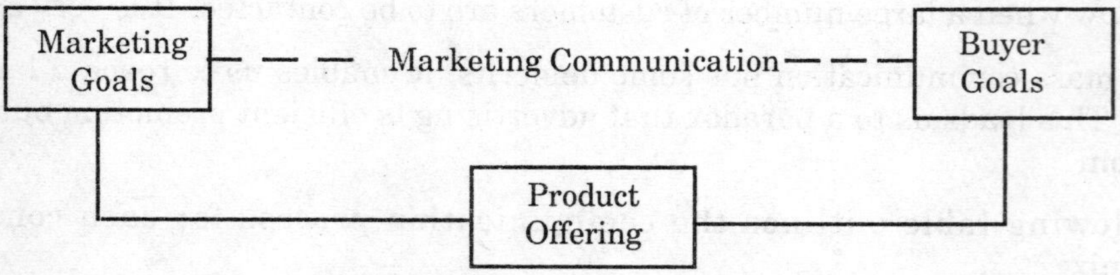

Fig. 9.6 : Role of Marketing Communication

Over and above goal compatibility, marketing communication has to *inform, remind* and *persuade* the actual and potential buyers for the marketer's offerings.

Marketer-Market Dyad

Marketing communication is not restricted just to buyers alone. It also addresses itself to business intermediaries, suppliers and other institutions. It also gets directed to opinion leaders and pressure groups. Each of these need a different message. The distributors are not interested in the looks of the product. They are more concerned about the dealers schemes, the margins available, and how the products fare with the competitive products. Business to business communication is an important branch of marketing communication.

Communication from Non-profit or Social Organisations

CRY, Cancer Society, Help Age, Eye Bank — all these organisations use communications to reach out to their clients.

Integrated Marketing Communication (IMC)

Many a time, we find that marketing communication gives the customers a fragmented and hazy picture. It happens because there is no integration amongst marketing efforts on the one hand and the communication efforts on the other. IMC makes a single-minded focused communication. Its consistency and cost-effectiveness are its main merits. The IMC concept is difficult to implement because communications are handled by different organisations. Personal selling is thus handled by the sales department, whereas advertising is handled by an ad agency. There are separate direct marketing and PR functionaries. Switch over to the IMC needs some re-organisation.

Integrated Communications and Marketing

To put it simply, integrated communication rotates around a central idea. Advertising carries an idea but the idea needs support in order to grow, *e.g.,* Pepsi commercial makes Pepsi a choice of a new generation but what is required further to carry the idea through is the research, direct marketing, public relations and appropriate event sponsorships. In other words, the need of the day is a well-rounded communication package, with a communications budget rather than an advertising budget. What is, therefore, necessary is the upgradation of an ad agency into a communications group.

In India, agencies like Lintas have already started moving in this direction by add-ons like:

(*i*) Linstock for financial advertising.

(*ii*) Market Links Direct for direct marketing, direct response advertising and tele marketing.

(*iii*) Pathfinders — research division.

(*iv*) Public relations division.

Similarly, agencies like HTA, Trikaya Grey, Zen Communications and O&M have many add-ons to offer integrated communications. Integrated communications and marketing are cost-effective for the agency as well as the client. However, it is for the client to decide which services are to be used after proper case analysis.

Credibility of the Source

Communication is to be decoded by the target audience. The creditability of the source affects this process. Perceived honesty and objectivity greatly enhance the acceptance of the message. Respectable sources also contribute to acceptance. Messages originating from unreliable sources are dismissed. Intentions of the source does affect the reception. Informal sources exercise a greater effect, as they have no axe to grind. Competence and knowledgibility of the sources greatly affect credibility. Distributors and media do affect credibility. Audience attitudes affect credibility. Credibility of a source exerts a reduced effect over a period of time (sleeper effect).

DAGMAR Approach

It is felt that the task of measuring ad effectiveness will not be daunting if we clearly spell out the advertising goals. Russel H. Colley (1961) pioneered an approach known by the acronym DAGMAR — Defining Advertising Goals for Measured Advertising Results, where to establish an explicit link between ad goals and ad results Colley distinguished 52 advertising goals that might be used with respect to a single advertisement, a year's campaign for a product or a company's entire advertising philosophy.

These goals may pertain to sales, image, attitude, and awareness. Some of the goals are:

- persuade a prospect to visit a show room and ask for a demonstration.
- build up the morale of the company's sales force.
- facilitate sales by correcting false impression, misinformation and other obstacles.
- announce a special reason for 'buying now' (price, discount, premium and so on).
- make the brand identity known and easily recognisable.
- provide information or implant attitude regarding benefits and superior features of brand.

According to DAGMAR approach, the communication task of the brand is to gain (a) awareness, (b) comprehension, (c) conviction, (d) image and (e) action.

Advertising goals should be consistent with these communication tasks. Later performance on these counts and projected goals is compared. For example, a company setting a goal of 15% increase in sales advertises and achieves this objective. Its ad then is successful and effective.

DAGMAR pre-supposes the understanding of the dynamics of consumer behaviour as without this goals cannot be set. Besides, a thorough acquaintance of market environment is called for. DAGMAR is a planning and control tool. It may guide the creation of advertising. However, as will be appreciated, the basic input of DAGMAR are not so easy to formulate and may also inhibit creativity.

Ad Objectives and Ad Purpose

Our objectives should support the purpose for which we wish to use advertising. The most extreme purpose of advertising is to induce direct action. The other extreme is to influence the attitudes. In between these two extremes, we want advertising to encourage information search, to relate a product to their needs, to encourage recall of past associations. Advertising influences attitudes, modifies them and re-inforces them.

Advertising Strategy

Advertising objectives, mostly communication objectives, as we have seen, spell out our position with reference to heirarchy of effects like awareness, attitude and preference. The next logical step is to develop advertising strategy. It describes how to achieve the communication objectives. Advertising strategy has two components — a *creative strategy* that describes what we are going to say (content) and how we are going to say it (style), and a *media strategy* which describes in which media and what time the message will be put across.

Advertising strategy basically is a blend of the advertising message and the communications media. While doing so, it also considers the target audience and the product concept. Together, this makes up the *creative mix.*

Advertising message spells out what the company plans to say, and how it plans to say it. It is a combination of the copy and visual and production elements. We can combine these elements in a wide variety of ways. It is called *creative execution.*

The process of marketing and advertising planning described so far was good for large companies. Large companies start their plans at the top and come downwards. It is called *top-down planning.* Small companies, however, adopt what is known as *bottom-up planning.* They reverse the normal process. In practice, they try to spot a clever tactic first. Later it is converted into strategy. The elements of marketing mix are built around one tactic. The combination of tactic and strategy creates a position in the consumer mind.

Advertising strategy combines the task of selecting the media and designing an effective message. These two tasks are, in fact, inter-related. An effective message seeks to answer the following questions:

(*i*) What are our business goals?
(*ii*) What kind of people do we now sell to? What kind of people should we sell to?
(*iii*) How do these people think, feel, and believe our product, our organisation and our competition?
(*iv*) What do we want these people to think, feel and do?
(*v*) Which key thought should we put into the minds of those people to make them feel, think, do and believe the way we want them to?
(*vi*) What tone of voice will get these people hear and believe us?

While developing the message, we must first create a *copy platform* which is a document that guides the creative team. It puts the strategy in writing and considers the prospects of the ad, the appeals to be used, the product features related to consumer needs, the media used and finally the style or approach or tone of the communication. While strategy describes the direction a message should take, a big idea infuses life in it. The *big idea* is a bold creative initiative. It relates product benefit with consumer needs in an original way. It synthesizes the purposes of strategy. It compels the readers or audience 'to stop, look and listen.'

Message Presentation

Messages are to be structured keeping the objective of the communication and the audience in view. Messages are presented either centrally or peripherally. A central message takes a direct route to persuasion. It is a well-documented ad. It compares advantages and disadvantages of a product. This central presentation provokes active cognitive information processing. Voltas refrigerators incorporating rational appeals is an example. These ads are consistent with the self-image of the respondents.

Peripheral presentation provides pleasant association, scenic background, favourable inferences about the product.

These are distinct, rational and emotional appeal ads. The rational ads appeal to logic, give straightforward facts and figures. The emotional appeal ads, make use emotional and symbolic clues, e.g., an ad for a fire extinguisher. It is seen however that most ads are a blend of rational and emotional message. This has been discussed again in detail in the subsequent chapter on appeals.

Advertising Message Structure

Advertising communication effectiveness not only depends on the message content, though it is no doubt an important component, but on its structure as well. The important aspects of message structure are: Drawing conclusions, repetition, one-versus-two-sided arguments, and the order of presentation. We shall discuss them in detail one by one.

(i) Drawing Conclusion: The question often raised is whether definite conclusions should be drawn for the audience in the ad for quick understanding or should they be left to them. In many instances, it is best to let the receivers of the promotion message draw their own conclusions. Such consumers feel that the message which draws a conclusion is over-aggressive and an attempt at forcefully influencing their choice. Moreover, since conclusion drawing at best assists in an easy comprehension of facts and not in the process of attitudinal change, it will not affect very much the persuasive quality of ads which aim at a change in attitude. When the issue involved is simple and the audience is intelligent, to draw a conclusion will be merely to attempt to explain that which is obvious. It does not add anything extra to the persuasive quality of the advertisement. Moreover, if the communicator is perceived to be unworthy, the receiver may resent the attempt on his part to draw a conclusion for him and influence his choice.

When the issue is highly personal, the audience may resent the communicator's interference in drawing a conclusion. A typical example of this is the recent ad campaign sponsored by the Poultry-Farm Association in Gujarat, promoting the use of eggs among vegetarians. Eggs from the poultry farms were given a new name the "Veggs" and recommended for consumption in that segment of society which is fully vegetarian. Since this touches a highly personal issue concerning religious attitudes, the ad was resented, and much criticism was published against it in the Reader's Opinion column in popular dailies. Thus, even though promoters sought the sale of the product in a new segment by drawing specific conclusions, these were not accepted, but rather resented. However, conclusion drawing is favoured where the product is a complex or specialised one. The Farex baby food ad, starting with a sensational headline: "Your baby is born with a 3-month gift of iron. After 3 months, milk alone cannot give him the iron he needs." The ad closes with the conclusion: "Doctors recommend Farex. Baby's ideal solid food for rapid all-round growth." A long body copy goes on to explain that Farex is ideal baby solid food.

(*ii*) *Repetition:* Repeating an ad message is often beneficial, for it develops a continuity of impression in the minds of the target audience, and may increase the predisposition to think and act favourably towards the products advertised. Everything else being equal, a repeated message increases awareness and knowledge on the part of the prospect. Audience retention improves with repetition, and falls off quickly when repetition is abandoned. The relationship of repetition and advertising effectiveness has been dealt with in detail in the chapter on "Advertising Effectiveness."

(*iii*) *One-versus-two-sided Communication:* This raises the question whether the advertiser should only praise the product or should also mention some of its shortcomings. The most common approach in sales and advertising is a one-sided approach. However, on deep analysis, it is found that one-sided messages tend to work best with the audiences which is initially favourably predisposed to the claims made in the ad message. Two-sided arguments go well when audiences have an unfavourable opinion about the communicator's position. Also, a two-sided message tends to be more effective with educated audiences capable of sound reasoning, particularly when they are exposed to counter propaganda. A two-sided communication produces the greatest attitude change when people are opposed to the point of view presented. Also, a two-sided communication is effective in maintaining the belief level against a counter-attack by competitors. However, it is the single-side communication which is commonly used, for it is difficult for the advertiser to refer to the product's shortcomings and still effectively persuade prospects to buy it.

(*iv*) *Comparative Advantage:* Here a product is directly or indirectly compared with a competitive product to show the advertised product to advantage. This trend has been seen more and more in some recent compaigns, especially when new brands in parallel categories are springing up at a rapid rate. Most prominent among these have been the Pepsi, Savlon, and Captain Cook campaigns. The recent Rin-and-a-look-alike-Ariel compaign is also a pointer. Pepsi was branded by Thums Up as gulab-jamun-like or cough-syrup like or as a drink kept out in the rain. When Coke took over Thums Up, Pepsi retaliated by calling it Thoke. There are hits and counterhits in this game. Captain Cook, the free-flowing salt has been compared to Tata salt which is moist enough to stick. In fact, Captain Cook has translated its technological superiority into product superiority. Whisper sanitary napkins have also been introduced on comparative grounds of absorbence. The ultimate aim here is to create brand distinction. While doing so, the competitive product should not be denigrated. Besides, there is no end to competitive advertising. Coke is following a simple rule. The No. 1 brand should never compare itself to No. 2. Instead, compare ads are usually a tool for a smaller brand trying to build business. Continued warfare in ads gets boring for consumers.

Message Format

Message format an important step in message development. By format, we mean the organisation, plan, style or type of ad message. The message format is the scheme by which the message content and structure strategy are implemented. It is characterised by the type of media vehicle in which the message is delivered. In a print ad, the message format elements are headline, body copy, illustration and colour, whereas, in radio advertising, the format elements are words, voice qualities (speech rate, rhythm, pitch, articulation) and vocalization (pauses, sighs, yawns). The message format is important because a good message strategy may not click if it is put in a poor format. The message format for a print ad includes such things as the position of the headline, the position of the picture or illustration, the colour scheme, the size of the letters in the headline and the body of the message. Let us briefly discuss the scope of the concept of message development.

Message Development

There are so many media that carry the ad messages. There are so many products which are advertised in these media. A number of companies advertise their products. We have therefore a lot of communication in all directions — direct, indirect, zigzag and all-sided. Perhaps, there is over-communication. This leads us to the concept of clutter, and how to overcome it.

ADVERTISING APPEALS

Advertising has become expensive, time-consuming and an important marketing activity. Firms have a great stake in the success of their advertising campaigns, for their growth and, at times, even their survival, depend on it. A vast amount of time, money and energy go into the creative work of developing advertising appeals to influence the buying behaviour of consumers. Through various appeals, advertising influence, rationally or emotionally, the prospects' purchase decisions. For this purpose, they take the help of varying product features or attributes in their ad appeals, or seek to influence consumer perception of, and changes in consumer attitude to, the advertised product or brand. Ad appeals may be product-oriented or consumer-oriented. Since there is a large number of such ad appeals, it would be difficult to discuss them all. It would, therefore, be helpful to devise a framework for classifying advertising appeals.

Human Needs as Basis for Appeals

The basic concepts in marketing tell us that it is all about satisfying consumer wants and needs. Product and services are offered by the marketer to satisfy one need or the other. Most of the time, needs are well known; but sometimes it is the marketer who creates consumer demand. This is what we call creative marketing. Ultimately, all advertising appeals are created for the purpose of activating human needs and wants, and showing how the advertised brand can satisfy those needs and wants. The advertiser has to determine the needs at which the advertising message should be directed. Though it looks simple, it is, in fact, very difficult to arrive at the right human needs or wants which would be the basis for ad appeals. Psychologists themselves do not seem to agree upon what constitutes a set of basic human needs. However, there are some generally accepted standard lists of need structure, which provide some guidelines to the marketer for developing advertising appeals. The most popular and widely accepted need scheme is the one given by A.H. Maslow. Maslow's basic human need structure states five levels hierarchically. They are:

(*i*) *Physiological Needs or Creature Comforts (Hunger, Thirst, Sex, etc.):* These are biological needs, such as food, water, sleep, and so on, and are the most potent of all human needs. These are therefore placed at the first level of the hierarchy.

(*ii*) *Safety Needs (Security, Protection, etc.):* These are based on the needs for physical safety and security, and stress such things as preference of the familiar to the unfamiliar and for the known to the unknown.

(iii) *Love Needs (Affection, Belongingness, etc.):* These needs are atleast partially fulfilled by marriage, parenthood and belonging to organisations, such as the Rotary, Lions and others.

(iv) *Esteem Needs (Self-Respect, Prestige, Social Approval, Achievement, etc.):* As love needs become atleast partially satisfied, the need for such things as prestige, self-respect, esteem and status emerge. The desire for achievement, independence and self-confidence are also part of these needs.

(v) *Self-Actualization Needs (Self-Fulfilment, Self-Experience, etc.):* The desire for self-fulfilment, or becoming everything one is capable of becoming, is the essence of these needs. Included in them are aesthetic satisfaction, acquiring knowledge, and so on.

Maslow states that each "higher" need dominates the organism as the lower ones become satisfied or nearly (sufficiently) satisfied. A person who has basically satisfied his physiological and safety needs will become concerned about the satisfaction of progressively higher level needs (love, esteem, self-actualization). One of these five stages is always prepotent, even though the needs at other stages are still influential; that is, some needs from all the five stages may operate on an individual at the time that one stage is dominant. An important point to remember is that a consumer does have to satisfy one class of needs completely before progressing to other classes.

Taking a closer look at the human needs, we find that physiological needs are the most basic of the five basic needs structure of Maslow. The need for food and water is so essential that, without its satisfaction, life would cease to exist. An individual is first concerned about the satisfaction of his food, water, sleep, and other biological needs. In a society where basic physiological needs are not fulfilled, advertisers of food and related products have to depict them as a better way of satisfying the hunger needs. In contrast to this, where most people in a society have this need satisfied, the advertiser should depict the food item as one which can help to satisfy a higher-level need, i.e., love or esteem, for example. Once the physiological needs have been largely satisfied, every human being is concerned with the next level of his needs, i.e., safety needs. When these two basic needs have been largely satisfied, he is free from constant fear for his safety, health and security. Advertising of food products for the satisfaction of the needs of hunger is hardly necessary. However, advertising for economical housing societies, life insurance policies, cheaper but nutritious food, healthy drinking water and promotion of sanitary living conditions — these would still be relevant to our society.

Next to the safety needs come love needs. Every individual, whose first two levels of needs have been fairly satisfied, will seek to love and would like to be loved by others. Love, here, is not to be construed as synonymous with the physiological sense. Sex involves both physiological and psychological gratification. Sex is often used in advertising as a means of satisfying both physiological and love needs. Advertisers have made an extensive use of sex appeals in their advertising. However, these appeals are aimed at the satisfaction of the love need (affection).

Esteem needs are of two types: one, those which are related to how a person sees himself reflected in his personal achievement and self-confidence; and, second, those which are related to how, he believes, others see him. How others see him is reflected in the attention and recognition he receives from others as well as his reputation and prestige among other people. Suitings ads of Vimal, Dinesh and Digjam aim at increasing the self-confidence of the user. The jewellery ads of Tribhovandas in Mumbai stress the prestige you can enjoy by using such expensive jewellery. Advertising of any product which can increase the self-confidence and self-worth of those who use it makes this appeal — the satisfaction of the self-esteem need. Many ads use the prestige appeal which the user of such advertised products will enjoy.

Maslow's hierarchy of the need structure is the most widely accepted list of basic needs, a detailed knowledge of which is necessary for any advertiser. However, others have also given their own classification. Combs and Snygg are of the opinion that there is only one basic need — the need for maintaining or enhancing one's self concept. Berelson and Stenier have given a list of primary and secondary human needs. The primary needs are physiological ones based on the biological functioning of every human being. The secondary needs, according to them, are those which are acquired or learnt, and are not necessary for the basic biological functioning of an individual. The primary needs include:

(*i*) *Supply Motives:* Hunger and thirst.

(*ii*) *Avoidance Motives:* Avoidance of pain, fear, harm and other negative consequences.

(*iii*) *Species-maintaining Motives:* Reproduction, mating and nutritive motives.

The secondary needs include:

(*i*) *Acquired or Learned:* It is believed that secondary needs are learned because of the satisfaction of primary needs. One learns that one can better satisfy one's hunger-and-thirst need by acquiring property and other possessions;

(*ii*) Recognition needs;

(*iii*) Affiliation needs.

The following conclusions may now be drawn:

(*i*) Unsatisfied needs are motivators of behaviour and satisfied needs are not.

(*ii*) Much of human behaviour is motivated by subconscious and unconscious needs. These are needs we do not or cannot consciously admit to ourselves. For example, in one of the ads of "Sir Shirts," it was said: "This is the MAN SIR is made for." A handsome man, together with his lovely girl, is shown in the picture. Man has an unsatisfied (and unconscious) need for exhibiting himself as a "He" man to his sweetheart. Wearing a Sir Shirt is presumably a symbolic way of satisfying this unconscious need.

(*iii*) Generally, several needs operate simultaneously to cause a given behaviour response; but only some needs are more important in bahaviour than others. These "key" needs should be identified and appealed to, directly and indirectly in the advertising message.

Buying Motives

We have already seen that needs motivate us. The various buying motives are given here by way of illustration. Essentially, the advertisers appeal to some of these motives or needs in their ad message.

Different kinds of motives encourage people to certain goals. All of man's actions are guided by his cognition, i.e., his apprehension, his awareness and his anticipation. When we ask a question: Why do people buy? We are in reality asking the question of motivation of buying. Motivation is thus concerned with the why of human behaviour. Motives arouse and maintain activity and determine the general direction of behaviour of an individual. In essence motives or needs are the mainsprings of action. Need or motive is something in an individual that prompts him to action. The following are the important buying motives:

Unconscious Motivation: Freud invited our attention to the unconscious motivation. People are not really aware of everything they want, that they will often have tastes, biases or attitudes which strongly influence their buying behaviour. But they really cannot account for it.

Power Motive: Power is a very strong motivator. We buy many things so that we can exercise power over others.

Competence Motives: We have a desire to have job mastery and professional advancement. So a doctor buys many equipments according to competence motive.

Affiliation Motive: Man is a sociable creature. We seek the company of others to gain some impersonal reward. The desire to be with other people for its own pleasure is also known. In many life-style advertising of products like cigarettes and soft drinks, we make use of affiliation motive.

Security Needs: Investments decisions, medicines, insurance policies etc. are sold on the basis of this need. Hosieries, woollens, umbrellas, rainwear etc. also get purchased against this need. This need is operative both at the conscious and sub-conscious levels. Fear is used as negative appeal to emphasise this motive.

Social Needs or Motives: Needs for belongingness is one powerful motive. We want to be a part of national mainstream. So we wish to buy packaged tours to Singapore, Europe, Nepal, Kashmir and other destinations. We want to be members of Diners Card or BOB Card or Cancard. We want membership of Dynasty Cultural Club or Rotary Club or Lions Club.

Esteem Needs or Motives: These are the motives of distinction, achievement, status and independence. Pride and vanity motives also fall in this category. These, are important buying motives. Automobiles are sometimes bought because they give us social status. All premium products are sold against these motives.

Physiological Needs or Motives: Some of our motives are to survive — we buy food products because of this. We buy houses and flats also to survive. We buy textiles for protection and survival. These are all primary motives of buying.

Comfort and Convenience: Different kinds of furniture, interior decor, footwear, woollens etc., we buy for our comfort. Similarly, calculators and computers make it convenient for us to do our accounts, billings and all such other functions. Kitchen gadgets like grinder-mixers, fridges, cooking ranges etc. are bought against these motives.

Envy: As Shakespeare has put it: 'Envy, thy name is woman.' Women envy the gorgeous dress others wear, the cosmetics others use, the complexion the next-door-neighbour has, and the ornaments the cousins have bought. Men also do not lag behind. Onida Colour T.V. is 'the neighbour's envy, but the owner's pride.' Wardrobes, cosmetics, fashionwear, designer dresses are all sold against this motivation.

Fashion: Fashion over a period of time changes — in dress, in eating, in design, in make-up, in appearance etc. Certain things are considered to be in fashion and in style. Readymade garments, salwar-kurta, trendy tops and tee-shirts are all sold on fashion grounds.

Novelty: Newness itself is a strong buying motive. We now have adopted Odopic washing powder in place of earth or clay, Sanifresh toilet cleaner, Odonil air-freshners — all on the basis of newness. After a time, newness wears off and we search for something else. We formerly applied Odomos as mosquito repellent on the body, but now we say good night to the mosquitoes by using "Goodknight Heater."

Sex and Romance: As it is, sex is a primary need, like the hunger and thirst. Most of the personal care products, toiletries, textiles, cigarettes etc. are sold on this basis. Romance is a matter of feeling, a very exotic feeling. Romance could be in imagination also. Tourist destinations, honeymoon packages, jewellery etc. are sold on this basis. Of course, sex and romance are inter-related.

Greed: This motive makes us save and economise. We also like to avail of discount sales, free gifts, price offs, premiums, coupons etc. because of this motive.

Curiosity: This is also a good buying motive. We are interested to know about the known and the unknown things. Books, games, quizes, new tourists destinations, dictionaries, encyclopaedias, self-learning packages etc. are sold on this basis.

The above list is only illustrative, and not exhaustive.

A motive is a state of tension. It activates action towards a goal and sustains it till the goal is reached. Motivation can be conscious or unconcious. Motives make the behaviour of the individuals goal-directed. Of course, the means to achieve the goal may be different, e.g., you may achieve distinction by being a star athlete like Shiny Wilson or an ace gynaecologist like Shirodkar. Motives are inside the individual — a mental state. Buying motives indicate our buying intentions. Maslow has classified human needs (the manifestation of motives) into five categories, as we have already seen.

Appeals and Buying Motives: Both these are closely related concepts. Appeals are cues or provide stimulus. Appeals are made because there are buying motives leading to action. Appeals are developed thus on the basis of buying motives. Lower-priced Nirma has the price appeal, but it incorporates economy motive. Tonics give us energy but they incorporate health appeal. Tribhovandas Bhimji Zaveri gives exquisite jewellery. This beauty appeals to the buying motive of pride or possession.

Appeals and Advertising Message

We have mentioned that the advertising message should appeal, directly or indirectly, to those key needs which influence bahaviour response. Without going into communication theories and models, we shall deal with the message content, its structure and the format to be employed for the formulation of an appropriate message.

The message content refers to what the advertiser has to say to the target audience that will produce the desired response. It may be an appeal, a time, an idea or a unique selling proposition. In fact, the message content ultimately formulates some kind of benefit, motive or reason why the audience should respond to, or do, something.

Types of Appeals

Appeals are broadly classified as rational, emotional and moral appeals. *Rational appeals* are those directed at the thinking process of the audience. They involve some sort of a deliberate reasoning process, which a person believes would be acceptable to other members of his social group. They attempt to show that the product would yield the expected functional benefit. Although there may be some disagreement regarding which motives are rational and which are emotional, the following are some buying motives which are normally considered rational under ordinary circumstances:

(*i*) *High Quality:* People buy television, stereophonic music systems, furniture, refrigerators, electric gadgets; kitchenware and a host of consumer durables for their high quality. Many consumer goods, too, are bought for their quality, such as clothing, beverages, food items, etc., and not merely because of their taste or fashion, or style.

(*ii*) *Low Price:* Many people buy low-priced locally made air conditioners for their homes because they believe that these products will show a product performance similar to, or slightly inferior to, that of nationally reputed brands at higher price. Whether this is true or not, a person, as long he believes this to be true, thinks his reason will be accepted as a "good" one by his social group. In this case, he is exhibiting a rational motive.

(iii) *Long Life,* as of a car tyre that will give 30,000 kms, before its utility has been exhausted.

(iv) *Performance,* as of a ball-point pen that won't release excessive ink or skip under any circumstances.

(v) *Ease of use,* as of a screwdriver with a magnetised tip which clings to the metal head of the screw. Or a timer in the kitchen mixer which switches off automatically after a predetermind time period.

(vi) *Re-sale value,* as of a two-wheeler scooter. "Bajaj" has a better re-sale value than any other make.

(vii) *Economy* in the operating expenses of some brands of refrigerator is greater because they consume less electricity. Many two-wheeler vehicles claim a better mileage per litre consumption of fuel than similar other vehicles.

Industrial buyers are most responsive to rational appeals. They make purchase decisions in line with the technical specification of the product, product quality, etc. Most industrial buyers are knowledgeable about the product class, trained to recognise value and are responsible to others about their choice. Often, industrial buying decisions are made after a thorough comparison of various offers and after evaluating the various benefits of different makes. Consumer durables of high value are also often bought on the basis of rational appeals.

People are ready and willing to give rational motives if asked why they have made a particular purchase. Even when decisions are made on emotional grounds, people like to rationalise their decision to show that they are based on sound rational grounds. Most of us want others to regard us as rational human beings. That is why we like to give socially acceptable reasons for our buying decisions. We feel that rational motives will raise our status in the eyes of our associates and colleagues.

Emotional appeals are those appeals which are not preceded by careful analysis of the pros and cons of making a buying. Emotions are those mental agitations or excited states of feeling which prompt us to make a purchase. Emotional motives may be below the level of consciousness, and may not be recognised by a person; or even if he is fully aware that such a motive is operating, he is unwilling to admit it to others because he feels that it would be unacceptable as a "proper" reason for buying among his associates and colleagues.

Emotional appeals are designed to stir up some negative or positive emotions which will motivate product interest or purchase. Different emotional appeals, which are particularly important from the advertising point of view, are listed below. Following several motivation research studies, it has been found that negative emotional appeals are more effective than positive ones. We shall also, therefore, name the negative appeals first.

Negative Emotional Appeals: An advertiser may try to induce a particular behavioural change by emphasising either positive or negative appeals, or a combination of both. For example, an advertising campaign to get the target audience to buy fire insurance may stresss the positive aspect — low cost relative to other investment, the services the insurance company provides, early settlement of claims, and so on; or it may stress the negative aspect of not getting insurance — the danger of losing one's possessions or the ravages of fire. Positive appeals use the strategy of "reducing" a person's anxiety about "buying and using" a product, while negative appeals use the strategy of "increasing" a person's anxiety about "not using" a product or service. In general, a positive appeal stresses the positive gains to a person from complying with the persuasive message; the negative appeal stresses his loss if he fails to comply.

We give here the different dimensions of emotional appeals.

EMOTIONAL APPEALS: RESPONSE CATEGORIES

Dimension of response to emotional appeal	*Illustration*
Feelings of an up-beat mood evoked by music, humour and other such ad elements	Celebrate with Asian Paints Home Coming' Compaign.
Feelings of quiet and relaxed pleasantness used in cosmetic commercials bringing out sensuousness	'Lakme — she's a woman to me' campaign.
Feelings of heart-warming and tenderness	Cadbury's 'Mother-son' commercial.
Feelings of motivational, appetite desire to buy or consume the advertised brand/category	Food ads.

Apart from the above four categories, the emotional roles the products play in Indian context also affect the response.

Role category of the product	*Details*	*Example*
Background	Normal part of the scene Necessary to set the stage on which important things in life occur associated with emotion-laden events like marriage	Room furnishings, accessories, most appliances storwel cupboard of Godrej.
Mediator to interactions	Product necessary for interaction to occur	Cameras Souvenirs of events which enable reconstruction of these events (VIP luggage campaign Kal bhi, Aaj bhi, Kal bhi). Restaurant scene of Titan watch ad. Husband gifts the watch to his wife. The symbol of warmth is the watch. The interactive has heightened. Background music plays an important part.

Expression of Self	—	Clothes, apparel and accessory categories. Reminders of self-esteem. Raymond's 'complete man' campaign. Sharmila Tagore and Pataudi in Gwalior suitings campaign.
Products themselves become objects of emotion	High product involvement object becomes a substitute for human relations.	'Hamara Bajaj' campaign.

Precautions while using the emotional route:

1. The advertising should have relevance. If the product needs attribute-based rational advertising, emotional appeals should be avoided.
2. There should be a natural flow of feelings.
3. Execution should not be exaggerated. The level of emotionality should not exceed that experienced by the consumer.
4. There is a difference between a consumer's emotions associated with the product/brand and a consumer's emotional reaction to the ad copy itself. Preferably, these two should be compatible.

Emotional Magic

Shivajeet Kullar of Contract is all praise for Rath Vanaspati film which takes an emotional route. In this film, parents are shown cooing over a little baby in a crib. The sibling rivalry affects his brother watching the parents do this. He goes off and sits at the bottom of stairs. There is a feeling of being left out. He is hurt. He is angry too. But mum has caught on. She cooks up a little treat in Rath Vanaspati and takes it across to him. Slowly, he smiles. He recognises the fact that he is loved after all. It gives a sense of involvement.

In Telco film, a little boy is shown going to a school for the first time in a bus, feeling lonely and a little frightened too. He nervously watches other two boys playing with a toy. They notice this new-comer. He looks back wide-eyed. One of the boys spontaneously offers him the toy. At the end of the journey, they help him to get down from the (Telco) bus. They rush to school together.

This is emotional magic at work. It works powerfully. It works in an enduring fashion. Fear appeals have been treated at length elsewhere in the book.

Positive Emotional Appeals: Positive appeals highlight product benefits and attributes capable of influencing consumer behaviour. They are love, humour, pride, prestige and joy. Most baby food products have a mother's love appeal. Love for family is perfectly employed in an ad of Dettol soap which has been called "The Love & Care Soap." In the closing sentense, the ad appeals by saying: "Give your family the Loving Care of Dettol Soap." Mother's love for the baby has been appealed to in ad of Johnson's baby soap. It says: "Gentle as a kiss on your baby's tender skin." It further goes on to say: "Johnson's Baby Soap. Because Johnson & Johnson care for your baby almost as much as you do." Is this positive appeal not effective, when the advertiser shows as much care for a child as its mother does?

Advertisers have also successfully used messages communicating the joy and thrill (all those soft drink ads) associated with using the product. A humorous message attracts more attention and creates more liking and belief in the source, though it reduces comprehension. David Ogilvy, a well-known personality in the advertising profession, believes that humour has been over-used: "People are amused by clowns — they don't buy from them .... So many people in advertising are compulsive entertainers who seek applause rather than sales."

Other positive emotional appeals involving price, prestige or exclusiveness are often used in ads of suitings. Advertisements of suitings by Raymonds, Digjam, Dinesh etc., employ emotional motives. "Suitings for the Connoisseur," a Digjam ad campaign, is an example of appealing to those individuals who are experts in matters of taste and choice of clothing. Other emotional motives are illustrated in the following list:

(*i*) *Desire to be different,* as illustrated by people who build an ultra modern home in an area of traditional homes.

(*ii*) *Desire to conform,* as in the case of teenage boys and girls who want to be "in jeans" because all their friends wear jeans.

(*iii*) *Desire to attract the opposite sex,* as shown by a teenage girl who buys a new cosmetic in order to make her skin more beautiful.

(*iv*) *Desire for prestige,* as shown by a person who buys the most expensive automobile (Mercedes, Toyota, etc.) he can afford in order to impress his friends.

In making purchases, many combine both rational and emotional motives. In fact, a blend of buying motives usually is the basis of a purchase. An engineer may take up a management course at any of the prestigious schools because he feels it will make him look important in the eyes of his associates and help him in securing a better job in the industry and business. A woman may want to buy a new home in posh locality because it will improve her family's social status and because it is within walking distance of a good school for her children.

Moral appeals are those appeals to the audience which appeal to their sense of right and wrong. These are often used in messages to arouse a favourable response to social causes, such as prohibition, adult literacy, social forestry, anti-smuggling and hoarding, consumer protection, equal rights for women, social responsibility projects of corporations, rural development, siding weaker sections of society, employment generation, and so on. There are messages which appeal for generous donations for flood victims and for famine relief operations — these are often based on moral appeals. Many commercial advertisements are criticised on moral grounds. The most controversial ad campaigns are by multinational companies marketing baby food products. Many WHO experts are critical of these corporations which promote bottle feeding against breast feeding.

Sex Appeals in Advertising: Sex appeal is being increasingly used in Indian advertising to overcome the culture in the print as well as broadcast media and to grab attention. Sex appeals in contraceptive ads have become explicit, and are more visual than verbal. Does sex really sell? Or is it a negative influence on consumer? The answer is not either affirmative or negative for these questions, and depends upon a number of factors.

Effectiveness of ads is measured in terms of the objectives — creating awareness may be the objective, and then brand recall is a measure of effectiveness. The advertising objective may be to make the consumer buy — here buying intention is a measure of effectiveness. The following summarise the research studies in this context.

Research shows that non-sexual illustrations are more effective than sexual ones while undergoing brand recall. Men remember the sexy illustration and neglect the brand. Favourably disposed people to the use of sex had a higher brand recall of brand names that used sex appeals in their ads. Negatively inclined people to sex had a lower brand recall.

Research also shows that nude illustrations of female are least appealing, are associated with lowest quality product and least reputable company. Recently Seven's research shows that explicit sex appeals do not interfere with the ability to recall brand names.

It has also been observed that visual which is highly sexual interferes with the congnitive processing of the message since readers tend to spend more time on the ad as a whole. Information transmission is definitely adversely affected by sex appeal.

Functional sex appeals have highest recall and so also symbolism.

Inappropriate sex appeals have lowest recall. Fantasies are also used as sex appeals. Appeal which are consistent with the product lead to a higher recall.

There might be gender-related responses to sex appeal. Females may find the sexual ad offensive and so its use for a female-targeted product runs a risk. A lipstic ad showing a female model which is seductive may grab the attention of the male-audience rather than the targeted female audience.

Connotative sexual appeals like symbolism are more acceptable than explicit appeals.

The sexual appeals are justified in case of products like personal products, panties, bras, undergarments, swim suits. They may not go well with industrial products. The relevance of the appeal to the product is very important.

The manner of sex portrayal, the sex of the models and the target segment also affect the effectiveness of the ad. Blatant references to sex are suddenly the in-thing in American advertising. Marketers promoting perfumes, jeans, alcohols, gloves, watches and cars are resorting to this route. Media clutter may be one reason to the explosion of sexual imagery in advertising. Ads of perfumes have traditionally focused on the sensuous. For Calvin Klein, sex has always been a fovourite selling point.

The late Justice Hidayatullah had ruled that "where obscenity and art are mixed, art must be so prepondering as to throw the obscenity into the shadow." We tend to agree with him. Even an act of kissing has both sexual and non-sexual content. "Of no use to one, yet it is absolute bliss to two. The small boy gets it for nothing, the young man has to steal it and the old man has to buy it. The baby's right, the lover's privilege, the hypocrite's mask. To a young girl, faith; to a married woman, hope and to an old maid; charity."

Sex appeals are interpreted differently from time to time, region to region, person to person, country to country, and society to society. Even the same person reacts to them differently at diffeent stages of his life-cycle.

Do Sex Appeals Work?

Does sex appeal work in advertising? Mahesh Bhatt, who has made some ad films, answers in the affirmative. The benefit of being talked about goes to the product. Roger Pereira says sex may not always work, especially if it is unrelated to the product being promoted. But these days, to stand out in the clutter, it seems a heavy dose of sex is being used. Certain ads are blatant, whereas certain use these appeals subtly. Jitendra, a star with a Casanova image modelled for 30 plus. The ad had an undercurrent of sexuality.

Perhaps, a new permissiveness is sweeping through the country. Most of these ads sell sex and keep product in the background. Often one forgets the product, and remembers the model only. It is a rare ad like Kama Sutra which use sex successfully and with class. We give some examples of complaints received by ASCI for brazen use of sex appeals. Some of these were dismissed and some were upheld.

Some recent complaints which were not upheld by the council:

Product	*Ad*
Sabari tea	It showed a man serving tea to a woman.
Adam condoms	Some were offended by the condom ads. 'Show her who is the boss!'
Kohinoor condoms Kingston cigarettes	Mild sexual overtone was resented. A couple on a beach. The girl was clad in a bikini. The man had a cigarette in his hand.
Leela Kempinski: Leela Beach, Goa	Kiss a pink lady in Rio.
Palmolive Soap	In the TV commercial, Aamir Khan praises the complexion of a woman model.
Amul butter	Love bites.
VIP Champ Briefs	Suggestive / offensive
A. Sirkar (jewellers)	Gold item displayed on naked thigh.

The following complaints were upheld:

(*i*) ad featuring trousers open at the waist. The base line 'The all male place is soon opening up.'

(*ii*) 30-plus ad with the line 'Rediscover the power to perform.'

DIRECT AND INDIRECT APPEALS

This is yet another way of classifying advertising appeals. Ultimately, all ad appeals may be grouped into direct and indirect appeals, depending upon whether they are linked directly or indirectly with consumer needs. Sometimes advertisers are explicit about the need to which they are appealing, whereas, at other times, appeals are veiled or purposely kept ambiguous, and the consumer has to determine the relevance of the appeal to him.

Direct Appeals

Direct appeals are those which clearly communicate with the consumers about a given need, followed by a message which extols the advertised brand as a product which satisfies that need. In Industrial advertising, some ads may have a direct appeal, satsifying the customer's technical need; but, in consumer advertising, the direct appeal plays a very limited role. Examples of direct appeal ads for consumer products are rare. In America, the hamburger was once advertised with the hunger appeal. The ad said: "When you get a man-size hunger, eat a whopper hamburger."

Indirect Appeals

Indirect appeals are those which do not emphasise a human need, but allude to a need. Because advertisers understand the influence of needs upon selective perception, they leave some ambiguity in the message so that the consumers may be free to interpret it and the need to which the advertiser is appealing. Since this interpretation of the consumer is not difficult, there is no risk involved in keeping the ambiguity in the message.

Indirect appeals are either product-oriented or consumer-oriented, or may be a combination of the two. We shall now discuss each one of these indirect appeals in details.

Product-Oriented Indirect Appeals: They are grouped into three classifications:

(*i*) *Feature-oriented Appeals:* The basic message is about product features, characteristics and attributes. Examples: Instant Shine, Cherry shoe polish, "Promise," the unique toothpaste with the time-tested clove oil.

(*ii*) *Use-oriented Appeals:* The basic message emphasises specific in-operation and/or post-operation advantages of the brand advertised. Examples: Anne French hair remover ad: "How much cruelty can a woman's skin bear?" The head-line is a searching question. The ad message discards other methods of hair removing — they are shaving, waxing, and threading. Then it goes on to inform you how gently hair is removed with Anne French. Another example is of Stayfree beltless napkins by Johnson & Johnson. It highlights the fact that there is no need of belts or strings or pins. How convenient it is, taking away all the botherations of women!

(*iii*) *Product Comparison Appeals:* The basic message emphasises the differences between the advertised brand and the competing brands. The advertised brand, of course, has a net advantage over those with which it is compared; otherwise the whole exercise becomes futile. Think of those ads of electric fans, when the product features of various brands are compared in the ad in a tabulated form — such features as the number of poles of the motor, the number of bearings, the price, warranty period offered, etc. A refrigerator advertisement compares the types of compressors used, whether high speed or low speed, electricity consumption, noise level, the quality of the white enamelled body, extra tray, etc.

Consumer-Oriented Indirect Appeals: They are further divided as follows:

(*i*) *Attitude-oriented Appeals:* The basic message is one which is in line with the consumer's attitude — his value — belief structure. Example: The ad series by Shriram group, namely: "Indian Corporate Evolution. The Shriram Experience." In one of the ads, it says: "We are Indians. We must remember our roots." Then it goes on to state the group's belief in Indian traditions and the advantages it shares with the country. This message, refers indirectly to Maslow's esteem need.

(*ii*) *Significant Group-oriented Appeals:* The basic message emphasises the kind of group which uses or approves of the advertised brand. The group may be a reference group, a social group, or a peer group, or any other group which is significant for the consumer target. The ad says: "Some possessions define a character. Some distinguish it. A cigarette so distinguished, it's by appointement to your Majesty."

(*iii*) *Life Style-oriented Appeals:* The basic message emphasises an identifiable life style relevant to a defined target market. Example: An ad of Charminar cigarette making an appeal with its strong taste. For some hard smokers, a "strong" cigarette can only give relaxation, particularly after a day's hardwork. One needs a Charminar.

(*iv*) *Sub-conscious-oriented Appeals:* The basic message is distinguished and is directed at the consumer's sub-conscious (or unconscious) need. These messages are aimed at the buyer's dream world, but are veiled in some manner by messages appealing to the buyer's conscious mind. Example: 'Petals' brassiers of VIP are advertised with a dreamy message: "As you flower into a woman, you discover the epitome of international fashion. Discover Petals."

(*v*) *Image-oriented Appeals:* Although all advertising appeals create a brand image in the minds of consumers, the image-oriented approach is distinct in the sense that here the advertiser, consciously and purposefully, makes an effort to mould a brand image. There is an intention to create a specific brand image. One strategy in to create a brand image which "fits" either the self-image or self-ideal image of the target market.

Essentials of an Advertisement Appeal

(*i*) It must be thematically sound.
(*ii*) It must be communicative.
(*iii*) It must be interesting.
(*iv*) It must have credibility.
(*v*) It must have finality and be complete.
(*vi*) It must contain truthful information.

Selling Points and Appeals

Selling points are those product attributes which are listed in the advertisement copy to impress upon the consumer the significance of a product to him. They could be specifications, quality statements, composition statements, descriptive or narrative or performance statements. Some selling points are primary selling points and the rest are subsidiary selling points. Selling points in order to be effective must have the force to appeal to a particular buying motive. ***Limca*** is advertised as the thirst drink (selling point), which appeals to your biological needs or motives. ***Campa Cola*** is offered as fun drink like ***Coke*** (*Har Mousamme Rang, Coca Cola ke Sang*) thus appealing to your psychological motives or needs. So selling points successfully touch upon the buying motives.

CASE : BATHROOMS: WHAT DO THEY STAND FOR?

Parryware's ad elevate bathrooms to glamour rooms which they really are. In the West, it is the most private and personal place. The spectrum of human life plays out here. It is caught at its most naked and intimate. Bathrooms in the movies are metaphorical locations. They are enamelled substitute wombs — all warm protective water and distorted sound. The bath signals soft-focus feminity. The glamour room is a fantasy of marble and gold filigree — a leisure place to linger in. The erotic power of woman is indicated by wet shoulders, smooth legs, bursting busts. Men taking bath suggest waning potency. The racy use of split-screen to meld the tubs is the highlight of *Pillow Talk.* In movies, it is shown as a place where most accidents occur, next to the kitchen. A lot of bathwater has undergone since Rock Hudson and Doris Day played in the tub in 1959. Sharone Stone's bathroom in *Silver* is a world in itself.

MOVIES FEATURING BATHROOMS

Movie	*Details*
Shoot and Moon	Dina Keaton surrenders to her demons as she soaks
Dennis	Five her old hero calms down in the tub. Enjoys bubbles.
Mr. Blandings Build his Dream House North Deallas Forty Dave	Real men take showers.
Charade	Fully clothed man.
Male and Female	Gloria Swanson hinting at her sunken assets below the water-line
Night without Armour	Marlene Dietrich in (birthday) suit — undraped.
The Women	Joan Crawford in undraped condition.
The Seven Year Itch	Marilyn Monroe in undraped condition
Harlow	Carroll Banker in undraped condition.
Cleopatra	Elizabeth Taylor in undraped condition.
Last Tango in Paris	Maria in undraped condition.
Leolo	Grandfather is stimulated by tap.
Psycho	A man dressed as a woman attacks a woman.
Psycho 3	Bath bound heroine Survives an attack
Squirm	Worms through the shower.
Night Kill	Boiling hot water.
Death Island	Water is replaced by acid.
St. Elmo's Fire A View to Kill Cocoon	Water sports.
Pillow Talk (1959)	Rock Hudson and Doris Day do a screen first split-screen melding of their tubs.
The Owl and Pussycat A Star is Born	Dive in.
About Last Night	Waves of hero/heroine.
Fatal Attraction	Blood-stained walls.
Sleeping with the Enemy	After-the-bath violation.
Nightmare on Elm Street	Metal claw between heroine who is asleep breaks the surface between her legs.
Look Who is Talking To Curtains La Fantome de la liberte	Bathroom humour.
Silver Bathroom Intimacies	Offensive bathroom world.

We would like students to understand the communicational possibilities of different objects. You can as well imagine how a lamp, a garden, a flower, a necklace can be used as potential communicators.

Semiotics

Semiotics deserve a mention in advertising and consumer behaviour texts. It is derived from the Greek word for sign. Derivation includes semantics and semaphore. It is the study of how symbols and symbol systems are used in the transfer of messages, verbal and non-verbal, and the codes and contexts that determine their meaning. Semiotics began to evolve into its present form in the early 20th century. The apprehension of meaning of words goes into the cultural and semantic context.

Indian advertising is conceptually western-leaning and the language used is English. The saving grace is of course the universalisation pop culture. Even then, many symbols and motifs are beyond the understanding of a big section of the masses. Some visible changes may well serve as bridges between cultures (the use of Hindi phrases instead of the French and Italian expressions).

Semiotics has expanded to include any system of signs, images, musical sounds, gestures, objects and complex associations of these as understood by different generations. The 'credibility gap' may well be the 'meaning gap'. Advertising practioners may as well study this discipline.

APPENDIX

Attention

Introduction

— Our sense organs are constantly being bombarded by stimuli.

— It is not possible for us to concentrate on all these stimuli.

— Therefore, we select and attend to only some of them.

— Thus, attention involves a process of *selection*.

Characteristics of Attention

(1) Attention involves a vivid awareness of sensation. When a person's attention is focussed on something, he is aware of the sensation and perceives the stimulus [artist pays attention to painting, he notices all details].

(2) Attention is no active behaviour and not a passive process. In order to pay attention to something, the person must be active and makes an effort. It is not automatic.

(3) Attention divides our field of experience into a focus and a margin. Those events or stimuli that we perceive clearly or attend to are at the focus as they stand out from the background. Other stimuli of which we are only vaguely aware of are at the margin of attention. Still other stimuli of which we are unaware or unconscious of are outside our field of attention. [transfer to a camera: main object focus, others in background, those at the back of the camera]

(4) Attention also shifts, what was in the focus can move into the margin of attention and vice versa. [e.g., - In a movie theatre, couple quarrels]

(5) Certain bodily adjustments are made when attending to a particular stimulus.

(1) Our bodily posture changes; we turn to the source of the stimulus.

(2) The involved sense organs fixes on the stimulus.

For example, leaning forward to hear/look at the object of attention. [e.g.: cat watching a rat hole] Muscles are tense ⟶ eyes fixed there

There are 3 types of attention:

(1) Voluntary: This requires effort. It is dependent on the individuals interest, past experience, expectations. For example, attention in a lecture, car driver's attention to the traffic ahead, factory supervisor's attention to defective articles.

(2) Habitual Attention: This attention is greatly influenced by the need and interest of the individual. For example, a botanist's attention to plants, designer's to what people wear, mom's to cry of baby, fashionable girl's to Ads, hungry man's to food].

(3) Involuntary Attention: This depends on the nature of the stimulus. The stimulus could be a strong factor that draws the attention of the individual. [*e.g.* One may be listening to an interesting radio programme, but the street fight, police siren, or thunder is bound to claim attention.]

Span of Attention

- It is the number of unconnected items that a person can attend to in a single act of attention.
- Children have a shorter span than adults.
- The initial experiments were done by WILIAM HAMILTON and by GEORGE MILLER.
- According to George Miller, our digit span is 7 ± 2. The time an individual can pay attention to without being distracted is 20 minutes.
- In experiments simple objects, letters and numbers are flashed on a screen for less than a second, the subject reports how many he can see.

Span of Apprehension

- It is the amount of information a person can obtain in a single act of attention.
- Items that are grouped together are likely to be remembered more easily. So span of apprehension ≥ span of attention.
- Words or connected digits are used for testing this.

Fluctuation of Attention

- It is a slight unnoticed shift of attention, our attention is never continuous, it shifts from one aspect to another aspect of the same object or it may move from one object to a new object.
- Sustained attention is when fluctuation occurs within certain limits. Interest helps to sustain attention as in the case of a painter, scientist. For example, a student reading a Text Book shifts his attention from line to line, idea to idea. Yet his attention to the topic is sustained for an hour or so.

Division of Attention

Attention cannot be divided but it is possible to attend to more than one task at a time when

(1) one of the activities is mechanical e.g. eating and reading at the same time.

(2) both activities are not intense e.g. ironing and listening to music.

(3) one can combine both tasks in a simple combination. e.g. playing an instrument and singing.

Experiment by *Hermandez Peon et al.*

Monitoring electrical activity in cat's brain – auditory nerve. Then, they presented a click sound. When presented with a rat, no activity.

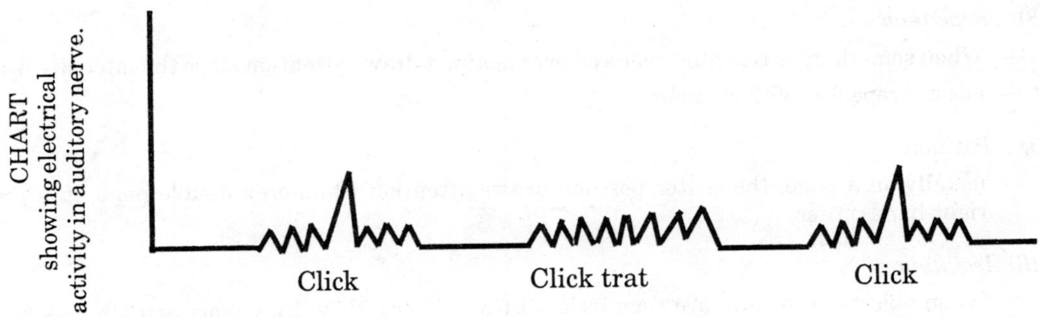

When one sensory channel is activated others are not. The cat was not able to divide attention between both rat and click sound.

[A] DETERMINANTS/FACTORS OF ATTENTION

Stimulus/Objective Factors

(1) Nature of the Stimulus

A visual stimulus is more powerful than an auditory stimulus.

Pictures draw more attention than words.

Also, coloured pictures draw more attention than black and white ones.

(2) *Intensity*

— A strong stimulus is one which is loud or bold. For example, loud sounds, bright colours, strong perfumes.

(3) *Size*

— Usually large stimuli draw more attention than small ones. For example, elephant, full page ads.

(4) *Change*

— When there is some change in the environment, it attracts attention. For example, factory – sounds of machine shop, changing ads.

(5) *Movement*

— A moving stimulus is more likely to draw attention than a stationary one. For example, rat moves in the room.

(6) *Contrast*

— When an object is seen in contrast with another, it is more likely and to be seen than when seen with another similar object. For example, spot on white dress, giant and pigmy, moon on a dark night, white diamond on black velvet

(7) *Novelty*

When something is out of the ordinary, it draws more attention.

— walking on our head

— sky-scraper for a villager.

(8) *Repetition*

— When something is repeated over and over again, it draws attention since the intensity is more.

— ads are repeated with changes.

(9) *Position*

— usually on a page, the center position draws attention while on a double page, it is the top right-hand corner.

(10) *Isolation*

— When objects or stimuli are seen isolated from others, they draw more attention — student sitting in a corner.

[B] OBSERVER/SUBJECTIVE FACTORS

(1) Motives and Needs

A stimulus that satisfies a need within a person has high attention value.

hungry man – food, youth – girl, sickman – dispensary

(2) Mental Set/Expectancy

It is the mental readiness and expectancies of a person to notice certain types of stimuli.

→ car driver → mother,

→ supervisor → expecting a friend

(3) Interests

— A person will attend to a stimulus that is interesting to him/her.

— Interests are of two kinds:

(a) Habitual – this kind of interest has been with a person throughout his life, so he reacts to the stimulus out of habit.

→ botanist

→ fashion designer

→ mechanic

(b) Transitory: This interest is temporary and only for a certain phase.

→ when in love

→ wearing a new dress

Distraction

Distraction causes a break in continuous attention. Distractors are factors which tend to break up sustained attention. In distraction, there is a conflict between the stimulus that a person wishes to attend to and the distracting stimulus.

Factors of Distraction

(1) The *degree of similarity* between the distractor and the main task. Sounds when listening to music.

(2) The *strength / intensity* of the distracting stimulus → police siren, sound of thunder.

(3) The extent of interest the individual has in the main task → painter, scientist, poet.

Types of Distractors

(1) External – These are stimuli in the environment.

(2) Internal – These are distractors within the individual. They are related to the persons thoughts, feelings, drives, etc.

Prevention of Distraction

External distractors can be controlled by two ways:

(1) Eliminating the distractor.

(2) Getting adapted to the distracting stimulus.

Internal distractors can be controlled by two ways:

(1) Concentrating more on the main task.

(2) Generating more interest in the task.

For examination, analyze an ad with reference to its factors of attention.

❑ ❑ ❑

10

GROUP INFLUENCES AND CONSUMER REFERENCE GROUPS

So far we have considered only the individual factors influencing a consumer. However, a consumer is not an island. He interacts with others, say his family or living group, his school or college-mates, his work group, his neighbours and a host of strangers. If your wife just casually remarks about the smart shirt you are wearing, it influences your purchase decision far more than a high-budget ad campaign of the company. The same applies to the remarks passed by our colleagues, friends and neighbours. We shall learn in this chapter how we get influenced by others and how we influence others.

Groups

A group is not any haphazard collection of people. Spectators watching a cricket match are just an aggregate collection. A group is defined as two or more people who interact to accomplish either individual or mutual goals. If we take our neighbours for a shopping spree, we are going as a group. A co-operative society which manages the affairs of our building is a formal group. We live together to attain our individual as well as common goals. In a group, people bear an explicit psychological relationship to each other. One student in Poona university and another in Mumbai University do not have any psychological relationship, and thus they are not members of a group. A group has persons who are interdependent. This influences their behaviour. As members of the group, they share an ideology, *i.e.,* a set of beliefs, values and norms. This affects their conduct.

Each group has a unique ideology. It distinguishes it from other groups. We come across religious groups, fan clubs, friendship circles, professional groups, cricket elevens and political collections. In a larger organisation, girls may form an informal group. There may be several cliques operating within an organisation.

When several groups form a larger collection, we get a *social organisation* such as a manufacturing plant which itself consists of smaller groups like officers' associations, supervisors' club, and a labour union.

Types of Groups

Groups can be classified on the basis of several criteria like the structure of the group, hierarchy in the group, membership or size. Though size is an important criteria, the largeness or smallness are relative concepts. When a person happens to know only a few from the members of the group, the group can be considered a large group. Sometimes our knowledge regarding the activities or roles of members is limited to a few members. As against this, in a small group, everyone knows everyone else and is aware of what others are doing. In consumer behaviour, we deal with such small groups because these very groups affect the buying behaviour of their members.

A *primary group* is one with which a person interacts regularly *e.g.,* a family. A *secondary group* is one with which a person interacts occasionally. A *formal group* is one where the structure of the group together with the roles of members and their goals are well defined. A housing co-operative society or employee's union is a formal group. A loosely defined group is called *informal group* e.g., a group of neighbours. *Membership groups* like a Pharmacist Association shows a member belongs to that group on the basis of eligibility criteria. A *symbolic group* does not offer formal membership, though a person acts like a member by accepting its norms. To an amateur cricketer, a professional cricket team is a symbolic group.

In consumer behaviour, our interest is focused on small, informal, primary groups since they influence the buyer behaviour most.

Consumer-Relevant Groups

Some specific groups exert a great influence on consumer behaviour *e.g.,* family, friends, social groups, work groups and shopping groups.

We shall study the influence of family in the next chapter. A family as an institution has the greatest effect on our buying behaviour. Next comes the *friendship group* which is an informal group. Affiliation motive encourages us to associate with people. It provides us sense of security. Camaraderie works in favour of our emotional fulfilment. It adds to our maturity since we establish an independent relationship outside the family fold. What our friends choose and prefer by way of products influences us in our own product choice. We come across many ads in which a friendship situation has been used. We arrive at a purchase decision by seeking the opinion of those friends with whom we share a common outlook. *Formal social groups* like Lion's club have influence of the buying behaviour, because members of such groups informally discuss products, services and distribution outlets. Another major influence is exercised by the *work group* as we spend considerable time on the job. In a formal work group, the relationships affect the consumption attitudes and activities of the members. Informal work groups, say a group of girls working in a bank, influence the consumption pattern on account of their interactions during the breaks, intervals and after-office hour meetings. *Shopping groups* are groups people who shop together. They are extensions of either the family or friends. Shopping groups provides a sense of reduced risk to the members as buying becomes a group decision. Besides, the congenial atmosphere in the preferred company is conducive to buying.

Structure and Function

A group survives if it fulfils some important functions for the individual. Family is an involuntary group. It is the first group in the process of socialisation. It provides biological maintenance. It gives a sense of belonging and identity to the individual. This generates a sense of physical and psychological security. A group also performs some secondary functions apart from its primary functions. A college is not just for imparting education. It is a place for meeting others, and establishing contacts with the opposite gender. A college enhances our social status and improves our employability. A group thus fulfils several needs and different groups fulfil different needs. This leads to the necessity of belonging to several groups. Each group influences our behaviour in its own way.

Conformity to the Group

A group always exercises pressure on an individual so that he falls in line with the group norms. In a voluntary group, he is free to leave the group if he is not in agreement with the group norms. A group has some mechanism to ward off non-conforming behaviour — sanctions or enforcing agents. A social group may indulge in gossip about a non-conforming member or may ridicule him. A community can ex-communicate him. A military organisation may resort to a court-martial.

In several studies, if has been observed that group influences consumption. In Venkatesan's study of suit selection and Wellerman's study of switch over from white bread to whole wheat bread, group did influence the consumption.

Reference Groups

A man is a social animal. He seeks the company of others to become aware, to protect himself and to enhance his identity. There is a tendency to evaluate himself either through non-social means or by comparing himself with the opinions and abilities of others.

The concept of a reference group was put forward by Herbert Hyman. A reference group, as the name itself suggests, is that group which a man uses as a *point of reference* so as to arrive at his own judgement preferences and beliefs. A reference group can be a single individual though the term group then becomes redundant. Generally, it is a group that serves as a point of comparison or reference for an individual to form his attitudes and behaviour. At times the reference group is a large aggregate of persons like a political party.

The concept is valuable because it improves our understanding of how an individual is influenced by other people as far as his consumption beliefs, attitudes and behaviour are concerned.

This concept has three dimensions — it is a *point of comparison.* It determines our own status, which depends on the group used for comparison. We may feel richer when we compare us with lower-classes, and poorer when we compare to the higher classes. Reference groups could be *groups of aspiration,* and we like to imitate their behaviour. There are certain groups whose *perspectives* are assumed by the individual. The very perspective becomes the frame of reference. We see the world through the eyes of this perspective. Though we may like or dislike this group, its perspective is assumed. We in India accept the liberal Western values inspite of our disagreements with them on many points. Perhaps, it is seeings the world through their eyes.

Normative Reference Groups

These reference groups influence our *broadly defined* values and behaviour. A family is thus a normative reference group. It has a role in our food habits, dress habits and shopping habits. It shapes what we call 'good' values.

Comparative Reference Groups

These are benchmarks for *narrowly defined* or specific attitudes or behaviour. We like to do the interior decor of our home just like our neighbour whom we admire. We may choose our car and vacations just like them. Such a group, say our neighbourhood family, is our neighbour whom we admire. We may choose our car and vacations just like them. Such a group, say our neighbourhood family, is then our comparative reference group.

Normative reference groups influence the basic code of behaviour. Comparative reference group has more to do with our specific expressions regarding attitudes and behaviour. These may depend to some extent on the basic values already shaped by the normative groups.

Reference Group Amplified

Over a period of time, the concept of reference group has amplified to accommodate both the groups with which an individual interacts directly and with which he interacts indirectly. Cinema stars, sports celebrities, political heroes, TV stars are some such groups with which we do not have direct face-to-face contract.

A person uses a never broadening variety of *referents* from a single individual to a family to a social class to a nation or culture. The following diagram illustrates this.

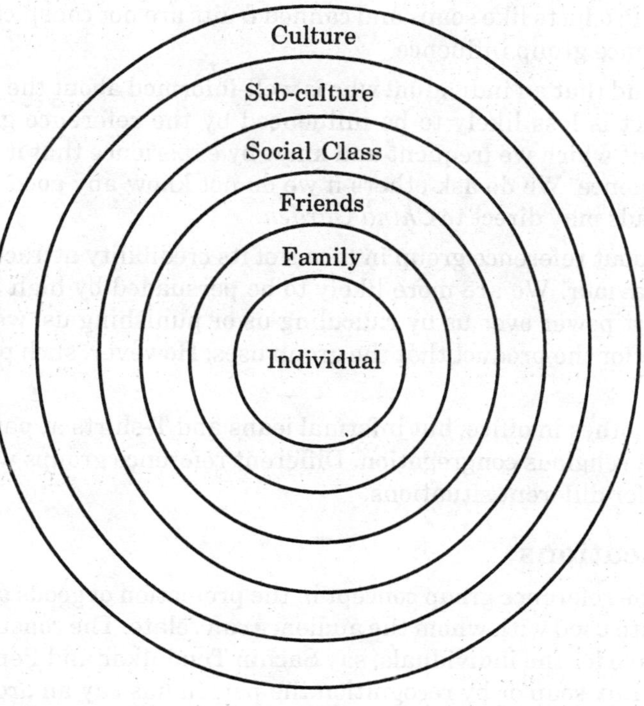

Fig. 10.1: Referents for a Consumer

Positive and Negative Reference Groups

A positive reference group inspires the members to behave in a manner congruent with its values. It has a positive influence on its members. A negative reference group is one which inspires an individual to behave exactly opposite to its own values. A reader of a political newspaper may despise its writing, and may vote exactly opposite to what the editorial material recommends. *Contractual group* is a positive reference group in which we have face to face contacts and whose ideology we approve. *An aspirational* positive reference group does not provide face-to-face contact, but inspires us to adopt its norms.

A *disclaimant group* is a negative reference group where there is face-to-face contact but disapproval of group ideology. An *avoidance group* is a negative reference group with them we neither have face-to-face contact nor we endorse their ideology.

Factors Affecting Reference Group Influence

Both the individual and the product determine the influence of the reference group on buyer behaviour. So also the social factors.

Certain type of products witness a high level of influence of the reference groups. Cigarettes, beer, and cars are chosen under the influence of reference groups, as claimed by Bourne. Clothing, furniture, magazines, and fridges as products are not chosen under the influence of the reference groups. But in these categories, brands do get chosen under the influence of the reference groups. Neither products nor the brands are chosen under the influence of the reference groups in case of soaps, canned peaches and radios. A conspicuous product either verbally or visually is chosen with an eye on the reaction of others e.g. luxury products or a new automobile or a mobile phone. Products like soaps and canned fruits are not conspicuous and hence are less amenable to reference group influence.

We can also contend that an individual who is well-informed about the product or who has *experienced* the product is less likely to be influenced by the reference group. We take our relations to a restaurant which we frequent and know by experience that it serves good food in the midst of right ambience. We do ask others if we do not know any good restaurant serving Chinese food. Our friends may direct to *China Garden.*

Our perception about reference group in terms of its credibility attractiveness and power also influence our behaviour. We are more likely to be persuaded by high credibility sources. When a group can exert power over us by ridiculing us or punishing us, we tend to follow the group norms, and go in for the product that the group uses. However, such power groups do not change our attitudes.

We wear formal clothes in office, but informal jeans and T-shirts at parties. We may were *dhoti* or a Burkha for a religious congregation. Different reference groups work on us at different points of time and for different situations.

Marketing Applications

We make use of the reference group concept in the promotion of goods and services. Either individuals or groups are used with whom the audience can relate. The consumers are moved by the admiration they have for the individuals, say Sachin Tendulkar and Pepsi or by aspiration, say a film actress and Lux soap or by recognition the person has say an architect and cement. There are four routes to endorsement copies — use of celebrities, use of an expert, use of a common man and use of an executive. Mostly these individuals appeal in the form of testimonials and endorsements. Sometimes, when a common man is used, we prepare a *slice of life* commercial.

Celebrities

Celebrities have high recognition value. They are admired by people. Their fame reaches far and wide. They are successful cinema stars, sports persons and media peronalities. They may be celebrity models also like Sushmita Sen and Aishwarya Rai. People consider them as their ideals; and they would like to adopt many things these celebrities do. People react favourably and positively to the association of a celebrity with the product. There is a definite identification of a product with a celebrity.

Celebrities who have used the product personally may give *testimonials* verifying the quality of the product. Vimal used newsmakers in its promotion for 'the finest suiting for professionals in the age group of 35-plus'. Sachin uses Visa card, and is all praise for its power. Celebrities mostly *endorse* the products. Lux is a very famous example of this type of copy. This soap came in the 30s and still is a powerful brand. It is presented as a soap for film actresses by getting the most popular actress vouch for it. The message is clear — a clear complexion and beauty care. Film actresses made it sound credible. There is complete product-personality synchronization.

A celebrity sometimes only acts as a character in the commercial. He does not either testify or endorse it. Amir Khan and Aishwarya have acted in Pepsi commercial. Shah Rukh acts in a Santro commercial. The brand and the product must be balanced in terms of image.

Celebrities can become spokesperson for the brand. These days they are made Ambassadors of the brand. The brand and the personality are associated. Cindy Crawford is an ambassador for Revlon.

Credibility of the celebrity is important. How far the celebrity is reliable? Do people feel that the celebrity honestly speaks about the product or brand? What is the *expertise* of this celebrity to talk about the brand? Credibility goes down if a celebrity endorses competitive brands and a variety of products. Money motivation becomes too obvious.

Celebrities are not used by all the companies. Celebrities may not be readily available. In future, celebrities may be held legally responsible for their endorsements.

Expert

An expert has some special training or is an outstanding professional, or is highly experienced. He facilitates our understanding of the product. We come across ads featuring nurses, doctors, architects, dentists and scientists. Some ads combine both the celebrity and expert.

Common Man

A common man is ubiquitous. He can be any ordinary male or female consumer. He endorses a product with which he is satisfied. Dove soap uses this approach. Common housewives narrate their experience of using Dove. Ariel uses this approach when it presents a dialogue between a mother-in-law and daughter-in-law. Surf Excel's husband which says *'Kuchh pane ke liye kuchh dhona bhi padta hain'* is a recent example of this approach. Mostly the advertised product is offered as a solution. A shoe-shine boy is shown offering a Surf Excel sachet to remove stain of polish on the trouser of a customer.

When real-life situations are presented, it is called a slice of life approach. These are the situations with which we can identify. Ujala liquid brings shine and whiteness to the clothes after they are dipped in water mixed with three or four drops of Ujala.

CASE: SLICE OF LIFE COMMERCIALS

David Ogilvy said if you can't think of anything else, go in for slice-of life. It works every time. When one can't think of a totally differentiated idea with a clear USP, one can opt for a life-style. Though it gives positive results yet soon it tends to look alike the other such commercials to the point that one can change packshots without the consumer noticing. Consider the family slice-of-life commercials for VIP luggage, Singer Sewing Machines and Appliances, Limca, Thums up, Hamara Bajaj among others. These commercials violate the basic rule of advertising; differentiate your product and your communication in every way. Though recall rate for this type of commercials is very nigh, the consumers may forget the brand. They are mistaken for other brands too — normally for ones that spend most media money.

Executives

Top executives are well-known. They can be effective influences. Vijay Mallya is used in an ad where he advises moderation in drinking. Lee Iaocca has been used for Chrysler ads. A top executive inspires confidence in the consumers. Instead, we can use a spokesperson of the company, say an employee who tells us how they build a great product.

Other Reference Points

When a product is featured in a reputed media, it influences our behaviour. A reputed store can also influence us by stocking a particular brand. Cartoon characters also serve as endorsers. Seals of approvals by professionals associations, objective product ratings, consumer reports — all these serve as frames of references.

Merits of Reference Group Appeal

It has two fold advantage. It increase the awareness of the brand and reduces the perceived risk in purchasing a specific product. Celebrities invite attention to the promotion. Products are differentiated by using reference group appeals.

APPENDIX

Concept of 'Social Group'

(1) Man is a social animal. So, he rarely lives in isolation.

(2) Hence, most social behaviour takes place in the context of social groups.

(3) This is one of the most distinctive characteristics of human beings i.e. to live in groups.

(4) Because of this inherent need, man is continually creating new groups and new symbols with which these can communicate.

(5) General Definition

Definition: A 'group' is a collection of individuals interacting with each other in an orderly way on the basis of shared expectations about each others' behaviour.

- According to GISBERT – A social group is a collection of individuals interacting with each other under a recognizable structure.
- According to MACIVER – A social group refers to any collection of human beings who are brought into social relationships with one another.
- Horton and Hunt have pointed out specific USAGES of the group

Usages of the Group

(1) Physical collection of people

(2) Certain common characteristics

(3) Sharing patterns of recurrent interaction

(4) A consciousness of membership and interaction.

If the above points are missing, it is not a social group.

— Social group must be differentiated from a Quasi Group (Potential Group). This is a mere collection of people having common characteristics but no recognizable structure, no interaction and no relationship. e.g. people waiting in a bus queue.

Two Types of Quasi Group

(1) A Social Category

— It is a collection of people performing a similar role and holding a similar status. e.g. MBA students, all MBA teachers, all doctors, lawyers.

(2) A Statistical Aggregate

— It refers to people who have certain socio-economic characteristics in common because of which they can be logically thought of as being together. e.g. All 16 yrs old girls, all people who are 5'6" tall.

— It is used in scientific analysis.

Conclusion

There are four essential characteristics of a social group

(1) A physical collection of people.

(2) A Recognizable structure. [Common interests, ideas, etc.]

(3) A pattern of interaction

(4) A social relationship

Classification of Social Groups

(1) Simmel: According to him, a group may be classified into size i.e., DYAD (2 people) and TRIAD (3 people). He has also introduced the concept of MONAD (1 person).

(2) Giddings: He uses membership as the criteria and divides groups into two – the genetic group (the hereditary group which one is born into e.g. family, religion, sex).

The Congregate Group (the voluntary group that you choose to belong to e.g. peer group, college, occupation).

(3) Anderson: He classifies groups on the basis of structure and membership into three groups:

(1) Voluntary Group – the congregate group

(2) Involuntary Group – genetic group

(3) Delegate Group – representative group. e.g. – Parliament, student's council

(4) Sorokin: He uses size into two kinds:

Horizontal Groups: large group like nation, state

Vertical Groups: smaller divisions within the horizontal group. e.g., districts, vertical groups can be horizontal also and vice versa.

(5) Summer: On grounds on membership into two kinds:

In-group – A group to which you belong

Out-Group – Those to which you don't belong

(1) These emerge when the boundaries of the groups are defined.

(2) The members who belong are specified as in-group and they identify with one another and with the group as a whole.

(3) 'Ingroupness' leads to a sense of belonging which is the essence of the group.

(4) The members of the in-group feel that they should be concerned with the personal welfare of each member. Hence, they share between them a considerable degree of sympathy, solidarity. They display co-operation, goodwill, mutual help and respect for each other.

(5) The In-group is expressed by the term 'WE' and sets members apart from others.

(6) Outgroup consists of those persons towards whom one feels a sense of indifference, avoidance, competition and even conflict.

(7) They are expressed by the terms 'THEY'.

(8) When the boundaries of these groups are not clear-cut, they tend to overlap and the difference between them becomes situational.

Membership and Reference Groups

(1) These were advocated by Sumner.

(2) Membership group is one to which the person belongs.

(3) Reference group is a group that a person wants to imitate. Man is an imitative animal who imitates behaviour better than his own. This is called reference behaviour.

(4) Two reasons behind this:

(a) Socio-Economic Reasons i.e., high status, better money.

(b) Psychological Reasons to develop a better aptitude, thinking level.

(5) There are three kinds of members here:

(a) *Aspiring Members:* not part of the reference group but want to be a part of it. They identify themselves with the group and its ideas.

(b) *Potential Members:* have the capacity and desire to belong to this group but are not part of it for personal reasons.

(c) *Actual Members:* They are those who look to the group as a standard and are also a part of it, e.g. doctor – society of surgeons.

(6) A person looks to the reference group for ideal behaviour and imitates it.

(7) He compares himself to that group and tries to live up to their standards.

(8) A person can be made to feel inferior because of a reference group of which he is not a member.

Primary and Secondary Groups

Primary groups are small having few members who interact through direct, face-to-face and personal relationships.

These groups share a definite intimacy and close personal contact.

Relationships in such a group have an emotional depth i.e., one member can't be replaced by another.

— This group is homogeneous and enduring in its relationship.

According to MERRIL, functions of a primary group are as follows:

(1) Activity Function

The primary group offers its members the opportunity to express themselves and their creativity. The members take part in their various activities in order to be together.

(2) Defense Function

- They protect their members in various ways.
- Economically, socially and emotionally.
- More often than not the members look to the group for emotional and moral support.
- Thus, they function as the shock absorber for the individual.

(3) Personality Function

- Primary group plays a major role in the moulding of individual's personality character.
- That part of the character formed there has a lasting impact on the individual's development.

(4) Communication Function

- It links the individual with larger society.
- It is the intermediary between the individual and society.
- The individual learns societal needs and expectations from this group.
- All these and functions denote that the primary group is very significant in an individuals life.

In COOLEY's words, the Primary Group is the Nuclear Cell of the social structure:

(a) He says it is important because it gives the individual emotional satisfaction.

- Several researchers found that people not belonging to primary groups were very lonely and had felt like committing suicide. It helps an individual to maintain his mental balance or otherwise he is prone to nervous breakdown.

(b) It is important because it functions as an instrument of social control. It passes on norms which are obeyed by members as they do not want to be ostracized. The members have their own system of rewards and punishments to get an individual to conform to society's norms.

(c) It mediates between the individual and society. It passes down societal norms, information and knowledge to its members. It is the medium through which people acquire and transmit culture in society.

Conclusion

- The primary group does not loose its significance even in a modern, complicated society.
- At times, the secondary group appears to take over but the primary group still survives because of its spontaneous living and because it provides stimulus (emotional satisfaction) to its members.
- In a modern advanced society, the primary group does not become redundant.
- Primary groups will always continue to exist in society.

Secondary Groups

They are large horizontal groups:

- Found in complex societies.
- Do not have emotional ties between the members.
- The relationships are utilitarian, contractual, impersonal and indirect, e.g. industry, army
- Within this group, the person becomes functionary and could be described by a number or by terms like 'manager,' 'officer' etc.
- One person can be replaced by another easily.
- Such groups emerge because of industrialization and urbanization.
- There is an emphasis on heterogeneity and anonymity.
- One is not concerned with the person but with the functionary.

Functions

(1) It is Goal-oriented. It will achieve its goals at any cost. e.g. academic excellence is the goal of a large institution. To fulfil this, personal relationships have to be kept aside.

(2) It has efficiency.

- To achieve this, tasks are specialized i.e., divided.
- Every individual is expected to perform to the best of his ability.
- Efficiency is achieved through + ve and – ve means. By giving incentives and punishments.
- Every individual has to put up with these systems because they know they can be replaced easily.

(3) It takes over several primary group functions. For example, socialization, education, vocational guidance, social welfare.

- The primary groups in a secondary society look to the secondary group for support.

Importance/Significance

From these functions, we find the importance of secondary group in society.

(1) It helps in framing policies and making rules and regulations to ensure that there is order in society.

(2) It provides society with resources – both human as well as material to function efficiently and achieve objectives.

(3) It gives rise to a hierarchy which is very necessary for smooth functioning of society or else there would be chaos.

(4) It opens up channels of opportunities for individuals so that they can exercise their various talents. Today, there are different fields, occupations, areas in which individual can fit themselves.

(5) It broadens the outlook of people in society. They become modern and secular. These ideas (cosmopolitan) which they develop are necessary for development of society.

Ferdinand Tonnies

German Sociologist. He divides groups into two:

(1) Gemeinschaft – small groups like family, small village, neighbourhood.

(2) Geselleschaft – large groups like cities, towns.

- He also divides groups in community and association.
- The social life of people is affected by the type of community that we live in.

•The term community was originally used. (1) to denote a collection of people occupying a definite territory or a geographical area. (2) collection of people sharing a common culture.

MacIver's Definition

"Wherever the members of any group, small or large, live together in such a way that they share not this or that particular interest but basic conditions of common life, we call that group a community."

Fr. Gisbert

A community is a permanent social group embracing a totality of ends and purposes:

— Any definition denotes that the community refers to a Pioneer Settlement.

— According to MacIver, as a pioneer settlement, community is based on two major factors.

(1) A Common Locality and an External Structure

— This is the geographical area occupied by the people, the territorial boundaries of the community. It also includes the facilities available. All this together is called the HABITAT. Habitat refers to a structural pattern into which the various units are fitted.

(2) A Community Sentiment

— When people share a common territory, there emerges a kind of 'positive-feeling', a sense of solidarity among them.

— This community sentiment also gives rise to a ROLE FEELING. This means that everyone in the community feels they have to contribute to its working.

— It also gives rise to a DEPENDENCY FEELING. People in the community depend on it for support and refuge – physical, emotional and social.

— Community sentiment varies from group to group, and by society to society. If the group is smaller, the sentiment is more and vice versa.

Association

(1) Association is a group of people who organise themselves to pursue a common interest or goal or a group of related interests.

(2) They come together either spontaneously or deliberately.

(3) MacIver's Definition

"It is a group which is organised for the pursuit of an interest or a group of interests in common."

(4) Gisbert

An association is a group of people united for a specific purpose or a limited number of purposes.

(5) What emerges as most important is the interest or activity of the group.

(6) Associations are formed on several bases

(i) Duration: They may be temporary, permanent, short-term or long-term.

(ii) Power: e.g. the Parliament, state, sovereign and non-sovereign associations.

(iii) Function: Biological (kinship groups, family), recreational (clubs), philanthropic (SPCA), vocational (trade unions)

— All these different bases can overlap. One association can have more than one basis/ conditions.

(7) Associations also have common methods of operation

(i) An association may own some property:

— This may not be owned by all the members.

— The members owning property have more authority and a greater say in the decision making.

(ii) The association may have funds which the members can't use as they please. They have to approach each other for access to them.

(iii) An association may possess certain powers, duties, rights and privileges which the members can't exercise as they please.

— All these 3 points indicate that an association has a Corporate Character.

— When all these are made legal, the association can become a corporation.

DIFFERENCES BETWEEN ASSOCIATION AND COMMUNITY

Criteria	*Association*	*Community*
(1) Purpose	The purpose for which an association is formed is a specific one or it involves some related goals and objectives. Largely speaking, an association is deliberately created.	It includes the whole circle of common life. It has no beginning and is much more spontaneous and comprehensive than the association.
(2) Type of Group	An association is an artificially created grouply and is formed for the pursuit of definite objectives and is an organisation within the community.	It is naturally formed group which grows spontaneously out of living together in the some locality and out of sentiment and we-feeling.
(3) Type of Membership	Membership to an association is limited. An association being a transitory (changing) group of people, is significant for a member as long as it serves his purpose. Also, membership is voluntary.	Membership to a community has a much wider connotation or implication. The community embraces the whole purpose of life and it does not exist for any one specific purpose. Membership to a community is generally hereditary.
(4) Sentiment	It does not regard sentiment as an essential feature. The main objective or the goal is most important.	Here, the sentiment or positive feeling is extremely important as it gives rise to the role and dependency feeling.

11

THE FAMILY

The most single most significant effect on consumer behaviour is exercised by the family group. What constitutes a family is difficult to define; in different societies different roles are assigned tc members of the family. Conventionally a family means two or more persons, related by blood, marriage or adoption who reside together. A family, however, is the basic social group living together and interacting to satisfy the personal and mutual needs.

In consumer research, we come across the term households. A household is a group of persons, not necessarily related by blood, marriage or adoption. Thus a household may or may not be a family. It could be a live-in couple, friends living together, roommates under one roof and so on. While studying consumer behaviour, however, we treat the concept of family and household synonymously.

In India, we traditionally had *joint families,* consisting of some three generations living together. Thus we see grand parents, their sons and unmarried daughters, and the children of the sons. The male earning member contribute to the family kitty. The eldest male member is generally the head of the family or *karta*. The joint family system is a good cushion against economic insecurity and emotional well-being. However, it fosters inefficiency amongst its members. With urbanization and the growing awareness of individual rights, the joint family system has disintegrated and has given rise to a family consisting of a *married couple.* As soon as children arrive on the scene, it gets converted into a *nuclear family*. The nuclear family is the bed-rock on which the family life is based. If either husband's or wives parents stay with the nuclear family, if becomes an *extended family*. There are many *single-parent* families on account of separations and divorces. Here we find either a father and a child or a mother and a child. There could be more than one child associated either to a father or mother.

The family structure differs from culture to culture. In urbanized India, we find nuclear families are quite common. In rural India, we still come across joint families or extended families. In a metropolitan city, with its working woman culture, we find many extended families because a parent is needed to do baby-sitting and minor household chores.

Socialization

A family fulfils several functions. As we are aware it promotes economic well-being and lends us emotional support. A family also nurtures a life-style. However, the most important function from consumer behaviour point of view that a family performance is that of socialization.

In the process of socialization, children receive their basic values and code of conduct in keeping with their culture. Mostly, these pertain to religious practices and inter-personal skills. We also learn how to dress and are groomed to face to world around us. We learn our etiquette and manners. We decide what our career would be. We grow to become responsible citizens. Socialization is both direct and indirect. Direct instruction comes from the parents. Indirectly, we learn by observing the behaviour of our parents and other siblings. Socialization is the foundation on which later experiences in life are placed one by one. Marketers target parents often to influence socialization.

Consumer socialization is of special relevance to the marketers. This is the process by which children get equipped with the skills and knowledge and wear attitudes necessary to act as consumer. Children pattern their consumption after their parents. Here parents act as role models. Till the pre-adolescent stage this remains so. As adolescents and teen-agers, we tend to accept our friends as models of acceptable behaviour.

A child is in tow when a mother shops. It results in the development of the shopping skills. Co-shopping is a way of spending time with children while accomplishing a necessary task. Parents use a carrot and stick policy to motivate their children. Children are rewarded for a particular behaviour, and punished to keep away from a particular behaviour.

Consumer socialization can be directly related to consumption. At times it is indirectly related to consumption *e.g.,* a teenager in periods is motivated to use sanitary napkins. Indirect socialization has more relevance to the marketers as it leads to the understanding of the why of consumer behaviour. Direct socialization is of academic interest.

Socialization is a continuous process and not restricted to childhood. It extends to our entire life. A newly set-up household has to adjust to challenges of living alone, and consume to satisfy their needs. It is an extension of the process of socialisation. A retired life is also an extension of socialization.

Socialization is a two way process — between a young person and the family members; and friends. He is influenced, and also influences those who are socializing him. It indicates why children are targeted by the advertisers to influence their parents.

Family Roles

Each member of a family performs some task either alone or together with others. Thus we have a housewife who cooks, a daughter who mops, a son who runs errands for the family and a father who earns livelihood. Of course, the roles keep on changing in a dynamic environment. We have a large number of working women now, adding quite a lot to the family kitty. We also see husband's sharing household chores with their working or non-working wives.

In matter of consumption, we come across the following types of roles in a family, each signifying the type of interactions at the time of consumption decision.

- *Influencers:* These family members influence the buying decision by providing the information inputs.

- *Gate keepers:* These control the flow of information about consumption items into the family.
- *Decides*: These take the ultimate decision of buying, consuming and disposing of the consumption items.
- *Buyers:* They actually buy the consumption items.
- *Prepares:* They convert the consumption items into a form suitable for use.
- *Users:* They either use or consume.
- *Maintainers:* They maintain the product in a functional condition.
- *Disposers:* They either initiate or carryout the disposal or discontinuation of a product or service.

Which role will be performed by whom is a matter which varies from family to family. A single family member may perform several roles. A single role may be performed by more than one family member. In some situation, we may not need some of these roles. A teenager may borrow a book from the library. He may do of his own accord, without getting influenced by others. He himself is the *decider,* the *buyer* (one who hires or borrows) and in one sense, a *gatekeeper.* But once a borrowed book enters the household, he alone may not *use* it. Several other members my share the book with him. Some products are used by several family members e.g. Amul butter or a soap. Some products are meant for the whole family *e.g.,* furniture in the living room or a common TV set in the hall.

Consumer Decisions by Husband and Wife

Wolgast has found that we come across several joint decisions about consumption taken by a husband-wife team. One member of this team may become dominant. The consumption decisions are husband-dominated or wife-dominated. In some decisions, they exert equal influence, whereas some decisions are unilateral. In most middle-income families, this joint decision making is common. When the couple is young, the joint decision making is related to the extent of husband-wife communication. But in case of older couples, role specialisation is more rigid.

While deciding jointly, the husband and wife team generally attempt to influence each other so as to arrive what they perceive to be the best decision. There are six *influence strategies* which we come across.

- *Expert:* One of the spouses assumes an expert's role to influence the other spouse.
- *Legitimacy:* The decision is legitimised on the basis of position in the family.
- *Bargaining:* Influence exerted by a spouse at present which will be exchanged with the other spouse in future.
- *Reward:* A reward is offered to the other spouse to influence the decision.
- *Emotional:* Emotionally charged response affects the other spouse.
- *Impression:* Persuasive approach to influence the behaviour of the other spouse.

These strategies are adopted when there are conflicts and disagreements with the other spouse. We know how different family members have different preferences for holiday locations.

The relative influence of husband and wife is product-related. To begin with, purchase of a car was husband-dominated. Purchase of food products are wife-dominated. These days women consumers decide about a second car for their own personal use. According to one study, the decisions about when to buy a car, where to buy a car and how much to spend for a car are husband-dominated. However, the decision about the brand of a car and its model is a joint decision with equal say for both the spouses. The decision of the colour of the car is wife-dominated.

A family's orientation towards sex roles also affects the consumption decisions. A gender equality approach is the hall-mark of a modern family. Gender discrimination is a cultural aspect. In some cultures, husbands take major decisions. Sub-cultural factors also affect the decision making.

In the decision-making model, we see distinct stages of problem recognition, search for information and final decisions. There are variations in the roles of the husband and wife at these different stages of decision making. Generally the person who initiates the decision making process completes it. But in some cases, there are stage-to-stage shifts. The decision to buy a washing maching is that of a wife (problem Recognition) but the final purchase of the washing machine is done jointly by both the husband and wife.

Children's Influence

Children put forward their own demands as soon as they acquire talking skills. They need all kinds of toys, crayons, 'baba-suits', chocolates and toffees. As they grow, they start participating directly in the consumption process. They influence the purchase decisions of a home PC, a music system, a video game and a holiday destination. When parents make a purchase according to the bidding of their children, they have in a sense *yielded.*

Children love TV commercials. They recite ad jingles. Nursery kids develop an ability to distinguish between the commercial and the TV programme. TV commercials of adult products also affect children. Girls get favourably disposed to products like lip-sticks.

As children grow, they develop the capacity to understand the symbolism in advertising.

CASE: CHILDREN AND TV

Dr. Anne Colby, Director, Henry Murry Research Centre of Radclife College, Harvard University who is a licensed psychologist believes that TV can widely assist in a child's intellectual, emotional, social and moral growth. Research has proved that children view TV actively and not passively. They try to relate the stories to their own life experience. Children's attention span is not affected because of TV watching.

Most of the myths instilled into our mind could be attributed to Marshall McLuhan who gave us the famous maxim 'The medium is the message' after television entered our lives. According to McLuhan, it was the nature of the medium that was more powerful than the message itself. Research has proved him wrong. It is the message — sex, violence etc. — that comes strongly, and this message comes form diverse sources. Other media are as culpable in the progress or regress of a child's development as television.

According to Dr. Colby, children who watch moderate amounts of TV a week show better school performance than those who watch little or no TV. It is not watching television *per se* that affects a child's development but the quality of what they are watching. She suggests parental control for viewing hours and parental censor for viewing programmes.

Children who remain at home after the school-hours while their parents are on the job are specially targeted by the marketers. Teenagers are more interested in sports-wear, T-shirts, denim clothes, mopeds, deo sprays, perfumes, entertainment, fitness products. They themselves are the buyers of a large number of products and services. They also influence the parental decisions. Besides, their age is impressionable. The consumption pattern they learn spills over to their adult life. College-going children have their peculiar needs. They are interested in books, personal clothes and fuel for their bikes. They attend discos and concerts. They like to spend holidays at some exotic place. They develop brand preferences and shopping habits more firmly. Mothers and daughters tend to share many brand preferences and shopping habits. But outlooks do differ about broad beliefs regarding the market such as price-value-equation between them. Collegiates are not only current consumers, but potential future ones. 'Teens Today' reaches this vital segment. FM channel programmes also address the needs of this segment.

CHILD MODELS

Children are used in TV commercials as models. Casting directors have to face their tantrums on the sets many a time. They may not be 'in a mood to shoot'. They are shown indulgence. Being a child model is not easy — they have to juggle between a school and modelling assignments. Child models get work only after video tests. Abroad, a child model works only after parental consent in writing. There is legal protection in terms of hours of work and working conditions. Child models are even insured. Shooting has to take place after school hours or on holidays. Such legal protection is not available in India. A top child model is paid between Rs. 2000 Rs. 40000 for a single contract. Such remuneration makes parents accommodative. The efficacy of child model depends on how it has been used. A child is considered a good endorser for products like the kids soap. He is also an influencers for a great many products.

Child Models

Kids were used to model for products aimed at children. They are now modelling for a lot of products unconnected with children like fridges, TVs, toothpastes, investment schemes, soaps etc. Children have a certain appeal and a charm. They attract more attention. Besides, advertising is now directed to a household or a family. The child is, therefore, the best medium to set the message across. Children evoke pure feelings — innocence, goodness, freshness, nurturing, caring, impulsiveness. The parent-child bond is used to convey the bond between the product and the user. The feelings evoked are used by advertisers.

Benaf Dadachandji is one of the more successful child models today. Formerly only cute children were selected as models. But more important these days is their ability to be natural and spontaneous, *e.g.,* Le Sancy model is not cute by conventional standards but is spontaneous and natural.

The child model is paid anything from Rs. 5,000 onwards for film advertisement. Some of them reportedly get Rs. 20,000 depending upon the film and the contract.

Children as Influencers

Kids in India influence family purchases in all kinds of product categories. This is the key finding of Cartoon Network's latest survey on Indian kids (2001). The level of influence children have on purchase and brand decisions is called Pester Power. Cars, computers, refrigerators, microwaves and televisions are some of the items where children directly or indirectly contribute to brand choice. Against international comparison of the degree of influence on parents purchases, India happens to be in the middle by registering 43 par cent as children influence, whereas Korea and Japan are at the top-end and Singapore and Malaysia at the bottom. Four out of 10 kids claim to read newspapers and/or comics. Animation on TV is their favourite programming genre. Sports and movies follow cartoons in terms of preference. Computer and internet usage are on the increase among children. Interestingly, after computers Internet is their next favourite medium. Children love humour in ads. TV is the best medium for entering contests. Delhi kids have high purchasing power given by pocket money. Bangalore has the lowest. Kids from smaller towns have high purchasing power than children in metros. Majority of children get less than Rs. 100 per month by way of pocket money. The New Generation 2001 survey was conducted in 14 Indian cities and had a sample of 3253 children and 735 mothers.

Children's Influence on Buying

Children accompany parents to the shopping malls. They influence the parents in buying decisions for a wide variety of products such as refrigerators, papa's office shirt, entertainment items (steros, TVs, home theatres). Children suggest a particular brand of cell phone, a particular brand of TV set and even an insurance firm. Advertisers are seeking them out for products for the entire family or only just for the parents in two ways — child's happiness or admiration for the parent or child's actual opinion about a product. Research shows children influence adult categories like ACs, cars, cell phones, insurance, music systems, travel holiday, and computers. To what extent children influence the purchase decision? Substantially. Schools are considered prime advertising platforms. Children under 10 are vulnerable however to harmful ads. Some children from poor families tend to have materialistic aspirations difficult to attain.

Global Teenager

'Global Teenager' is a myth. Our teenager is similar in some respects with his Western counterpart; but he is different in both attitude and outlook.

(*i*) He enjoys the family bonds and avails of the support system till be turns out to be 21.

(*ii*) He is more conservative and shows more respect for authority.

(*iii*) He is not as materialistic as his Western counterpart. He is less cynical.

(*iv*) This family socialization conditions him differently. He consults his parents for marriage.

Four Characteristics of Teen Social Group

They show the following four characteristics.

(*i*) Fashion tastes

(*ii*) Music interests

(*iii*) Socialising activities

(*iv*) Indulgence practices (alcohol, tobacco, drugs)

Motivation

Teen in one market selects a brand to show his rebellions spirit, but an Indian teenager may do so to conform to the market trend abroad. A teenager elsewhere may opt for the brand as a safe option.

FAMILY LIFE CYCLE

Concept of Family Life Cycle

People go through several phases in their lives. Family Life Cycle (FLC) refers to the series of life stages through which individuals proceed over a period of time.

In other words, FLC describes the process of family formation and dissolution.

To illustrate, a young man or a woman marry to form a family, in which children are born and live with the family till they grow up, and later move out. At last, the couple grows old and fends for itself. Each life cycle stage differs from previous stages in terms of (a) structure, (b) financial position, (c) consumption pattern, and (d) product need and preferences.

Traditional or Conventional FLC

The FLC is a progression of several stages.

(1) *Young and single* bachelor stage. The career has just started. However, in absence of burdens, they are free to spend as they wish. They tend to buy personal consumption items of food and clothing, are fun-loving and buy entertainment, have time to be on vacations and tours, move about on bikes, mobikes and other two wheelers, read novels and thrillers.

They buy some basic utensils and furniture.

(2) *Newly married couples* have household burdens and go through an expenditure phase in life. They generally buy consumer durables like furniture, wall paints, refrigerators, TVs etc.

(3) *Young married with child* directs their income to bringing up the child. They buy toys, medicines, tonics, baby foods, formula milk etc.

(4) *Older, married with children* are fairly stable income wise. They like food products, music, educational services and a wide variety of other products.

(5) *Older married with dependent children* have high income, but do rational purchases. There is replacement buying.

(6) *Older, married with no children* become interested in self-education, saving schemes, hobbies, luxury appliances, magazines, health products.

(7) *Old, single, retired* people lead an economic life style. They are interested in health care and other services. They've budget constraints.

Revised FLC Concept for the 90s

Conventionally, family was considered a single unit throughout the life-time of an individual. However, this assumption is not true these days. There are families due to second marriages, with a legacy of children from previous marriages. There are deserted wives. There are divorcees. Several families are single parent family, where the parent could be either a father or a mother. Again, the ubiquitous working woman makes the traditional FLC model invalid.

Let us consider the following dimensions of Indian families in 90s.

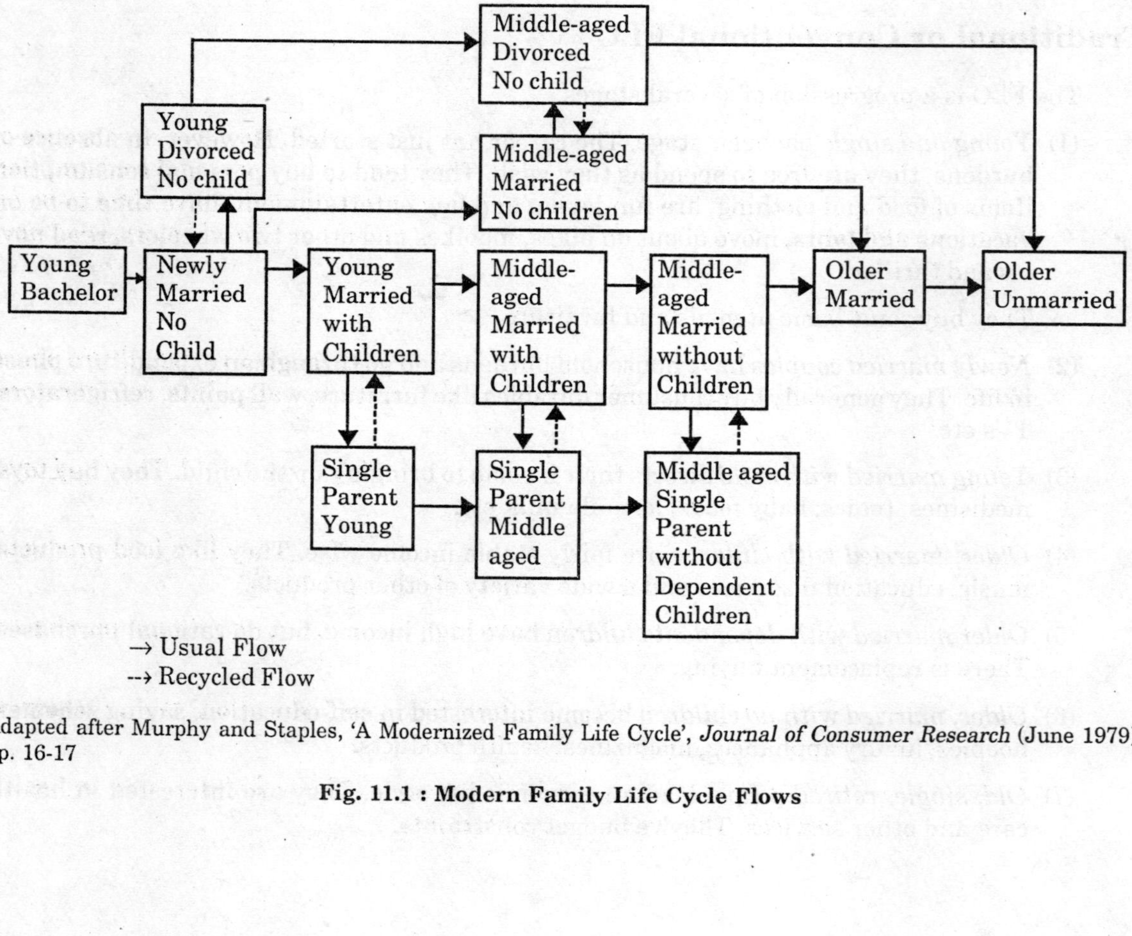

Adapted after Murphy and Staples, 'A Modernized Family Life Cycle', *Journal of Consumer Research* (June 1979) pp. 16-17

Fig. 11.1 : Modern Family Life Cycle Flows

CHARACTERISTICS OF FLC STAGES

Bachelor Stage	*Newly Married Couples*	*Full Nest I*	*Full Nest II*	*Full Nest III*	*Empty Nest*	*Empty Nest*	*Survivor—*	*Survivor—*
		Young Married Couple with Young child	*Young Married Couple with Child over Six*	*Older Married Couple with Children*	*I Old Married Couple with No Children*	*II Old Married Couple, No Children, Retired Bread-winner*	*Spouse no more. But still Working*	*Spouse no more and Retired*
• Financial freedom • Entertain ment and recreation oriented • Fashion conscious *Products bought:* Basic uten sils, basic fur- niture, vaca- tions	• Less wor- ried about finance • Think of buying housing and dura- bles to settle down *Products bought:* Furniture, fridges, TV, two-wheel- ers, honey- moon pack- ages	• Worried about finances • Interested in rearing up the child • Like innovative products • Buy house- hold items *Products bought:* Appliances, paediatric products, sports items	• Working woman, and hence two salary cheques • Better offfinancially • Interested in bargains *Products bought:* Food products, music systems, bikes	• Better off fi- nancially • More work- ing women • Supple mentation of income by children at times • Average buying of durables *Products bought:* Tasteful fur- niture, fancy appliances, dental services	• Pilgrim ages, travel plans • Self- education • Not inter ested in new products *Products bought:* Vacations, luxuries, home im provements	• Income curtailed • Keep in doors *Products bought:* Health- related products	• Loneliness • Sell off as- sets like a big house • Likes social interaction and social work	• Curtailment of in come • Health conscious • Depen- dence needs

Young, Married, with Child and Dual Income: Here both the husband and the wife work, and get two income cheques. The pace of the life is faster and there is less time for children and also for one another. The consumption pattern therefore shows preference for convenience goods like washing machines, grinder-mixers, rice cookers, grinding mill (gharghanti) etc. Women manage on two fronts — domestic chores and work. Husbands share the responsibilities of running the house to some extent. Instant foods, creches etc. appeal to such families. To compensate for the time babies miss with parents, there is a tendency to buy costly garments for kids, games for kids, prams etc.

Single Parent Families: The single parent family needs security and buys all the products that offer physical and psychological and financial securities — *e.g.,* burglar alarms, teddy bears, insurance, saving certificates etc. When the child grows, he may be put in a boarding school/public school.

Divorced: They buy money saving products, lease or rental housing, child care, time saving appliances, instant foods. They are short of cash.

Older People, Married or Single: They are also cash poor, and health conscious. They need security. They also need recreation.

Some researchers have done a detailed analysis of the Family Life Cycle, and their product preferences. They have considered the FLC in as many as nine stages which are outlined in Table given on page 200.

The family-life cycle concept, as conventionally understood does not consider a large number of marriage terminations, single parent families and married couples without children. To compensate for these lacunae, a modern family life cycle has been framed, and is presented in Fig. 11.1.

SEGMENTATION STRATEGY ON THE BASIS OF FLC

Product	*Segment*
(i) Cosmetics	Young single and young married women who are cash rich are a potential segment for beauty products like face creams, moisturizers, compacts, foundation make up etc.
(ii) Vacations	Middle-aged families need facials, sauna baths and such related products. Newly married couples are sold vacations at the time of marriage in the form of honeymoon packages. Middle-aged couples with no responsibility of children are the most attractive segment to sell vacations in the form of packaged tours. They are cash rich and free from encumbrances.
(iii) Housing	Young, married with children need starter housing. Middle-aged couples need housing — 2 bedroom flats etc. Bachelors need liberal and professional education. They are career minded. They can be sold courses like private secretary, computers etc.
(iv) Education	Middle-aged with children buy education for their children — home tuitions, coaching classes, public schools etc. They buy education for self also to improve their career — *e.g.,* distance education programmes of IGNOU.

Parents generally take a personal interest in monitoring transmission of cultural values to child. However, today this function is being taken over by other institutions like schools, domestic servants, creches. Despite this, the family still remains as one of the most primary agencies of socialisation and culture transmission.

Sustenance and Maintenance: Man can't live without human response and it is in the family that this kind of care, protection, security is offered. It is not just material and economical but is also emotional. The family accumulates property and passes it down from generation to generation. There is an affectional bond within the family which creates a very strong 'we feeling' within the family and so is very important. Family channelizes the handing of property.

Social Placement of the Young: Legitimate birth of an individual in a family gives the child an identity in society and brings about stability. From the family the child inherits the name, status as well as property. Life's opportunities do depend on this status which is passed down.

FEATURES/CHARACTERISTICS OF FAMILY

(1) The Family Regulates Behaviour of the Members: It sets down norms and values for every form of behaviour and places individuals on prescribed path of society.

(2) Replacement of Members: Every society needs a system of replacing members from generation to generation. Hence, it needs a system of Decent/Lineage/Nomenclature. This lineage can be traced through the father and through the mother. If it is traced through father, it is called PATRI-LINEAL DESCENT and through the mother, MATRI-LINEAL DESCENT. Some societies have MATRI-PATRI LINEAL DESCENT.

(3) Family Circle: It can be based on blood ties called consanguine family coming from Latin word 'sang' meaning blood. When it is based on marital ties, it is conjugal family. Joint family has consanguine and conjugal ties.

(4) Type of Residence:

If owned by father	PATRILOCAL residence
and by mother	MATRILOCAL residence
and by uncle	AVUNCULOCAL residence
and by mom and dad	MATRI-PATRI LOCAL

(5) Emotional Basis: Family rests on primary and secondary emotions. Primary emotions are feelings that come close to instincts like mating, reproduction, parenthood. Secondary emotions are: A very important law in the family is LOVE and DUTY is another law. The wheel of duty has to be greased with love. Family is the Buffer or outlet for pent-up emotions.

It helps an individual to absorb the shocks of society.

(6) Formative Influence: It is a major influence in moulding character and personality of the individual. First formative years are very important. During this, members develop their personality.

(7) Responsibility of Members: The family makes continuous and heavy demands on its members far more than any other group. People generally work very hard for the sustenance of the members of their family and make several sacrifices which they would not do for any other group.

(8) Permanent and Temporary Nature: Family is permanent as an institution and is temporary as a group.

Procedures of the family remain more or less permanent. When people get separated due to death, birth, divorce then family is like a group and is temporary.

(9) Dynamism: It is a dynamic institution. It is subject to constant change. Any change in society brings about a corresponding change in family as members of family are a part of society.

For example, during war, family gets closer, they save up as rations are scarce. Some person may die in war.

TYPES OF FAMILY

(1) Matriarchal Family: It is also called 'Mother-Right' family. The eldest woman is generally the head of the family. She has complete authority over the family. In such a family, descent is matri-lineal and residence is matrilocal. Even though property is owned by mother or female-head, it is managed by a male. This male is either the husband or the maternal uncle or brother. For example, the Nair family is called THARWAD. Here, the woman is the head. But the male i.e., KARNAVAN runs the THARWAD. The Karnavan is always the husband of the female head. All the property is in the lady's name.

However, the relationships in a matriarchal society are always based on CONVENANT i.e., mutual understanding and not on authority.

(2) Patriarchal: It is much more universal, relevant and accepted. The eldest male is the head, called the 'patriarch.' He owns and manages the property. The residence is Patrilocal and descent becomes Patri-lineal. In such a family, the father-son relationship is very important. The birth of a son is very auspicious. This type of family originated in ROME where it was called PATER-families meaning Father-Right Family. The Roman Patriarch, however, was the absolute head with respect to other members. He had total authority. He could beat, sell, kill them. They had no say. Today, the role is not so authoritative – it is more paternalistic – like a father figure – the Protector of the family. This also prevails in the Indian joint family.

(3) Joint Family: The joint family is a combination of a consanguine and conjugal unit. There are several generations under one roof. The head is generally the eldest male or the grandfather. In the Hindu joint family, the head is called the KARTA.

There is a collectivist approach i.e. the whole family functions as a collective unit. The family functions considering three main factors with respect to collectivism. They are:

(a) Joint Property and Joint Income: (i) It owned by the male head and transmitted through male members of the family. (ii) All members are supposed to have equal share in the property. (iii) Property is in form of Land and Business Decisions of the head are binding on the family. But, he cannot sell or give away property without consulting the other members, generally male. The other male members are co-parceners i.e., co-owners. So, if property is fragmented, the joint family is also fragmented.

(b) Joint Kitchen: (i) food cooked under one roof also keeps the family together. (ii) Customary and traditional cooking re-inforces family solidarity. (iii) However, there are time when norms relating to food-habits may change and temperaments clash. Then, the need to cook separately may arise. Also, decision making with respect to food is important. Who will plan the daily menu? Who will eat first? Whose favorite food will be cooked? These are the questions that arise. A balancing factor is required. So, with respect to roles and statuses allotted to family members, they can dilute or strengthen family norms.

(c) Joint Worship: Prayer in an Indian family is important and common prayer is a binding factor. The family observes festivals, ceremonies together. There are certain norms that have to observed here. The role of head and other elders becomes very significant because they pass on the heritage, the way of carrying out the task.

Advantages

(1) Economically advantageous as incomes are pooled in. Hence cheaper to run the family.

(2) It functions like a welfare state i.e., it looks after the handicapped, old, widow. So everyone is looked after.

(3) Heritage is preserved and transmitted from generation to generation mainly because of presence of elders who know what is to be done.

(4) Presence of elders in the house provides a sense of security and a check on the children.

(5) A joint family provides economic and social stability. Social stability is a result of control over the members and the members having developed an identity.

(6) Elders help out in the decision-making.

Disadvantages

(1) There may be a clash of temperaments and personalities leading to friction. (e.g: clash over property, generation gap).

(2) The head may be very authoritative leading to friction and problems.

(3) A joint family can encourage idlers. Some might put in a lot of money but others might not. They are parasites of the family.

(4) Woman lose out on their individuality.

(5) There is no privacy.

(6) Decision-making has to be joint and not individually.

Nuclear Family

The process of industrialization and urbanization has led to the emergence of the nuclear family which is becoming more popular in the urban setup.

(1) Here, in an urban setup, the conjugal relationship between husband and wife is given more importance whereas the larger kinship ties are not so strong.

(2) Residence is mainly NEOLOCAL.

(3) Such a family is individualistic as against a collectivistic joint family. It is centered round its own individual needs.

(4) This family is also egalitarian in approach i.e., it is more permissive. Especially women get more freedom, have an important say in the decision-making.

(5) It has also emerged because of the demands of industrialisation where the living conditions demand a small-family setup. So, the nuclear family norm becomes more common.

(6) The nuclear family turns to other agencies for support. e.g., schools, creches, banks, domestic servants, media, etc.

(7) Children in the nuclear family are appreciated for their value as individuals and are given definite importance not just as economic assets.

(8) Parents do not receive any economic gains from the expenses incurred on bringing up children and the latter are more an economic liability.

(9) Individual goals become important and members expect the freedom to pursue them.

Dysfunctions (Disadvantages)

(1) Burdens – Several burdens are imposed on the family. Married partners demand a lot from each other.

(2) It is severely affected by any disorganisation. e.g.,death/prolonged illness of bread- earner, mental disorders can throw family out of gear.

(3) If expections are not fulfilled, then there is much more discontent in the nuclear family than in a joint family.

(4) Problems of AGED: They may have no role to play in the nuclear family and they might end up feeling very lonely and unwanted.

(5) Economic independence of women makes women career-conscious and a lot of compromises have to be made. So, very often, the nuclear family goes through a phase of stress.

(6) Tremendous competition in today's society can pose severe stress on nuclear family.

Advantages

(1) Freedom and Privacy: They can make their own norms. They have the freedom to develop their own individuality.

(2) There is equality with respect to status of men and women.

(3) Change in sex-roles: Women have a say in the decision-making. Tasks are shared and they can carry out the functions of the family more efficiently.

(4) Neo-local Residence is becoming more popular. Both have an equal share in the family over the home.

(5) Individualism and Egalitarinism is replacing collectivism and authroitarianism. Because to develop your personality you need to be given freedom. It makes you more ambitious.

(6) Women have more rights to think freely, opportunity to exercise their individuality, to grow, to voice their opinion.

(7) Family members have a closer relationship.

❑ ❑ ❑

12

SOCIAL CLASS AND CONSUMER BEHAVIOUR

Purely economic explanation of consumer behaviour fails to satisfy us as far as choices of products and services go. Social stratification based on differentiation and evaluation goes a long way in explaining the consumer behaviour. The most primitive societies also had some differentiation. One person used to head the tribe, and his word was respected. Societies later started respecting the persons with curative powers. In India, we had the priestly class, the warrior class, the trading class and the lowly class. Different individuals have been valued differently, as the role they played differed in importance. If all are on par, there is no differention and evaluation, and consequently no satisfaction. In a society, a doctor is valued much more than a scavanger. All occupations do not carry the same prestige. We all are conscious of the class differences. Social classes are the *strata* in the society. It makes society hierarchical. Social classes group people statuswise. Each class has people having more or less the same status. Status is a function of wealth, power and prestige. In marketing, we consider status with respect to household income, occupational choice and academic achievements. Divinity, supernatural considerations, spiritual attainments, public service also affect the social status. Heritage, religion and caste also affect the social status.

Social classes are open ended, and people from one social class can aspire to move to the higher social class. As opposed to this, the caste system prevalent in India is close ended. A caste is an endogenous group. We are born and die in the same caste. We also marry within the same caste. Caste system does not provide any opportunity to move upwards. Class mobility is more on account of industrialisation and urbanisation. Marketers can make use of social classes in segmenting the market. Each social class has certain shared values and attitudes, and show certain characteristic preferences. This helps the marketers to understand consumer behaviour. Each social class serves as a frame of reference. It shapes the behaviour and attitudes of its members. A sense of belonging stimulates the consumer to look upto the social class for behaviour norms. Lower classes aspire to imitate the behavioural patterns of the higher classes.

Status Symbols of Teenagers

A & M conducted a survey (Jan 15 1998 issue) and has arrived at the following status symbols for the teenagers.

TOP 10 STATUS SYMBOLS

Symbol	*Score*
Career ambition	6.69
Parent's background/profession	4.03
Branded clothes	3.66
Pocket money	3.43
Choice of music	3.26
Room to yourself	2.74
Holiday destination	2.73
Mode of travel to college	2.50
Internet connection at home	2.43
Cellphone	2.31

Categories of Social Classes

Warner has classified the society into six classes. The following table summarises his categorisation.

Class	*Description*
1. Upper-upper	Microscopic. Elite. Wealth inherited. Gracious living. Value family reputation. Believe in pedigree. Socially responsible.
2. Lower-upper	2 p.c. of population. Wealth of first generation. Neo-rich. A shade less than upper-upper. Choose good schools for children like Doon School and Mayo College. Future generations have chances to move to top class. Class of top corporate executives, successful professionals and proprietors of large business. Emulate etiquette of the top-class.
3. Upper-Middle	Larger than the above two classes. Well-off financially. Income above average. Moderates successful professionals and businessmen. Emulate upper classes. Degree of success puts a dividing line between them and the two upper classes.
4. Lower-Middle	A large class. Supervisors, non-managerial staff, traders, clerical staff, sales people. Respectable living. Value education.
5. Upper-Lower	Largest class. Wage-earners. Working class. Strive for respectability.
6. Lower-Lower	Lowest income unemployment. Underdevelopment. Uneducated. Daily wage earners. Low occupations.

Marketing to the Rich

They are a *profitable niche*, which is expanding fast. Segments are quicker to *adopt* consumer habits considered premium. *Stereotypes* are no guide to marketing. Exotic perfumes have been sold to the stereotyped South-Indian who is quite traditional. If there is value, consumers do not mind paying a premium. Rising income means less expenditure on household products, and more *spending* on out-of-home activities. *Social acceptance* and *status* are powerful drivers. Many offerings lose their premiumness over a period of time. Some categories are premium for different income groups. There are variations in the choice of categories however, for different income groups at times. We cannot generalise while marketing to the rich. We have to understand their need for 'specialist' products, personal grooming, and concern for fitness.

Middle-Class

Though middle-class is difficult to define, it has three components – cultural, consumption pattern and psychographics. A middle-class is a matter of attitude or a state of mind. Income is an easier criterion to define middle-class. Here the data given by National Council of Applied Economic Research (NCAER) comes handy. Let us consider the income in terms of take-home packet.

TAKE HOME PACKET PER ANNUM

Household	*2000-2001*
Low Income	₹ 33,750
Lower Middle	₹ 33,751 – 67,500
Middle Income	₹ 67,501 – 1,05,000
Upper Middle Income	₹ 1,05,001 – 1,44,000
High Income	More than ₹ 1,44,000

Low income households are poor, and high income households are very rich. The other three categories are lower middle income, middle income and upper income. They add up to 60.5 million households. The following is their distribution in population.

CLASS DIVIDE 2001-02

Type of Household	*Strength (in Million)*
Low Income	32.8
Lower Middle Income	40.00
Middle Income	13.00
Upper Income	7.5
High Income	6.7

As we have seen, the middle Income categories constitute 60.5 million households. If we take an average of five individuals per household, there are 302.5 million individuals in this middle income category. It is a useful surrogate for middle class.

❑❑❑

13

THE INFLUENCE OF CULTURE ON CONSUMER BEHAVIOUR

We have seen the concept of individual differences by travelling to higher and still higher aggregations. This encompasses a wide field ranging from psychology to social psychology and sociology. In the present chapter, the vantage point is cultural anthropology.

Culture is thus the broadest parameter of a society and is thus rightly called the *personality of the society.* It represents the character of the society and includes factors like knowledge, laws, languages, religions, customs, rituals, art, music, technology, products, work patterns and all those artifacts that impart a distinct flavour to the society. It is thus a highly stretchable concept that includes a wide spectrum of aggregation.

Essentially, culture can be defined as a set of *learned* beliefs, values, attitudes, habits and forms of behaviour that are *shared* by society and are *transmitted* from generation to generation within that society. Culture as an aggregation directs the consumer behaviour of members of a particular society.

Beliefs are verbal statements indicating what a person knows and how he assesses something. Values are also beliefs but they meet the criteria of being *few* in number, *enduring* enough, *not specific, widely accepted* and channels for *culturally appropriate* behaviour. Values and beliefs in short are *mental images* leading to a variety of attitudes which affect the behavioural response of an individual. We choose a product like a car on the basis of general *values* like perceptions about workmanship, and a quality of a particular brand of a car and specific *beliefs* about its design, aesthetics and status it provides. In the definition, we have referred to forms of behaviour. By it we mean *customs.* Customs are culturally acceptable or approved way of behaviour with respect to specific situations. Taking a bath after return from a crematorium is a custom. Removing hair from the head after the death of a kin is also a custom. Routine behaviour such as adding milk and sugar to a cup of tea is also an example of custom. Beliefs and values are mere guide-lines for behaviour. Customs are acceptable forms of behaviour. Thus understanding of culture of a society enables a marketer to predict the adoption of their products. What we seem to do most naturally and automatically is perhaps attributable to our cultural background.

We realise the significance of culture's moulding our behaviour when we visit a region where different customs are followed. The contrast between us and them enables us to see the role culture plays in our life.

We in India are habituated to have a daily bath. Sometimes we bathe more than one time to get relief from the sultry tropical climate. There are, however, societies where they do not take bath daily. It is a cultural difference.

Culture is a great help in our need satisfaction. It provides guidance to us for various activities *e.g.,* what and what not to eat or what and what not to drink. Cultural norms provide satisfaction, and require modification or replacement when they do not do so. Products are sold as they satisfy our individual needs, and the larger societal needs. They are modified when such need satisfaction does not take place. Consumers are likely to change their values and customs. Girls these days would like to be slim, and this figure-consciousness make them accept gym lessons, exercise equipments, jogging and low-cal products. The change in values and life-style is a signal to marketers to do the necessary adaptation.

Culture is Learned

We inherit our physical characteristics from our parents *e.g.,* our complexion or the colour of our eyes. However, culture is not an inheritance. It is *learned* either formally or informally through family and friends and the environment. Promotion enhances cultural learning. The messages are repeated, so as to re-inforce the learning. At one stage, the benefits being promoted are *inherently* desired due to cumulative exposure. Advertising *teaches* the audience to expect certain benefits from the product category.

Acculturation

Cultural norms are effective when they become internalized by an individual. When we learn a new culture which is not our native culture we call it acculturation. Marketers marketing global brands must know about acculturation.

Enculturation

The process by which we learn our own culture is called enculturation. In other wards, we are talking of socialization. Our own culture is called native culture.

Language and Symbols

A common language facilitates the acquisition of a common culture. A common language enables communication to be completed by sharing of meaning. Communication is symbolic, and the symbols could be both verbal and non-verbal. Logos are an example of non-verbal communication. Symbolic nature of human language makes it quite distinct. A symbol represents something. All the words which make up the language are symbols. A storm makes us conjure up the images of hard-blowing winds and mad sea. It evokes apprehension in our mind. Our capacity to process the symbols gives us the advantage of experiencing a thing even vicariously. It is not necessary to have direct experience always. Our ability to understand symbols makes it easier to market the products on their features and benefits. Shared language and culture enable us to form definite images, and interpret them. A symbol can be interpreted by several ways. It is necessary to assess how it is being perceived. Price is used as a symbol of quality. Elements of marketing mix can be used as symbols.

Rituals

Consumer research so far neglected religious rites and rituals as a part of culture. Rituals are example of repetitive behaviour of a particular sequence on the part of individuals over a period of time. We follow rituals from cradle to grave. Thus we have naming ceremonies or christening, communion or thread ceremony, marriage ceremony and funeral rites. Rituals can be civic or religious. They can range from simple chanting of 'Om' or 'Bismillah' to an elaborate prayer procedure for 'yagna' or 'namaaz'. They can be private ceremonies or public ceremonies (marriages). All rituals are however not based on religions. Some are pure etiquette or grooming techniques. Ritualistic behaviour is pre-scripted. It flows in a particular sequence. It occurs repeatedly time and again. Thus at the end of every function, there is a ritual of singing the national anthem — *Jana Gana Mana.*

Marketers are concerned about the products associated with rituals. Many catering packages are sold to celebrate rituals of birth and death. Products like watches and pens are gifted as a part of ritual of passing a public examination. Champagne is sold as a celebration drink. Plaques are sold to distinguish people who achieve in the field of sports. Clothes are sold so that people can celebrate the weddings, Deepavali or Christmas. Cards are sold to greet people on various occasions.

A ritual, as we know by now, is just a practice. *Ritualistic behaviour* is behaviour that is patterned on a ritual. Beauty care techniques adopted by youngsters are examples of ritualistic behaviour. A facial involves cleansing the face by deep cleansing milk, moisturization by a moisturizer, steaming by hot water, putting a facial mask to remove dirt and applying an anti-astringent lotion to tighten the pores.

Much of the Western culture derives its set of shared value and beliefs from the Judeo-Christian heritage. The US culture is based on the Protestant ethic. India's cultural heritage is traced to the *sanatan dharma,* though other cultural practices co-exist with the Hindu traditions to make India's culture a mosaic of composite culture. Middle-East follows the Islamic traditions though some practices can be traced to pre-Islamic era.

Culture is Shared

A cultural characteristic is one which is shared by the society. Group customs thus provide cultural linkages. Common language enables value, experience and custom sharing. Institutions like family, schools and colleges, places of worship and mass media play a great role in the transfer of culture.

Advertising and Cultural Values

Today there is give-and-take of culture. No matter how hard the traditionalists try, there is no stopping the tidal wave of pop-culture. Adopting Chinese cuisine does not imply selling our souls to the Chinese civilization. The give-and-take of culture which advertising brings about in its contemporised form is a symbol of universal togetherness. But when we strip these Western culture enthusiasts of their borrowed veneer of Westernisation we, discover a conservative Indian who believes in traditional values.

Culture is a basic part of human nature. It also determines a person's wants and behaviour. Culture is learned. There is socialization of a child right from the time it comes into this world. The child acquires a basic set of values, perceptions, preferences and behaviour. The socialization is done through the institutions of family, school, church, friends etc. Advertising also shapes our cultural values. The other maxim is also true; the cultural values shape up our advertising. In fact, both inter-act with each other.

We have several cultural values as Indians. We want to be successful. We want to be efficient. We are oriented towards our family. We seek comfort from external environment. For the sake of our family, we can postpone our own gratification. We like to be youthful etc.

Indian advertising asks us to save for the marriage of our daughter or for the education of our child. We are other-centred, and not self-centred. So the advertisements reflect this cultural value of ours. Besides, there are advertisements for the well-being of the family, for the betterment of the child, for a gift to a loved one etc.

We, as a cultural group, prefer advertisements of products like incense sticks (agarbattis), bindi (Shilpa), kajal (Jai Kajal), ornaments (Tribhovandas Bhimji), shaloos (marriage sarees), bidies (smoking device).

We love fun (Thums-up), hospitality (Rasana), health (Chyavanprash), long hair (Keokarpin, Coco Raj), thick hair (shampoos), complexion (Vicco Turmeric Vanishing Cream).

So the advertisments we see are steeped into our cultural ethos. But at the same time, some advertisements make us receptive to the denim and pop culture. We change our cultural values under the influence of these advertisements.

But core cultural values are not affected much by the advertising. It does affect the subsidiary cultural values.

Culture is Dynamic

Culture keeps on evolving to meet the newly emerging social needs. Women were confined to the four walls of the home some years back. They have now come out of the closet and kitchen. We find them working and earning a sizeable income. Several male bastions have fallen and female presence could be seen in such exclusive male preserves. All this has implications for the marketer. The gender roles have changed drastically. Decision-making for purchasing is thus affected. Male-female roles have also undergone changes. Many products which were consumed only by male population are now also targeted at women e.g. some types of liquors, insurance policies, cigarette's etc.

Measuring Culture

There are methods like projective techniques and attitude measurements which are popularly used to study culture. Apart from these, we can undertake direct *observation* of the consumer while they buy a particular product, say spectacles. The observer may also participate in the process, say by posing as a sales person. Depth interviews and focus group methods are used to notice emerging cultural trends. Content analysis of advertising also indicates the change in culture. Value instruments are used to assess what people feel about such concepts as comfort, peace, security and freedom.

Core Cultural Values

Every culture has some core cultural values which affect and reflect its character. India is a vast continent-like country with a number of sub-cultures, each having its own cultural values. Indian society is dynamic and is undergoing a constant cultural transformation. There are some contradictory values in Indian society which lead to confusion. Thus though Indians show high attachment to parents, they also love individualism. Indians choose a wide array of products and services which reflect their-style. India is a country of paradoxes and a society in transition.

Core values are, however, pervasive, and enduring. India tries to balance the values of dharma, artha and kama. It is a deeply religious and spiritual society. However, it has a long tradition of trade and commerce. It was a liberal society once upon a time, but sex became a taboo under the influence of Victorian values. India believes mostly in monogamy. Its society is highly tolerant and believes in prosperity for all. There is too much other-centred approach and less emphasis on 'I-centred' approach. There is a tendency to postpone gratification rather than have immediate gratification. Indian Constitution has given 'freedom of speech and expression' as a fundamental right. Indians are philanthropic. They express their social obligations by building institutes like schools, colleges, hospitals and temples. All these core values are not exclusively Indian. Some of these have been accepted by our contact with other cultures. Some of the values which are deeply ingrained in India have now travelled to other regions of the world. These values reflect our character. They are relevant for consumer behaviour. Core cultural values are respected by the marketers. It is difficult to change them.

Sub-Culture

In the same society, we have sub-sets of culture which possess distinct cultural values and beliefs, and constitute what is known as sub-culture. In each of these subsets, the shared values are transmitted from generation to generation. These sub-cultural sets conform to many of the norms of the dominant culture. However, when these norms are not compatible with their sub-culture, they tend to deviate from them.

Sub-cultures are formed on the basis of many dimensions. *Nationality* is one important dimension. Thus we have Indian sub-culture in the United States. *Religion* is also a very common dimension for a sub-culture. Thus we have Muslims in India having their distinct sub-culture. In some countries, *race* also becomes a dimension. Thus we have the Blacks in America. In India, regions produce a sub-culture, thus we have North Indian sub-culture, South Indian subculture. *Castes* also become an important factor. Brahmins have a distinct subculture. Sometimes, caste and region together generate a subs-culture, *e.g.,* Palghat Brahmins and Konkanastha Brahmins. Sub-cultures are based on age (teenagers, middle-aged and elderly), social class and gender.

MTV-IMRB Survey of Young Indians

The primary objective of this survey was to map out values, attitudes, life-style, music and music-related preferences. It covered 2745 respondents in the three metros, Kanpur, Lucknow and Bangalore. The age-group interviewed was 15-34 years. The following propositions and the percentage of people who favour them are illustrative of how a young Indian defines himself.

Proposition	*People who favour it (in per cent)*
People recognise that what I buy is the best.	64.4
I always seek the advice of friends regarding brands and products.	52.19
I wear what suits me, irrespective of whether it is fashionable or not.	69.44
Life should not be taken too seriously.	57.55
One should rebel if someone is being unreasonable.	57.46
College education is very important.	67.61
Job security is more important than money.	Many favour it
Pre-marital sex is a way of life.	29.33
Couple should live together before marriage.	31.55
Friends are the centre of my activities.	53.07
I try to obey my elders even if it hurts.	65.63
It's okay to take parental help to make it in life.	Not many in favour
Television is the ultimate entertainment.	55.22

O and M survey talks of controlled freedom that today's youth prefers. There is a strong individualism and a desire to maximise opportunities but tempered by a strong sense if family engagement.

ORG-MARG Survey called Youth Track-96 finds Indian youth admire the west for the elements of modernity. But he is also conscious that west has given us wrong values like smoking, drinking and pre-marital sex. They admire Indian values such as respect, hospitality and the patriarchal system. What they dislike are the corruption, dowry and caste system.

Though Indian youth is outwardly westernised, it is still rooted to its moorings as far as community and marriages are concerned. Indian youth today is out for western trappings and accepts the Indian values. Many still believe that both the Eastern and Western values can co-exist.

Marriage is considered necessary for raising the family. The festivities of marriage like the band, the song and dance are liked.

Mostly, youth believe in conformism, since non-conformism is seen to reduce the chances of success.

Today's youth wants to remain marketable. The emphasis is not philosophical values and intellectual activity. Ideologies have failed them. Money has become all the more important. They prefer glamorous careers, rather than the conventional careers.

Age-subgroups of the Indian population might be considered as separate sub-cultures. Each stage of the family life-cycle can be treated as a separate sub-culture. Generation X group is of people between 18-29. Baby boomers correspond to the people between 30 and 40. The elderly consumers have reached their 50th birthday. Sex is also a sub-culture, with males and females showing distinct characteristics, and playing different roles. Women's role is gradually expanding giving rise to working woman's culture.

OPENNESS IN RELATIONSHIPS

In recent times, relationships in the family itself have opened up a lot. Consider the ad of Stayfree. Here the relationship between the youth and the parent is reflected. Earlier, a sanitary napkin was introduced to a young girl by a progressive older sister or a friendly aunt. But not the mother. The mother was usually an amazed, passive, naive and side-lined character. Stayfree shows a bewildered young girl looking upto a more confident mother, who advises her to be carefree and carry on with life.

It shows an openness and a new order of parenting. It shows a less inhibitive society.

Cross-Cultural Consumer Behaviour

In these days of globalisation, the world is becoming a small place. Multinationals are registering their presence in many countries of the world. They should, therefore, know to what extent the consumers of two or more nations are similar or different. It is called cross-cultural consumer analysis. This enables the marketers to design an appropriate marketing programme. The more similar the consumers are, the greater are the chances to adopt universal marketing strategies. To the extent they are non-similar, we shall have to adapt the marketing strategies. Kellogs can become successful to sell breakfast cereals if it first understands the breakfast habits of the market it has entered, and then tries to modify these habits so that they become conducive to the use of Kellog products. It is a dual acculturation process. The differences in culture should be understood properly. These differences could be because of semantics. Sometimes, the segmentation opportunities are different. Two societies may have different consumption pattern. Though one product is perceived as giving certain benefits in one society, it may be perceived as giving altogether different benefits in another society. Products can be evaluated differently in different societies. Socio-economic conditions are different. Market structure is not the same. Research techniques may need modification to accommodate cultural differences.

GLOBAL ADVERTISING

Global Advertising is conceived as a response to global marketing enabling the agency to channelise advertising from trans-national corporations into trans-national media. The same product brand that was once sold nationally can now be sold to the whole world backed by the same advertising.

Customer needs and desires have homogenised and globalised. Global Corporations sell standardised products in the same way everywhere. Global advertising promotes a global product. Coke has been using the same standardised advertising in all countries. Pepsi adapts the common theme to the national culture.

Global advertising is defined as any paid form of non-personal presentation and promotion of idea(s), good(s), or service(s) by an identified *global sponsor* of a product to a *global customer*.

Objectives

(*i*) to keep up the world wide corporate image.

(*ii*) to reduce production and creative costs.

(*iii*) to avoid message confusion in international areas of media overlap.

Degree of Standardisation

It is dependent on the product category. Culture-bound home use products of Nestle and require a large degree of adaptation. Coke is less culture-bound.

It is aimed at younger generation, whose cultural norms are fluid. Coke appeals to the same segment the world over. Therefore it can run a universal campaign targeted at the common beliefs of these people.

Single-Theme Success: Types

(*i*) *International Advertisements*: Universal campaigns are used here as the target consumer is the same all over the world, e.g. a Coke.

(*ii*) *Semi-international*: Partial adaptation of the universal campaign. Foreign product is shown in one's own environment, e.g., Camay. The theme used is the same but the copy is adapted to suit each local market.

(*iii*) *Provincial category*: Full adaptation of universal theme. Even execution is adapted to the local market. The basic reason is that the target customer changes from country to country; e.g., Renault in France is a 'super-car', in Germany a 'safe' car, and in Italy, a 'speedy' car.

Trade off between Adaptation and Standardisation

This should work in Indian Market depending on product category, budget constraints, promotional constraints, competition, cultural diversity of the target segment in India and in the parent country. Lufthansa adapted whereas Tang did not. Coke may also have to go the Pepsi way in India by adapting "pattern standardisation." Indian companies have to formulate strategies while advertising a global product into India and while being a global marketer to other countries.

Agency: Global Marketer/Advertiser

The global company prefers to keep the same ad agency to do global advertising.

Celebrity Endorsements

Global companies are endorsed by global celebrities like Michael Jackson endorsing Pepsi worldwide.

INTERNATIONALISATION OF ADVERTISING

Internationalisation, globalisation call it what you will — is an evolutionary process, requiring some encouragement and guidance with restraint. But at the same time local values are to be protected. The dilemma is resolved by two words: 'know thyself' or 'know thy purpose.'

An ad has to perform two functions — it has to be sold by the agency to the client which is its customer and thereafter the ad must persuade the consumer in its favour. And selling the client and persuading the consumer do not always coincide.

Advertising is a body of techniques in communication. Individual advertisements are meant to be used by the consumer to help the decision-making. As soon as the ad appears, it no longer belongs to the advertiser. It becomes the property of the consumer.

Consumer puts a final stamp on an ad and so the labels like internationalisation or protection of local values are to that extent irrelevant.

All Advertising is Local

Internationalisation is an advertiser's view-point. The consumer is concerned only with his satisfaction.

Globalisation in advertising has originated because business has become global in coverage but continues to be controlled from a central point of authority and impetus. Secondly, globalisation results in *economies of scale* in the production and implementation of ads. Thirdly, there is a need to influence the market *with speed.* It translates into 'selling the same things in the same way everywhere.' But perhaps it is too much to expect that basic needs and aspirations are essentially the same, whether a person stays in Mumbai or in New York. Perhaps, globalisation strikes at a basic freedom — the freedom of choice.

Nevertheless, it is true that the world is becoming a global village — the world of commerce is shrinking. Segments of populations are becoming demographically similar in terms of rising incomes and higher aspirations. People buy brands and are not aquiring products. At the same time, ethnic awareness is coming into focus when people look at their glorious cultural heritage, which becomes a point of inspiration for them.

As human beings, basic motivations are the same everywhere. But there should not be deceptive generalisations. Research in the market place of consumer psyche is a must. The thing that matters is relevance. Without relevance, no advertisement will be effective.

With a true understanding of relevance, many ads of international brands could be adapted or adopted or created to suit the Indian environment. Globalisation of execution and globalisation of concept are different.

Internationalisation vs. Localisation

Americans believe that some successful US ads can be effectively used in the rest of the world. They feel young people everywhere are the same. This similarity is becoming more apparent within time and with development. The French disagree with this thesis. They believe that advertising is a part of culture. Global appeal ads are developed because big creative ideas are not easy to come by. Also because ads for different countries become costly.

The success or failure of an ad, in other countries depend upon three factors:

Target Audience: Mercedes-Benz or BMW German cars have a strong upper middle class orientation in Japan. But in Germany taxis are either BMW or Mercedes-Benz. If the same ad is launched in both the countries, it is bound to be a disaster in at least one.

Market Share Position: A brand leader may be a late comer in a foreign country. Its copy strategy should be different.

Competition: How many major competitors a brand has is a very major consideration.

International Advertising

Advantages

1. Savings on production costs. These savings can finance more number of ads. Lintas campaign for IBM ran in 26 markets. The cost of production was around 1,50,000. Had there been a separate film for each market, it would have cost around 4 million.
2. Commonalities in consumer rather than differences make it more efficient to have global marketing plan and global advertising strategies.
3. Harmonised international messages reduce consumer confusion.

Pitfalls

1. Different markets have different marketing environment. In Poland, mothers enter the hospitals to deliver babies only if they are seriously ill. AT & T US-made commercial featuring a woman who had just delivered a baby in hospital thus could not be run in Poland. Women in Saudi must have their heads covered. In UAE, left-hand's use for food related action is a taboo. Even brand names require a change in different markets. Unions in Australia who control TV production insist on having Australion-media films for at least 80 p.c. of their advertising time.

2. TV format has no world wide standard. Great sound tracks can get spoilt in markets where both the sound track and picture are started at the same time. There should be ½ second gap.

Adaptation of International Messages

To suit the Indian ethos, international companies are changing their media communications appropriately, though keeping the basic platform unchanged. GE uses emotions worldwide, but gives them an Indian face here. 'If light wasn't an expression of joy, they wouldn't have created a festival in its name'. The obvious reference in the ad message is to Diwali. Shell has released the highly visible messages of *Namaste* Shell and *Suhana Safar* on bill-boards across the country. Regionalisation of communication makes the messages more relevant though at the same time global competitive image is retained. There should be a trade off between a global equity and regionalisation. Wrangler Jeans from India dilute cowboy brand. MNCs are attempting to bring an Indian perspective to their image.

ADAPTATION OF INTERNATIONAL CAMPAIGN

Campaign: Camay Soap

Visual in Campaign	*Country*
A beautiful bathing woman in the bath-room	Universal campaign
A man was included in the bathroom	Venezuela
Only a man's hand could be seen in the ad.	Italy and France
Man waited outside the bathroom	Japan
Man walked into the commercial much after the woman was dressed.	India

Source: Lajwanti D'Souza, TOI, Feb. 4 1996

Case for Internationalisation

Internationalisation is justified on four major grounds:

1. Building brands and creating brand equity is expensive. For a transnational it is economical to make a similar brand offering globally.
2. In competitive markets, it is sensible to pool resources instead of fragmenting them amongst local agencies creating local campaigns.
3. Satellite media do not know national boundaries and uniform ads in such media are more sensible.

4. In marketing mix, advertising and packaging are kept uniform since consumers travel more and their experience with a brand gets more uniform. The product may however be adapted to suit the local needs.

Learning from one market is transferred to another market to evolve a global strategy which is cumulative local strategy.

India may be diverse. But beneath this diversity, there is unity. The main thing is the big idea which can cut across the markets. Ideas can be made global, like Marlboro's cowboy who does not have anything common with a Japanese or an Indian. Visual metaphors must be found to transcend the boundaries. The Cathay Pacific commercial's target audience consists of well-travelled executives with international exposure. And so it works. Pepsi stands for a set of values in the US and the same set of values apply to India. Creativity here is commercial creativity, and not art for art's sake. The more global the creative appeal is, the better is the time utilisation. Besides, advertising serves a business purpose. It is the business point of view that over-rides the creative point of view.

Lintas (Delhi) has done a campaign for Mastercard in India which is more or less similar to international campaign. Or the Pepsi campaign where Amir fetches a bottle for a demanding girl. Agencies may have reasons to do a campaign different from the international campaign e.g. Motorola in India.

Case Against Internationalisation

India is too culturally diverse to allow this to happen. The target audiences of Europe and the US at least have something in common. We do not have even a common link language, which is an essential requirement for creative communication. A fantastic idea in English cannot be put as effectively as in a language, say Tamil.

In India, there is a vast rural market where Fido Dido or a Remo may not be relevant. Multi-nationals have manuals which specify the main elements in any ad campaign e.g. logos, print size etc. We are being asked to live in a furnished room. We have to juggle around the elements they may specify. Transplantation of creative may work with certain categories and in certain target groups. Aerated cans can appeal to the US youth as much as they could to the Indian metro youth. But a weather beaten Rajasthani seeks a valid reason to quench his thirst with a can. Narrow segments in Indian population on par with America in metro can benefit from international ad transplantation.

We have to think global, but act local. Globally Ariel stands for *outstanding clean* but locally it is interpreted as *stain-remover* and *whitener.*

❑❑❑

14

OPINION LEADERS AND PERSONAL INFLUENCE

An opinion leader is a person who influences informally the actions and attitudes of others. Others may be just *opinion receivers* or may be active *opinion seekers.* Though this influence is verbal, at times it can be non-verbal too. Two housewives talking about the cleaning powder they use in washing the utensils are engaged in a product-related conversation. It is a *word-of-mouth* communication. Such communication is informal and happens between two or more persons. It is interpersonal, and so mostly face-to-face or telephonic. The party that expresses an opinion and offers advice about specific product or product category is called opinion leader. An opinion leader may play the role of an opinion receiver in case of some other product or product category.

The following situations illustrate how opinion leadership operates-

1. In office, an employee expresses a desire to own a CD music system. His colleague recommends a particular brand.
2. Two friends see an album of marriage photographs. One friend suggests the use of Kodak Gold film which works better in low illumination, and has high colour fidelity.
3. A person moves in a new flat. He feels the need of one more fan in the hall to make it airy. He visits a neighbour to know the name of a 'reliable electrician' to fix the fan.

Research in this area focuses on how opinion leaders influence the consumption patterns of others. We can use the broader term personal influence in place of word-of-mouth. The investigation of personal influence embraces the four areas of activity: (1) fashion (2) movie-going, (3) public affairs (politics) and (4) marketing, (which is related basically to brand choice).

Opinion Leaders and Persuasiveness

Opinion leaders persuade others in favour of certain products. Their influence is derived from the perception that they are objective in their assessment and are doing simply a food turn by proffering advice. Such advice reduces the anxiety level of the new buyer. Opinion leaders also express both pros and cons of a product. We can, therefore, avoid brand and products which attract negative comments. Opinion leaders not only narrate their experience with the product but also offer an advice regarding buying or not buying. Interpersonal communication with an opinion leader guides regarding the choice of a brand, the usage of a product, the place where we can shop for the product and the service level of a service provider.

Opinion leadership is category specific. We may seek a person's opinion while buying a two-wheeler for our teen-ager son. The person who acts as opinion leader regarding bike-choice may himself become an opinion seeker while deciding about the future career of his son. Opinion leaders are specialists in certain product categories. Research of Katz and Lazarsfeld does not support a generalized opinion leaders. Opinion leaders are specialists in certain product categories. Opinion leadership is thus a two-way process. One and the same person can be an opinion leader or an opinion seeker, depending upon the situation. Besides, an opinion seeker may also influence an opinion leader during the course of the conversation.

"Influentials and influences may exchange roles in different spheres of influence." — *Katz*.

Opinion leaders are more knowledgeable, and have greater exposure to mass media. The communication flows form mass media to opinion leaders, who spread it across horizontally. It is thus not a 'trickle-down' but a 'trickle-across' approach.

An opinion, leader by analogy is a 'shepherd' of a flock of sheep (group) of which there are, many in the society. Each flock of sheep or group has its own shepherd or opinion leader. But as we have already observed, there are role reversals in the personal influence process, and like any analogy, this one too is not perfect.

Opinion leaders belong to the same primary groups of families, friends and co-workers. Opinion leaders are characterised by many interpersonal contacts (Gregariousness) and by above-normal exposure to media.

Motivation and Opinion Leadership

We have to consider the motivation of both the opinion leaders and opinion receivers.

Opinion leaders seem to satisfy some need of theirs *e.g.,* self-improvement, social acceptance etc. Sometimes an opinion leader tries to bring down his own post-purchase dissatisfaction by asking others to fall in line with his own product choice. It is just a reassurance for himself that he has made the right choice. An opinion leader may be seeking attention to himself or may be trying to impress on others how knowledgeable and aware he is. He wants to pass on the impression that he is in possession of knowledge which others do not. He wants to prove his superiority. He may get the satisfaction of having won others to his own view-point. All this is self-involvement.

Apart from self-involvement, an opinion leader may be motivated by *product-involvement, message involvement* and involvement for *others.* Product involvement indicates a high degree of satisfaction or dissatisfaction with a product which an opinion leader wants to share with others *e.g.,* his preference for a particular brand of a car. Message involvement indicates the influence of ad messages. Ad slogans and messages become pieces of everyday conversations. Thus people talk about 'the real pleasure', *dhoondhate reh jaogey* and a 'right choice'. Involvement for others uses product-related conversation as expression of friendliness, love, affection and neighbourhood feeling.

Opinion receivers satisfy various needs by receiving information from the opinion leaders. As we have already observed, the anxiety factor is reduced. There is also no need to undertake an extensive search. Besides, the product selected meets the approval of an opinion leader. The choice of an opinion leader is a matter of the socio-cultural background of the opinion receiver. Purchase pals are those who accompany us on our shopping sprees. They can be males or females. Male pals play a role of opinion leaders. Female pals are used as moral support and to instil a sense of confidence in the buyer.

The following chart summarises the motivations of opinion leaders and opinion receivers.

Motivation	*Opinion Leaders*	*Opinion Receivers*
Self Involvement	• Reduce cognitive dissonance • Invite attention • Impress knowledgeability • Satisfaction of having converted others	• Risk reduction • Reduction of search time
Product Involvement	Express satisfaction with a product	• Learn about innovations • Learn about usage
Message Involvement	An exciting ad is made a piece of conversation	—
Involvement for others	Expression of friendliness and neighbourliness through product related discussions	Buy products which will meet the approval of others. A search for acceptance.

Measuring Opinion Leadership

What is the extent of influence of the opinion leaders? It is a question of measuring opinion leadership. We shall consider four techniques of measurement: (1) self-designating method, (2) socio-metric method, (3) objective method, and (4) key-informant method.

Self-Designating Method

Here we ask others what role they have played in influencing the consumption of others in recent past, (say six months). A straight question could be:

In the past six months, have you been asked to advise or give your opinion about .... products? (Specify products on the blank)

The answer could be 'yes' or 'no'. It classifies them into leaders or non-leaders. But such straitjacket compartmentalisation does not reflect a range of opinion leadership activity. The questions therefore can be qualified by using time-denoting adverbs like 'infrequently influencing others' or 'sometimes influencing' or 'frequently influencing'.

Illustration:

1. Friends and neighbours *frequently* seek my opinion on .... products.

....	....	....	....	....
Extremely Agree	Agree	Neither Agree/Disagree	Not Agree	Extremely Disagree

2. Sometimes, I influence what .... products my friends buy.

....

3. Often, I render advice on .... products.

....

4. I can count at least 3 people who have asked my opinion about .... products.

....

5. My friends regard me as a good source of advice about .... products

....

Recently, researchers have also compiled scales for measuring susceptibility of consumers to the influence exerted by others. A typical statement may read as follows.

I buy fashion clothes only when I am sure my friends would approve them.

The agreement is taken on a 7-point scale; extremely agree, fairly agree, agree, neither agree/disagree, not agree, fairly not agree and extremely not agree.

Socio-metric Research

Here a self-contained population is examined to verify consumer-related conversations. To illustrate, we can study the inmates of university hostels in terms of influencing others or getting influenced by others. A wider socio-metric study beyond a self-contained community is difficult to manage as it involves tracing all those individuals who are named by the primary group, irrespective of their location.

We can ask Bombay University Hostel Inmates the following questions to assess them an two dimensions — providing information to others and receiving the same form others.

Providing Information

1. At the hostel, did you tell any one about the movie *Taal* in the past one week?

   Yes .... No ....

   If yes, then proceed.

2. Whom did you tell about it first? ....
   (Name the person)
3. To whom others from the hostel did you tell about it? ....
4. Did you recommend them to see or not see the movie?

   See .... Not see .... Other ....

Receiving Information

1. Which first comment do you remember about *Taal?*
2. Do you remember who made this comment?
   Yes .... No ....
   If yes, proceed.
3. Who made this comment? ....
   (Name the person).
4. Is he a hostel resident?
   Yes .... No ....
5. Did he recommend you to see or not see the movie?
   See .... Not see .... Other ....
6. Did you talk with this person prior to seeing *Taal* or after seeing it?
   Prior .... After .... Not remember ....
7. Can you specify other hostel residents who talked about *Taal*?
   ....
   ....

Objective Method

It is a type of controlled experimentation. Here new products are placed in the hands of a chosen group, and then interpersonal communications are examined. Natural opinion leaders influence others to fall in line with them. Non-leaders are ineffective in doing so. In objective method, opinion leaders are artificially placed to act as such, and the results of their efforts are measured.

Key Informant Method

Instead of studying a sample or a whole self-contained community, we can identify a key informant who will name the opinion leaders in a particular group. To illustrate, a college professor may know which one or two or several students are most likely to be the opinion leaders of a particular class. A professor who identifies opinion leaders in a class is thus a key informant. Sales people may act as key informants to identify opinion leaders which influence other customers. Purchase manager may act as key informant to pinpoint those who are likely to influence a purchase decision.

Profile of an Opinion Leader

As we have seen, it is necessary to identify the opinion leaders so as to direct our promotional messages to them. Though research has been carried out to prepare a profile of an opinion leader, it is not an easy task. First, an opinion leader may himself becomes an opinion seeker for some different product category. Still in general we can say an opinion leader is having higher *involvement* with the product. It makes him knowledgeable about the product, and he spreads this *knowledge* He also reads the print *media* and listens to and views the electronic media much more. He is a consumer *innovator* who tries new products, and passes on his experience to others. He is *self-confident* and *gregarious*. He is *differentiated* from others and chooses to act differently. He belongs to the same social class as that of the consumer to engage in horizontal interpersonal communication. Consumers choose old people to know their opinion in respect of certain product categories, but choose young people to know about fashions. Opinion leaders are more likely to read special interest magazines devoted to specific product categories in which they 'specialize'. Opinion leaders belong to the same age group and socio-economic group as their opinion receivers.

Overlap of Opinion Leadership

Opinion leadership is pretty common and every third person could be an opinion leader or sometimes every other person. Is opinion leadership generalizeable? In others words, is an opinion leader in one sphere likely to be an opinion leader in another? Overlap of leadership is possible across certain product categories with similar interests e.g. cosmetics and personal grooming, books and periodicals, haute coutre and hair styles etc. We can say that opinion leaders in one product area are opinion leaders often in other related product areas. Barring this, a generalized opinion leader is not supported by research. Yes there can be a generalized *marketing leader* whose opinion matters as they have marketing expertise. They are distinguishable from opinion leaders as their influence is not a result of their product experience. Marketing leaders of today are good at electronics, computers, space travel, automobiles and the latest theories in science and technology.

Two-step Flow of Communications Hypothesis

We become interested in identifying the opinion leaders after Lazarsfeld, Berelson and Gaudet (1948) put forward "the two-step flow of communications hypothesis". It was observed that certain members of the social system are more exposed to the mass media and tend to operate as filters and transmitters of information for the remaining members of the social system. We now understand that this differential knowledge implies differential influence. Thus the concept of opinion leadership crystallised. They are the direct receivers of information from mass media and transmit (and interpret) this information to masses. They are a link between the mass media and the society at large.

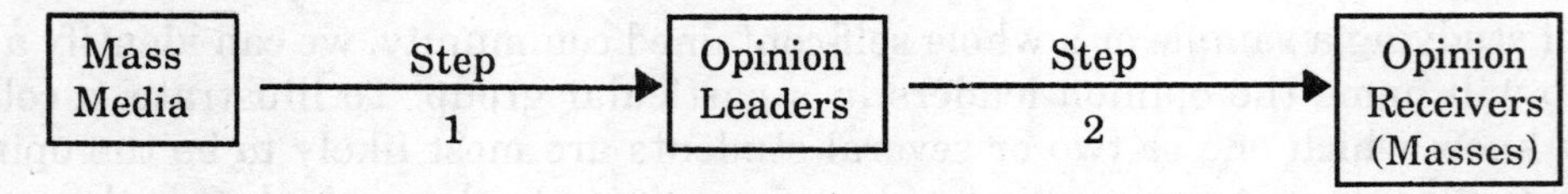

Fig. 14.1: Two-step Flow of Communication

The above diagram illustrates this hypothesis. It's major contribution is its emphasis on social interaction between people. It is a method of conveying information, whereby attitudes are developed, and behaviour is stimulated. It rules out that mass media alone can influence the selling of products, ideas or persons. Opinion leaders transmit the information, interpret it at times and legitimize it. The receivers are friends, neighbours and acquaintances, who comprise the 'masses'.

The theory is fallacious since it is not a true picture of information and influence flows. Mass media may affect both the opinion leaders and opinion receivers. However, opinion receivers are more likely to be influenced by opinion leaders than by mass media. Opinion leaders do not initiate all interpersonal communication directed at opinion receivers. Sometimes opinion receivers may initiate communication. Opinion receivers are also likely to offer advice to others, and opinion leaders themselves. Opinion leaders are more likely to receive and seek advice than those who are non-leaders.

Multi-step Flow of Communication Hypothesis

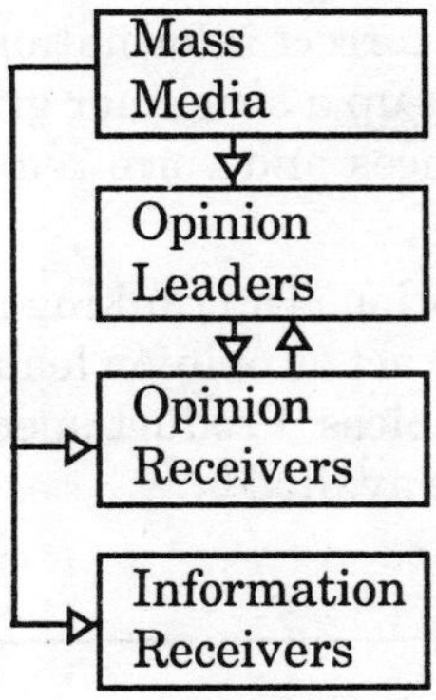

Multi-step flow is a broader view of the flows in interpersonal communication. It accounts for the fact that the interaction between opinion leaders and opinion receivers both in terms of giving information and being influenced is a two-way process. The diagram 14.2 illustrates a multi-step flow.

Communication flows the flow information from the media both to the opinion leaders and opinion receivers and information receivers. Information receivers do not either influence others or get influenced. Opinion leaders and opinion receivers both pass information and influence to each other.

Fig. 14.2 : Multi-step Flow

Opinion Leadership	Opinion Seeking: H	Opinion Seeking: L
H	Social Integration	Social Independence
L	Social Dependence	Social Isolation

We can form a matrix of opinion leadership and opinion seeking.

Viewed from the matrix, there emerges four patterns of interpersonal communication -

- High opinion seeking, and leadership combination leading to *social integration*
- High opinion leadership but low opinion seeking leading to *social independence.*
- Low opinion leadership but high opinion seeking leading to *social dependence.*
- Low opinion leadership as well as opinion seeking leading to *social isolation.*

It puts consumers into four types rather than into two types as opinion leaders and opinion seekers.

Opinion Leadership and Promotion

Word-of-mouth communications and other informal communications have greater credibility than the formal paid ad messages or personal selling. It is an acknowledged method by which a consumer reduces his perceived risk. New product designers respect word-of-mouth comments, and the design is made in such a manner that there is something to talk about it by the consumers. Walkman owes its success mainly to word-of-mouth. Movies sell more on word-of-mouth. Sometimes word-of-mouth publicity is not spontaneous, but is simulated. Ads and samples are used to persuade people to tell others how they like the product. A direct marketing programme can be run to provoke a discussion about the benefits of the products. Informal communications about a product are inter-woven in commercials. It is necessary to keep in mind that informal communication is difficult to control. There may be negative comments and rumours which are not true. There may be a feeling that the product is harmful to health or causes diseases like cancer. Or it is a 'foreign' product which harms our national interest. A toll-free number can be set up to set at rest the negative publicity by giving correct information. A good Public Relations programme is called for. It is also necessary to set up a consumer grievance redressal cell. When consumers get a mechanism to their grievances and voice redress them, the chances of bad word-of-mouth publicity are reduced.

It is possible to make use of opinion leaders strategically for promotion. Top ranking students can be given a set of books as a prize by a publisher to allow them to act as opinion leaders for the other class-mates. Sports captions can be used to express their choices. Product-specific opinion leaders can be created and their enthusiasm for products can be availed of.

BUZZ OR WORD-OF-MOUTH PROMOTION

Word-of-mouth promotion has become an important force capable of bringing obscure products into the centre-stage. It is wrong to think that only outrageous products are buzz-worthy. Viagra, has become successful by word-of-mouth publicity amongst doctors and consumers. Viagra is a research product. Fosamax by Merck which is a product for osteoporosis became significant by making this debilitating bone condition a common topic of discussion between women and their doctors. All products are not buzz-worthy however. To be so, they must have some unique attribute. Secondly, they must be highly visible. Word-of-mouth publicity does not just happen. It is increasingly the result of carefully managed marketing programmes. It is necessary to put the products into the hands of those people who have greater influence in shaping public opinion. A limited supply of products is another strategy to make people crave for what they cannot get easily. Celebrity endorsement also supports buzz. A product can make to a list to become a guide to consumers to focus their attention. A management institute can be 3rd or 4th in *Business Today's* list, and that guides the unknowing students to consider it. Product loyalty must be cultivated widely across the whole community. Who starts the word-of-mouth? Not always our own customers. There may be unexpected vanguards, and identifying them is a matter of research. Often a counter-culture has a greater ability to start word-of-mouth.

It is not correct to assume that trends are best exploited by the companies who enter first. Even market followers also benefit from the trends if they can correctly assess when to exploit the trend and when not. It is not advisable to use media and advertising too early to generate buzz. It may provoke the opinion makers reject a highly promoted product which they would have otherwise adopted. Companies should concentrate on consumer-to-consumer communications. This is the birth-place of all buzz. We should encourage consumers to talk about a product or to use the product in such a way that it is noticed by other people. In this age of globalisation, word-of-mouth travels across national borders. Word-of-mouth would flourish in this borderless world of Internet and mobile telephony. Word-of-mouth will become a dominant force in the shaping of markets.

* Based on HBR article.

❑❑❑

15

DIFFUSION AND ADOPTION OF NEW PRODUCTS

Spread of innovations within the market represents diffusion. In other words, diffusion leads to acceptance of the innovation. Acceptance occurs because of communication process to members of a social system over a period of time.

Innovation itself has several interpretations. Booz, Allen and Hamiton have given the following six categories of innovative products.

(1) **Technological Breakthroughs:** That really give a unique product, *e.g.,* an anti-cancer drug, an AIDS vaccine. These products are quite different from the existing products. Nylon or transistors when first introduced were technological breakthroughs. These products are new-to-the world, and will create their own market.

(2) **Significant Improvements:** These products are significant improvements over the existing products, *e.g.,* instant coffee replaces the usual brew coffee. These have greater perceived value.

(3) **Modified Products:** These are revisions in the existing product, *e.g.,* addition of a new flavour or perfume, a new package, a revised size etc.

(4) **Products New to the Company;** These products are new to the company but not new to the market. They are imitative products. These allow the company to enter an existing market with a *me-too* product.

(5) **Repositioning:** Existing products are targeted to new markets or market segments.

(6) **Cost-Reductions:** The products remain functionally the same, but the prices are reduced.

Innovations can be considered with reference to the company. They can be considered with reference to the product. Product innovations are *continuous* when they disturb the existing pattern the least — they are just modifications. Product innovations are *dynamical continuous* when they disrupt a continuous innovations somewhat, but still do not change the established behaviour pattern *e.g.,* Sony Handycam, CD players, disposable diapers. Product innovation can be *discontinuous* when the consumer behaviour pattern is changed e.g. diagonostic strips for diabetes, fax machines. Innovations with reference to the market means either it has been purchased by a small percentage of the total potential market or it has been on the market for a relatively short period of time. Innovations are more appropriately defined with reference to consumer perceptions.

Discontinuous Innovation		**Dynamically Continuous Innovations**		**Continuous Innovations**
Basic Telephony Rotary Instrument	→	Push-button Phones Cordless Phones Cellular Phones Video-Phones Satellite Phones	→	Instruments in different designs, colours, and styles

Fig. 15.1 : Product Innovations

Market Evolution

Market for a product evolves over the four stages of product life cycle. We shall first consider the evolution of market at the introductory stage.

Market Evolution: Introductory Stage

Here a new product is introduced. The sales are still low. This stage continues till sales begin to rise rapidly. Some products can have a very long introductory stage. Some products do not cross this stage at all. We call them product flops. Technological breakthroughs start an altogether new product life cycle, *e.g.*, transistors, photocopiers, radial tires, new antibiotics. Being new, there are obvious difficulties in assessing the market reaction. There may not be precedent to fall back upon. Perhaps, the product has not fulfilled the expectations of the buyers. Since consumers have no experience with the product, they cannot vouch for its benefits. Consumers would like to know more about the product. Even marketers do not know how best to market the products. In this introductory stage, a market evolves on the basis of the rate of diffusion and adoption of the new products. These concepts are illustrated here.

New Product Adoption Process

The new product's acceptance by the consumers is called its "adoption." It is a six-step process in which the consumer passes through the awareness, information, evaluation, trial, adoption and confirmation.

Stages	*Activities Involved*
(i) Awareness	Person is exposed to the new product. He becomes a prospect.
(ii) Information	He solicits information about the new product by becoming interested in it.
(iii) Evaluation	He studies the merits of the new product mentally.
(iv) Trial	He tries the new product in a limited manner. He prefers a small quantity for trial.
(v) Adoption	Here he decides whether to accept the new product in a full-fledged manner.
(vi) Confirmation (Post-adoption)	The new product is adopted. He needs a constant reassurance about his choice.

The stage of information is also called 'interest' stage. The above progressive stages suggest that the marketer of a new product should facilitate the movement of the prospect through these stages. In India, many prospects are interested in a dish washer, say, a Maharaja Whiteline Dishwasher, but there is an uncertainty about its functioning. They may be given a demonstration of a dishwasher. A mail order company selling garments might induce the prospects to place a trial order, and may ask the consumers to return the goods if not satisfied within a specified time. A product may be offered on a trial basis with an option to buy if the results are satisfactory. It may be noted that the ultimate adoption or acceptance is a result of the adoption process.

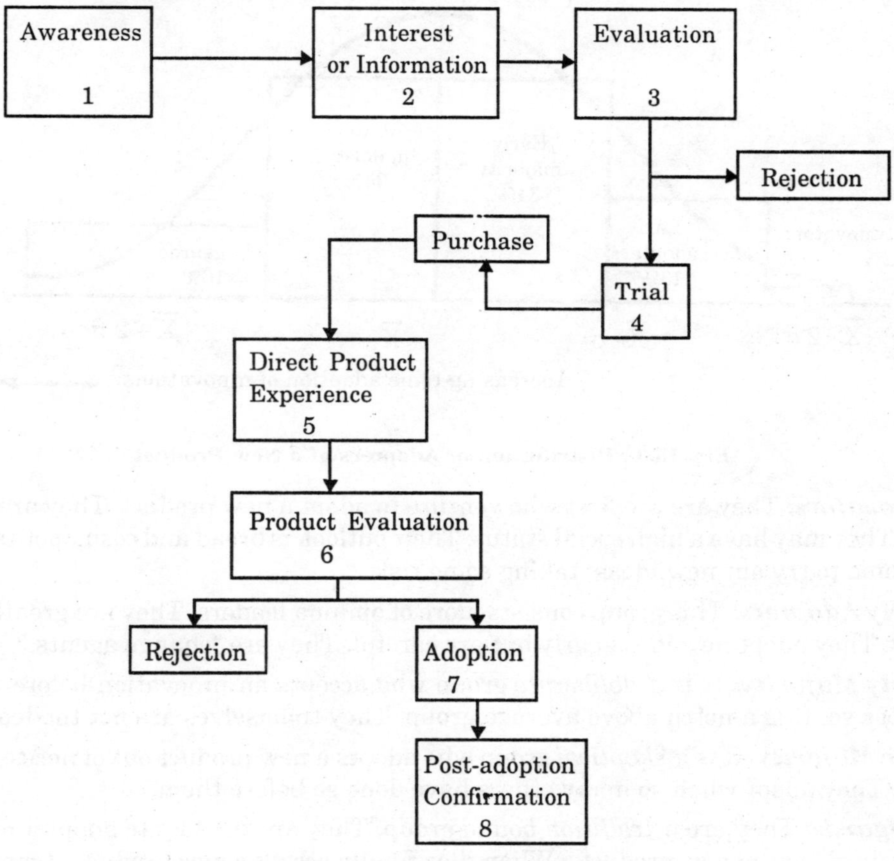

Fig. 15.2 : Trial-Adoption Model

Between the stages (4) trial and (5) adoption or rejection we can add *direct product experience;* and *product evaluation*. The above diagram illustrates the adoption process.

Awareness starts the adoption process, leading to *interest* in the product, and its *evaluation.* The product then can be either *tried* or rejected before or after the purchase.

If tried, we get *direct product experience* resulting in confirming the *product evaluation*, leading to either rejection or adoption. The post adoption *confirmation* is a reassurance about our choice.

Some adoptions affect us minimally, whereas some drastically. Thus cars, fridges and TV have a major impact on society.

Adopter Categories

Some people accept a new product quickly while others take time. There are some who never adopt a new product. Research studies put adopters into five categories depending upon the time taken to adopt a new product. The following diagram illustrates this:

The adoption process is represented as a normal distribution over time. First, there is a slow start. Increasing numbers adopt it later. The adoption reaches a peak. It then diminishes, leaving very few non-adopters.

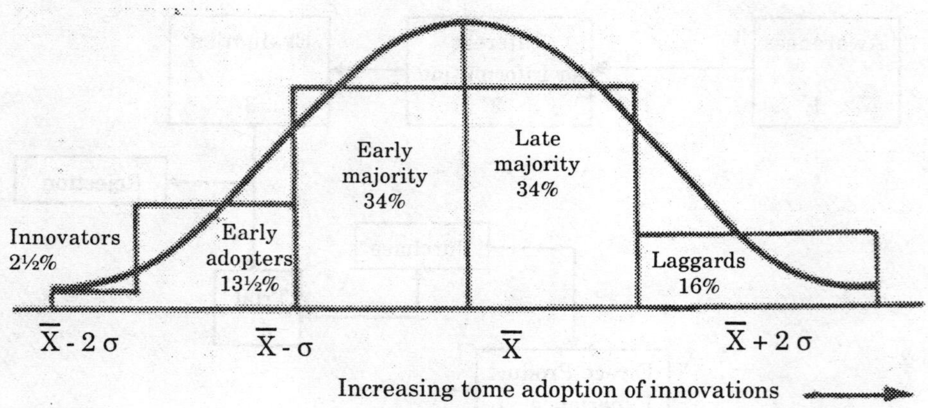

Fig. 15.3 : Distribution of Adopters of a New Product

Innovators: They are the first who venture to adopt a new product. They are likely to be younger. They may have a high social status. Their outlook is broad and cosmopolitan. They are venturesome to try out new ideas, taking some risk.

Early Adopters: This group consists more of opinion leaders. They are greatly respected in society. They adopt new ideas early but are careful. They are "change agents."

Early Majority: It is a *deliberate* group who accepts an innovation before the average person does so. It is a notch above average group. They themselves are not the leaders.

Late Majority: It is a *skeptical* group who adopts a new product out of necessity or social pressure. They adopt when so many others have done so before them.

Laggards: They are a *tradition bound* group. They are the last to adopt a new product. They are suspicious of new products. When they finally accept a new product, it may so happen that the innovation might already have been discarded by the innovators. These people are comparatively older. They are at the lower end of social and economic scale.

These slots help the marketers to study the media habits of each slot differently. There is no overall innovative trait in an individual. He may be an innovator in certain areas and may be a laggard in others. A person may be conservative in dress habits, but may accept exotic dishes. Each marketer has to study the characteristics of likely early adopters in a given product category

NEW PRODUCTS
Between each new technology and man, there is a period of courtship. There is an inherent resistance to change symbolized by new technology and there is a desire to enjoy the novelty and excitement. Telephone took 50 years gestation period before its wider acceptance. We have to see how fast Internet gets accepted. Some inventions are awaited. As soon as they happen, they find acceptance, e.g., TV. Some inventions are resisted, e.g. electricity. It took quite some time to accept this deadly invisible power. Some innovations are accepted with warmth but the initial enthusiasm then wears off, e.g., the airships which were welcomed but the fervour waned when there was an air-crash. Some inventions like car and washing machine were initially viewed with suspicion and hostility. There was a red flag law for the cars. A man with a red flag ran ahead of the cars to warn the public of the coming monster. The washing machine was saddled as a luxury item. It is only now that these have become a way of life. The public remains indifferent to any concept of electric cars, whereas a potential traffic hazard like Walkman (1979) has been successful. It is to be seen how cellular phone will be accepted, considering the antipathy to the public display of private function of telephoning. We have to see how on-line shopping will be accepted in future.

Characteristics of Innovation Affecting Adoption Role

There are five characteristics of an innovation which affect its adoption rate.

Relative Advantage: This is the degree to which a new product scores over the old ideas. It maybe the benefit of a lower cost or some other advantage. The greater the advantage, the faster the adoption.Fax machines have a great relative advantage as they transmit a document at low cost and great speed. They score over the traditional methods like mailing and couriering.

Compatability: This is the degree to which the new product lives up to the cultural values and experiences of the prospects. A music system may be highly consistent with the life style of an upper middle class home. It is difficult to shift men from the ritualistic wet-shave to dry shave of Philips and Braun.

Complexity: The degree or level of difficulty in using a new product or in understanding and mastering it. A professional camera may take a longer time for adoption since it is difficult to master its various functions. The *technological fear* acts as a barrier.

Divisibility or Trialability: This is the degree to which a new product may be tried in a limited manner. The hire purchase scheme increases the rate of adoption of an air-conditioner. Central air-conditioning system is having a lower trialability than a new variety of seed which can be tried on a small plot of land.

Communicability or Observability: This is the degree to which the results of the use of a new product can be observed or described. An innovation whose use can be demonstrated to others diffuses faster in the social system. Products with high degree of social visibility like fashion items diffuse better than the private products like a toothbrush.

Apart from the above, personal influences, initial pricing, scientific credibility and social approval also affect the rate of adoption. All these factors must be carefully studied by the marketer, and are used as inputs while designing a new product.

Diffusion

Rogers has defined a diffusion. It is the spread of an innovation in the mass of ultimate users or adopters. Diffusion starts from the source of invention or creation and ends with the users or adopters. Diffusion is the process by which the innovation is communicated within the social system over time.

Resistance to Innovation

Some products are well-received, whereas others do not strike roots for years together. To understand the differences receptivity to new products, we have to understand the diffusion and adoption better by studying resistance to innovation. The innovation with reference to product characteristics decide the extent of resistance. There is more resistance if the relative advantage, compatibility, trialability and communicability are low. There is higher resistance to complex products. The following model of consumer resistance is presented with reference to cultural, social and situational factors.

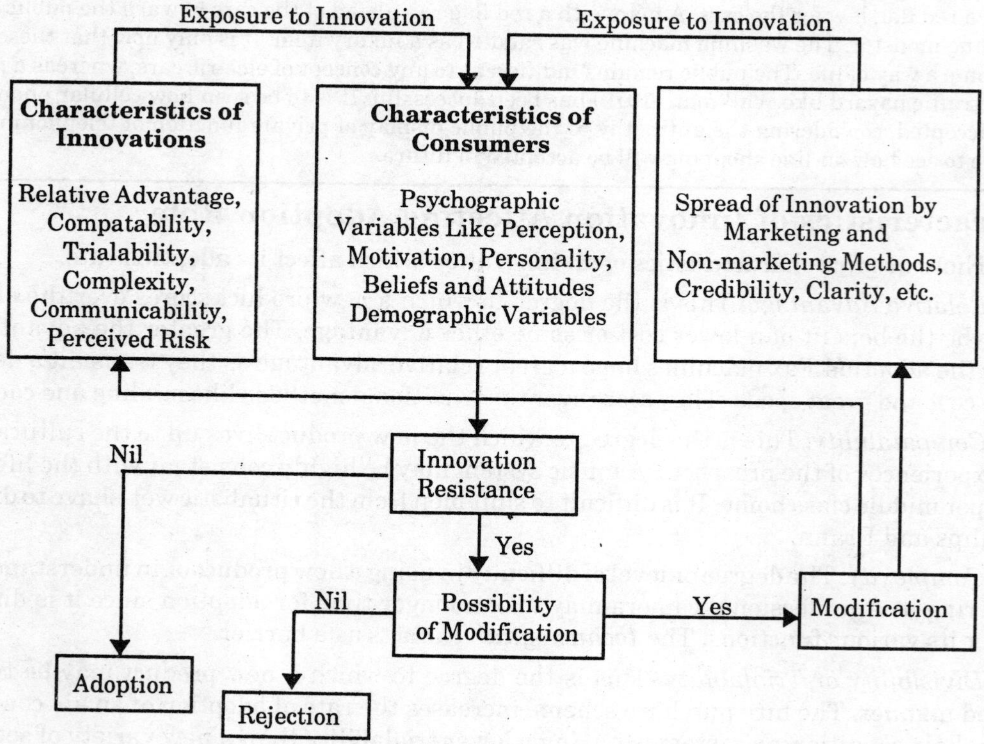

Fig. 15.4 : Innovation Resistance Model

Adapted after S. Ram, *A Model of Innovation Resistance, Advances of Consumer Research* (1987)

Resistance to innovation can be reduced by adopting suitable marketing strategies. If usage is resisted, packaging can be improved upon, and market development strategy can be followed. If there is less value offered by a product, we can improve product performance and positioning or can reduce price. Perceived risk is reduced creating brand equity, proper promotion and trial inducements. Tradition bound consumers can be set free from the shackles by suitable education of the consumer and by using change agents. We cannot just dismiss the age-old trading lightly. Image barriers are countered by creating suitable brand image and in short-term by shaking off negative connotations humorously.

Limitations of Adoption Process

The adoption process model has many limitations. It tends to ignore the problem recognition stage that precedes the awareness stage. It fails to consider the possibility of rejection by the consumer after the trial stage. It also ignores the possibility of the six stages occuring not in a sequence. It also does not recognize that evaluation occurs all through the decision-making process.

Innovation Decision Process

To overcome the above limitations of the adoption process, a general decision-making model called *innovation decision process* has been proposed. The revised model has five stages - *knowledge* due to exposure to the product, *persuasion* or attitude formation, *decision* of either adoption or rejection, *implementation* of putting the product to use and *confirmation* for re-inforcing his innovation decision. The following diagram illustrates this model.

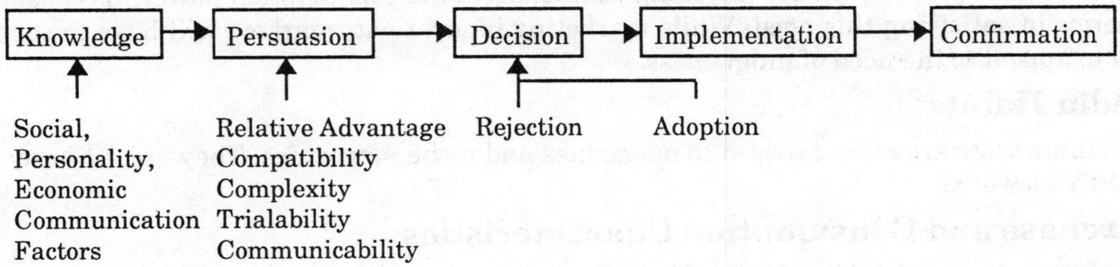

Fig. 15.5 : Innovation Decision Process

Adapted after Rogers, *Diffusion of Innovation* (3rd Edition)

Consumer Innovator

He belongs to the earliest users of the product. Sociologist put them in 2.5 per cent of the social system. Innovator is to be understood with reference to the consumer-definition of innovation. In terms of time, if the innovation is what is available for a period of two months then the innovator is one who buys in these two months. Another way to consider an innovator is his adoption from new products some minimum number of items. A consumer buying for instance eight fashion clothes out of ten available is an innovator when compared to a consumer who just buys one fashion dress and remains a non-innovator.

Interest

A consumer innovator has greater interest in products than either early adopters on non-adopters. He is more likely to seek greater information from a variety of sources.

Personality Traits

He is open-minded and less dogmatic. He approaches new products with openness. He relies on his values and standards. In other words, he is inner-directed. He is a variety seeker. His receptivity to the unfamiliar things is more. He loves informative promotion. His optimum stimulation level is high *i.e.,* a life-style that prefers novelty, complexity and unusualness.

Opinion Leader

There is a strong inclination for opinion leaders to be innovators. Innovators pass on their experience and advise others about the innovations. Others who receive such information fall in line. A product to be successful must influence an innovator favourably.

Perceived Risk

A consumer who perceives little or no risk while trying a new product is likely to be an innovator.

Venturesomeness

It indicates his willingness to accept the risk of purchasing the innovation. On buying intention scale, he shows a definite intention to buy new product. Those who are hesitant are not innovators.

It is, however, to be noted that an innovator in a particular product class may not show the same behaviour with the purchase of later innovations in the same class.

Need for Uniqueness

There is evidence to support the proposition that innovative behaviour has something to do with a *need for uniqueness.* Anything that changes the consumption pattern is considered superior in satisfying this need. While marketing innovations, markets will have to consider how to appeal to the need of uniqueness.

Media Habits

Innovators are more exposed to magazines and niche magazines. They are, however, not avid TV viewers.

Purchase and Consumption Characteristics

Innovators are not brand loyal. They are prone to the effects of sales promotion deals. They buy a larger quantity. They find new applications for products.

Social Characteristics

Innovators are socially accepted. They represent many social groups. They are opinion leaders.

Demographic Characteristics

Innovators tend to be younger, However, age is related to product category in question. They have higher disposable incomes. Their professional status or occupational status is higher. They have formal education. They tend to be more up scale.

Generalized Innovators

It is not necessary that consumer innovators with respect to one product category are innovators for other product categories too.

Innovativeness overlaps across similar product category . Innovativeness within a product category continues. A person using silver classic credit cards is more likely to be receptive to gold cards. A person using credit cards like Master or Visa is more likely to use charge cards like Diners or AmEx. Such a pattern suggests that marketers should first address themselves to those consumers who are using a particular product category. The following table illustrates the difference between the innovators and non-innovators.

DISTINCTION BETWEEN INNOVATORS AND NON-INNOVATORS

Characteristic	*Innovator*	*Non-innovator*
Personality	Open-mind More venturesome Less perceived risk Inner-directed Rich life-style	Closed mind Less venturesome More perceived risk Other — directed Mundane life style
Product Interest Media Habits	More More magazine exposure More reading of niche magazines Views TV lesser	Less Less Magazine exposure Less reading of niche magazines Views TV more
Social Factors	More social integration Higher mobility across occupation Belongs to more groups	Less social integration Lesser mobility Lesser groups
Purchase and Consumption Pattern	Less brand loyal More interested in SP More usage	More brand loyal Less interested Less usage
Demographic Variables	Younger in age High disposable income More educated High occupational and professional status.	Older in age Lower disposable income Less educated Lower status

Trade off between the Fidelity and the Convenience

Kevin Maney has recently authored a book *Trade Off — Why Some Things Catch On and Others Don't.* He discusses two things. There is fidelity of buying a product or service. Fidelity is the total experience of something, say your presence at a live music concert. It becomes a part of your identity. The convenience of buying a product or service is another factor. Convenience is all about how easy it is to get something, which includes price. The fundamental point that Kevin Maney makes in his book is that people are willing to trade the fidelity or quality of experience for the convenience of getting it and *vice versa*. This phenomenon is called the fidelity swap. Though attending a live IPL match is highly inconvenient, it is a terrific experience. On the other hand, an iPod song is so convenient that one can forgo buying a CD. ATM machines are successful as they are highly convenient, contrary to popular belief that banking is all about fidelity. The products and services that excite the customers most are those that have a clearly defined identity either as fidelity or high convenience. When something does not have enough fidelity to make people forgo convenience or enough convenience to displace fidelity, people get confused about why they should buy this product. It is called *fidelity belly*. Blue ray discs are an example. The technology does not improve fidelity enough to make people spend more and buy a whole new player. It is risky to try to achieve both high fidelity and high convenience e.g. RAZR phone of Motorola which dropped prices, and made it a mass market product. It will be interesting to see how China fares while trying to establish high fidelity brands, though so far it produced only high convenience brands. It will also be interesting to see how an electric car overcomes its convenience problems of refuelling and range.

It is easy to conclude that products that are both high on fidelity and convenience would be highly successful. However, according to Kevin Maney, it a difficult to be both high fidelity and high convenience. Fidelity refers to the total experience of something – it is about tactile, visible, sensory aspects of a product or service. Fidelity has more to do with experience, rather than cost, though in many cases people pay a premium for a high quality, high fidelity experience. A live musical concert makes you see the real person perform in real time. It is authentic and is much more valuable than a music CD. It is a huge high fidelity experience. Convenience refers the ease of access. Cost is an essential part of convenience since low costs imply ease of buying for most people. It is less painful and thus more convenient. McDonald's is essentially a convenience outlet — they are everywhere, economical and clean. However, an attempt to make McDonald a high quality experience simultaneously fails. Similarly, Starbucks is a high fidelity coffee experience. Extensive network dilutes this position.

❑ ❑ ❑

16

CONSUMER DECISION MAKING

In our day-to-day life we have to take so many decisions right from the time we wake up to the time we retire for the night. We have to choose between several brands of toothpaste for brushing our teeth. We have a variety of soaps to take our bath out of which we choose one. We decide what we shall have on our breakfast table. We commute to our office using a specific mode of transport and a specific vehicle to carry us. We have to decide what clothes we will wear. We decide the mix of products we shall use either for our lunch or dinner. Then there are decisions regarding our means of entertainment, cosmetics, sanitary products, health care products, books, magazines and periodicals and the academic courses and institutions. We have to decide for ourselves, and for others. We give advice to others, and receive advice from others. All these decisions are *choices from several alternatives available.* It is necessary to decide whether to buy or not to buy, and if we want to buy, which product or brand to buy. If there is no choice then it is called a *Hobson's choice.* The freedom to choose is an essential value of the Indian society. The following table summarises the types of purchase decisions we take:

Alternative X	*Alternative Y*
Whether to buy	Or not to buy
Buy brand A	Or buy brand B
Buy a usual brand	Or buy another brand
Buy a no-frills basic model	Buy add-on functions or luxurious model
Buy a new brand	Buy an established brand
Buy a standard quantity	Buy something more or less than this quantity
Buy a national brand	Buy a local brand.
Buy from a from a specific store, say a departmental store	Buy from some other retail outlet
Buy from outlet	Buy from other outlet
Buy indoors	Buy outdoors
Buy from neighbourhood store giving local convenience	Buy from down-town or up-market store
Buy cash	Buy on card
Outright purchase	Purchase by instalments

Economic Man

In perfect competition which is a utopion concept, we visualize an *economic man* who behaves *rationally.* This man knows about all product alternatives, ranks them correctly in terms of merits and demerits, knows about prices and buys the best product. But such assumptions are fallacious in the real world. Our ability is limited. We have limited values and goals and all of us operate in an imperfect world. We will not be in a position to maxmise the decisions such as price-quantity or marginal utility or indifference curves. Instead, we shall settle down to satisficing ourselves by buying something that is good enough. Economic man model has theoretical value, and is not operative in the real world.

Passive Man

In contrast with the economic man who is rational about his choices, we imagine a passive man who is subject to the high pressure selling, marketing and promotional efforts of the organisations and yields to these passively. He tends to be irrational and impulsive purchaser. The conventional attention-interest-desire-action (AIDA) model of selling presumes a passive customer. This model robs the customer of his critical faculties. It fails to recognise an important role he plays in the buying process. He seeks information about product alternatives and selects the product from which he derives maximum satisfaction. We know that consumer as an individual shows his motivation, perception, learning, attitudes, communication and opinion leadership. All these factors affect his buying decision, and thus to say that he is passive is far from the truth.

Cognitive Man

Here a consumer is considered as one who seeks to solve his problems by seeking products and services which satisfy his needs, and improve the quality of his life. His choices are governed by certain processes such as seeking information and forming preferences. As against an economic man, the cognitive man obtains only the sufficient information so that he can settle for a reasonably good product. He may develop certain short-cut methods to arrive at a decision. He may use certain decision rules. He thus falls in between a purely rational economic man and a purely irrational passive man. Though he is not in a position to take perfect decisions, he attempts to take satisfactory ones. His consumption decisions are based on information. He is thus well-informed. Consumer behaviour literature equates a consumer with a cognitive problem-solving man.

Emotional Man

Each of us is a bundle of emotions such as love, happiness, hope, fear, fantasy, sexuality and even some out-of-world experiences like magic. These influence our product choices a great deal. These emotions involve us with a product. We may have several handkerchiefs, but if we lose one gifted by the beloved we go to great lengths to find it. There are people who wear talisman with 'Om' incarnation or 786 digits, and believe these have great protective power.

Certain products link us to the past, and give us a sense of nostalgia. They comfort us while travelling to an unknown and precarious future. A photograph of the loved person on the battlefront provide us the hope to have jolly good times once again indicative of normalcy.

Many of our purchases are driven emotionally without any information seeking and alternative evaluation. Purchases are governed here by moods and whims. This does not necessarily mean that an emotion-driven purchase is not rational. The goal of emotional satisfaction is also a rational decision. Brand choice is a matter of emotional preference, and has little to do with rationality. Ritu Beri's clothes are preferred because we feel better wearing them. Promotion is becoming more and more feeling-oriented.

Mood is a state of mind, and it also affects our consumption. It is a response to particular environment. It pre-exists when a consumer enters a retail outlet or is face-to-face with a brand or a product. It influences shopping and therefore a retailer tries to create a mood for shopping. A positive store image does affect a shopper's mood. So also the shopping ambience. It is also a matter of mood for the consumers as to how long they remain in stores. A positive mood is a great help in product recall. However, it does not mean that such a mood created on the spot by music and POP (point-of-purchase) will influence brand choice, unless some previous evaluation has already occurred.

The Consumer Decision Process

Consumer behaviour does not consist of discrete acts, but is a process. A woman who joins a slimming centre first recognises the need to reduce her obesity. She then seeks information about various methods of slimming down, and chooses a slimming centre as the best alternative for her. She then decides in favour of a particular centre, considering the cost of the total slimming plan, its credibility and the track record. After choosing the centre, she may or may not be satisfied with the results. All this is a part of the *purchase decision process.* It is not just the decision but a whole series of decisions.

The following diagram shows a simplified model of consumer purchase decision process.

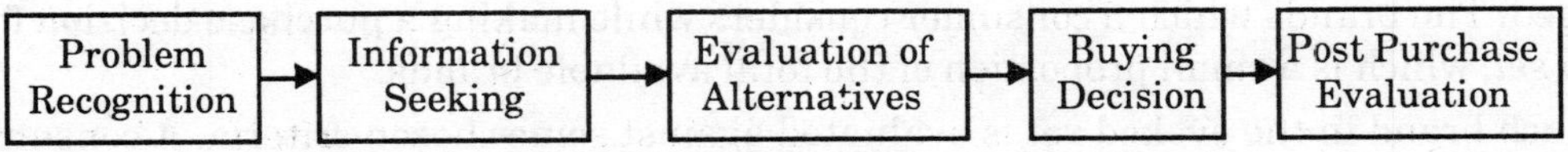

Fig. 16.1 : Consumer's Buying Decision Process.

The five stages in the buying decision process are:

1. Problem recognition
2. Information seeking
3. Evaluation of alternatives
4. Buying decision
5. Post-purchase evaluation.

It will be appreciated that the process starts much before the actual purchase, and continues beyond it.

Problem Recognition: Problem recognition in fact is the beginning of the buying process. It is a matter of perception. We realise what we should ideally have and what we have at present. The decision to buy a two-in-one music system is triggered by the gift amount received on the occasion of the birthday. Mrs. Y may go in for a fridge because Mrs. X has already got it. A perfume bottle of Charlie may be purchased when one sees it in the window of a shop. We may decide to buy another paste, when the current one is on the point of running out. Problem recognition is generally a slow process, but can occur fast when purchases are made impulsively.

Marketing efforts facilitate the problem recognition stage. Ads goad us to buy many a thing Similarly, a window display also acts as an incentive to buy. Personal selling makes us realise what our unfulfilled needs and wants are. Psychological factors do influence problem recognition stage.

Information Seeking: This follows the problem recognition stage. More-often-than-not, there is little knowledge about the alternatives available. The search is mostly directed towards the products that are consistent with our needs. A housewife buying a mixie might start visiting the shops selling appliances and might start discussing the need with her friends. She is interested in knowing which brands are on offer and their features.

The amount and type of information that is collected is related to the product in question, and the consumer's personality. To buy consumer durables like fridges and ACs, we need a great deal of information from different sources. To buy fast moving consumer goods , we need limited information. To buy petty items, there is hardly any need for information seeking, except to know what size is available, and at what price. The beauty of brand marketing is that it makes the consumer loyal to the brands. These consumers then continue to buy the same brands, and do not seek any information at all.

Information seeking starts with cognitive internal search — recalling information stored in memory. This may lead to further stages of buying decision process. Alternatively, the consumer may start external search; seeking information from sources other than memory.

The major external sources are peers, friends, colleagues, relatives whom we trust. In addition, we get information from different marketing communications, media, distribution channels and consumer's own experience.

Evaluation of Alternatives: When, the consumer seeks information, he realises the alternative choices available to him and gets the background against, which of these choices can be judged. The brands which a consumer considers while making a purchase decision forms an *evoked set,* which is a small proportion of the total available brands.

Each brand in the evoked set is evaluated against some chosen criteria. A consumer buying a mixie for example considers the following criteria.

- Band name
- Price
- Functions performed
- Appearance
- Attachments like a juicer, a chutney jar
- Reputation of the company marketing it
- Warranty
- Technical specifications
- After-sales service available.

Each of the above criterion is assigned some weightage, which may differ from consumer to consumer. After this, it is all a matter of perception. To illustrate, flavour of sharbat may have equal importance for two different consumers. One feels Rasna orange has very good flavour whereas the other feels that it is awful.

Promotion, especially advertising, provides information to the consumer enabling him to evaluate the different alternatives.

Buying Decision: After the alternative choices are evaluated, the brands are ranked, and the top-ranking brand may be purchased. The ultimate buying decision may undergo a change, if the preferred brand is not available. In such a situation, the second-ranked brand may be bought. The ultimate buying occurs only when the consumer finds a suitable outlet where the brand is available, and price negotiations are complete.

Post-Purchase Evaluation: Now the product has been bought and consumed. It is the stage for post-purchase evaluation. The consumer may either be satisfied or dissatisfied. A satisfied consumer stores the product information in his memory and uses it next time at the time of problem recognition stage. A dissatisfied consumer may go in for another brand next time he is out to buy. He will seek additional information, and will consider another set of brands. To illustrate, a consumer dissatisfied with Fiat may consider other small cars like Maruti 800, Zen, Hyundai Centro, Tata's Indica etc.

Types of Purchase Decision Behaviour

Consumer behaviour changes depending upon the nature or type of buying — a razor blade may be purchased without much fuss but a colour TV set purchase takes time and deliberation. The nature or type of purchases give rise to three types of buyer behaviour:

(*a*) RR (Routinised Response) behaviour

(*b*) LPS (limited problem solving) behaviour

(*c*) EPS (Extended Problem Solving) behaviour

RR occurs where there is low product involvement, the consumer knows the brands available and criteria of choice, and the stakes are not so high in terms of price; *e.g.*, bread, soft-drinks, pastes, soaps etc. Here the customer expects a consistent quality in the products. New customers are drawn by sales promotion and product improvements.

LPS occurs when the consumer knows the brands available, but still needs additional information to make a correct choice, especially when a new or unfamiliar brand confronts him. Thus, Ariel or Surf Excel enzyme detergents must convince the housewife that they are superior to conventional detergents due to the presence of enzymes and so the housewife feels the necessity of searching aditional information. The marketer here has introduced a new brand in a well-known product category. The promotion here should explain complete features of the new brand, and build up consumers' confidence to facilitate the purchase decision.

EPS occurs when a new product category comes on the scene. Here extensive information is needed on both the product category and the brand being made available, *e.g.*, micro-wave ovens introduced by Kelvinator first explain the concept of micro-wave cooking as distinguished from conventional cooking, and then sell the brand. Colour TVs as a product category, a particular brand of TV (say Onida or Videocon) and a particular model (say PIP: Picture-in-Picture or Surrounded Sound System) do need information at three levels. Promotion should satisfy the needs of information at these three levels, and especially, how the advertised brand has a unique set of positive attributes. This concept is most applicable to new products, maybe new to consumers. For a tribal, even purchase of a toothpaste may involve EPS, whereas for us it is just RR.

Model of Buyer Behaviour

Research workers have developed various models to explain the influences on buyer's behaviour of purchase. Howard-Sheth model which has been developed by an Indian Jagdish Sheth in collaboration with Howard explains the behaviour of an individual consumer. There are separate models for group consumer behaviour and organisational buying behaviour.

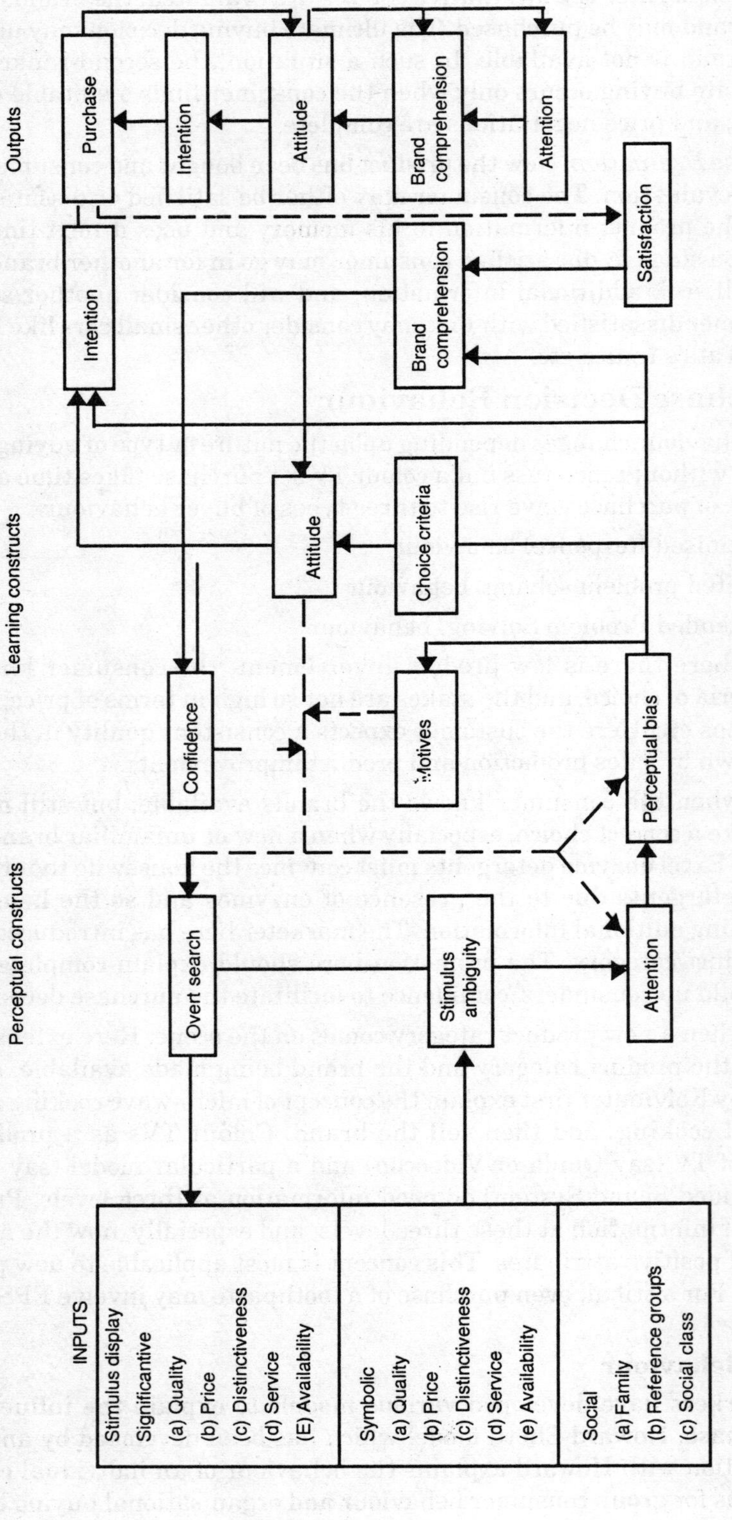

Fig. 16.2 Howard-Sheth Model: Simplified Adaptation

Howard-Sheth Model

The decision process is influenced by four major sets of variables, *e.g.*, (1) Inputs, (2) Perceptual and Learning Constructs, (3) Outputs, (4) External variables.

(1) Inputs: These are stimuli to purchase decision. Significative stimuli are tangible product characteristics provided by the marketer. Symbolic stimuli are intangible or perceptual characteristics of the product, *e.g.*, the overall quality. The actual price may be significative stimulus, and the price being on high or low side for the bargain is symbolic stimulus. Social groups like the family, reference groups and social class are the social stimuli.

(2) Perceptual and Learning Constructs: These are psychological variables, *e.g.*, motivation, attitudes, and perceptions affecting the buyer. The interpretation of the stimuli are influenced by stimulus ambiguity and perceptual bias. Ambiguity of stimulus means the consumer is not sure of the meaning of the stimulus and his response thereto. Perceptual bias makes him distort the information received to fit his previous experience and his established needs.

His interpretation of the stimuli results in brand comprehension — his understanding of the brands and their ratings. High rating build up his confidence, resulting in the purchase decision.

(3) Outputs: The purchase decision itself is an output. Product trial may give him satisfaction. It reinforces his positive attitude. Then there is reinforcement of purchase intent and brand. He is favourably inclined to receiving stimuli which further improves his brand comprehension. On getting dissatisfied with the product, he may develop negative attitude, insensitivity to stimuli, poor brand comprehension and negative intention to purchase.

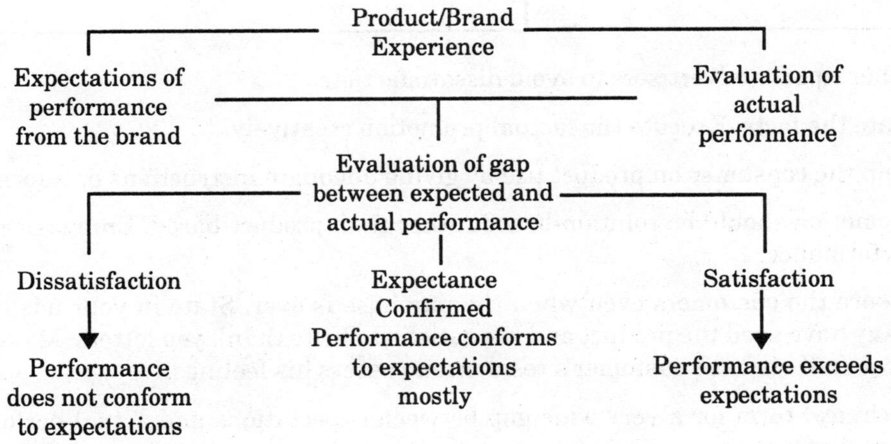

Fig. 16.3

(4) External Variables: These are not part of the decision process in the model, but are improvement to the extent they influence a buyer. These differ from buyer to buyer and include, status, relevance of the product, social class, personality traits etc.

Post-Purchase Behaviour

The desire to study the behaviour of consumers after the purchase has been made is a 'true' marketing orientation, an identification with the consumers and seeing things from their perspective. Purchases are purposive and motivated. Post-purchase behaviour indicates to what extent these purposes have been met and motives achieved. Post-purchase activity gives an indication as to whether the customers are going to again patronise a firm in future, and also whether they will be in a mood to recommend a product to potential customers.

Formation of Satisfaction/Dissatisfaction

A purchase may lead either to satisfaction or dissatisfaction. Satisfaction is a result of expected outcome — when the product meets our expectations. Dissatisfaction means it does not perform as per our expectations. Dissatisfied customers may discontinue their association with the company, may spread negative word of mouth, may send a formal complaint, or in extreme cases, may sue the company. The communication strategy depends upon the expectation-performance disparity.

Disparity	*Communication Strategy*
Minimised by adjusting perceived expectations with performance	Overstate product claims
Magnified	Reasonably understate product claims
Negative feeling	Consistent claims with performance
Minor disparities minimised Major disparities magnified	State product claims above the actual performance marginally but within the overall acceptance range of the consumer.

The other tips for advertisers to avoid dissatisfaction:

(1) State the facts. Execute the factual promotion creatively.

(2) Help the consumer on product use by giving adequate instructions or information.

(3) Promotion should be solution-based rather than product-based. Emphasise products' performance.

(4) Assure the customers even when the purchase is over. State in your ads the fact — many have used the product and are satisfied. Write thank you letters. Make the technical staff visit the customer's residence to assess his feelings.

The technical term for a very wide gap between expectations and actual performance is post-purchase dissonance.

Schiffman-Kanuk Model of Consumer Decision making

It takes care of the two types of individual consumers — cognitive or problem solving and emotional. It has three components — input, process and output. The following diagram illustrates this model.

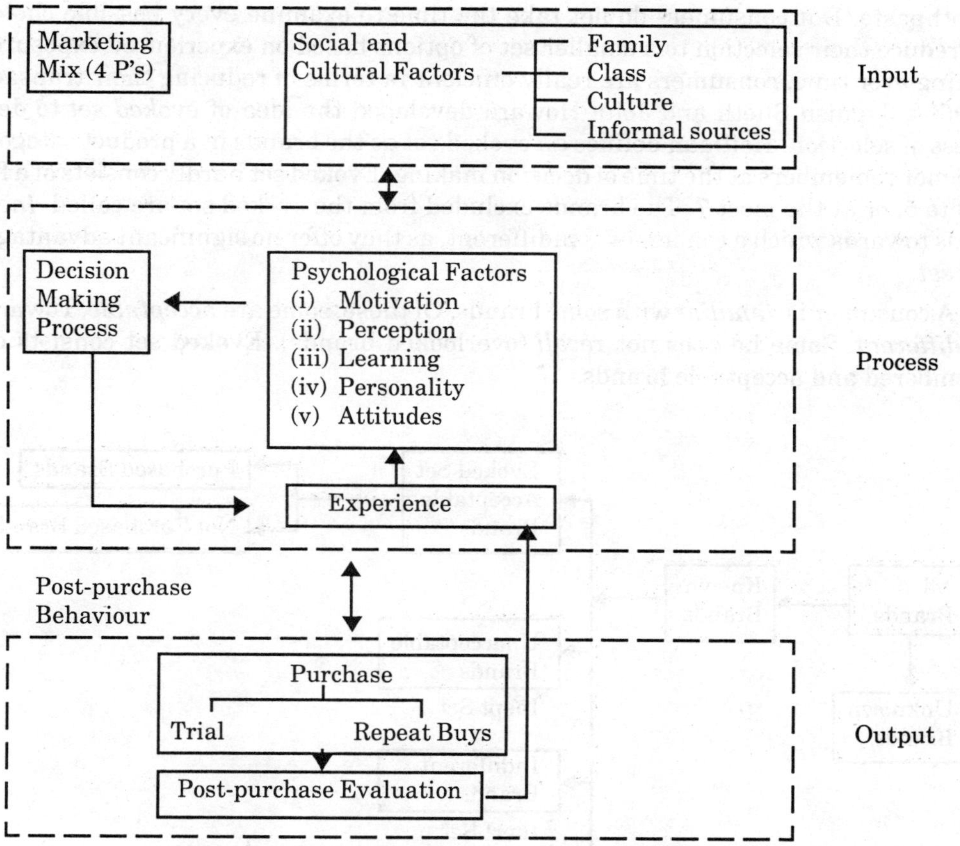

Fig. 16.4 : Schiffman-Kanuk Model

Marketing mix and its perception largely affect the buyers. Apart from this word-of-mouth publicity, social class and culture affect a consumer's evaluation and ultimate adoption of the products. The input is processed by the consumer while he takes the decisions. The decision making process is affected by the psychological factors. Here we have to understand two key concepts — *perceived risk* and *evoked set*. While buying products, consumers cannot anticipate the consequences of their decision, and this is precisely the perceived risk. The product may not function as expected (functional risk). The product may harm us (physical risk). The product may embarrass us socially (social risk). The product may affect ego adversely (psychological risk). The time taken to buy may be wasted over a non-performing product (time risk). Risk is perceived with respect to product categories e.g. there is higher risk while buying a computer than that while buying a book. Shopping situation also contributes to the perception of risk, e.g. some may not like to buy by mail order. This perception may change by positive feedback. Perception of risk differs from people to people, and so consumer research regarding risk behaviour of one country cannot be generalized.

Consumers handle risk in a variety of ways. Their risk reduction strategies consist of information search, brand loyalty, buying an established brand, buying from a reputed retailer, buying the next expensive brand or model, and seeking confirmation about a buy.

Evoked set consists of brands which a consumer *considers* while buying a brand in a specific product category. On the shelf, there may be 30, 40 brands of shampoo or 20,30 brands of toothpaste. But consumers do not take the time to examine every possible choice. Rather, they reduce their selection to a smaller set of options based on experienced exposure. Through learning over time, consumers are really efficient in terms of reducing their transaction costs. In 1960s, Jagdish Sheth and John Howard developed the idea of *evoked set* to describe this process of selection. Hoffman defines an evoked set as the brands in a product category that the consumer remembers at the time of decision making. Evoked set hardly consists of a few brands, say 3 to 5, or at the most 7. The brands excluded from the evoked set are called *inept set.* The brands towards which a consumer is indifferent, as they offer no significant advantage, form the *inert set.*

A consumer is *familiar* with some brands. Of these, some are *acceptable.* Towards some he is *indifferent.* Some he does not *recall* (overlooked brands). Evoked set consists of familiar, remembered and acceptable brands.

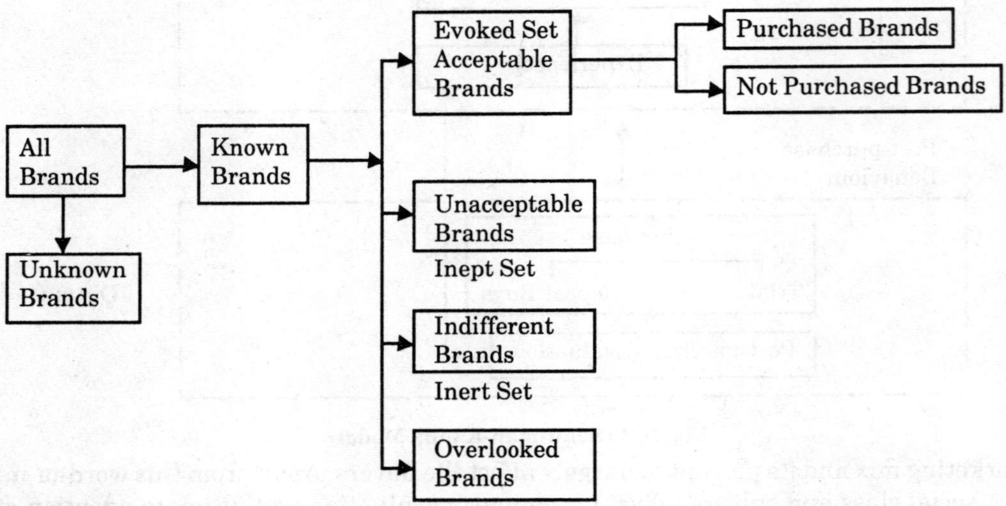

Fig. 16.5: Evoked Set

The results depend on how we sort out the products or possibilities into categories. The way this information is recorded in memory can influence consumers' preferences for brands and whether the brand will be considered for purchase. According to Dannon and Yoplait, if yogurt is arranged by brands first and then by flavour within the brand, consumers tend to select their flavours from the same brand. On the other hand, if the yogurts are classified flavourwise first, say all strawberry yogurts; then consumers would most likely choose which flavours they wanted first, and then choose which brand name they would most like for that particular flavour.

American supermarkets display meats sorted into types – beef, chicken, pork etc. The next division is by cuts. In Australia, meats are arranged by the way they might be cooked, and stores use more descriptive labels – a ten-minute herbed beaf roast. The result is that Australians buy a greater variety of meats.

The classification of products changes our choices. The compensation of the set of final possibilities can have subtle effects on choice. Thus brand choices can be influenced (without changing the actual preference for a brand *per se*) merely by changing the content of the consideration set.

This can be extended to appointments, nominations, board seats, speakers, and all such hiring decisions. Decision makers start with an evoked set of possibilities – the people who immediately spring to our mind.

We have already considered the decision making process; and the post purchase behaviour. We shall consider *consumer decision rules* in the evaluation of products. These rules make complex decisions simpler for the consumer.

Compensatory decision rule is one where a brand is evaluated as a summated score of all relevant attributes. It allows the choice of a brand carrying the highest score. A brand may have positive evaluation on one attribute and negative on some other attribute. These are balanced out in compensatory decision rules. To illustrate, performance of a car compensates high fuel cost. In *non-compensatory decision rules,* such balancing positive and negative evaluations of brand attributes is not allowed. In non-compensatory decisions, we can follow a minimum cut off point for each attribute to qualify a brand. This is called *conjuctive decision* rule. Here a brand is rejected if it falls below this cut off point. However, a brand is accepted if it is above this cut off point and it is called *disjunctive rule.* When more than one brand cross the minimum cut off requirements, another decision rule can be applied or the first brand exceeding cut off is accepted. *In lexicographic decision rule,* various attributes are ranked in terms of relevance and importance. The single most important attribute is chosen to compare other brand alternatives. The brand that scores highest, against this attribute is chosen. If two or more brands score highest the process is repeated against second highest-ranked attribute. The process is continued till we select one brand. In lexicographic rules, the attribute ranked high is indicative of consumer orientation. These decision rules are combined to form new variations.

It is possible that consumers retain in their memory their overall evaluation of the brands in the evoked set. It makes the individual attribute evaluation unnecessary. He is likely to select the brand that provides highest perceived overall rating. It is called *affect referral rule.*

The knowledge of decision rules enable marketers to design a suitable promotional programme.

We have to appreciate that so far we have concentrated only on brand choice / product choice decisions. But consumer behaviour goes beyond this.

We have to consider *experience* of consuming and the sense of pleasure derived either from consuming or possessing. Possessions link us to the past. Some objects are treasured memories. Gifts are not ordinary and routine purchases. They have symbolic meaning. Some acquisitions are self-gifts. They are a result of certain circumstances. To illustrate, a hefty bonus at Deepavali time may be an occasion to celebrate and may lead to many purchases.

Signalling Value of Products

Geoffery Miller in his recent book *Spent — Sex, Evolution, and Consumer Behoviour* proposes that consumerism is an evolutionary concept. All animals have a tendency to show off and try to attract the opposite sex for mating by doing so. The same tendency is displayed by human beings when they buy the most expressive and impressive consumer goods they can afford. That is extension of the show off tendency. In social groups in the evolution process, image and status mattered. That was necessary for survival as well as for attracting mates, impressing friends and rearing children.

According to Geoffery Miller, many products are signals first, and material objects later. A Hummer H 1 Alpha sport utility vehicle is not a good rationaly buy for the price paid. Yet some people feel the need to buy it, and biology offers an answer.

In experiments, it was seen that men went in for conspicuous consumption when interested in mating whereas women think of conspicuous charity.

Physical appearance, especially facial appearance, is used as an indicator of fertility in most primate species. Cosmetics do extend this fertility even while ageing. Later after meeting people, we judge them on other traits i.g. intelligence, kindness, faithfulness etc. We then consider products such as an IIT or IIM degree, and donations to animal welfare funds.

If a company wants to make a decent profit, its product must have a special signalling value beyond its nominal function.

Relationship Marketing

The emphasis these days is to retain the existing customers against the onslaught of competition. Such customers who are loyal to a company and its brands are in effect more profitable to the marketers than the new customers. Relationship marketing is thus building of long-term relationship and trust between an organisation and its customers for mutual benefit. It enhances the consumer retention index. Considering that it costs several times more to acquire a new customer than retain an existing one, companies are taking all efforts to please the existing customers. This relationship extends to the members of the distribution channel and the suppliers. These relationships are based on high quality products, fair pricing and effective servicing.

Relationship marketing has been informally practised by many a shopkeeper. We know how a local grocery store in a small town is the meeting place for the customers, who contact socially at this place.

In a marketing transaction, satisfaction is derived from the product and service offered, and the relationship between the marketer and customer. The values thus flow from two sources — offerings and relationships. The ultimate satisfaction is a subjective experience. A customer seeks relationship values while shopping; over and above the transactional values. When most of the offerings are on par in terms of quality and performance, a customer values the personal equation which becomes the deciding factor in buying.

In mass marketing, the relationship perspective is often lost. To restore relationship perspective, it is necessary to concentrate on building one-to-one relationship with an individual customer. All customers may not qualify for such long-term relationship arrangement. It is necessary to understand what the customers actually want. In relationship marketing, customers are the basis for differentiation in terms of their unique needs, rather then the products. Strategically, it pays more to gain more business out of existing customers by understanding their requirements.

In relationship marketing, customers collaborate with the business to generate new business by providing feedback and ideas. Frequent interactions with the customers guide the company about how they think, what they prefer and why, and how they rate the company. These days when physical products are almost the same, the service factor differentiates a caring organisation practising relationship marketing. Though it is difficult to maintain consistency in the quality of services, it is possible to rectify the damage of deficient services by providing superior service next time.

The data-base of the customers maintained by computer based information system greatly helps relationship marketing by providing us the profiles and needs of our customers accurately.

Building brands that establish a relationship between the customer and the marketer is one of the key elements in relationship marketing, along with other elements. Elle allowed its customers to create their own shades. Sabah Mansoor, a 15-year old school girl from Bangalore created Elle 18 by squeezing some glitter-glue into some varnish. It has been named 'Sabah Sparkle' after her. Pond's interactive efforts now make the customers well-informed about the ceramides, collagen, elastins and alpha-hydroxy-acids.

If a customer repeats buying our product for a life-time, it makes up a tidy sum. HTA research has shown that the life-time value of one cigarette smoker is 1.1 lac over a period of ten years. It amounts to 7000 times the value of a cigarette pack approximately. In relationship marketing, retaining the customers becomes important, and desertions are monitored, and the reasons for these desertions are studied. A sale is not just the end of the transaction. It is just the beginning of a long relationship. In conventional marketing, the communication is one-way through mass media. In relationship marketing, it is one-to-one communication. It develops an interactive relationship.

Bank of America greatly believes in relationship marketing. It has re-named its customers as clients, since client denotes a long-term relationship, and customers conjure up a one-time transaction image. In a Mystery Shopping programme, surrogate customers rate the bank's employees on relationship friendliness. This score is tied to compensation packages.

Relationship marketing is practised in consumer durables sector by after-scales contact with the consumers through phone operators, technicians, franchisees and dealers. Relationship marketing addressess itself to both entry level sales and replacement demand. In case of fast moving consumer goods, relationship marketing focusses on the delivery aspect of the product attributes. Besides, there is a need to cater to market niches. Service industry has greater need for relationship marketing. It is very important to have the right kind of sales staff and organisation's internal relations with them. The internal relations reflect on external relationships.

DISTINCTION BETWEEN TRANSACTION MARKETING AND RELATIONSHIP MARKETING

Transaction Marketing	*Relationship Marketing*
• Emphasis on single sale	• Emphasis on customer retention
• Product-oriented	• Customer- oriented
• Short-term	• Long-term
• Limited customer services	• High customer services
• Limited customer contact	• Extensive customer contact
• Quality is production-driven	• Quality is everybody's concern.

Relationship Marketing: Synopsis

It is an attempt at a long-term relationship and is an exercise in brand building, with interaction between the brand and the consumer. It goes beyond conventional marketing, and seeks to establish an enduring relationship with the consumers. It is not just one transaction. It is an antithesis of sales promotion which is a short-term exercise — a temporary incentive for people to buy.

To institute relationship marketing, we have to start with the data on consumers. Mattel Toys has been able to create phenomenal demand for its Barbie dolls worldwide by settling up kiddie clubs. It is an interactive club where children can emulate the role model. The new members of the Club write to Barbie and she replies to them. It is fun with learning. For children, involvement levels and attachment to characters and products are very high.

Leo has built a 21,000-strong data base. The Club has 12,000 active members between the ages of 6-12. Every year, around 5,000 new members join; though there is subscription fee of ₹ 95/-. They have been successful at developing a cult for Barbie. The Club members are hard-core Barbie fans, and they correspond regularly with the company. The relationship marketing exercise has helped the company sell 1.5 million Barbie dolls so far.

Parle Agro has also formed Frooti Funtoon Club targeted at youngsters to carry over the brand appeal to the second generation. These members will be parents twenty years hence and will still have a fondness for the brand. The club organises plant visits, animation film shows and quiz contests. Birthday cards are sent. The scheme aims at building up a solid data base plus a consumer segment.

Hawkins Cookers trains its 500-odd dealers to deal with consumers. Incentives are offered from time to time to keep the dealers on their toes. Salesman visit families to demonstrate cooking. The company builds up a data base on the guarantee card counter foil returns. Miniature Hawkins for children have been introduced to train them to use cooker and help the mother brand.

Companies may offer schemes to its regular customers during sales and special offers.

Service industry like banks and hotels can also make effective use of relationship marketing. Communication here is more focused and effective.

Relationship marketing opens a two-way communication channel with consumers. It has the potential to win their loyalty.

Inside Out – Outside In

Ranjay Gulati, HBS, has written Reorganize for *Resilience – Putting Customers at the Centre of Your Business.* There are two approaches – inside-out and outside-in. The inside-out perspective is fundamentally one where you say I know what the market wants. The job of the company is to produce, distribute and sell. There is some idea of what the customers want, but the organisation is not sure. In the outside-in perspective, the business is not defined by products but by the markets to be served. Apple's iPhone is 90 per cent outsourced, and only 10 per cent made in. There are almost a lac of applications for iPhone but not even a single one is made by Apple. Inside-out is closed architecture, where everything is made in. The outside-in model has mastered the ability to understand where the markets are moving. Customer – centricity does not mean blindly listening to the customer. The customers do not design the iPhone. Apple just understood the right trade-offs between ease of use and other things. Everyone claims they are customer-centric. Either it is a matter of luck or some design. Progressively, companies get disengaged from customers. The myopic view and the arrogance of knowing better come in the way. The companies are not organised around customers. Outside-in starts the reverse way – the mission for which the company is established. A hospital can be managed with a crew of specialists. But it can serve the younger people with isolated problems, but not the ageing population with several interrelated problems. The configuration of delivery system could be inside-out and not outside-in. Al Ries is of the opinion that customers do not know what they want till they are given a real world choice. The companies should do what they do best, and outsource the best. The companies should not confuse between core and critical. Core things give An unique edge in the market-place. Critical things are necessary to do business, but do not necessarily give an advantage. Power is needed to run a industry, but that does not mean that you need to own a powerplant. The idea is shrink the core. Bharati considered coverage a core factor. Today it is a hygienic factor, taken for granted. At one point of time, owning towers was the differentiator. The tower must have electricity. The diesel to generate electricity was bought by Bharati. It was the second largest buyer of diesel after the Indian Railways. Bharati then hived off the towers into a separate company. It is not worried about diesel anymore. It now focuses its energy on marketing and new business development, and service innovation. The idea of shrinking core means how I can do less and less for myself.

❑ ❑ ❑

17

CONSUMER PROTECTION IN INDIA

Like labour movement, the consumer movement also exercises considerable influence on the socio-economic environment of business. A strong consumer movement is the **sine qua non** of a healthy house-hold sector in an economy.

Why Consumers Need Protection?

(1) In Indian economy today because of imperfections in both product and factor markets, some sort of exploitation of consumers often results.

(2) Here the masses are illiterate, less informed and have little purchasing power. Therefore, they need protection as well as guidance.

(3) India is ideologically wedded to giving social justice, and so consumer protection is a natural corollary.

(4) In our country, because of chronic inflation, different anti-social elements have emerged and they indulge in malpractices. The need , therefore, is to be more alert to consumer protection.

(5) Indian business community till date treates the consumer non-seriously. This is because they are operating in seller's market. Slowly we are moving towards a buyer's market. In this transitory period, consumers need all the more protection.

(6) Consumers are lured into buying shoddy products by promising advertisements. Here, they need guidance and protection.

(7) Consumers need protection from monopolistic and restrictive trade practices.

Protection of consumers could be at the level of traders like FTPA or at the level of government which legislates in favour of the consumer.

Protection of consumers could be at the level of consumers as a consumer movement, at the level of traders like FTPA or at the level of government which legislates in favour of the consumer.

Rate of Consumer Guidance Society of India (CGSI)

Consumers who are not organised are exposed to several unfair practices of the trader and the manufacturers and their distributors. So they need to be protected. Consumer movement is a movement that protects consumers themselves. It is a self-protection. CGSI is an association of consumers for protection and guidance.

Born in Bombay, 1966, it was pioneered by housewives and social workers. Its main purpose is to protect consumers and guide them in their product-related problems.

It fights for *consumer rights.* It makes them *conscious* of these rights. It's membership is open to individuals and associations. It has branches in several major cities.

Role:

(*i*) It employs democratic and peaceful means to fight unfair practices.

(*ii*) It disseminates accurate and relevant information.

(*iii*) It has quality testing laboratories.

(*iv*) It co-operates with state agencies.

(*v*) It ensures the compliance of consumer protection laws.

(*vi*) It undertakes to educate the consumer by various means.

(*vii*) It uses mass media to educate the consumers.

(*viii*) It publishes a house journal of guidance.

(*ix*) It maintains a complaints cell. It receives complaints, takes up matters with the concerned parties, and seeks redressal. It gives a follow up to complaints.

(*x*) It fights for the right of consumers, It makes them conscious of their rights.

In short, it directly and indirectly takes steps to protect and guide consumers. It publishes consumer guidance literature, and observes 'Consumer Week'. At times, it takes the matter to a court of law. Still, its efforts are not enough. The reasons are:

(*i*) There is a need to protect rural consumers whereas the society is urban-based.

(*ii*) There are limited resources to undertake a gigantic task.

(*iii*) The approach is ad hoc.

(*iv*) There is some politicisation.

(*v*) There is lack of leadership and management.

(*vi*) There is lack of consumer education.

These defects have to be removed and the society should be strengthened. Here the consumer councils have a role to play.

Present Position of Consumer Guidance and Protection in India

At the level of traders, we now have Council of Fair Business Practices (formerly FTPA) which is an association of business community formed primarily to protect the consumers in terms of price, quality and availability of products. The attempts, however, are very feeble and not strong enough to earn Indian business a fair name.

At the level of government, there is a wide array of enactments to protect a consumer. Despite all this, the Indian consumer is subjected to a number of unfair practices. There enactments fall short of providing adequate safe-guards. Besides, whatever little protection is available is piecemeal. There is no branch of law dealing specifically with consumer trade practices. Legislation like the MRTP Act has not really protected the vast majority of consumers. There is an urgent need today for legislative control of a misleading and deceptive advertising and sale of products not meeting safety standards. One most important point. Ours is a mixed economy with a vast public sector. In India consumer needs more protection against government as a supplier of such important services like health-care, transport, tele-communication, drugs and medicines, sports, iron, steel, minerals, gold, agricultural produce, cooking gas, petroleum etc.

At the level of consumers, now a consumer movement has started in the form of consumer associations in Urban India. But these are very weak financially and concentrate on post-office like functions of receiving complaints and forwarding them to the concerned parties. The recent comprehensive legislation of consumer protection with a district level Consumer Council, State-level machinery and national mechanism perhaps will take the movement a few inches forward.

Consumer Education: Education means imparting information, guidance, training to consumers. All this should be tied up with their protection and safety. It is in this sense different form conventional formal education. This consumer education makes them aware of sharp business practices and how to blunt them. It gives an added confidence to consumers to fight the menace of business malpractices. Consumer education arms them to protect themselves. They become conscious of their rights. As our general education does not cover all this, separate specialised consumer education is needed. This education is universally needed.

Significance: Indian consumers are less informed or illiterate. They are gullible too. So, they need consumer education.

Indian business is known for sharp practices. Therefore, consumers need this education.

Indian consumers are poor, and accept any substandard product. They are not choosey and fastidious. Hence, they need education about their rights and remedies, and about being selective.

Consumer education paves the way for consumer movement which could be the only answer to business malpractices in the long run.

In short run also, consumers emerge as a pressure group in several pockets due to consumer education and the gains are then spread for one and all.

Education makes consumer a watch dog, but not a blood-hound.

Agencies of C.E.: The education of consumers could be at different levels. See the following chart:

C.E.
(Consumer Education)

Consumer Level	**Government Level**	**Business Level**
Through Consumer Associations (Seminars, Lectures Exhibitions, Use of Mass Media, Advertisements)	(i) Conferences, (ii) Use of TV and radio, (iii) Use of government publications (iv) Talks, discussion press (v) Extension services, (vi) Adult Literacy Mission.	(i) Brochures, (ii) Circulars, (iii) Publicity, (iv) Business mags, (v) Guidance through press

Consumer Movement

Consumer movement, like labour movement, is a reaction to the exploitation of the consumers by organised and unorganised business. It is a response of consumers to business mal-practices. It is a collective response, a united response, a concerted response, and it creates an impact on business which slowly starts to behave. Scattered individuals as consumers are too weak to fight alone. They need an organisational mechanism for this right for self-protection and self-help. Consumer movement checks sharp business practices, Ideally, it is a non-political movement. It seeks to protect, educate, guide the consumer and ensure his welfare.

The organisational mechanism for this movement is a consumer council. These can exist in several tiers. Consumer movement, strong enough to blunt sharp business practices, is the need in all developing economies.

Advantages:

(1) Consumer movement avoids exploitation. Consumer gets a fair deal. He pays reasonable prices. He becomes immune to unfair, restrictive trade practices.

(2) Consumers develop a sense of belonging and each help all, and all help each.

(3) Consumers become watch dogs but not blood-hounds.

(4) Consumer movement when advances on right lines eliminates middlemen and takes distribution upon itself.

(5) Consumers are protected in adverse business conditions.

(6) Consumer movement makes government pre-consumer, makes it enact consumer legislations, give teeth to these legislations and enforce them effectively. Most important, the government also as a supplier of goods from public utility services and public sector enterprises starts being more vigilant about dealing with consumers.

(7) Consumer movement imparts consumer education which is like insuring a consumer against exploitation.

(8) Consumer movement acts as a pressure group on business people.

(9) Consumer movement creates public opinion against sharp practices.

(10) Consumer movement ultimately results into grievance handling cells, consumer co-operatives, fair price shops, fair business councils, distribution of consumer goods for self-services and self-helper.

Limited Consumer Movement: Reasons: Consumer movement has so far not made any substantial dent on Indian business. The reasons are not far to seek.

(1) The movement is very young, and will take time to mature and take roots.

(2) Low level of literacy and general backwardness are conducive to consumer exploitation.

(3) Poverty also results into helpless acceptance of all that is offered, irrespective of quality.

(4) The movement has to spread itself in rural areas.

(5) The movement has adversaries in the form of powerful business houses and public sector which is callous.

(6) There is no systematic effort of consumer education. It is all ad hocism.

(7) Consumers are indifferent towards their rights.

(8) Consumer movements lacks resources, expertise, and government support.

(9) There are miscellaneous reasons like vast size of the country, lack of communication infra-structure, emasculated and over-burdened enforcement agencies, lack of leadership, caste-ridden divided society, society in transition etc.

Rights of Consumers

Consumers are those for whom the business exists. Business has to earn its profits through consumers satisfaction. Consumers have certain rights and duties which should be known to them. Consumers' rights give foundation to business marketing. Kennedy referred to the following four rights of consumers.

(i) the right to safety, (ii) the right of information, (iii) the right of choice, (iv) the right to be heard.

Consumer rights give direction to marketing firms. They also protect the consumers. These rights exist in free market economy. These rights should be respected by traders. It is in their own interest in the long run. Consumer movement safeguards these rights. Consumer education makes us aware of these rights.

Let us consider these rights in brief.

(i) Right to Safety: It pertains to his health and safety. He is to be protected against hazardous goods. We have to be extra vigilant about electrical appliances, food items, children's toys, medicines, ect. For all items consumers should be given instructions of use. These items should be standardised. Stringent quality control and quality audit are necessary here.

Suitable laws regarding product-liability are called for. Houses which crumble within a short-time taking a toll of human lives or the glycerine tragedy at J.J. Hospital are glaring examples of how safety requirements are flouted. Adulteration is also rampant. We see scented supari with Saccharin which is Carcinogenic, and edible oil which is adulterated and can cause paralysis. Media has a great role to play here in educating consumers.

(ii) Right to be Informed: Consumers have a right to get full information about the product he is buying. The information should be correct and quick. This is to be done through labelling, brochures, booklets, packing and advertising. Misleading ads giving incorrect information should be banned. Consumer needs proper training to make use of the information.

(iii) Right to Choose: It is an unbridled right to select any article out of available right to select any article out of available assortment. There cannot be compulsion to buy a particular commodity. Competitive market automatically gives this right. Advertisements also help in free choice. Tie-up sales are against the right to choose (buy a burner when LPG Cylinder is alloted). In a sellers market, this right has limited scope. Legal monopolies also come in the way of full implementation of this right. (We have to get a phone connection from MTNL only).

(iv) Right to be Heard: Consumers have a right to express what they feel about marketing mix of the firm — price, product, product feature, product quality, packing, branding, distribution, advertising etc. It gives them an opportunity to give suggestions and to raise objections, and register complaints. Apart form these four basic rights, the consumers have the following additional rights:

(1) The Right to Redress, (2) Right to Clean Environment, (3) Right to Form an Association.

Consumer movement has not succeeded, but it must succeed. For its success realisation of consumer rights is a step in the right direction.

Business Malpractices

Business is an exchange through the medium of money of need satisfying products and services to generate consumer satisfaction. The transactions in money are conducted in such a way that the revenues generated cover all the operating costs and still leave a surplus called profit. However, consumer satisfaction is the over-riding consideration and not the profit. Still profit motivation not checked by any other consideration leads to many malpractices. These practices are harmful to consumers and to community at large.

Business malpractices is a blanket term — it could happen in any operational area of business. We can have malpractices in terms of product and its quality, pricing of the product, proper distribution and availability of product, and truthful advertising of the product. These malpractices could be tax evasion, violation of fiscal laws like FERA, speculative activities in commodities and stock, unfair accounting standards etc. The list is almost endless.

These malpractices could be monopolistic, restrictive or unfair. There are legal distinctions, but for us they are wafer thin, All these malpractices affect the consumers, or other parties dealing with business, or community at large. Thus, malpractices having impact on other parties do affect the consumers too, albeit indirectly.

Consumers have to pay the price of eternal vigilance to keep away form these malpractices.

Usual Malpractices:

(i) Adulteration: Generally, it occurs in food products. The food is not what it purports to be. It is blended with a cheap or injurious substance. This is done to reap more profits since it is concerned with human life, it is most detestible malpractice. The malpractice can be fortunately detected in a laboratory. We need to have many such laboratories considering how rampant this problem is. Besides though there is Food Adulteration Prevention Act, but its implementation is very slack. Even when implemented, the dealers come off acquitted in the trial as there are many loopholes in the laws. Adulteration may lead to many physiological problems, which could be as minor as slight skin rash or as major as a dreaded disease like cancer. Many have suggested that adulteration should attract criminal liability also.

(ii) Lack of Safety Measures and Quality Control: We pay a price for the product. We should get commensurate quality or else, it is outright deception. Indian manufacturers are indifferent to quality. Quality is built into a product right from the idea stage. We have to be careful about quality of raw materials, quality of process, quality of components, quality of spares and quality of finished products. We have to exercise Quality Control physically as well as statiscally through control charts. There should be Quality Audit periodically. Quality has to be thought in terms of product design, product contours and product performance.

Quality of poor nature may also make the product less for us. Quality in performance against specification, therefore, must be checked.

Japan was once considered to be a country with poor quality but has now acquired a status of a quality conscious country. We in India should leave as J.R.D. Tata says **'the chalega'** attitude and think in terms of producing quality products.

(iii) Short Weights and Measures: Many commodities are sold in terms of weight of a particular quantity for which we are paying, but in reality the weight might be less than what it is stated to be. We get this experience while buying in retail any item like milk or kerosene. But even when we buy products of organised industries like cement, we find a bag contains less than

what it should. Either the manufacturer or the distributor plays the mischief, and we are taken for a ride. The practice is so widely prevalent that legal steps to prevent it are grossly inadequate.

(iv) Misleading Advertising: There are advertisements, mostly in the field of personal care and health, which make very tall claims but the product offerings fail to measure up to our expectations. Thus we are promised a complexion — fair and lovely — with which we are born, or a hair-growth on bald head or a cure for infertility. Then there are advertisements which show before and after effects: a skinny young man becoming a muscular Tyson, a pimpled lady in distress becoming a dimpled beauty — the contributing factor being the advertised product. It is all Utopian.

(v) Black Marketing and Profiteering: Here goods are sold at an unofficial premium to reap excessive profits, by making use of adverse business conditions or a wide unfulfilled demand. Who has not heard that till the other day a well-known brand of scooter commanded a premium of a few thousand rupees? Of late, even our small car did command a premium. Then there are shortages of edible oil, sugar and such other sensitive commodities and consequent over-charging. All this affects national economy, results into consumer exploitation, and puts genuine consumers at a disadvantage. Regular supply channels also dry up.

(vi) Illegal Trading: Gambling, speculation, smuggling, FERA and COFEPOSA violations, and such similar practices are too well-known to need any further explanation.

Regulation of Malpractices

Basically, the very purpose of business is to create a customer. It is the consumer who pays a price either to survive or grow further. No customer, no business. Anything that harms him, therefore, is out of place in business. It is like cutting the very branch on which you are sitting or killing a hen laying golden eggs.

Business also exists in a society and uses social resources. It has, therefore, to be responsible to all members of society. It cannot afford to be anti-social. It has to advance the civilization. It owes dividends to shareholders, taxes to the governments, payment to suppliers. Business cannot be at the cost of human safety and human life. Of course there are perpetual dilemmas: say whether to promote smoking or not and whether to ask people to eat more ice-cream and lead to caries (tooth-decay) and whether to allow people the use of disposable containers but environmental pollution. Social cost benefit analysis and social audit is a fast developing area and business has to do a tight-rope walking over there.

Business malpractices may lead to a bad bargain and consumer's post purchase dissatisfaction.

Business malpractices also make consumers worse off rather than better off.

For all these reasons and for the overall gain of the country and economy, we have to put a stop to business malpractices.

Legislative Regulation

Those trade practices which are not favourable to consumers must be regulated. This regulation occurs at the trade level, a the consumer level, or a the government level. The government cannot remain a silent spectator to business malpractices, and so intervenes by enacting suitable legislations for consumer protection. Consumer protection legislation exists in all countries to control unfair trade practices. The important measures introduced in India are.

1. Weights and Measures Act, 1958 (As amended in 1967): It gives protection to the consumers regarding weights and measures. It has introduced uniform weights and measures in the country (The Metric System). Short weights is now punishable. Inspectors visit markets and check weights and measures. Surprise checks are made. Offences are registered against defaulters. This legislation, though good in intent and purpose, needs vigorous implementation.

2. The Prevention of Food Adulteration Act (PFA), 1954: It is a designed to protect the health of the public by prohibiting adulteration of food. Its provisions influence the product and promotion decisions of food product companies. According to its provisions, manufacturing, selling, storing, distribution of adulterated or misbranded foods are prohibited and its violation attracts both civil and criminal liabilities. It defines both adulterated and misbranded products.

Certain other related legislations are:

(*a*) Drugs and Cosmetics Act, 1940
(*b*) Drugs and Magic Remedies Act, 1954
(*c*) Dangerous Drugs Act (DDA)
(*d*) Poisons Act, 1919
(*e*) Narcotic and Psychotropic Substances Act.

An adulterated food article is *injurious* to public health. It is deemed to be injurious when:

- the product quality is not as demanded or claimed.
- it contains an injurious substance
- any constituent of the article has been taken away;
- it had been prepared, packed, or kept under unsanitary conditions;
- it is unfit for human consumption because it is filthy, putrid, rotten, decomposed, insect infested, etc;
- it is obtained form a deceased animal;
- it is poisonous or deliterious;
- it contains a prohibited preservative;
- its quality or purity falls below the prescribed standards.

A food product is said to be misbranded when:

- it is a deceptive imitation of or resembles an existing product;
- it is not plainly and conspicuously labelled so as to indicate its true character;
- it is falsely stated to be a product of another place or country;
- it is sold by a name which belongs to another article of food;
- a damaged article is so processed as to conceal its damage;
- it makes false claims;
- its contents are not conspicuously and correctly stated on the label;
- its package contains false or misleading information about its contents.

The Act provides elaborate rules about the quality of different food articles and imposes both civil and criminal liabilities (Sec. 16), for violation of its provisions.

3. The Drugs and Magic Remedies (Objectionable Advertisement) Act, 1954: The provisions of this Act influence the advertising decisions of companies marketing drugs for certain types of ailments specified in it. It aims to prevent advertisements tending to cause the ignorant and unwary consumer to resort to self-medication with harmful drugs and appliances. According to this Act (Sec. 3 and 4) advertisement are prohibited in respect of certain diseases and disorders such as prevention of conception, sexual impotency, menstrual disorders, epilepsy, fits, etc. and others given in the schedule. It also prohibits advertisements making false claims for the drug. It imposes both civil and criminal liabilities for the contravention of its provisions (Sec. 7).

4. The Packaged Commodities (R) Order, 1975: Under DIR provisions of emergency, this Order came into being. It pertains to the right labelling of the products. There should be product identity, net wt., date of package and maximum retail price on each package. Even retailers are expected to display retail prices. This Order is honoured by most manufacturers.

5. The Essential Commodities Act, 1955: The essential Commodities Act, 1955, controls the production, supply and distribution of essential commodities in order to maintain or increase the supply of such commodities or for securing their equitable distribution and availability at a fair price. For this purpose, the Act empowers the Government to regulate production by licensing, control price, regulate storage and transportation, prohibit sale and to buy products at a specified price. It imposes both civil and criminal liabilities.

Several commodities are declared as essential under this Act. It ensures a regular supply of essential commodities. It checks black transactions and hoarding. The competent authorities can do searches and seizures under this Act.

6. The Monopolies and Restrictive Trade Practices Act 1969 (MRTP, 1969): It attempts to regulate the monopolitic and trade restrictive practices of companies. It applies to companies whose assets are more than 100 crores and to dominant undertakings. MRTP Commission has come into existence under this Act. MRTP Commission not only monitors monopolistic and restrictive trade practices, but also entertains consumer complaints in this matter.

7. ISI and AGMARK: ISI Certification Mark Act, 1952 for ensuring standards of products and AGMARK standards for agricultural products help, guide and protect the consumers.

8. The Indian Sale of Goods Act, 1930: Governs the transactions of sale and purchases. It, thus, influences the selling decisions of companies. It defines contract of sale as a contract whereby a seller transfers or agrees to transfer the property in goods to a buyer for a price. It divides the terms of sales into conditions and warranty. Condition is a stipulation essential to the main purpose while warranty does not. Warranty entitles to only damages. The Act proclaims the principle of 'caveat emptor' which has possibly made many people in the Indian Business sales-oriented. It lays down rules for the performance of the contract of sale.

9. The Trade and Merchandise Marks Act. 1958: The Trade and Merchandise Marks Act, 1958 influences the product and advertising decisions of a company, particularly with regard to the trade and merchandise marks. The registration of trademark under this Act, endows on its holder the right of exclusive use of trademark for a maximum period of seven years each time. It lays down conditions for the registration of the trademark. An infringement of the rights of the trademark holder attracts injunction, damages, and submission of an account of profit and its payment by the person who has infringed the rights of the trademark holder. It also attracts criminal liability in certain cases.

10. Immoral Representation of Women in Advertising Act: This Act recently enacted prohibiting the portrayal of women in an immoral manner in commercial messages.

Over and above these, there are other acts:

(*i*) Fruits Products Order, 1955

(*ii*) Agricultural Produce (Grading and Marketing) Act, 1937

(*iii*) Household Electrical Appliances (Q.C.) Order, 1976

(*iv*) Emblems and Name (Prevention of Improper Use) Act, 1950

(*v*) Patents Act, 1970; Copyright Act, 1957

(*vi*) Forward Contracts Regulation Act, 1952

(*vii*) A Comprehensive Consumer Legislation of 1958.

Curbing of Unfair Practices

At the trade level, many unfair practices can be curbed. Here the initiative is taken by the manufacturers and traders. The Associations like Fair Trade Practices Association (FTPA), other trade associations and chambers of Commerce. Education through seminars is a must of manufacturers and traders. Profit motive comes in the way of fair practices. Apparently both are contradictory but in reality they are complementary. These measures, though welcome, are not enough. The consumers must be organised and there should be state pressure. When these pressure groups are strong, voluntary compliance is forthcoming.

Restrictive Trade Practices

The MRTP Act also prohibits restrictive trade practices of companies covered by it if these are found to be prejudicial to the public interest on an enquiry by the Monopolies and Restrictive Trade Practices Commission or otherwise. The Act defines (Sec, 2 (0)) a restrictive trade practice to mean a trade practice which has or may have the effect of preventing, distorting or restricting competition in any manner and the particular:

- Which tends to obstruct the flow of capital or resources into the stream of production; or
- Which tends to bring about manipulation of prices, or conditions of delivery, or to affect the flow of suppliers in the market relating to goods or services in such manner as to impose on consumers unjustified costs or restriction.

As is clear from the provisions of this Act, not all restrictive trade practices are prohibited; only those practices which are prejudicial to the public interest are banned. However, in order to determine their prejudice or otherwise, the Act requires (Sec. 33) companies to register with the MRTP Commission the following types or restrictive trade agreements:

- Any agreement which restricts or may restrict by any method the persons or classes of persons to whom goods are sold or from whom goods are bought;
- Any agreement requiring a buyer, as a condition of purchase, to buy some other goods (e.g. forcing slow-moving goods with the fast-moving ones);
- Any agreement restricting a buyer from acquiring or otherwise dealing in any goods other than those of the seller or other persons;

- Any agreement to purchase or sell goods only at prices or on terms or condition agreed upon between the sellers and the buyers.
- Any agreement to grant or allow concessions or benefits, including allowances, discounts, rebates, or credit in connection with or by reason of dealings;
- Any agreement to sell goods on the condition that resale prices will be those stipulated by the seller unless it is clearly stated that lower than stipulated price can be charged;
- Any agreement to limit, restrict or withhold the output or supply of any goods or allocate any area or market for the disposal of the goods;
- Any agreement not to employ or restrict the employment of any method, machinery, or process in the manufacture of goods;
- Any agreement to exclude any trader from the trade association;
- Any agreement to sell goods at such prices as would have the effect of eliminating competition or competitor; and
- Any agreement considered trade restrictive by the Central Government.

Limitations

(1) It offers no protection to consumers against false or misleading advertisements or other similar unfair trade practices.

(2) There is justification for exempting Government or Government controlled/owned undertakings from the provisions of this Act. It is an irony that in a democracy the public sector should not be subjected to a law that is designed to protect the interests of general public.

(3) There should be data-base of goods produced or services rendered for the effective implementation of this Act.

The following table illustrate how we have moved forward to further the consumer rights:

CONSUMER RIGHTS

Year	*Legislation / Activity*	*Remarks*
1915	Passengers and Traffic Relief Association	—
	Women Graduates Union, Mumbai	—
1960s	Consumer Guidance Society of India (CGSI)	—
	All India Bank Depositors Association	—
	Bombay Civil Trust	
	Surat Consumer Association	—
	Kennedy committed to promotion and protection of consumer interests	—
	International Organisation of Consumer Union.	—
1969	The Monopolies and Restrictive Trade Practices Commission (MRTPC)	Powers to grant interim relief.
1970s	Mrinal Gore started *dharnas* and picketing	—
1976	Pune Grahak Panchayat	Fought rampant food adulteration
1977-80	Mohan Dharia and later A.K. Antony appointed as Consumers Affairs Ministers.	—
1980s	Consumer groups were formed rapidly.	Their number is 1500 today.
1986	Consumer Protection Act (CORA)	Consumer Courts at three levels — District, State and National.
1990	Synergy amongst the Voluntary Consumer Organisations (VCOs)	—
1999	Ban on diesel-run commercial vehicles and relocation for small industries out of residential areas by the Supreme Court.	—

❑ ❑ ❑

18

CASE STUDIES

CASE 1: SCENTS AND SENSIBILITY

The ultimate inspiration for perfumes is nature itself. The flora and fauna has its own fragrance. It is due to the volatile substances and essential oils. It is an art to blend these substances of different levels of volatility to create a perfume.

Perfume was first used by the Egyptians as a part of the religious rituals. They burnt incense, and applied fragrant balms and ointments. The word perfume comes form the Latin *perfume*, meaning *through smoke*. The reference is to incense. In medicine and body care, perfumed oils have been used since long. They have been used in religious rituals and festivals since 1580-2085 BC. The use of perfumes spread from Egypt to Greece, Rome and the Islamic world. *Attar* derived from the Arabic *aettr,* means fat or extract. Attars are aromatic oils extracted from flowers, plants and herbs. Attars in the market are not only single-fragrance but can also have a mixed bouquet. With the fall of the Roman empire the use of perfume declined. This decline was reversed in the 12th century, with the development of international trade.

As early as in the 15th century, Oleum mirabile, an alcoholic extract of rosemary and resins was produced for medicinal purposes. As time went by many modifications were made in its composition. The most important change was that the resin extract was left out. The rosemary distillate, now diluted with alcohol, was incarnated as hungarian water – the fore runner of *eau-de-cologne.*

In the 17th century, perfumes came of age. They entered France in a big way. In 18th century, Eau de Cologne was invented, which gave a fillip to this industry. Originally, it consisted of a mixture of rosemary, neroli, bergamot and lemon. Perfume bottles imaginatively crafted gave a further fillip to this industry.

So far, perfumes were prepared form crude plants. The emergence of chemistry laid the foundation of modern perfume industry in the 19th century. The process of perfume development by chemical methods was initiated.

In post-revolution France, perfumes became the choice of people along with other luxury goods. Grasse, a little town on the coast of France, became the perfume capital of the world. Grasse has the raw materials of perfume — Jasmine, rose and orange. In 1724, Paris emerged as a counter balancing centre to Grasse. This tiny village has over 65 international perfume companies jostling for space. These firms generate 50 per cent of the French perfume turnover and eight per cent of the world's. The turnover of France in perfume is 1.05 billion euros. Bottling of perfumes got added importance. In 1930's, family fragrances and floral scents became popular. In 50's, the perfume industry in France reached its peak. Christian Dior, Jaques Fath, Pierre Balmain, Nina Ricci and other designers started creating their own brands.

As observed earlier, complex blends are popular today rather than single flower scents. In fact, Coco Channel used to say that women did not want to smell a bed of roses. Channel 5 thus emerged as a complex blend. Still, certain scents of lily are still popular.

Origin of Perfumes

Technically perfumes are mixtures of substances, some vegetable and others of animal origin. Some may be wholly or partially artificial. Dissolved in alcohol, these various mixtures of volatile fragrant substances release their scent at normal temperatures. Only the mixture which contains a large proportion of fragrance concentrate, and the least possible alcohol is called 'perfume' Any mixture containing a larger percentage of alcohol is called 'eau'. Some fragrance solutions are diluted with oil. Compact or cream perfumes are produced by mixing fragrance oil with solids such as paraffin or other waxes.

Most of them are derived from flower essences. They are floral perfumes. Another perfume family is derived from the greens like resins, mosses and ferns (called chypre family) or leaves, grasses and buds. Greens can be combined with flowers. Greens are crisp and fresh. Woody fragrances are derived form barks, roots, timbers, ferns and moses. Channel 19 is a famous example of this group. Woody perfumes are foresty, smoky, earthy flavours. They are known for their masculinity. The fragrances are most appealing. They are soothing. They are used generally as top notes, followed by florals and greens. De Lancome, Gio of Armani, Escape of Calvin Klein, Witness of Bogart's, Sunny Fruity of Escada are famous examples of the fruity flavours.

The following table illustrates the broad perfume families.

Type of fragrance	Details	Examples
Floral	Suitable for romantics. Suitable for all occasions. Very feminine	White Linen, Lady Stetson, Burberry Weekend, Chancherel's Amor Amor, Carolina Herrera
Fresh smelling	Suitable for exbuberant and people on the move. Lend a fresh feeling they smell citrus or fresh dew.	Lalique, Azzaro 9, Ralph Lauren Polo Sport, Calvin Klein's CK, One Boss by Hugo, Cool Water
Spicy and Oriental smelling	Strong whiff can travel far. Make a statement. Suitable for go-getters and confident	Laura Biagiotti, Sunflowers, All about Eve, Dunhill, Elysses, Sensi, Poison
Exotic woody	Suitable for those who look for class and ooze with sensuality.	Chanel No. 19, Paloma Picasso, Opium, Obsession, Burberry Brit for Men, Halston, Farenhit, 212, H 20 Men

Apart from these broad sources, perfumes are made to resemble so many different substances in nature.

Indian Market

Indian fragrance market is pegged at 40 million prospects (men and women) and that will rise each year. About 60 p.c. of all fragrance purchase stems from fragrance for women.

Symphony in Perfumes

Like notes in music symphony, a good perfume has three district notes.

The Top Note (First Impression)	These lightweight notes introduce a perfume. It reaches our senses first. Most volatile of perfume ingredients make up this note. It is the initial impact that the perfume creates. It is also called the head note.
The Middle Note (Heart Notes) (Bought Notes)	These notes last during the entire period of the wearing of the perfume. These notes emerge gently when the top notes begins to fade. It is made up by less volatile substances. It calms itself.
Bottom Notes (Base Note)	These are the notes that linger. It has the slowe s t evaporation rate. It reveals the true personality of the perfume.

A fragrance retarder binds these three stages together so that a perfume does not break up into three stages each smelling differently. This way well-balanced perfumes move easily from one note to another.

Fragrances are also related to the bio-chemistry of the person who wear them. The time and season also affect the effect of perfume. Lighter fragrances like Eau de Cologne are preferred during day time. In the evening, we may use concentrated ones. In summer we use fresh, flowery notes like Eau Fresh, Escada Sport and Ocean. In winter, we wear exactly opposite perfumes like Montanna Parfum de Peau. The choice also differs from nation to nation. Japanese women prefer the floral family. Europe and the US prefer stronger, less subtle smells. The seven families of perfumes are (i) greens (ii) florals (iii) aldehydic (iv) chypre oriental (v) tobacco-leather and (vi) fougere (fantasy, rarest-line, semi-oriental *e.g.,* Jicky).

Personality and Perfumes

Choosing a perfume is quite challenging, especially when it comes to matching it with the personality of the user, especially women users. A perfume reflects the personality of the user, especially that phase of personality at that given point of time. The following table lists some famous perfumes and the personality type of women for whom they are created.

Brand	*Organisation*	*Type of Perfume*	*Created for*
Opium	Yves St. Laurent	Oriental, warm, spicy with touches of flower	An extremely sensual, mysterious, luxury loving woman.
Poison	Christian Dior	Exotic, aromatic, spicy with tinges of floral	A warm, sensual, sultry, strong yet feminine woman.
Chanel No. 5	Coco Chanel	Classy floral, subtle, mild	An intelligent career woman. A go ahead woman. An elegant, sophisticated woman. Anytime,anywhere perfume. "The only thing I wear to bed is Chanel No. 5" - Marilyn Monroe
Paloma Picasso	Paloma Picasso	Floral and full-bodied and yet not too intense	A dignified elegant woman
Armani (for women)	Giorgio Armani	Combines spicy, woody, floral and fruity	A mature woman of strong character.
Scoundrel	Revlon	Spicy-Fruity	An assertive, exuberant, voluptuous woman.
O De Lancome	Lancome	Light, delicate and soft	A spontaneous, serene and confident woman
Paris	Yves st. Laurent	Floral-woody	A romantic, graceful dreamer woman.
Laughter	Yardley	Woody-spicy. Strong, seductive	A sensual, bubbly, spirited, younger woman
L' Air Du Temps (1948)	Nina Rici	Floral. Mild	A reserved, gentle, intelligent younger woman. Fresh and feminine.
Magriffe	Carven	Floral, mild	A quiet, shy, introverted younger woman
Rive Gauche	Yves St. Laurent	Floral, woody	An active, extroverted, daring, spontaneous bright woman who is strong but not aggressive
Anais Anais	Cacharel	Fresh, light scent	A half-child half-woman who is romantic and gentle, youthful and soft.
Guerlain Shalimar	Guerlain	Simple, elegant, subtle composition. Queen of orientals	Speaks of the mystery of being a woman. Shalimar in Sanskrit means temple of love.

ZODIACAL SIGNS AND PERFUMES

Zodiacs put the mankind into 12 slots, each with peculiar personality traits, who need peculiar type of perfumes. The following table summarises the sign-trait-perfume matching.

Zodiacal Sign	*Personality Traits*	*Attributes Expected in a Perfume*	*Brands*	
			For Men	*For Women*
Aries	Strong, appetite for life, get ahead	Dazzling, overwhelming memorable	Gucci Envy Paco Rabane PH	Acte Z Carolina Herrera
Taurus	Irresistible Sensuality de	Likes foresty and floral smells	Herrera for men, Escada Sport, Oscar de la Renta	Escada en fleurs, Tocade, Amarige Givenchy
Gemini	Curious, everchanging	Drawn towards youth. Spring time scents	Paco Guy Le Roche	L'eau Issey, Mystere
Cancer	Imaginative Sensitive Romantic	Florals	Escada Pour Homme, 5th Avenue	Magaretha Ley, Fleur D'eau
Leo	Generous Honest Positive	Bright, shiny colours should leave a fragrant trail. Heady scents	Escada Sport, 5th Avenue, Byzanc, Gucci Envy	Envy, Madame Rochas, En Fleurs
Virgo	Prudent, shy, discreet	Natural, well-Structured light notes	Jovan Ginseng Red Door	True Love, En Fleurs
Libra	Polite, tries to please others	Wears perfume like a second skin. Light, floral but	Escada Sport, Sunflower, Eau de Rochas sensual fragrances	Femme, Gucci Accenti, Magaretha Ley
Scorpio	Determined yet idealistic. Two opposites blended.	Attracted to unusual scents. Sensual and oriental	Escada Pour, XS Pour Homme	Gucci No. 3, Mystere Escada Collection
Sagittarius	Citizen of the world. Defender of human rights. Audacious, Adventurous	Wild flowers and freedom they represent	Escada Sport Paco Rabane PH	Madame Rochas, Chanel
Capricorn	Dependable Responsible Disciplined	Rejects superfluous woody smells. Loyal to a perfume	Aqua de Gio Escada Sport	Issey Miyake Femme, Truest

Aquarius	Creative	Testing new fragrances. Trying out contrasts. Warm and citrus or deep and light.	Escada's Seasonal Fragrances, Salvador	Sun, Moon, Stars Narcisse
Pisces	Idealistic Romantic Sensitive Intuitive	Like water. Marine and amber notes Sweet-fresh harmonies	1881 PH Acte 2	1881 PE Chloe

Life Style Classification

Some experts have made an attempt to match life-styles and perfumes.

Life Style	*Likely Perfume*
Always up with the dawn. Juggling more than one project at a time. Loathe sitting around.	Green notes. Citrus-like smells. Men's fragrances which are sporty. Brand: New West Skinscent
Escape to rural idyll. Relaxed, meditative mood.	'Ozonic' and 'oceanic' fragrances. Callone, the active ingredient, lifts the spirits. Brand: Escape (Calvin Klein) Dune (Christian Dior)
Hedonist, believer in seductive power of perfume.	Soft vanilla overtones. Spicy sensuality. Brand: Spell-bound (Estee Lader) Heritage (Guerlain)

Mood Classification

Here mood is linked to a fragrance. Colour is considered to be very close to the emotional centre; which governs our responses on the most intimate level. To identify client's mood, colour preference, is therefore assessed. It is possible then to predict fragrance preference.

Colour Preference	*Type of Perfume*	*Bramd*
Grey	Classic understated perfumes.	Safari (Ralph Lauren)
Green	Reject powdery sweet smells. Tends towards fresh, sharp fragrances.	Vent Vert (Balmain)
Rosy	Reject woody, dry notes. Opt for well-rounded harmonious bouquets.	L'Heure Bleu (Guerlain's)
Orange	Reject classical fragrances. Tend towards enlightening fresh smells.	New West (Armais)
Black	Fragrance full of refinement but totally individual.	Feminine du Bois (Shiseido's)

Top Selling Woman's Scents in US and Europe

Chanel No. 5	(Chanel)
Tresor	(L'Oreal)
Vanderbilt	(L'Oreal)
Opium	(YSL/Elf Sanofi)
Anais Anais	(L'Oreal)

Chanel No.5 was launched in 1921. It is by Coco Chanel and is 'a woman's fragrance that smells like a woman'. Top notes include ylang ylang, neroli and aldehydes. Jasmine and mayrose are at the heart, and the dry down consists of vetiver and sandalwood.

Top Selling Men's Scents in US and Europe

Draker Noir	(L'Oreal)
Pool and Crest	(L'Oreal)
Aramis	(Estee Launder)
Obsession	(Unilever)
Eternity	(Unilever)

Uni-Sex Perfume

cK One (Calvin Kelvin) appeals to both sexes

Carolina Herrera for Men is wearable by both sexes. The Paco Rabanne fragrance brand for men and women is part of the $ 800 million Spanish Pulg Group which also sells Carolina Herrera and Nina Ricci.

THREE TYPES OF SCENTS

Eau de Parfum	Highly concentrated. High percentage of oils	Last 5-8 hours
Eau de Toilettes	12-20% oil Mix of oil and spirit.	Last for 4 hours
Sprays	Little perfume oil.	Not more than two hours.

Choosing the Right Fragrance

The image or moods one likes to project and the enhancement of personality are the two factors which influence the choice of a perfume. A fragrance chosen indicates the type of person you are, and the way you would like others to perceive you. We may need different scents to highlight different facets of our personality. A scent chosen is compatible with our body chemistry. The occasion also influences the choice of a perfume. An evening party may lead to a sensual perfume with oodles of spiciness. A daytime perfume could be fresh and under-stated.

Paco Rabanne (French House)

Paco Rabanne has introduced fragrance line called Ultraviolet Men in India. It is a fresh, woody and ambergris fragrance. It stands out as a new generation sensual new-technology tag aimed at young men in the age group of 18-35 and will be sold at MRP of ₹ 2250 for 100ml and ₹ 1700 for 50 ml. In 2000, the Ultraviolet Women's range was launched.

OTHER LAUNCHES

April 2002	Ultraviolet Woman Aquatic Plastic
October 2002	Paco Rabanme Pour Homme
April 2003	New Perfume for Women

Paco Rabanne Brands Available in India

Ultraviolet for Women
XS for Men and Women (1993)
Paco Rabanne Pour Homme
Paco Rabanne Sport
Paco (1996)
Paco Energy (1998)

Appendix C
How to choose the Right Perfume?
For Women

Personality	*Fragrance Type*	*Chamber*	*Brands*
Feminine	Floral	Light-hearted, sweet-natured, feminine in her dress Happy (Clinique) Aqua de Gio (Armani)	Joy (Jean Patou) Channel No. 5 Diorissimo (Dior)
Discreet	Chypre	Discreetly feminine, stylishly understated Femme de Rochas	Miss Dior (Dior)* Mitsouko (Guerlain)
Seductive	Oriental	Overtly feminine, flirtatious Angel (T. Mugler) Must de Cartier	Shalimar (Guerlain) Opium (YSL)
Sporty	Ozonic	Sporty, active casual	Polo Sport Woman (Ralph Lauren) Escape (Calvin Klein) L'Eau d'Issey (Issey Miyake)

* Miss Dior from Christian Dior was introduced in 1947, and has been reinvented as Miss Dior Cherie. It is floral, woody, powdery and green. It is perfectly sophiticated, pretty and young.

For Men

Mr. Natural	Dry woody	Natural Equipage (Hermes)	Vetiver (Guerlain)
Bon Viveur	Oriental	Likes finer details	Santos (Cartier) Egoiste (Chanel)
Masculine	Fougeres	Deeply masculine Paco Rabanne Mouchoir de Monsieur (Guerlain)	Xeryus (Givenchy)
Understated	Citrus understated, discreet	Appealing, Monsieur Givenchy, cK One	Eau Savage (Dior)

SOME TRENDY SCENTS

Nature	*Company*	*Brand*	*Price*	*Constituents*
Earthy	Christian Lacorioc	Bazar	₹ 2750	Sweet notes of nectarine and roses
	J.Lo's	Glow	₹ 2700	Zingy orange flower, grapefruit and vanilla.
	Azzaro	Orange Tonic	₹ 1950	Bergamot and ginger
Chic Sophisticated	Dolce and Gabana's	Red	₹ 3405	Cedar and roses
	—	Cindy Crawford	₹ 2300	Magnotia and lemon
	Carolina Herrera	Carolina	₹ 2800	Hyacinth and iris
Carnal	Elizabeth Arden	Arden Beauty	₹ 2850	Sandalwood and white amber
	Pacco Rabanne's	UV Woman	₹ 2800	Ambered vanilla and osmanthus
	YSL	Opium	₹ 3260	Clove and patchouli
Romantic	—	Dailystyle	₹ 2400	White gardenias and freesia
	Christian Dior	Eau de Dolce Vita	₹ 2985	Apricot, peach and cardamom
		Babydoll	₹ 2850	Wild rose, freesia, rhubarb, red currant and grapefruit

Indian Attar

Also called *itra,* India along with Persia and Egypt, has a long history of perfume production. All these are natural perfumes or essential oils. Attar distillation process is about 300 years old. Blending is done as per the secret formule handed down from generation to generation. Kannauj is well-known for attar production since the 14th century. Its fragrance of *juhi, mogra, harsingar* and *gulmehandi* are well-known. Aligarh is famous for its rose attar. Jaunpur prides itself on its *chameli. Kewra* from Orissa is also justly famous. Distillers of attars are able to duplicate any fragrance, even the undefinable smell arising from the parched earth after the first rains. Dhanulaad is an expensive attar produced from the trees growing in Assam.

Perfumes

Creating a perfume is a fascinating process. It has a mystery of its own. The direction is known. But reaching the goal straight is not always possible. The perfumes are created by a 'nose' - who is more of an artisan than an artist. It takes a great deal of time and experience to become a nose. The olfactory memory of a nose should be trained to remember several thousand scents.

A perfume is a way of expressing. The fragrances of the past can be recreated new. The ideas come from available fragrances regional peculiarities, off beat notes. Each fragrance has a power seduction since they have a sense of memory and intuition. There is often a feeling of escape - a hint of another place, suggested by its exotic components.

Each perfume ensures its quality by the blend of perfect ingredients. It is a marriage of poetry and the most modern science. Perfumes and chemists are mutually indispensable.

The chemist brings the formulas to the level of the perfumer's imagination. However, it is perfumer alone who measures out the relationship of a minute drop of essence and the capture of our senses.

Basic ingredients are chosen. First they are cultivated and harvested. Depending upon the type of plant or fruit and the country of origin, harvesting takes place at different times af the year.

Plant/place	*Harvesting time*
Citrus fruits (lemon, mandarin, bergamot)	November – February
Orange blossoms (North Africa)	Spring - for 4 - 5 weeks.
Roses In Grasse	Late spring Between 8 - 10
Jasmine (In Grasse)	Last few days of July

The Essences

Examine the following sources:

Raw material	*Place*
Jasmine	Grasse
Bergamot Mandarin	Calabria
May Rose centfolia	Grasse
Damascena (Rose)	Isparta, Turkey
Irises	Tuscany
Ylang ylang	Comora Islands, Madagascar
Lemon	Sicily

The essences obtained are different according to the plant, the orientation and their maturity. The fragrance is not stored in the same place e.g. the fruit of lemon tree is used, whereas the fragrance used in Chanel No 5 and No. 19 are in the orange flower.

A fragrance has many dimensions. No. 5 Chanel is floral (say vanilla). It smells of ylang ylang. It has notes of base. It is a scent of mystery. Of course fragrance is very subjective.

A harvester gathers an average of 2100 roses, about six or seven kilos, an hour. The Turkish roses are more difficult to collect. A harvester collects only two kilogrammes of roses an hour. To get a yield of one kg. of essence, we have to obtain 3500 kgs. of flowers. And 350 kgs. of essence yields only one kilo of absolute.

The Distillation

It depends upon the nature of the plant or its part and the type of essence needed. Expression is used for citrus fruits. Sometimes, alembic distillation is used. May roses are not distilled. The product is obtained as a concrete which is transformed in to an absolute.

Damascena (Turkish Roses) are left on huge carpets. Oils then come to the surface. Then they are distilled. The rhizomes of iris plant are stored for 1-3 years after drying. They are then crushed. They are later subjected to hydro-distillation or steaming or extraction, using either alcohol or solvents.

Ylang yland produces essences of different quality depending upon the time taken for distillation.

Ultimate Aim

The ultimate aim for a perfumer is not the development of a number of perfumes. It is to develop a few perfumes which can withstand the test of time. Chanel introduces perfumes at about 10-year intervals. Each Chanel fragrance has a loyal following. Each fragrance developed should become a classic.

At Chanel, they do not invent anything. They just transform the values which are unique to them. They want success and they have success.

Celebrity-endorsed Perfumes

Kate Moss has lent its name to a perfume. The late Elizabeth Taylor pioneered this trend with the launch of White Diamonds in 1991. Jennifer Lopez endorsed fragrance is called Glow. More than 30 celebrity scents have been launched in the UK in 2007. celebrity-endorsed perfumes create instant awareness. But few perfumes survive the first year of their launch. Celebrity-endorsed perfumes appeal to the younger consumers. Perfume market is over-crowded, and even the best selling fragrances account for only a 5% market share. The product life cyles are very short. In 2006, 220 new perfumes were launched.

Boutique perfumes

This is another emerging trend. These are niche perfumes. Fashion houses such as Prada, Hermes and Dior are creating private collections of limited edition perfumes. They are sold mostly in their own boutiques. Coty dominates this sector. It acquired Calvin Klein from Unilever in 2005. L'Oreal owns brands like Giorgio Armani and Ralph Lauren. L'Oreal entered mass market by purchasing The Body Shop. Chanel concentrates on its three leading brands.

10 Best Scents of Seduction

Brand	*Company*	*Remarks*
Rose	Paul Smith	It contains Turkish rose oil, green tea, magnolia in cedar wood. Fresh and sensual.
Dream of Pink	Lacoste	Base note-sandal-wood, Heart note-Lotus and rose, Top note-Red berries.
The One	Dolce Gabanna	Defiant and gorgeous.
Incredible Me	Escada	Mascarpone, coffee, chocolate and biscuit. Generous warmth.
Dreaming	Tommy Hilfiger	Fantasy world.
Mediterranean Breeze	Elizabeth Arden	Fruity, florals couibined with sensual woods and addictive musks. Reminds of a warm, summer day.

Issues: Move around in the market to get a feel of Indian perfume market. What possibilities do you see? Critically examine the personality and the perfume matching.

CASE 2: STATUS SYMBOLS: A & M – AC NIELSEN – SURVEY, 2000

Such a survey was first carried out in 1994. It was repeated in 1997. The third has been conducted in 2000. These surveys have been conducted at three year intervals. The list of 30 symbols is pre-selected. It now includes the new realities such as the Internet connection and swimming pool. In the surveys conducted previously, it was all-male sample, but in the present survey, about a third of the sample is women. Car ownership, other than the entry-level Maruti 800, is a criterion for being included in the sample. The present survey covers eight cities – Delhi, Mumbai, Chennai, Calcutta, Bangalore, Hyderabad, Pune and Ahmedabad. For two salaried men, one was a self-employed male. There was one working women for every two housewives. Out of 30 symbols, the most powerful 10 status symbol were ranked. Respondents were asked to name a brand for each symbol.

The following are the top all India symbols.

Symbol	*Score*
Educational Degree	7.29
Car	6.27
Home Location	3.57
Cellphone	3.53
Child's School/College	3.38
Credit Card	3.29
Air Conditioner	2.72
Holiday Abroad	2.57
Job/Business	2.54
Club Membership	2.26

Educational degree has overtaken home location. The most coveted qualification is MBA. The car comes next. Home location is the third. Cellphone is no. 4. Credit Card has upgraded itself from no. 10 to no.6. The brand of the card has become more important. AC has re-entered the top 10. Holiday abroad and club membership are at no. 9 and 10 respectively. Club membership has downgraded itself from its previous score. Farmhouse no longer is a part of top 10.

In Mumbai, the car is no. 1 status symbol, followed by educational degree. In Ahmedabad, credit card is at no.10. Even cellphone is not as important in Ahmedabad as in other cities. Farm or beach house or orchard form a part of top 10 in Ahmedabad.

In AC category, the top brand is LG; which has displaced Voltas, with Carrier being a runner up. National and GE are strong in Mumbai. Nokia is the leader amongst cellphones. In Mumbai, the most happening place is Malabar Hill along with Bandra. In Pune, Deccan and Koregaon Park are the areas to live. Salt lake wins in Calcutta. In Bangalore, it is Indira Nagar. Greater Kailash and Golf Links are prominent places in Delhi.

CASE 3: AMEX SURVEY ON CONSUMER SAVINGS

AmEx conducted a survey on savings motivations of 1000 people across several nations by utilising the services of Taylor Nelson Sofres. The following table summarise the data for the reasons to save.

WHAT PEOPLE AROUND THE WORLD ARE SAVING FOR

	USA	*France*	*Germany*	*Italy*	*UK*	*Hong Kong*	*India*	*Japan*	*Singapore*	*Taiwan*
Retirement	48	16	18	9	23	12	19	21	15	15
A vacation	3	7	17	7	12	4	1	2	3	1
Emergencies	12	22	16	39	10	57	30	21	38	25
Major purchase	5	8	12	4	6	5	2	7	1	3
Child's college education	11	6	7	12	6	12	31	9	14	21
Purchase of first home	4	9	7	6	5	3	12	3	4	4
Others	17	32	23	23	38	7	5	37	25	31

All figures in per cent
Source: American Express Bank.

The financial concerns uppermost in India were children's education (56 p.c.) and retirement (51 p.c.). In US, retirement is the biggest financial concern (47 p.c.). In UK, it is 31 p.c. People in France are worried about unemployment (44 p.c.). In Italy, the same fear grips 60 p.c. people, and in Hong Kong 75 p.c.

The top motivation for savings in India was children's education (31 p.c.). Emergencies (30 p.c.) and retirement (19 p.c.) come in next as savings motivations. Japan is not clear about its savings motivations. (36 p.c.).

Issues: What strategies the educational institutes and financial institutes must adopt in India to boost savings considering children's education being the topmost priority for saving?

As Indians do not save for vacations, how can holidays and vacations be marketed?

CASE 4: STYLE CLANS — AN EMIC CLASSIFICATION

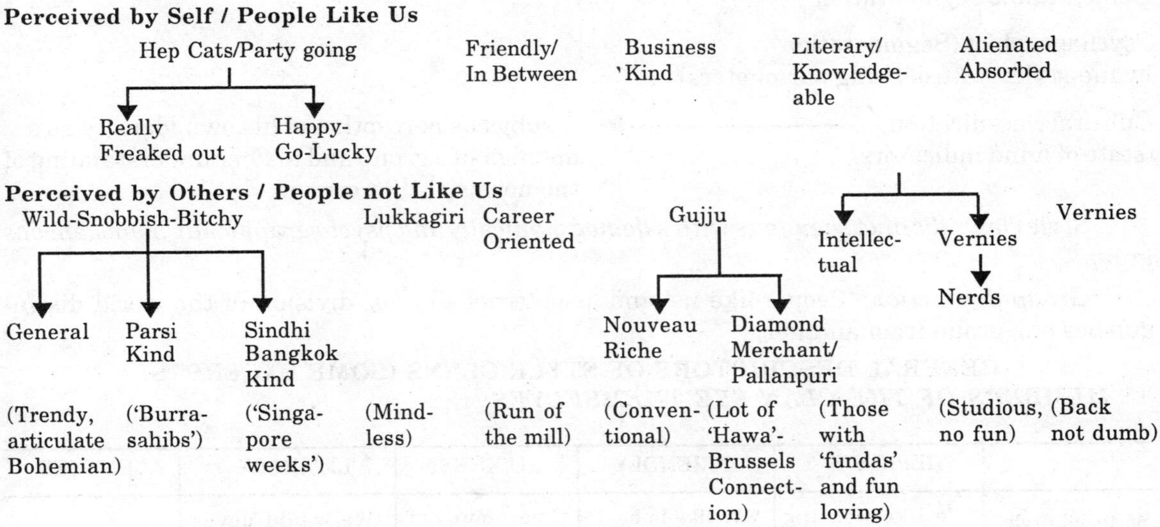

Dr. Ragini Prakash, Associate Research Director, Quest (the Qualitative Research Division of MARG) and Rama Bijapurkar, Dy M.D. MARG won the MRSI award for the best paper in year (1992) — "Cultural Classification. A Different Way of Segmenting Consumers". One example of cultural classification is *style clans.* These were so far recognised at intuitive level *e.g.,* ads like *anything karega for Go Cool,* Pepsi ad with Remo Fernandes or Limca with zero-level and 'isotonic salts' — all these appeal to different style clans within the youth market.

The 25 in-depth interviews revealed that style-clans existed within a very homogeneous target group. The respondents identified and labelled are given in the above diagram.

Contradictions

1. Hedonistic people were alert to the call of share market.
2. Snobby bitch types will keep away form the vernacs but will go to Kamuthipure to distribute condoms for the prevention of AIDS.
3. The friendly lot mixes with nerds and vernacs to get votes for student union elections.
4. The literary/intellectual is disdainful of materialism but holds symposia in the exotic surroundings.
5. The Gujarati/Business/Diamond merchant type would desire conventional bride, but would want her to be a wanton Hep Cat when alone or in the company of select friends.

Notes: Age Cohorts are contemporaries who have experienced major political / social events at about the same age; *e.g.,* partition sufferers, Raj nostalgics.

For effective communication this system of cultural classification is very useful.

Demographic Segmentation
|
Psychagraphics (Segmentation by life-style: state of being parameters)
|
Cultural classification (state of mind indicators) ——→ A subject's perception of his own identity as a member of a group and his/her understanding of the norms of that group.

Style clans: distinct segments with a demographically and psychographically homogeneous group.

Group distinction: 'People like us' and 'people not like us' division of the world distinguishes one group from another.

GENERAL DESCRIPTORS OF STYLE CLANS (SOME EXCERPTS)

AS MEMBERS OF THE CLAN SEE THEMSELVES

	HEP CATS	FRIENDLY	BUSINESS	LITERARY	ALENATED
Sartorial Style	"We like wearing trendy stuff.. real classy."	"We like to be presentable and formally dressed."	"Feel out of sorts in fancy clothes.. not just our kind."	"We would never like to wear clothes which attract attention, expose our body".	
Accessories	Chunky jewellery Boys-earring/cross in one ear.	No accessories	Matching accessories	No accessories	White elastic belts, matching shiny shoes, etc.
Make-up	"We like to use real sophisticated, subtle make-up everyday."	"On some occasions we like to use.. when we have the time."	"We like to use make-up which matches with our dress."	"Do not use, It's too frivolous."	"We do not like to use make up".
Hair Style	Perm/crimp/crew/punk	"No time for fancy cuts... have travel in trains/buses... it will get messed up anyway"	Well kept conventional, presentable.	Not bothered by styles of hair	Plaits, hair clips, gajras in hair.
Music	"We are most inspired by charts."	Music of 70s, Rock, old Hindi songs.	Ghazals, Hindi music, Western but not loud.	Jazz, Hard Rock, ghazals, bhajans - not governed by charts.	Hindi or Marathi. Not much western.
Favourite Haunts	Open House, RG's, 1900, Cellars, Go Bananas, Croissant	"Would never go to Nepean Road because it is full of Gujjus"	5 Star Hotels, but not to discos, generally.	"We can hang around anywhere ... doesn't matter."	"Now with the Cable and Star Plus, there is so much to do at home."
Ambition	"We will write SAT, TOEFL or pay our way to go to the USA for MBA."	"Like to go to USA on a scholarship."	"We will join a professional course in India, but if it is too tough we will pay our way to USA."	"We will by to get a scholarship but will definitely want to come back to India... don't want to live like second class citizens."	"We are not too ambitious and have little possibility of going abroad. "

Personality traits pereived by self	"We love the company of the opposite sex.. it is electric."	"Would never run after guys with cars."	"Our family expects us to take over the business we only get time on weekends."	"We enjoy discussing and participating in things which have relevance."	"We do like to mix about but not if it is not reciprocated."

AS PERCEIVED BY "PEOPLE NOT LIKE US"

	Smart, aloof, snobbish, always hanging around with opposite sex, late night party, spoilt brats.	No hang ups in life, easy going.	Move in Gujju crowd, keep to themselves.	Talk and involved with politics and world affairs, usually sit in the library, very brainy and knowledgeable.	"Brainy but cannot converse in Ennglish."
	"May be they are proud because they are fluent in English."	They get involved in all kinds of college activities since they want fame."	"They are very keen on the stock market and keep in touch with it."	"They only like to talk high 'funda' stuff."	"They like to stick together, are quite conventional and introverted."

Issues: Cultures affects consumer behaviour. Style clans is cultural classification. Describe the clans as members see themselves and others.

CASE 5: SPIRULINA OF SUNOVA

Spirulina is blue-green algae rich in chlrophyl and dozens of high-value nutrients. It is a superfood, 1 KG of which equals 1000 KG of assorted vegetables. Sunova is an associated company of Dabur accounting for 100 crore turnover of the overall market of Rs. 2300 crore. This product has been promoted on low pitch, and the company expects that world-of-month recommendations will do the rest of the job. Today 50 p.c. of turnover goes into advertising handled by Mudra. Press and outdoor hoardings are in use.

Issues:

What is the role of world-of-mouth publicity?
How can Sunova adopt life-style advertising?

CASE 6: STONEY-HEART ROMANCE

India is a gold loving country. Diamond selling is a challenging task. De Beers promoted diamonds for the last three years, and sales have started rising. India was woefully ignorant about diamonds. Consumers were educated through ads about the four Cs — Clarity, Caratage, Cut and Colour. Prices are printed alongside the stones. TheIR myth that they are 'beyond the reach' was shattered. Apart from weddings where diamonds were purchased (65%), it was necessary to conceive more use occasions, and cherish the gift culture. If an occasion is promoted with a strong association of diamonds, it must work. Diamonds will be as desired in the coming millennium as they are in this. They are forever.

Issues: Instead of a vacation, a woman gets diamonds from her man. How emotional appeal has been used to promote diamonds? See the end of the copy. It tells about the four Cs. Is it necessary to use the rational appeal and physical attributes of the product in the copy? Why?

CASE 7: SOCIO-ECONOMIC SEGMENTATION (SEC)

Socio-economic segmentation (SEC) is a classification made by the marketing research agencies about 6-7 years ago when it was felt that the income classification does not present a true picture. Perhaps, people are reluctant to state their real income, and the income stated implies different things in different parts of the country. SEC classifications are based on income-education combination. There are five SEC groups from A to E. Each of these are further sub-divided. The full classification chart is given below.

SOCIO-ECONOMIC CLASSIFICATION GRID

Occupation	*Illiterate*	*School upto 4 years. literate but no formal schooling*	*School 5-9 years.*	*SSC/ HSC*	*Some College, but not graduate*	*Grad/ Post-grad-uate General*	*Grad/ Post-graduate Professor*
Unskilled workers	E2	E2	E1	D	D	D	D
Skilled workers	E2	E1	D	C	C	B2	B2
Petty traders	E2	D	D	C	C	B2	B2
Shop owners	D	D	C	B2	B1	A2	A2
No of Employees							
Business people (None)	D	C	B2	B1	A2	A2	A1
Industrialist One to Nine	C	B2	B2	B1	A2	A1	A1
More than 10	B1	B1	A2	A2	A1	A1	A1
Self-employed professionals	D	D	D	B2	B1	A2	A1
Clerical job / Salespeople	D	D	D	C	B2	B1	B1
Supervisory level	D	D	C	C	B2	B1	A2
Junior officers / Executives	C	C	C	B2	B1	A2	A2
Senior officers / Executives	B1	B1	B1	B1	A2	A1	A1

Issues: You are marketing a luxury mid-segment car; costing around Rs. 5 lacs. How SEC is useful to you?

CASE 8: SOCIAL ADVERTISING

Advertising can be used to promote a cause, say 'don't waste water', or 'don't waste' fuel or 'don't kili animals.' It is necessary to use strong appeals to break our stupor or indifference. The ad here asks asks you a straight question, 'Would you murder a woman just because you liked her skin?" The denial is linked to a plea for not murdering animals for their hide. The tag line is also very effective — 'Be human. Let Animals Be'.

Issues: Can we use communication to promote social causes? What are your comments on this copy?

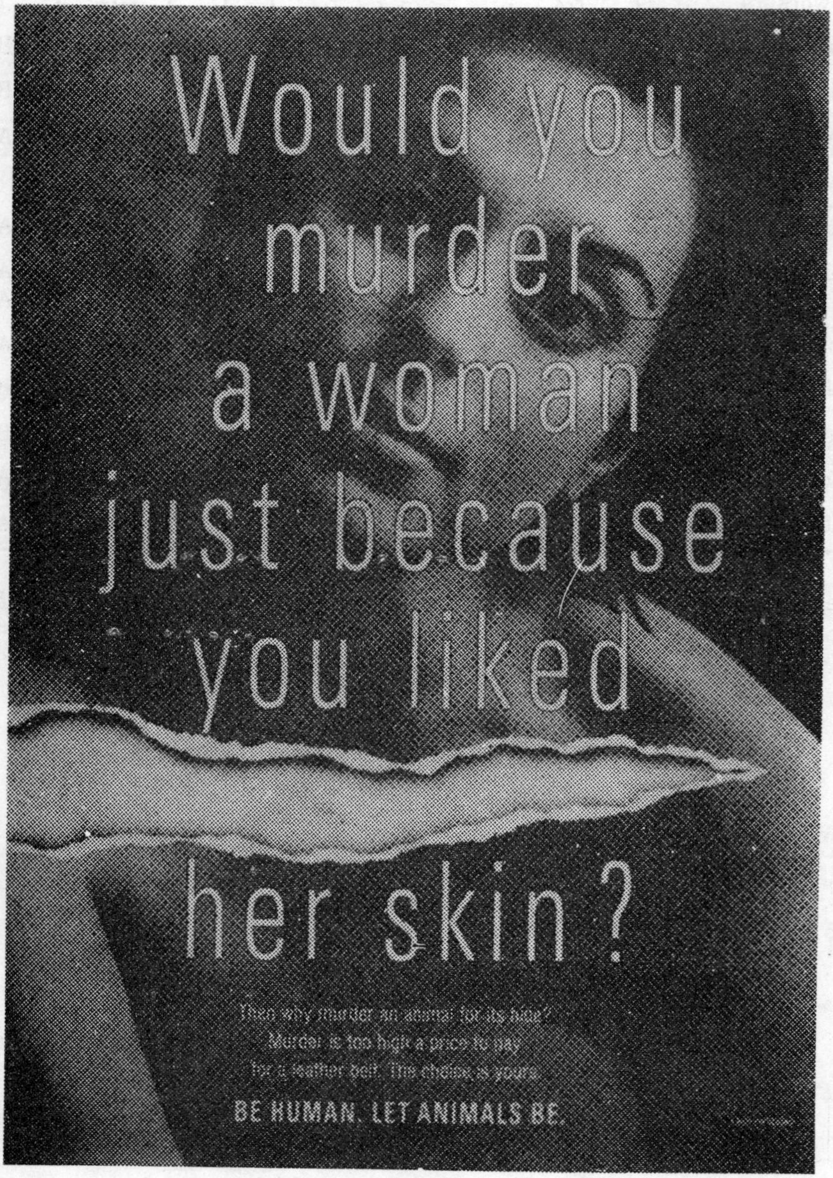